Wiltshire Record Society

(formerly the Records Branch of the Wiltshire
Archaeological and Natural History Society)

VOLUME 54

FOR THE YEAR 1998

Impression of 500 copies

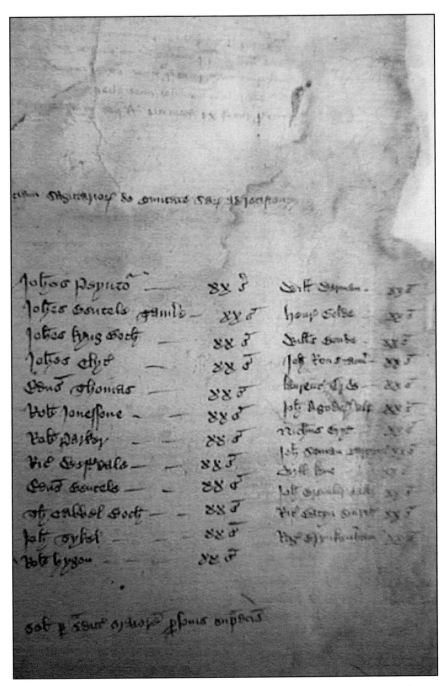

Detail from f. 107 (see **317***). The names of Salisbury archers (and sums paid to them) who were sent to resist the siege of Calais in 1436. Note the typical water damage to text above this entry.*

THE FIRST GENERAL ENTRY BOOK OF THE CITY OF SALISBURY 1387-1452

EDITED BY

DAVID R. CARR
University of South Florida, St. Petersburg

TROWBRIDGE

2001

ISBN 0 901333 31 X

Typeset by John Chandler
Produced for the Society by
Salisbury Printing Company Ltd, Salisbury
Printed in Great Britain

CONTENTS

PREFACE

The Wiltshire Record Society acknowledges with gratitude the formal permission to publish this manuscript of Salisbury District Council, its owner.

Professor Carr wishes to thank the University of South Florida for supporting his efforts through a Faculty Research Enhancement Award from the College of Arts and Sciences, a Research and Creative Scholarship grant from the Research Council, and a semester of release time from teaching responsibilities at the St. Petersburg Campus. He acknowledges too the Travel to Collections grant provided by the National Endowment for the Humanities. The editors of the *Wiltshire Archaeological and Natural History Magazine* and *Southern History* have kindly allowed material which originally appeared in those journals to be used in the introduction to this volume.

Professor Carr and the Society are grateful to the staff of the Wiltshire and Swindon Record Office in Trowbridge, who not only provided hospitality and kindness while the manuscript was consulted there, but also permitted its temporary transfer on two occasions to London, to the University of London Institute of Historical Research and to the British Library. The assistance of the staff of each institute is also gratefully acknowledged.

The translation and interpretation of this difficult manuscript have been immeasurably improved by the painstaking labour of Professor Christopher Elrington, the President of the Wiltshire Record Society, who has not only examined the text in its entirety, but has also prepared the index of persons, and contributed to the index of places and subjects and the introduction. I have assisted with the indexing and a limited amount of checking, with which I acknowledge the help of Steven Hobbs of the Wiltshire and Swindon Record Office. Professor Carr wishes to place on record the editorial help and encouragement of Christopher and myself, and our friendship shown to him during his visits to England. His principal debt, however, is to his wife, Guna, who has patiently encouraged him throughout the quarter of a century consumed by this project. While she took to referring to the manuscript as 'the other Mrs. Carr,' her patience with and faith in him have sustained his effort.

JOHN CHANDLER

ABBREVIATIONS

The following abbreviations have been used in the citation of books and articles.

Ballard, *British Borough Charters*	*British Borough Charters, 1042–1216*, ed. A. Ballard (Cambridge, 1913)
Carr, 1990	David R. Carr, 'The Problem of Urban Patriciates: Office Holders in Fifteenth Century Salisbury', *Wiltshire Archaeological and Natural History Magazine*, vol. 83 (1990), 118–35
Carr, 1997	David R. Carr, 'From Pollution to Prostitution: Supervising the Citizens of Fifteenth-Century Salisbury', *Southern History*, vol. 19 (1997), 24–41
Chandler, *Endless Street*	John Chandler, *Endless Street: a History of Salisbury and its People* (Salisbury, 1983)
H.M.C. *Var. Coll. IV*	Royal Commission on Historical Manuscripts, *Various Collections, Vol. IV* (H.M.S.O. 1907)
Hatcher	Robert Benson and Henry Hatcher, *Old and New Sarum, or Salisbury* (London, 1843, published as part of Sir Richard Colt Hoare's *History of Modern Wiltshire*)
Sarum Charters	*Charters and Documents Illustrating the History of the Cathedral, City, and Diocese of Salisbury in the Twelfth and Thirteenth Centuries*, ed. W. H. Rich-Jones and W. D. Macray (Rolls Series, London, 1891)
Street	Fanny Street, 'The Relations of the Bishops and the Citizens of Salisbury (New Sarum) between 1225 and 1612', *Wiltshire Archaeological and Natural History Magazine*, vol. 39 (1916), 185–257, 319–67
VCH Wilts.	*The Victoria History of the Counties of England: Wiltshire*, vols. iii (1956), iv (1959), v (1957), vi (1962)
Wilts. Borough Records	*List of Wiltshire Borough Records earlier in date than 1836*, ed. Maurice Rathbone (Wiltshire Archaeological and Natural History Society, Records Branch, vol. v, 1951)

INTRODUCTION

The first extant minute-book or general Entry Book of the city of New Salisbury relates to the years 1387–1452. It contains valuable and unique information about the administration and the social and economic life of the city. While it is a formal record of meetings of the citizens, with long lists of those attending the meetings and of those assessed for taxes, it illuminates many facets of the city's history. Interspersed among the records of meetings are miscellaneous memoranda, notes, and documents related to the business of the meetings.

THE MANUSCRIPT

The book is the first of a series of eight which runs to 1836, and it was traditionally known as 'Ledger A'. It is one of the earliest such minute-books for an English town. It was formerly kept in the Council House at the east end of the market place, and it was badly damaged by water used to extinguish the fire which damaged that building in 1780.[1] It was transferred from the Salisbury District Council muniment room at Bourne Hill, Salisbury, to the Wiltshire (now Wiltshire and Swindon) Record Office at Trowbridge about 1981, and was given the call number WRO G23/1/1. The volume consists of 163 paper folios, measuring approximately 40cm high by 28cm wide, and numerous interfoliated sheets, usually of parchment but occasionally also of paper. All the folio sheets, though used over a period of 65 years, have the same watermark, the outline of a steeply-roofed church surmounted by a simple Latin cross. The precise origin of the paper has not been traced, but it is most likely to have been imported from the continent, perhaps France, as a single shipment.[2] A local mercer trading through Southampton could have been the supplier.

The manuscript was repaired and rebound at the Public Record Office in London in 1951, perhaps at the instigation of Dr A. E. J. Hollaender, who in 1949 listed and numbered the city's accumulated records.[3] No record appears to survive at either the Public Record Office or the Wiltshire and Swindon Record Office of the repair and rebinding, which seems to have retained the arrangement of an earlier rebinding made, apparently, about 1907.

---

1   *Wilts. Borough Records*, 69; *VCH Wilts*. vi. 87.
2   British paper production began only in the late fifteenth century, and regular production did not occur for another century beyond that. Mercers came to control the importation of paper by the mid fifteenth century: Richard L. Hills, *Papermaking in Britain, 1488–1988: A Short History* (London, 1988); F. H. Norris, *Paper and Paper Making* (London, 1952).
3   *Wilts. Borough Records*, 68.

The volume is made up of twelve gatherings, with two additional gatherings, one at the front and one at the back, each of four modern leaves glued to a guard round the adjoining gathering. The collation of the volume is set out below, on pages xxxi–xxxiii, where each folio that is not marked as an insertion or as 'single' is one half of one of the double leaves that form the gathering. Four of the gatherings are each of sixteen folios (eight double leaves), two are each of fourteen folios (seven double leaves), and four others are variously of ten, nineteen, seventeen and fifteen folios, those with odd numbers of folios containing just one single leaf. The last two gatherings, of four and seven folios, each contain only one double leaf. Many smaller pieces of parchment or paper have been sown into the book, including royal writs which are shown by internal evidence to have been inserted when the manuscript was being compiled.

The gatherings are in general in chronological order, following the dates which are recorded on them or may be inferred, and accord with the different enumerations of the folios as described below. Meetings in the period July to December 1393 (**194–200**) appear out of order on folios 63v–66 between two of November 1418 (**193, 202**) on folios 62v and 67, the recto of folio 63 being blank and the lower part the recto of folio 66 and the verso of the same folio being used for a rental of 1419 (**201**); the most likely explanation is that the scribe who entered the meeting of 11 July 1393 began on a new page, the verso of the third folio in the gathering, leaving blank pages for meetings that had not been recorded, that when the record was resumed in or after January 1393 the scribe went back to the first gathering, and that later, in February 1417 (**174**, with which folio 61 and gathering V begins), the partly used gathering containing the record of the meetings of 1393 was taken back into use. Some other documents are out of chronological order as a result of using blank pages or parts of pages for infilling.

The folios are numbered in at least four different sequences, with a fifth surviving on seven folios and matching one or another of the more continuous enumerations. All the enumerations are in arabic figures. That designated as *a* in the list below is the most nearly complete and the most prominent, and for those reasons is the one which is used in this edition. It is of large pencilled numbers at the top right-hand corner of each folio, added apparently in the eighteenth or nineteenth century, perhaps when the book was repaired after the fire at the Council House in 1780. It treats insertions in the book as additions to the original pages, giving each the number of the preceding or following folio with the suffix a, b, or c. The enumeration *a* is missing from f. 24 and from the insertions following ff. 70, 98, 104, and 119, has been omitted from f. 132 (of which the recto is blank), and for reasons which are not clear is discontinuous at the end of the book, the last two folio, following f. 161, being numbered 171 and 172. On five folios (29, 34, 54, 56, and 62) the pencilled number has not been added, because it would have duplicated a number written earlier in ink, part of the fragmentary fifth sequence of numbers mentioned above.

An enumeration in pencil, *b* in the list below, appears to be of the nineteenth or twentieth century and may have been added at the rebinding of *c*. 1907. The numbers are small and inconspicuous, often hardly legible, at the lower left-hand corner of the rectos of the folios. Some of them have apparently been trimmed away. They treat the insertions as part of a single sequence of numbers, but four folios have numbers with A or B added, presumably to rectify mistakes in numbering.

Of two earlier enumerations that designated *c* in the list below is in ink, usually faint or badly written, and may be contemporary or nearly so with the compilation of the manuscript. It ignores the insertions, and appears to contain mistakes. The numbers are in the top right-hand corner of the rectos; some may have been trimmed away, while a few have been crossed out. Also in ink and at the top right-hand corner of the rectos are numbers, designated *d* below, which appear to be slightly later and are much blacker. They are in only three parts of the book, are far from complete, and have in some instances been crossed out.

The damage sustained by the book in the fire of 1780 is extensive, and is most marked in the earlier folios of the volume and in the upper ends of the folios. It has not prevented historians from using the valuable evidence which it affords but has made full and systematic searching of its contents extremely difficult and discouraging. A report of 1907 on the city of Salisbury's muniments by the Royal Commission on Historical Manuscripts included eight pages of extracts from the book, but those extracts are mostly devoted to entries relating to national history rather than to the local matters with which the book is largely concerned and for which it is such a valuable source. The report stated that little of the book was legible before the reign of Henry V [1413–22], and its remark that none of the volumes 'shed as much light on public affairs as might have been anticipated in the records of so important a municipality as Salisbury'[1] assumes that local affairs were not public affairs. As for legibility, Fanny Street considered everything to be illegible before folio 68,[2] which relates to the year 1419, and the *Victoria County History* followed an earlier author in saying that little was legible before *c.* 1406.[3] Several previous attempts to produce a published edition of the book were abandoned.

The book takes the form of a record of successive meetings of citizens. In most instances the meeting is entitled *Convocatio*, translated in the edition as 'Assembly', but in some it is in fact a meeting of the council or of the mayor's court. The formal record of the meetings is in Latin but some interpolated documents are in French or, increasingly towards the end of the period covered, in English. The various hands in which the book is written are, in general, regular and good, though at times the scribes appear to have written hurriedly.

MEDIEVAL SALISBURY

THE BISHOP'S CONTROL OF THE CITY

Salisbury, or New Salisbury, was a new town created by the bishop. That circumstance made it exceptional among English episcopal cities and unusual even in comparison

1   HMC *Var. Collns. IV*, 192–200.
2   Street, 220.
3   *VCH Wilts.* vi. 96 n.; *Wilts. Borough Records*, 69 n.

with continental towns controlled by their bishops.[1] Other English cities which were under the control of their bishops, including Bath, Wells, Durham, and Ely, did not owe their establishment to the bishop.[2] In Salisbury whatever civic authority was exercised had been derived from the bishop, who in turn had received his authority from the Crown, and all the liberties enjoyed by the citizens had been bestowed by the bishop. It has been argued that episcopal lordship gave Salisbury advantages, particularly in securing additional privileges and in avoiding negotiations with royal officials,[3] but other episcopal cities had the same advantages. That Salisbury maintained its relative importance as an economic centre later in the medieval period than comparable towns was not because it was under the bishop's control, nor was it because the citizens maintained superior relations with their bishop. In fact there was a prolonged conflict between the citizens and the bishop. After a temporary settlement in the early fourteenth century, the conflict between the bishop's exercise of his rights and the wishes and ambitions of the citizens resulted in a relationship that was peppered with hostility, if not outright violence, during the fifteenth century. The hostility came to a head with the murder, perhaps by a Salisbury butcher, of Bishop William Ayscough in 1450 during Cade's rebellion.[4] It hindered the progress towards the greater formal independence for which the citizens wished, and they enjoyed few privileges superior to other contemporary episcopal cities. Salisbury offers a clear example of the struggle in which several English medieval cities were engaged to carve out independent governmental functions in the face of repressive episcopal lordship.

Repeated confrontations between the citizens and their bishop resulted only in the reaffirmation of episcopal domination. Very slowly, however, a substructure of civic administration developed beneath, beside and in conflict with the episcopal administration and jurisdiction. The painstaking acquisition of functions by civic officers was frequently contested by the bishop or his officers and was wielded by civic officers largely *de facto* rather than *de jure*. Although the city did not secure political autonomy in the period to which it relates, the Entry Book amply demonstrates activities by which the citizens gradually won from the bishop a measure of control of the administration and jurisdiction of the city.

In 1220 Bishop Richard Poore relocated his cathedral from the hilltop city of Old Sarum to a new site in one of his manors, just above the confluence of the rivers Avon and Nadder. His motives, whether stemming from the loss of his authority over the old city, from a desire to augment his income, or from the apocryphal complaints of

---

1   Far more commonly new towns were created by kings and powerful princes: M. W. Beresford, *New Towns of the Middle Ages* (London, 1967), *passim*.

2   The relationship is studied in depth in David R. Carr, 'The Role of the Episcopacy in English Municipal Politics during the Middle Ages' (unpublished PhD dissertation, University of Nebraska, 1971.

3   Chandler, *Endless Street*, 160–1.

4   For a general history of the city see *VCH Wilts*. vi. On the conflict with bishops see Street, and on Cade's Rebellion in particular J. N. Hare, 'The Wiltshire Risings of 1450,' *Southern History*, iv (1982), 13–31.

the canons that howling winds drowned out their chants, are not certainly known. Simultaneously he founded a 'new town' abutting the close of the new cathedral. This site proved a fine one for both commerce and manufacture.

The bishop's powers in the new city were greater than in the old. In 1226 and 1227 Henry III confirmed his earlier privileges and granted further extensive liberties. The bishop and his successors gained freedom from the jurisdiction and fines of shire and hundred courts and the right to impose and claim at the Exchequer amercements of all his lands, fees, and free tenants save those arising from pleas of the Crown. The bishop's court was to have the view of frankpledge, held by the Crown's official but giving the bishop the fines and forfeitures arising from a wide variety of offences. The Crown's officials were not to enter the bishop's lands or to have jurisdiction over the free tenants of the bishop, dean, and canons except in pleas of the Crown. The bishop and his land were made exempt from a broad selection of aids, pleas, fines, gelds, and tolls, and the bishop might himself levy tolls. Freedom from toll, pontage, carriage, stallage, and pannage throughout the kingdom placed the bishop and his citizens in an enviable economic position.[1]

The bishop's judicial and administrative control of the city was exercised by his officers, of whom the most important in the daily life of citizens was his bailiff. The bishop's bailiff received the oaths of the officers elected by the citizens, including the mayor, aldermen, and reeves, and admitted them to their offices. In the absence of the bishop's steward he presided in the court leet, where he held the view of frankpledge for the Crown and the assizes of bread, ale, and wine, and he executed the return of writs. He presided also in the fortnightly court held in the Guildhall, which belonged to the bishop. He collected the bishop's market dues and might hold pie powder courts for the rapid settlement of disputes arising in the markets or fairs. His presence was necessary for the transfer of property, whether by gift, sale, or demise, within the city.[2]

In 1225 Bishop Poore granted the free tenants of New Salisbury the right to hold their plots by what amounted to burgage tenure, though it was not described in those words: they were to pay a fixed money rent, or quit rent, for all services and to have freedom to transfer their holdings by gift, sale, or mortgage, other than to a church.[3] Henry III's charter of 1227, granting that Salisbury should be a free city under its bishop, said that the citizens were to enjoy the same liberties as the citizens of Winchester, with the usual freedom from tolls and customs. It also gave the bishop the right to demand tallage and other reasonable aid whenever the king tallaged his own demesnes.[4]

In 1302 Bishop Simon of Ghent levied a tallage which the citizens refused to pay on the grounds that the bishop had never demanded a tallage before. When the dispute came before Edward I and his council, the bishop pointed to Henry III's charter

---

1   *Sarum Charters*, 24, 175–82; Hatcher, 36–7, 44.
2   Hatcher, 44.
3   Ibid. 43, 728; *The Tropenell Cartulary*, ed. J. S. Davies (Devizes, 1908), i. 187–8; Street, 190–1; *VCH Wilts.* vi. 94.
4   *Sarum Charters*, 175–8.

which bestowed the right upon the bishop and provided that the bishop's rights should not lapse through disuse, while the citizens claimed immunity from tallage on the basis that Bishop Poore had freed them from such impositions in exchange for quit rents. The king found in favour of the bishop, but permitted the citizens a choice. They could either retain their 'liberties' and pay the tallage, or lose them and avoid the tallage. They chose to avoid the tallage and renounce the liberties, but soon realized the disadvantages of not enjoying the freedoms allowed by the bishop with regard to regulating markets, fairs, tolls, and a wide variety of commercial activities. A settlement was reached in 1306, when the bishop granted a charter to the city. In return for unspecified rents and services and for recognition of the bishop's lordship, the community was permitted to choose its own officers, as they had evidently done before the dispute of 1302. Additionally the citizens were excused from obligatory attendance at the bishop's court more than twice a year.[1]

Following the agreement of 1306 the mayor and others of the city's officers played a role alongside the bishop's bailiff in the bishop's court,[2] but they were clearly in a subordinate position.. The bailiff's authority was strengthened by royal confirmations from Edward III, Richard II, and Henry V.[3] Repeated attempts to avoid the requirement that the officers elected by the citizens had to be sworn and admitted to their offices before the bishop's bailiff met with stiff opposition from the bishop.

The proliferation of civic offices, discussed below, might seem to suggest growing independence, but the authority of the bishop's bailiff could severely limit the power of the city's officials, who, though elected by the citizens, were sworn and admitted to office before him. His court, held in the Guildhall, might displace all others within the city. The bailiff might tallage the citizens, act as constable, justice of the peace, and more.[4] Surprisingly then, the Entry Book contains relatively few specific complaints about episcopal authority during the first half of the fifteenth century, and makes no direct mention of the violence during Cade's rebellion. Other sources, however, make it clear that the struggle between bishop and citizens over political authority and economic privilege was active at the time.[5] In 1472, after a protracted dispute, the citizens agreed that the mayor should take his oath before the bishop in person.[6] Not until 1612 was the city freed from episcopal dominance.

THE CITIZEN BODY

The citizens of Salisbury as a group had no corporate status. They nevertheless had a strong sense of community and their meetings performed many administrative functions. The record of their meetings forms the framework of the Entry Book, but the record is

1 Street, 198–202; Hatcher, 75.
2 *VCH Wilts.* vi. 95.
3 Hatcher, 43, 748–50, 759–60.
4 For an account of episcopal authority see *VCH Wilts.* v. 60–1.
5 Street, 224–33, which depends heavily on the *Liber Niger* of Bishop Beauchamp.
6 *Wilts. Borough Records*, 63–5.

far from complete. Apart from the damage which has made large parts of the book illegible or only partly legible, it is clear that by no means all the business conducted was minuted, and some of the meetings may not have been recorded at all. The book generally describes each meeting as a *convocatio*, a word rendered in this calendar as 'Assembly'. One meeting was described exceptionally as a council of neighbours (**160**), and three, in 1445, 1447, and 1449, as of the mayor's council (**395, 410, 432**). Those attending the meetings are often named as the mayor and fellow citizens. The citizens were distinguished in 1415 from other inhabitants (**146**) and then and in 1420 from other neighbours (**148, 213**). Some meetings, notably the annual meeting at which the mayor, aldermen, and other officers were elected, held usually on All Souls' day (2 November) though in 1412 and 1413 apparently on St. Martin's day (11 November) (**113, 128**), are not described other than as an election. The annual meetings were apparently not usually included in the Entry Book before 1415 (**155**), though the meeting in 1393 (**198**) is an exception. Up to 1414 the usual order of entries has the record of a meeting in October followed by notes of accounts for the preceding year and then the record of the first meeting under the new mayor in November or December. Although it is possible that the record of a few of the annual meetings is missing because of the damage to the manuscript, it is more likely that the annual meeting, held by 1393 in St. Edmund's church (**198**) as noted below, was regarded as different from the other meetings and recorded separately. Many of the meetings recorded under the heading *Convocatio* were evidently not general assemblies of all the citizens but were in fact meetings of the mayor's court (e.g. **177**) or of the councils of the Twenty-Four or the Forty-Eight, which are discussed below.

The agreement of 1306 provided for the establishment of a guild merchant, a name which in other cities and boroughs was used of an administrative body. Salisbury's guild merchant is not known to have had any administrative function. As provided for in 1306 it comprised merchants, craftsmen, and others to the number of some 300, and it may have been the reconstitution of a body which had existed from the foundation of New Salisbury. The mayor and commonalty of the city were joined for religious and social purposes in the guild or fraternity of St. George, which may have been another name for the guild merchant.[1] In the Entry Book are frequent references to the fraternity, which was clearly distinct from the meetings of citizens held for administrative purposes.

Those meetings were held at apparently irregular intervals, except for the annual meeting on or near All Souls' day at which elections were made. From 1416 freeholders of the city were penalized 6d. 'and ale' if they failed to attend a meeting to which they were summoned (**419**, an entry summarizing an ordinance that is not found earlier in the book; cf. **203**). The numbers of men named as attending the meetings fluctuated widely, from as few as seven (**189, 291**) to nearly one hundred (**300**). For a large proportion of the meetings, however, the Entry Book is illegible, while for some no list of those attending was included in the Entry Book, and in many the list of names ends

1 *VCH Wilts.* vi. 97, 133.

with 'and others' or 'and others whose names appear on the list' (e.g. **146**), indicating that the Entry Book was not the only (or indeed the primary) record of attendance.

The question whether Salisbury had an urban patriciate has been addressed elsewhere. The conclusions are that the city's élite was drawn from a wide range of occupations and that neither a single class of great merchants nor a small group of families was dominant.[1] Within each mayoralty, however, there appears to have been a group of between five and eight men whose attendance is regularly recorded,[2] but there is no evidence that such a group had any formal existence. Larger and formal groups of senior or influential citizens were the councils of the Twenty-Four and the Forty-Eight, of which the Twenty-Four was the inner or superior body. They were in existence by 1364;[3] the Twenty-Four is first mentioned in the Entry Book in 1413, when the assembly ordered that its members, along with six advisers, were to wear a silken livery (**128**), and an election of new members of the Twenty-Four, to fill vacancies caused by death, is recorded at the All Souls' day meeting in 1417 (**185**). The Entry Book first mentions the Forty-Eight by that name only in April 1445 (**397**) and election to it in September of the same year (**399**). In 1419 an ordinance requiring that members of the councils present in Salisbury should attend the masses for citizens who had died mentions members of the Twenty-Four, who were to be fined 2 lb. of wax for non-attendance, and those of the other Twenty-Four, for whom the fine was 1 lb. of wax (**127, 206**): the other Twenty-Four was perhaps a temporary alternative form of the Forty-Eight. The fines in wax were later demanded for non-attendance at council meetings (**397, 399–400, 407. 499, 411**). A few lists of those attending meetings clearly distinguish members of the two councils (e.g. **438**), but more are simply arranged in a way that appears tacitly to acknowledge the distinction (e.g. **425**). The more important of the city's officials, including the mayor, aldermen, serjeants, and reeve, seem invariably to have been drawn from the Twenty-Four while constables and chamberlains were usually from the Forty-Eight.[4] A larger select group of sixty citizens was mentioned in 1393, when its members were to be dressed uniformly in silk for a visit to the city by the king (**194**). Later references in the Entry Book suggest that the silk liveries were worn only by the Twenty-Four and the city's legal advisers (**128**), and only on special occasions, including Christmas (e.g. **170, 268**) and visits by the king (**300**) and other great men (**253**). In 1412 a man who had served as a collector of taxes (e.g. **71, 109**) was fined £2 for wearing the livery when he was not one of, presumably, the Twenty-Four (**113**).

The damage to the book makes it difficult to know precisely how frequent the meetings were, and it seems that the principle on which it was compiled was not consistent. In the 47 years from 1406 (when the record becomes more or less continuous) to 1452 there were nearly 320 meetings, not counting election meetings, an average of

1 Carr, 1990.
2 A similar inner group is described in thirteenth-century Lincoln: J. W. F. Hill, *Medieval Lincoln*, (Cambridge, 1948), 295.
3 Hatcher, 79, 111.
4 Street, 220.

a little under seven each year. The average is increased by the relative frequency of meetings recorded between 1410 and 1420, when there might be twelve or more meetings in a year. Later the number of meetings recorded each year was usually between four and six. In 1449, however, twelve meetings were recorded, five of them in the five week period from 6 June to 8 July, but in that period a high proportion of the meetings recorded were apparently not of the citizens generally but of the councils of the Twenty-Four and the Forty-Eight, whose meetings may not have been regularly recorded in the earlier years covered by the Entry Book. Since meetings were evidently called to deal with particular pieces of business, including the business of the mayor's court, they might be at very short intervals: the assembly of 15 Nov. 1415, the first of a new mayoralty, was followed the next day by one to deal with the king's writ demanding the levy of a tax (**156–7**).

The meetings of the citizens and their councils were held in various places, which are not recorded in the earlier parts of the Entry Book. The mayor paid rent in 1406 for a house where accounts were audited (**54**), which stood opposite the Guildhall (**64**) and was used for discussions (**71**). The Council House, apparently the building by St. Thomas's church[1] and perhaps the house being built next to St. Thomas's cemetery in 1408 (**71**), was mentioned by name in 1409–10, when the city's reeves were paying rent for it (**89**). The mayor paid the rent in 1410–11 (**98**) and the city chamberlains in 1413–14 (**140**) and 1419–20, in the latter year to the dean and chapter (**217**). The Council House was to be used to keep goods and chattels distrained upon for non-payment of rent in 1417 (**179–180**), in 1419 a coffer containing money was kept in a chest there (**212**) and a charter was kept in the common chest there (**462**). From 1430 the mayor's chest was kept there and payments were made there (**270, 275, 282, 343, 459**), a bond was to be brought there 1440 (**354**), and accounts were audited there 1449 (**423**); in 1416 the common chest had been in St. Thomas's church (**130**; cf. e.g. **108, 158**). Meetings were held at the Council House from 1416 (**160, 189, 205, 214–15, 266, 291, 294, 313**), but they were also held at the bishop's Guildhall (**177, 181–2, 231, 293, 295, 341**) and the annual meeting for elections on All Souls' day was held by custom in St. Edmund's church (**198, 299, 309, 418**). In 1428 the assembly was said to be at the Council House because the Guildhall was in use by the king (**258**). The meetings in 1445, 1447, and 1449 of the mayor's council were held at the Council House (**395, 410, 432**).

CIVIC OFFICERS

Of the English cities controlled by their bishops, Salisbury had the most articulated administration, and the number of offices recorded increased during the fifteenth century. The proliferation of offices was perhaps intended to spread responsibility.[2] The Entry Book mentions in the late fourteenth century the mayor, aldermen (**14**), serjeants (**33**),

1   *VCH Wilts.* vi. 87.
2   A. R. Bridbury, in *Economic History Review*, 2nd ser. vol. 34, 1–24, following Hill, *Medieval Lincoln*, 254–68.

and collectors and assessors (**15**), while reeves, constables, and coroners are known from other sources. To them were added by or in the fifteenth century attorneys, a city clerk, chamberlains, overseers of wards, a steward of the borough court, and a subwarden of the almshouse. To most of those offices the Entry Book describes the holders as being elected, a word may which may mean no more than 'chosen', not that the men were voted into office. Elections of the mayor, the members of parliament (**233**), and the chamberlains, however, were made following nominations to those offices, and the wording of a resolution of 1445 that the members of parliament, the serjeants, and the priest of the fraternity of St. George should be resident in the city suggests that a vote was held in the selection of those office-holders (**396**).

Men paid fines to escape from serving the offices of mayor, reeve, and alderman, to avoid either the responsibility or the loss of time involved. To be excused serving as mayor one paid the large sum of £20 before 1398 (**11**) and in 1408 another paid £10 (**71**). Neither the introduction of an annual fee for the mayor nor the increasing dignity of the position was enough to persuade all candidates to accept the mayoralty: in 1444 one paid £3 to be excused the office in perpetuity (**394**), in 1449 three men were similarly excused in perpetuity for 40 marks (£26 13s. 4d.) each (**432**), and in 1450 another three paid £20 each (**440**). To be excused serving as reeve some men were ready in 1418 to pay a fine of £3 (**202**), and one, having refused the office, refused to pay the fine (**211**). The fine was only £2 in 1432 (**418**), 1445 (**401**), and 1449 (**436**), £1 6s. 8d. in 1437 (**333**) and 1438 (**341**). Fines for being excused the office of alderman were levied at £3 in 1421 (**227**), 1428 (**260**), and 1429 (**264**), £5 in 1432 (**418**), at 6 marks (£4) in 1437 (**333**), £2 in 1438 (**341**) in 1440 (**354**), and £4 in 1443 (**387**); from 1442 a fine of £4 excused men the offices of both alderman and reeve (**373**, **394**, **401**, **415**, **422**, **436**, **448**, **456**).

The Mayor

Salisbury may have had a mayor, acting as the leader and representative of the community, from the foundation of the city, but neither the charter of 1225 nor that of 1227 mentioned any organization of city officers. The first documented reference to the mayor was in 1249, when he carried out a decision in a civil case made by the court of Salisbury over which episcopal officers presided.[1] In 1290 and 1303 the mayor witnessed conveyances.[2]

The mayor presided at meetings not only of the citizens generally and of the councils of the Twenty-Four and the Forty-Eight but also of what was in effect, if not in law, a mayor's court. Before him appeared people accused of slander (e.g. **165–6**), commercial malpractice (**266**), and irregular trading in the market (**250**). In 1417 it was agreed that the mayor and community should hold the seal of the deputy aulnager for

1 *Crown Pleas of the Wiltshire Eyre, 1249*, ed. C. A. F. Meekings (Wiltshire Archaeological and Natural History Society, Records Branch, vol. xvi (1961), 255; *VCH Wilts.* vi. 95. Hatcher, 735 and note, and *Wilts. Borough Records*, 63, give 1261 as the date of the first record of a mayor.
2 Street, 197.

Salisbury and Wiltshire (**175**), which gave the meetings presided over by the mayor greater authority in regulating the cloth trade (**180–1, 186, 190**).

Until 1409 the mayor was not only the city's leader but also its chief financial officer. The tax gathered by collectors in the four wards of the city was handed over to him (e.g. **280**), and he received the rents and other payments due to the community. From those receipts he met a wide variety of expenses, in fees and payments in kind to the city's officials, in travelling, subsistence, and entertainment, in gifts (often in the form of wine) to dignitaries and outside officials, and in providing liveries for the members of the councils and for the city's officials (e.g. **216**). In 1409 it was decided that the chamberlains should levy and receive all payments due to the community (**79**), as mentioned below, and in 1445 it was decided that the mayor should not receive any payment due to the city except by the hands of the chamberlains (**400**). The mayor presented his accounts, usually towards the end of his term of office. The mayor who presented his account apparently in Sept. 1410 agreed to forgo the repayment of some of his expenses (**84**). Though most if not all of them were ultimately reimbursed, the mayor's expenses may have reduced the attraction of the position. In 1416 the outgoing mayor was thought to have performed the office so well that he was given an allowance of £10 in addition to his expenses, and it was agreed that any future mayor who held the office twice should have a similar sum beyond his expenses (**167**). A regular yearly allowance for the mayor was discussed but not agreed in 1419 (**212**), and one of £10, paid about that time to a former mayor and one about to take office (**218**), was approved by the assembly in 1420 (**221**). In 1424 the retiring mayor was allowed an additional £5 at the end of his fourth (and second successive) term (**244**). Five years later the retiring mayor was allowed 5 marks beyond his fee of £10 because when prices were high he had sold corn cheap (**264**).

An evident increase in the importance of the mayor's office during the fifteenth century was accompanied by practices which add to its dignity. A deputy mayor was recorded in the second decade of that century (**79, 171–2**). From 1420 the mayor was to be attended by the chaplain of the fraternity of St. George (**216**). The chaplain was to live in the mayor's house, the mayor receiving an allowance for his board (**221**) and paying him 1s. a week if he was too ill to stay with the mayor (**244**). In 1429 it was ordered that maces were to be carried in front of the mayor by the serjeants (**265, 275**), and in 1435 that the third serjeant or macebearer should wait on the mayor. That serjeant was salaried and liveried (**303**) and came to be known as the mayor's serjeant (**413, 450**), while the maces were gilded in 1447 (**414**) and one of them was to be mended in 1450 (**440**). For two annual gatherings at midsummer, recorded from 1440 when all were to wear their best clothes (**352**), the mayor was reimbursed for providing firewood and two casks of good ale (e.g. **367**); men were fined for not coming to watch with the mayor (**410**), and in 1451 it was ordered that each member of the Twenty-Four was to have an armed man to accompany the mayor on those nights (**442**).

The mayor was elected annually at the meeting of citizens held usually on All Souls' day. Two references to a mayor elect (**134, 184**) apparently result from the retiring mayor serving out his term after the election of his successor. For the seventy-four years

1380–1453 the Entry Book gives the names of forty-nine mayors (assuming that the mayors of 1429–30 and 1449–50 were not the same as their namesakes more than forty years earlier), and a further four may be added from the list given by Hatcher.[1] Eleven of those men were mayor for more than one term, three of them for, respectively, three, four, and five terms.[2] After 1453 three of the mayors of before that date held the office again.[3]

In 1428 the assembly agreed that anyone who had been mayor was to be quit of the office for five years, provided that there were three other suitable men who might be nominated from the Twenty-Four for election by the commons, (258) a rule that was confirmed, without the proviso, in 1429 (264) and 1451 (448; cf. 419B). The rule, which was repeatedly ignored in the rest of the fifteenth century, may have been designed to prevent a mayor from serving a second term within a short period, but it is more likely that it was to spare him from serving again an office that was seen as burdensome. Perhaps unusually large fines, as mentioned above, were intended to discourage avoidance.[4]

While the Entry Book does not indicate the occupations of many of the mayors, the lists which it includes of taxpayers place them normally in the highest or second highest level of wealth. In 1436 twelve of the seventeen people assessed for 10s. or 13s. 4d. had been or were to become mayor (321A–D). Not all the mayors were uniformly chosen from among the ranks of the great merchants, the mercers and drapers. Two grocers, for example, were successively mayor 1392–4 (197, 200).

The aulnage returns of 1396–7 and ward lists of 1399–1400[5] reveal something of the range of economic status among the mayors. The average number of cloths held by ten men who had been or were to become mayors was 55, but the numbers ranged from a minimum of 5½ cloths to a maximum of 131. Similarly the ward lists reveal an average assessment of 5s. 4d., with a range from 4d., the lowest possible assessment, to 13s. 4d,, the highest recorded. Both in the aulnage returns and in the ward lists the averages for the mayors are substantially above those for the city as a whole, especially in the ward lists where most people paid only 4d. or 6d.. That the averages for mayors are not higher implies not that the mayors were fairly close in wealth to the citizens at large, but rather that the office was held by men from within a wide economic range, a testimony to the ability of citizens to rise from relatively modest beginnings.

Reeves

The functions performed in some other towns by bailiffs[6] were performed in Salisbury by reeves elected by the citizens, apparently annually at their meeting on All Souls' day

1   Hatcher, 995.
2   See list of mayors below, pp. xxxiii–xxxv.
3   Hatcher, 996, including John Port (or a Port) for an unprecedented six terms in all.
4   Cf. J. I. Kermode, 'Urban Decline? The Flight from Office in Late Medieval York,' *Economic History Review*, 2nd ser. 35 (1982), 179–98.
5   Chandler, *Endless Street*, 257–72.
6   e.g. Alice S. Green, *Town Life in the Fifteenth Century* (London, 1894), i. 318–20; N. M. Trenholme, *The English Monastic Boroughs* (Columbia, Missouri, 1927), 35. At Ipswich the offices of bailiff and reeve were synonymous: Ballard, *British Borough Charters*, pp. lxxxv–lxxxvi.

(e.g. **155**), but responsible among other things for collecting dues to be paid to the bishop (**89**). In 1412, the assembly ordered the inspection of the reeves' rolls, probably to ensure that they had properly accounted for the bishop's income (**113**). The only mention of portreeves in the Entry Book (**15**) is presumably of the same officers. The book contains a single reference to the election of bailiffs, in 1417 when two were elected (**185**). They were presumably the same as reeves, of which the city had had two in 1265.[1] An officer was described as city reeve in 1410 and 1411, when he was to have a livery, suggesting a single reeve, though the record of the same meeting in 1411 also mentions a payment to the bishop by the city reeves (**91, 98, 185**); it may be that one reeve was appointed by the bishop and another was elected by the citizens. The man mentioned as the liveried reeve in 1411 was called bailiff in 1418, when the question of his livery was deferred (**203**); in 1420 and 1423 he was to have his livery with others paid by the city (**217, 237**). He was not one, however, of any of the pairs of city reeves who were recorded and elected between 1414 and 1418 (**140, 155, 169, 202**). From 1418 various men agreed, as mentioned above, to pay a fine to be excused the office of city reeve. Later in the century the two reeves were elected at the annual meeting on All Souls' day, a new pair each year (e.g. **273, 279, 299**).

Aldermen

Each of the four aldermen of medieval Salisbury presided over one of the wards or aldermanries into which the city was divided.[2] The aldermen occupied the second most significant urban office, ranking immediately below the mayor.[3] They were responsible for both peace-keeping and tax-collection, though the assessment and collection of taxes was done by men elected for those tasks (see below). From 1415 onwards the election of the four aldermen at the meeting on All Souls' day was regularly recorded in the Entry Book after the election of the mayor (e.g. **155, 185**). The assembly sometimes required them to supervise the execution of particular orders within their wards. Several men paid fines, as mentioned above, to be excused the office of alderman, sometimes the office of reeve also. In 1423 a royal writ ordered the mayor, aldermen, and community of Salisbury to desist from compelling a clerk in holy orders to serve as alderman by reason of his tenement in the city and to reimburse any fine imposed on him for refusing the office (**239–40**). The mayor and aldermen replied that they had not compelled him and that he had willingly sworn to perform the office (though his name does not otherwise appear in the Entry Book), appointing a deputy in his place (**241**).

While mayors usually had held several other civic offices, the aldermen often held only a few and were drawn from a broader spectrum of occupations. The alderman

---

1 *Sarum Charters*, 342.

2 In some other cities and town an alderman was the chief official of a guild: Ballard, *British Borough Charters*, p. lxxxviii.

3 Cf. the position of aldermen of Exeter, who functioned merely as 'wardsmen with few powers': Maryanne Kowaleski, 'The Commercial Dominance of a Medieval Provincial Oligarchy: Exeter in the Late Fourteenth Century', *Mediaeval Studies*, xlvi (1984), 362.

elected for Market ward in 1418 (**211**) was apparently a cordwainer (**213**). The alderman elected for St. Martin's ward in 1436 (**323**) was evidently a dyer (**319**) whose only other known office was that of collector (**318**). The alderman for Market ward 1449–50 (**436**) was a glover who had been a collector (**400**) and was later reeve (**456**). The alderman for Meadow ward 1436–7 (**323**), however, was apparently a member of the Forty-Eight (**431**) and served in a variety of offices and not only in Meadow ward (**253**, **371**, **385**, **400**, **461**). Residence, or at least long residence, in the city was evidently not required of those elected as alderman since men from Fordingbridge (**279**) and Bristol (**368**), neither of whom are found elsewhere in the Entry Book, were elected, and one from Warminster was dispensed from the office, promising to give £3 (**155**).

Assessors and Collectors

Regularly throughout the Entry Book the election is recorded of assessors and collectors of levies for a variety of purposes, including the repayment of the mayors' expenses and loans and taxes demanded by the king. Each of the four wards had at least two assessors and two collectors in each instance. Collecting taxes was, as ever, an unpopular task, and in 1449 it was agreed that in future the collectors of a fifteenth and tenth should be paid a fee for their work (**407**).

Coroners

In 1410 the mayor obtained a writ which allowed the community to choose two coroners for the city (**89**) and the election of one or two coroners is recorded from time to time as vacancies occurred (e.g. **128**, **358**). The office was sometimes held by the mayor (**275**).[1] Coroners held the pleas of the crown and saw that the reeves were just administrators.

Constables

The city had two constables, who were elected either to fill vacancies as they occurred (e.g. **81**, **262**) or as a pair (e.g. **242**). The two chosen in 1416 were said to be appointed to keep the watch (**163**). The number was increased in 1449 to four, one for each ward (**427**), and the following year to two for each ward, to keep the peace (**438**), reflecting, like other decisions recorded in the Entry Book, the uncertainty of the times. The increase to eight was apparently temporary: only four were elected and sworn in 1451 (**442**), but in that year it was agreed that there should be watchmen and wardens of the city by night 'during these days of unrest', to be sworn in by the mayor and constables (**444**). Most of the constables went on to higher civic office, often as members of parliament or mayors.

---

1   Cf. *VCH Wilts.* vi. 99.

Serjeants

Two serjeants were elected at the annual meeting on All Souls' day in 1416 (**169**) and regularly thereafter. They served for just one year (e.g. **185, 202**) until the 1430s, when the same pair of men began to be elected each year (e.g. **309, 323**). They were sometimes mentioned as serjeants at mace or serjeants of the gaol, reflecting their functions as, respectively, ceremonial officers and the custodians of prisoners (**205**). They summoned the citizens to attend meetings (**350**) and to appear before the mayor (e.g. **107**). In 1430 they were put in charge of the common ditch surrounding the city, with the responsibility of scouring and repairing it and paying 13s. 4d. a year for the profit which they could make from it (**269**). In 1451 one of the two serjeants was to have a house in which he was to live and keep any prisoners, and the two serjeants were to look after the city's weigh-beam and take its profits, for which they were to pay 13s. 4d. a year (**450**). In 1416 it was agreed that there should be a third serjeant because of the king's expected visit (**170**). In 1435 the assembly ordered that a third macebearer or serjeant should be appointed, with a wide range of responsibilities: he was to wait on the mayor, act as a chamberlain in collecting rents and seeing to the maintenance of buildings belonging to the city (being paid for that £2 a year like the chamberlains), and was to act as subwarden of Holy Trinity hospital for a wage of £1 6s. 8d., receiving also a gown and food and drink (**303**, cf. **313**). In 1439, when the assembly was evidently trying to economize, the need for the third macebearer was in question (**349**), but the following year one was appointed at a salary of 6s. 8d. with food and clothing (**355**) and in 1450 the salary was 13s. 4d. (**450**), which may have come, as in 1447, from the profits of the city's weigh-beam (**413**).

The City Clerk

The assembly appointed two clerks of the city in 1404 (**43**) apparently for distinct purposes:[1] in the following year, when their wages and their right to a livery were mentioned, one of the men was described as the city's attorney in the Common Bench and for searching the rolls to identify outlaws, while the other was then clerk of the city (**44**), as later (e.g. **64, 203**). The city clerk was presumably responsible for recording the proceedings in the assembly and the mayor's court, and for prescribed fees he wrote and enrolled the deeds by which people held city property (**292**), which were sealed with the city's common seal (**33**). In 1420 it was ordered that no deed should be sealed with the mayoral seal, evidently distinct from the common seal, except by the city clerk (**216**).

The office of clerk grew in importance and was lucrative. The attorney appointed in 1404 and 1405 became city clerk in 1420 (**215–16**) and in 1442, after nearly forty years' service, retired on a pension (**370**). He had been paid an additional fee in 1421 for work in trying to obtain letters patent relating to the city's liberties (**220**) and in

---

1 The clerk for the recognizance of debts, who is mentioned once in the Entry Book, in 1403 (**41**), was appointed by the Crown, not by the citizens: cf. *Calendar of Patent Rolls, 1350–4*, 45.

1424 was to ride to London on legal business (**310**). His successor, having agreed in 1448 to resign (**422**) in favour of a notary, was in 1449 reappointed to the office (**424**), but was discharged in 1451, and the notary was appointed after the king had sent a writ in his favour (**445**). The new clerk was elected to the Twenty-Four later that year (**448**).

Attorneys

The citizens of Salisbury retained both an attorney, salaried and liveried as mentioned above, and other legal advisers who also received salaries and liveries. One of the two advisers retained in 1405 was John Gowayn (**44**), who in 1393 had been the bishop's steward (**196**). Counsel retained in 1417 (**185**) and 1418, as in earlier years (**203**), was still retained in 1435 at his old wages and livery (**310**). Other salaried advisers were appointed in 1447 (**412**) and 1449 (**431**), and in 1452 a member of the Forty-Eight and the former city clerk were paid annual fees for giving advice (**455**).

Chamberlains

Although Hatcher wrote of mention in the mid-fourteenth century of a chamberlain who was receiver and treasurer of the city,[1] the assembly's decision in 1409 to elect two chamberlains to receive all payments owed to the community, with a comptroller to keep a counter-roll (**79**), appears to have been a new departure.[2] While references to the comptroller later in the Entry Book are rare (**90, 179**), the chamberlains assumed functions previously performed by the mayor (**80, 135, 227**), gradually acquiring greater control of the city's finances (**136, 149, 171, 221**). The chamberlains were sometimes renewed in their office from year to year (e.g. **133**); the replacement of the two in 1419 (**208**) may have been either because they had been unsatisfactory or because they deserved to be relieved from an onerous task. A new chamberlain was elected from time to time, to replace one of the two previously in office (**280, 285, 293**).

Auditors

Although there is little evidence of the activity of the comptroller of the chamberlains, references to auditors of various accounts and assessments, mentioned in 1404 when they were to be chosen by the mayor and a select group (**43**), become increasingly frequent. Audit was made a regular practice in 1417 (**188**), and auditors were drawn from those with experience of civic office. In 1446 the mayor, two former mayors, and two others were to supervise both the assessment and the collection of a levy for the expenses of the members of parliament (**403**), and in 1447 the assessors elected for the year, presumably of all accounts, were the mayor, two members of the Twenty-Four, both former mayors, and two members of the Forty-Eight (**414**).

---

1   Hatcher, 79.
2   Cf. Street, 223.

Other Officers

Besides numerous functions performed by members of the city's councils, the Entry Book refers intermittently to minor officers. In 1433 a supervisor (who was later to be mayor, 1452–3) was appointed for the weigh-beam which the chamberlains were instructed to provide (**293**), which in 1435 all were required to use (**310**), and which was later controlled by the serjeants, as mentioned above. The assembly agreed to the removal of the subwarden of the almshouse, otherwise Holy Trinity hospital, and the appointment of a successor in 1418 (**204**) and 1419 (**208**); the mastership of the hospital was vested in the mayor for the time being,[1] and the mayor's serjeant came to act as subwarden, again as mentioned above. In 1443 the assembly agreed to a levy for the wages of a 'raker' or refuse collector (**388**). The four porters, one for each of the city's gates, whose appointment was sanctioned by the bishop in the mid fourteenth century,[2] find no mention in the Entry Book; their office may have lapsed, and the watchmen and wardens who were to be sworn in 1451 served some of the same purposes (**444**).

THE BUSINESS OF THE ASSEMBLY

In addition to recording the names of those present at meetings and the election or appointment of civic officers, the Entry Book reflects the varied business of the assembly. That business included the election of members of parliament and the payment of their expenses, the presentation by officers of their accounts of receipts and expenses, arrangements for the assessment and collection of taxes and other dues, supervision of charities and city property, disputes between citizens, and the regulation of trade and hygiene.[3] The attempts by the citizens to wrest greater independence from the control of the bishop and his officials do not feature strongly in the Entry Book, though there are indications that it was a lasting preoccupation of the mayor and his colleagues, as in the order that the bishop's clerk of the market should not enter the city to perform his office (**353**), in the deputation to discuss with the bishop the revival (as the citizens saw it) of the city's liberties (**389**), and in the raising of 23 marks to appease the bishop for granting the 'old customs' (**392**). The Entry Book is largely silent about Cade's rebellion of 1450, which though more than a local feud resulted in the murder of the bishop of Salisbury by the hand of a Salisbury man. It does include, however, the king's certificate of a commissioner sent, following the rebellion, to inquire into sedition in the south-west (**436A**) and the writs mentioned in the record of an assembly of 1451 (**445**) may have resulted from acts of violence committed during the rebellion.

Parliamentary Representation

The assembly elected the city's members of parliament. The usual practice appears to have been to elect one senior and one less experienced man (**231**). All those elected

1   *VCH Wilts.* iii. 357.
2   Hatcher, 83.
3   Cf. Carr, 1997.

were citizens except perhaps for a man described as esquire who served in the parliament of 1442 (**375**). Some citizens repeatedly represented the city, and many of the representatives had or would hold the office of mayor. The assembly imposed a levy from which to pay the members' expenses, normally at the standard rate of 2s. a day, though between 1447 and 1449 the assembly, apparently in an economizing mood, paid only 1s. per day (e.g. **408, 425**). The totals could be large: the members attending the parliament of 1433 were paid for 118 days (**296**).

Taxation and Finance

Much of the assembly's attention was devoted to the collection of various levies. Besides the expenses of members of parliament, on the one hand were the taxes granted to the king by parliament and loans demanded by the king, and on the other were local requirements, either occasional, like the money raised for the purchase of the George Inn (**43**) and for the payment of soldiers recruited in Salisbury for the defence of Calais (**317, 321**), or the recurrent reimbursement of expenditure by the mayor and other civic officers. National taxes were assessed as a notional tenth or fifteenth of the taxpayers movable goods. For the loans the citizens asked for sureties of repayment, which was often to come from the customs on wool paid at Southampton (e.g. **150**).

The money held by the city's officers was presumably kept in the common chest (**108**) or in the small chest with two locks in the mayor's keeping (**121**). The assembly elected keepers of the keys of the common chest (e.g. **310**), and in 1447 the chest was to have four keys, one with the mayor, one with a member of the Twenty-Four, and two with members of the Forty-Eight (**414**). In 1440 the common seal of the city and the common purse were to be placed under no fewer than six locks (**354**). The assembly's care with the money in its custody is shown also by the appointment of auditors, as mentioned above.

The Economy of the City

Cloth manufacture accounted for the bulk of Salisbury's economic prosperity in the period of the Entry Book, and the occupations most frequently recorded were connected with the making and selling of cloth. Apart from dealing with sub-standard cloths (**180–1, 186, 190**), the assembly was much concerned about the imposition of new tolls at Southampton in 1411 (**92–4, 102**) and about the introduction of new standard measurements for cloths (101, 115), which it was alleged made it impossible to produce to the legal requirements the striped cloths, or 'rays' (**104**), for which Salisbury was famous.[1]

The craftsmen of the city were organized in trade guilds, which the Entry Book mentions infrequently. In 1441, in connection with the completion of the great ditch, it named the stewards of nineteen guilds, comprising thirty-eight specified trades. Some of the groupings of trades within a guild are surprising, cooks with barbers, saddlers

---

1   Cf. *VCH Wilts.* v. 125–8.

with cutlers and other metal-workers, vintners with fishmongers, bowyers and fletchers with building trades (**362**). In 1421, when the assembly restricted the sale of cloths made in Salisbury (**219F**), the book listed the names of the stewards and members, both masters and journeymen, of two of the most important guilds, the weavers and fullers (**219B–E**).

The Regulation of Retail Trade and Nuisances

The market was under the control of the bishop's officers, but the citizens' assembly and officers contrived to involve themselves in the regulation of retail trade. In the exercise of the assize of bread the mayor was on equal footing with the bishop's bailiff,[1] and the Entry Book records the punishment in 1401 of bakers who sold defective bread (**40**). It is perhaps surprising that that is the only record in the book relating to the assize of bread. In 1417 the mayor's court, sitting in the Guildhall, heard a case against a man for regrating (**177**). The assembly made orders in 1416 about selling outside the hours of daylight (**167**), in 1438 about the hoarding of grain (**344**), and in 1439 about the sale of cooked meat (**349**).

Most of the assembly's orders in relation to the market and retail trade were clearly intended to avoid nuisances, particularly from the butchers' trade. In 1415 the stalls of the outside butchers were relocated next to the ditch behind Butcher Row, where the street was to be improved (**145**). The orders were different for outside and for resident butchers presumably because the outside butchers slaughtered their animals and disposed of the offal before coming to the city. In 1423 the assembly ordered that animals should be slaughtered not in the street in front of Butcher Row but behind the row (**236**), an order that apparently needed reiteration in 1434 (**295**, **298**), and the removal and rendering of the offal was to be done at night (**236**). In 1437, however, the assembly agreed that at a cost of £3 the butchers' stalls should be moved back from the common ditch to their former place by the market (**327–8**). In 1445 the assembly resolved that resident butchers should perform no slaughtering or scalding except at the newly constructed scalding house near Fisherton Bridge (**398**), and in 1447 that while the outside butchers should remain in the market the resident butchers should sell meat only from their own houses (**413**).

Fishmongers and the sellers of other produce that was liable to rot were also the subject of ordinances: in 1427 fishmongers were placed by the common ditch, with outside fishmongers apart from and behind the resident fishmongers (**260**), the resident fishmongers having their stalls opposite the Guildhall in 1432, and there was special provision for oysters and other shellfish. Dairy produce and fruit were to be sold in a particular place, and rabbits were to be sold only in the market (**286**). An order of 1418 about pigs, geese, and ducks (**203**, cf. **236**) was probably also intended to avoid nuisance. The assembly also sought to remove or limit the obstruction and hazard of animals brought into the city either carrying goods (**167**, **236**) or to be offered for sale (**260**): once pack-animals had been unloaded they were to be removed from the market and

---

1   Street, 208–11.

the streets, and animals offered for sale were to be kept at Barnwell Cross and Culver Street in the south-east corner of the city.

The assembly concerned itself with two other forms of potential nuisance. It provided, early in the period covered by the Entry Book, for two refuse carts manned by a team of four (**271**, cf. **294**). In 1438 it ordered that the mayor should negotiate with the dean and chapter (the bishopric being vacant) for digging a pit in market in which to put market refuse (**335**), and in 1445 it authorized the mayor to make a five-year contract with the refuse collectors (**396**), having two years earlier agreed to pay a 'raker', as mentioned above. To control a nuisance of another kind it ordered in 1433 that the prostitutes' brothel should be at the cottages in Friary Lane (**291**). In 1442 it was ordered that the prostitutes should live in Culver Street (**372**), as confirmed in 1450 with the addition of the penalty of imprisonment at the mayor's discretion if they did not obey (**440**), and in 1452 they were to be removed from Culver Street to outside the city, were not to loiter in the city, and were to wear striped hoods,[1] on pain of imprisonment (**451**).

Watercourses, Streets, and Bridges

The condition of the elaborate system of channels which carried water through the city was a recurrent concern. An ordinance of 1416 imposed a penalty on those who obstructed or fouled the watercourse running through the middle of the city (**167**). In 1429 it was ordered that willows planted in the common ditch were to be uprooted, the ground appropriated for them being remade, and all the defects in the ditch were to be made good under a surveyor appointed by the mayor (**263**). Apparently at about the same time a collection was made among the citizens for repairing the common ditch (**262**). In 1452 the condition of the ditch was to be discussed with the bishop, and a committee of seventeen from the Twenty-Four and the Forty-Eight was formed to oversee the paving of the streets and the ordering of privies, ditches, and sewers (**452–3**). The great ditch surrounding the city on the north and east sides, and forming part of its defences, was made the responsibility of the serjeants in 1430 (**269**) but two years later was assigned to one of the chamberlains (**286**). The same man still enjoyed the grazing rights there in 1441 (**359**), but in the same year major work was done on the great ditch (**362, 364–6**).

In 1393, with the arrival of Richard II impending, twelve citizens were made responsible for the repair and improvement of Minster Street and all broken streets (**194**). In 1452 when the paving committee was formed the assembly prohibited the use of sledges attached to carts and of elongated packs dragging on the ground behind pack-animals because of the damage done to the streets and ditches (**453**). The numerous

---

1   Leah Lydia Otis, *Prostitution in Medieval Society: The History of an Urban Institution in Languedoc* (Chicago, 1985), 77–83, discusses the restriction of prostitutes to certain areas and distinctive apparel. As with the French prostitutes, the peculiar clothing of the Salisbury women provided means of both punishment and publicity. See also Ruth Mazo Karras, 'The Regulation of Brothels in Later Medieval England,' *Signs*, 14 (1989), 399–433.

watercourses required bridges to cross them. In 1389 a group of men were given permission to build what appears to have been a temporary bridge to take a cart across the ditch at St. Edmund's church (**271**). Bridge repairs are not infrequently recorded: in 1406 and 1408, for example, the mayor claimed for money spent on work on the bridge carrying High Street across the common ditch (**64, 71**) and in 1414 the chamberlains claimed for more extensive work to the same (**140**). The maintenance of Fisherton Bridge, the way over the Avon into the city from the west, was mentioned in 1388 (**3**) and 1430 (**272**).

City Property

The city paid the 100 marks to the Crown in 1406 to secure the right to hold property in mortmain (**53**), a development which may have led to the appointment of chamberlains three years later and may also have resulted in less cordial relations with the bishop.[1] The citizens bought some property with money which they contributed, notably the George Inn in 1404 (before they had obtained the mortmain licence) (**43**), and the assembly gave its attention to the running or letting of that property (**78, 121, 130, 132, 203**). Other property was left to the city in wills (e.g. **113**). Yearly obits in the churches of the city commemorated those who had made such gifts (e.g. **206**), and rentals scattered throughout the Entry Book show the extent of the property (e.g. **126**). The city's chamberlains supervised the repair of houses (e.g. **140**) that were not to be repaired by their tenants (e.g. **209**). In 1431 an ordinance provided that all houses within the city still thatched with straw were to be roofed in tile (**275**): the fire hazard posed by thatched roofs in the close quarters of the city is obvious.

War, Civil Disturbance, and the Resolution of Disputes

The Entry Book records the city's involvement with fighting elsewhere. In 1405 the mayor paid the wages of archers sent to the king in Wales (**44**), and a further payment for men delayed in Wales was necessary in 1407 (**64**). It records that the king's letter for an array in 1415 was read and quotes at length the account of the Agincourt campaign (**154**). Men at arms and archers from Salisbury were sent at the city's expense to defend Calais in 1436 (**313, 315, 317, 321**), and preparations were made for a similar force in 1451 (**443–4**).[2] For defence at home in 1440 barriers were to be raised within the city, and guildsmen were to be mustered (**350**); a new north gate had been built (**354**), work was done on the walls around the city (**353**), and the construction of the great ditch began (**358**).

Before the Agincourt campaign, on an August Sunday in 1415, a fight broke out between some Salisbury inhabitants and the duke of Lancaster's men, who were camped to the west of Salisbury beyond Fisherton Bridge. The soldiers attacked the citizens

---

1   *VCH Wilts.* vi. 101–2.
2   The record of wages paid to soldiers sent to Southampton in 1457 (**56**) appears to have been inserted in the First Entry Book in error.

with swords and arrows and killed four of them after a chase (**151**). Afterwards the city provided for extra security and paid for the burial of one of the men who were killed (**153**). No other incident of comparable violence is recorded before Cade's rebellion, about which the Entry Book maintains a discreet silence.

Most of the disputes which came to the attention of the assembly or the mayor's court arose from offensive words, of a more or less serious nature (e.g. **446**). One man, William Reynold, appears to have been a trouble-maker, having been involved in a dispute about assessment for tax (**13**), petitioning the king about false imprisonment for speaking allegedly treasonable words (**34**), doing penance in 1416 for his wicked words against a fellow citizen (**161**), and being imprisoned in 1417 for accusing others of treason (**178**) and again in 1419 for scandalous words (**205**). There were, however, apparently two men of the name in 1399 (**138**), one of whom had been a tax collector (**15**, **17**) and was several times recorded as a leading tax payer and as attending the assembly. Other disputes arising from taxation that came to the hearing of the mayor and his fellows concerned violence against a collector (**64**), refusal to pay and to answer a summons for that refusal (**107**), an accusation against the assessors of perjury (**165**), and criticism of the mayor and the ward alderman (**166**). A member of the Twenty-Four was in 1425 removed from the office of constable, barred from meetings, and fined for infringing the mayor's regulations about trading in the market (**250**). Another member of the Twenty-Four, the mercer Thomas Freeman, was in 1426 fined a pipe of red wine and £1 for a breakfast for the Twenty-Four (**256**) for defaming the mayor, and three years later was charged with bringing a false plea of debt and an accusation of breach of the peace against another citizen; he was forgiven on the intervention of his friends (**266**) and later served as mayor for two terms, 1436–8.[1]

EDITORIAL METHOD

This edition is in effect a slightly abbreviated translation, which omits some common form and insignificant verbiage. It ignores running cancellations and corrections in the manuscript, and excludes marginal notes that add nothing to what is in the main text. While it indicates the arrangement in columns of lists of names, it does not necessarily note where other kinds of information appear in the manuscript in columns or tabular form.

The text has been divided into distinct entries which are numbered to facilitate indexing and to indicate chronological separation. Most entries are meetings of the assembly, but some separate items, such as royal letters and the accounts of the mayors, have also been made into separate entries, particularly where the item was not evidently included in the discussion of the assembly or where it is an attachment (often vellum rather than paper) bound into the Entry Book as a separate piece.

The folio numbers of the most nearly complete foliation (see above, pp. x-xi) are given in square brackets. Where an inserted piece is omitted from that foliation it

---

1 There were two men called Thomas Freeman in 1423 (**237**), one being a yeoman (**238**). There may even have been three if the merchant of the name (**376**, **378**) was distinct from the mercer.

has been assigned a folio-number according to the folio which it follows: e.g.: f. 27a; if two or more occur together, they have been designated 'a', 'b', etc., in sequential order.

Dates are given both in the form used in the manuscript and, in square brackets, in their modern form. In many places damage to the manuscript has made the date illegible, and where possible an approximate date is given in square brackets.

Damaged portions of the Entry Book have presented challenges. Much time spent with magnifying glass and ultraviolet lamp has resulted in the recovery of substantial passages which at first appeared illegible, but others, either damaged by water or obscured by repair material, have remained unread. Relatively short illegible passages are indicated by an ellipsis in round brackets (. . .). Presumed readings of illegible words are in roman type enclosed in round brackets, with a question mark to indicate those which are less certain.

The edition notes where an entry is in a language other than Latin. Where the actual words of the manuscript are thought to be of sufficient significance or difficulty they are added to the translation in round brackets and in italic type for words in Latin or French or, for words in English, in roman type in quotation marks. Where in an entry in Latin a word or phrase is in English or French it is put in quotation marks. Editorial corrections (including suggested revisions and words supplied to make good omissions) are enclosed in square brackets, and editorial comments are additionally in italic.

Surnames are given in the edition in the spelling of the manuscript, but forenames are given in their modern form. Place-names are, where possible, given in their modern form, with the manuscript form in brackets if it offers a point of interest. Sums of money and other figures, which in the manuscript are in roman numerals, are translated into arabic numerals, either with £ s. d. modernised or in marks. Sums of money which the manuscript expresses as more than 20s. or more than 12d. are translated in the edition into pounds and shillings.

THE COLLATION OF THE MANUSCRIPT
(see above pp. x-xi)

Gathering — Enumeration of folios

a	b	c	d
I (10 folios)			
1			
2	2	2	
3	3		
4	4	4	
6	6	6	
5	5	5	
7	7	7	
8		8	
9	9	9	
10		10	
II (19 folios)			
11			
12			single
13			

Gathering — Enumeration of folios

a	b	c	d
14	14	14	
15	15	15	
16	16	16	
17	17	(17)	
18	18	18	
19	19	19	
20		20	
21		21	
22	22	22	
23	23	23	
[24]			
25	25		
26	26		
27a	27		insert
27	28	24	
28		25	
29	30	26	

Gathering
Enumeration of folios

a	b	c	d	
III (14 folios)				
30	31	[2]7		
31	32	28		
32	33	29		
33	34	30		
34	35	31		
35	36	33		
36	37			
37	38	35		
38	39	36	38	
39	40	(3)4	(39)	
40	41	38	40	
41	(42)	(3)8	41	
42	43	39	42	
42[a]				insert
43	45	38	43	
IV (17 folios)				
44	47	39	45	
45		4(0)		
46	49	41	47	
47	50	42		
48		43	49	
49				
50		45	51	
51	54	46	52	
52		4[ ]	52	single
53	57	47	53	
53[a]	56			insert
54	55	48	54	
55	59	49	56	
56	60	5(0)	56	
57		51	57	
58				
59			54	
59[a]	64			insert
B59[c]				insert
60	66			
V (15 folios)				
61	67	53		
62				
63			6[ ]	
64	70	55		
65	71	56		
66	72	57		
67	74	58		
67a	75			insert
68	76	59		single
69	77	(60)		
70	78	(63)		
[70a]	78			
71	79	52		
72	80			
72a				a blank recto
73	82	64		
73	83			
VI (16 folios)				
75	84	46		
76	85	65		

Gathering
Enumeration of folios

a	b	c	d	
77	86	(8)8		
78	87	89		
78[a]	88			
78[b]				
78[c]	89			
78[d]	90			
78[e]				
79	91	78		
80	92			
80[a]	93			insert
81	94		83 (twice)	
82	95	(73)		
83	96	74	85 (twice)	
84[a]	97			insert
84	98	75		
85	99	76		
85[2]	101			insert
85[a]	100			insert
86	103	77		
86[a]	102	78		insert
87[a]	104			
88[a]	105			insert
88		79	90	
88[a]	107			insert
89	108	80	91	
90	109	58		
VII (16 folios)				
91	110	8[ ]	93	
92		87	94	
93[a]	112	(84)		
94[a]	113B			insert
94	113	8(5)	96	
95	114	(86)		
96[a]	115	87		
96[a]	116			insert
97[a]	117	88		
97[a]	117A			insert
98[a]	118	89	100	
[98[a]]	119			insert
99	120	90		
100[a]	122A			insert
100	122B	91		
101	123	92		
102	124	93		
103	125	94		
104	126	95		
[104[a]]	128			insert
105	127	96		
106	129	98		
VIII (16 folios)				
107	130	97		
108	131	99		
109	132	100		
110	133		112	
111	134	102		
111[a]	135			insert
112	136	103		
113	137	104		
114	138	105		

Gathering Enumeration of folios					Gathering Enumeration of folios			
a	b	c	d		a	b	c	d
115	139	106			X (14 folios)			
116	140	107			139	169	130	
a double leaf, unnumbered			insert		140	170	132	
117	142	108			141	171	133	
118	143	109			142	172	133	145
119	144	109 [again]			143	173	134	
[ ]	145		insert		144	174	135	147
120		110			145	175	136	
121	147	111			146	176	137	
121		113 [on verso]			147	177	138	
					148	178	139	
IX (16 folios)					149	179	140	
123	149	114			150	180	141	153★
124	150	115			151	181	242 [sic]	
125	151	116			152	182	143	155
126ª	152		insert					
126	153	117			XI (4 folios)			
127	154	118			153		144	single
128	155	119			154		14(5) [on verso]	
129	156	120			155		147	
130		(121)			156	186	148	single
131	158	123						
[132]			blank recto		XII (7 folios)			
132ª	160		insert		157	187	149	single
133ᵇ	162		insert		157ª	188		insert
133ᶜ	163		insert		158	189	150	single
133		124			159	190	151	single
133ª	161		insert		160	191	153	
134	164				161			
135	165	126			161ª	193		insert
136	166	127			171			single
137	167				172	195		single
138	168							

★ other numbers on the folio are 253 (crossed out), 153, and 35 (crossed out)

MAYORS OF SALISBURY 1380–1453
as recorded in the First Entry Book

Names in square brackets are from Hatcher, 695, with an asterisk to indicate uncertainty about the name or date.

Mayoral year	Name	No. of entry
1380–1	Thomas Chandler	447
1381–2	[John Buterleigh 1382★]	
1382–3		
1383–4	Thomas Hindon	447
1384–5	John Needler	447
1385–6	Robert Play[1]	447

1 Robert Play is recorded as mayor on 14 Nov. 1386, suggesting that he became mayor on 2 Nov. 1386, but since John Buterleigh rendered his account as mayor at Michaelmas 1387 it is likely that in 1386 the new mayor was not elected until after 14 Nov.

Mayoral year	Name	No. of entry
1386–7	John Buterleigh	1–2
1387–8	Thomas Boner or Boyton	1–2
1388–9	William Warmwell	40, 447
1389–90	John Heath 1388	271
1390–1	[John Wallop 1390★]	
1391–2	[John Baker 1391★]	
1392–3	John Salisbury, grocer	194, 197
1393–4	John Cammell, grocer[1]	194, 200
1394–5	? Thomas Boreford, [2]	8
1395–6		
1396–7	John Moner	15
1397–8	Richard Spencer	11, 14
1398–9	Edmund Enfield	27, 32–3
1399–1400	Adam Teffont	6
1400–1	Richard Leche	37–8
1401–2	John Newman	41
1402–3	William Walter[3]	74–5
1403–4	John Salisbury	42
1404–5	William Waring	43–4
1405–6	John Needler	51
1406–7	Nicholas Harding	42, 57
1407–8	William Bishop	65–6
1408–9	Walter Shirley	72
1409–10	William Sale	81
1410–11	Walter Nandre	91
1411–12	William Dowding	100, 112
1412–13	John Becket	113
1413–14	Thomas Mason	128
1414–15	John Lewisham	134, 142
1415–16	William Waring	156
1416–17	Walter Shirley	169–70
1417–18	John Judd	184–5
1418–19	Robert Poynant	127, 202
1419–20	Robert Warmwell	211
1420–1	Henry Man	219, 211

1   John Cammell was elected mayor on 2 Nov. 1393 and was named as such on 5 Dec. (no. 200), but he had been named other than as mayor on 7 Nov. when John Salisbury was named as mayor (no. 199), so it is likely that the election was not effective immediately.

2   John Boreford (or Brutford) is named by Hatcher for 1395 and as uncertain for 1394. The reference in the Entry Book to him as mayor is undated.

3   William Walter's mayoralty is dated 1402 by Hatcher. It is undated in the Entry Book, which records his account apparently in 1409, six years after the last preceding date for which no other mayor is known. At the same meeting William Waring accounted for his mayoralty, 1404–5.

Mayoral year	Name	No. of entry
1421–2	John Swift	227
1422–3	William Waring	233, 235–6
1423–4	William Waring	243–4
1424–5	William Warwick	246–7
1425–6	William Warwick	251, 256
1426–7		
1427–8	John Bromley	257–8, 260
1428–9	William Pakyn	261
1429–30	William Warmwell	264, 268
1430–1	Richard Gatour	274–5, 278
1431–2	Henry Man	279–80
1432–3	Henry Baron	286, 288–9, 418
1433–4	William Waring	293–4
1434–5	John White, mercer	299–301, 303, 308
1435–6	Stephen Cooper	309, 311, 320
1436–7	Thomas Freeman[1]	323, 326–7
1437–8	Thomas Freeman	333, 341
1438–9	Henry Man	342, 345
1439–40	William Warwick	348, 355
1440–1	William Warwick	356, 358, 366–7
1441–2	John Wyatt, mercer	362, 368, 370–2
1442–3	William Pakyn	373, 386
1443–4	William Hoare	387, 389
1444–5	William Swayn	394
1445–6	Richard Payn	401
1446–7	John Port	406
1447–8	John Wyatt	415, 420
1448–9	William Cormaille	420, 422, 427–8, 431
1449–50	John Cammell	436, 438
1450–1	John Hall	445
1451–2	William Lightfoot	448, 454
1452–3	Simon Poy	456

1 Presumably the merchant or mercer of than name, rather than the yeoman. Two men called Thomas Freeman attended a meeting in 1423 (no. 237).

GLOSSARY

Some of the vernacular or obsolete words or forms of words that occur in the text may not be immediately comprehensible and are explained below.

bocher, boucher, bowchere, i.e. butcher
bowier, bowyer, i.e. bowmaker
browderer, embroiderer
bruer, brwer, i.e. brewer
chapman, chepman, itinerant dealer or pedlar
chivaler, knight
corvasor, corvecor, corvyser (etc.), i.e. cordwainer or shoemaker
curreour, i.e. currier, leather-dresser or shoemaker
deiher, dier, digher, diger, i.e. dyer
dubber, beater of leather
dygyngs hous, the meaning is uncertain
fourbour, furbour, i.e. furbisher of metalwork
fysshere, fishmonger
habergeon, a jacket of armour
heliere, tiler of roofs
hosyer, i.e. hosier, maker of stockings or leggings
irmanger, irmonger, i.e. ironmonger
loder, i.e. loader, perhaps carrier or keeper of pack-horses
lymnour, lympner, limner, illuminator, painter
mark, a unit of money (13s. 4d., two-thirds of £1) used in accounting
motley, parti-coloured cloth
noble, gold coin value of 6s. 8d.
plomer, i.e. plumber
pynnere, i.e. pinmaker
pyx, chest or box
savernapes, presumably some form of table linen
solar, upper room or storey
sompnour, i.e. summoner, a petty official
soudyours, i.e. soldiers
touker, i.e. tucker, another word for a fuller
webbe, webbere, i.e. weaver
wefer, perhaps weaver
welere, i.e. wheeler, wheelwright
vynter, i.e. vintner
yeman, i.e. yeoman
yrmonger, i.e. ironmonger

THE FIRST
GENERAL ENTRY BOOK
OF THE CITY OF SALISBURY

[f. 1; *badly faded, the upper half mutilated*]

1. [Assembly:] (. . .) Michaelmas 11 Ric. II [*29 Sept. 1387*].

Account of John Buterleigh, mayor (. . .).

Account of John Forest and his fellow, collectors of the subsidy on cloth, for the preceding year. Nothing remaining; quit.

Account of the stewards at the feast of St. Martin (. . .).

Order that John Buterleigh pay £32 19s. to the commonalty; £4 10s. for rent; £9 19s. 4d. for the subsidy on cloth during the term of Thomas Boner mayor, successor of John Buterleigh.

2. [Assembly:] Wednesday after Easter 11 Richard II [*22 April 1388*].

Thomas Boyton, mayor. Elected to assist Robert Wotton and his fellows, collectors of half a tenth granted to the king: Nicholas Boukland, Robert Curlynstoke, Richard Folham, and William Walters. The sum of 100 marks 8s. 8d. was afterwards paid by Thomas Boyton 'bowiere' mayor at the assembly on Saturday before St. Kalixtus 10 Ric. II [*10 Oct. 1388*]. He answered for £9 19s. (4d.) for rents owed at Michaelmas when John Buterleigh was mayor in 11 [Ric. II], for £10 received (. . .) in the same year at St. Kalixtus [14 Oct.], of which £9 19s. 4d. (. . .) was paid to Thomas Boyton 'bowiere' as above (. . .). The same Thomas answered for £20 received from John Chaundiler from a sum of £24 1s. 7d., for £2 from the gift of William Becket, for 8s. from John Weolere for arrears of 2s. [a year] paid in full, for £10 (. . .) from John Forest from sealing the subsidy on cloth at St. Philip and St. James 11 [Ric. II, *1 May 1388*], £20 from the executor of John Shouve knight.

Allowances for the mayor's payments and expenses £76 19s. 2d.; he owed £53 0s. 2d. and paid £40 into the common chest; he owed the remainder of £13 0s. 2d.

Other debtors owed a total of £52 0s. 11d.: John Chaundelir £12 1s. 7d., John Forest £10 for sealing the subsidy on cloth at Michaelmas 11 Ric. II [*1388*]; rents at the same term, £9 19s. 4d.; John Taillor £20 for bonds. Afterwards paid.

[f. 1v.; *badly faded, the upper third mutilated, the remainder blank*]

3. Assembly: (. . .)

From Thomas (Boyton?) to (William?) Loord, £13; held from the time of William Warmwelle then mayor, £5.

John (Buterleigh?) for an old house at the upper bridge of Fissherton, £12 1s. 7d.; (. . .) (Buterleigh?) for allowances of (William?) Charlyng for the costs of two bridges over the common ditch and for repairs to the street next to the ditch flowing into the city, £11 1s. 7d.; paid by (Buterleigh?) to carpenters, William Woderove and John (. . .), for improvements to the (. . .) of the (upper?) bridge of Fissherton from a grant by the mayor and commonalty in the time of John (Boner?), mayor, 11 Ric. II, £1.

Paid to the mayor by (. . .) Ferour of his tallage of 4s. imposed by the mayor with the assembly's agreement, 19 (. . .).

Paid by Buterlegh and Warmwell (. . .).

[f. 2; *badly faded, the upper half mutilated*]

4. (. . .) Account of John Moner, mayor: given by the commonalty, £150. (. . .) Expenses for the obit of Hugo Bussele, £1 6s. 8d.; for William Warmwell, £5. Sum of expenses: £129 11s. 1d.

(. . .) Remaining in the hands of the said Richard [Spencer, *who preceded Moner as mayor*] £47 4s. 9½d.; he accounted for the receipt of the city's rents, of money from the subsidy on cloth sold, and of the common seal: Thomas Castelton for rent £15; John Goldsmyth for rent at the bridge 17s. 6d.; John Crablane for city's rent at the bridge, £2; rent bought from Walter Byterle £4 8s.; William Furbour for 16s.; John Forest for sealing the subsidy on cloth £3 15s. 4d.; from the common seal of the city of New Salisbury, £1 5s., of which was pardoned to John Chaundelere, 15s.; Robert Blake for the subsidy on cloth sold £6 13s. 4d. Sum received from Spencer: £34 0s. 2d. Sum received and existing in hand £81 4s. 11½d.

[f. 2v.; *the upper half mutilated and badly faded*]

5. (. . . Account of the mayor?) Thomas Andys owes (17s. 6d.?) for various agreements. Paid for 8 pipes of wine given to various lords as specified by Spence, £17 11s.; in the fees of William Stourton, John Gowayn, Robert Fraunces, Oliver Harnham, John Wykyng, and William Loord, along with their gowns (*slopp'*), £9; for gowns for two men during the king's visit £14 16s.; for holding the king's parliament of justices and other expenses, £22 2s. 4d. Sum of expenses £74 7s.

Elected as assessors of the sum allowed to Spence for the above expenses and payments:

John Forest senior, John Nyweman, John Nedlere, Robert Deverel; as collectors: Nicholas Hardyng, William Waryn, William Bysshup, Thomas Felde.

6. Friday before Whitsun 1 Hen. IV [*4 June 1400*]

Accounts made in the time of Adam Teffonte, mayor, and remade in the presence of the said mayor, John Mone(r), John Wollop, George Meriot, John Salesbury 'grocer', William Gys, Robert Deverel, John Nedler, William Walters, John Sydenham, William (Ha?)lle, William Baly, Thomas Rede, Stephen Edyngdon, William More, John Nouble, John Gilberd, Thomas Eyr, Thomas Felde, Nicholas Harden, John Judde, Robert Durant, Walter Orm, William Salle, Henry Suthewyk, John Mountagu, Thomas Chyld, John Gatecoumbe, and Roger Enterbusshe.

Found that all the money received from the Pyper' [*or* Pyx?] with the increment was expended and totalled as appears in the said account of the said John [*no surname*] and John Moner (. . .).

[f. 3; *badly faded, the upper half mutilated*]

7. (. . .) Wednesday (. . .) Order that the house called George's inn, surrendered by Alice, wife and executor of William (Teynterer?), be granted to William Warmwell, co-executor with Alice; done on Thursday after the feast of (. . .) by the order of the mayor. (. . .)

8. (. . .) Memorandum that the mayor and commonalty claimed forfeiture of George's inn by Alice (and by William Warmwell?) executors; the holding of the tenement by the fraternity (of St. George?) in perpetuity to be approved by the whole assembly, which was to buy from the heir the perpetual possession of the tenement, by view of a court composed of these citizens: Richard Spence, William Warmwell, William Gys, John Nyweman, Richard Leche, Robert Juwel, John Forest, William Waite, John Nedlere, Thomas Castelton, William Balys, John Bakere, William Bysshop, William Waryn, William Salle, John Pope, John Levesham, Stephen Edyngdon, William Hute [*sic*, Shute?], Walter More, and others.

Elected as serjeants to levy and collect debts owed to the mayor and commonalty from the subsidy on cloth sold: John Cary and Stephen Edyngdon. Joan who was wife of William Cotton is bound to the mayor and commonalty for the subsidy with a total owed of (. . .).

Memorandum that John Byterley citizen of New Salisbury, in the presence of Thomas Boreford mayor and the citizens written below, in the assembly gave to the mayor and commonalty £100, through the sale or alienation of one of his tenements, whether he lives or dies, for the benefit and use of the city; present: John Moner, William Warmwell, John Cammell, John Bakere, Edmund Enefeld, Richard Leche, Richard Spencer, Robert Deverel, John Forest, John Nedler, John Nyweman, William Gys, John Chaundeler,

Richard Juwel, John Eceshale, Walter Orm, John Dogton, John Drewery, Robert Body, Thomas Castelton, William More, Thomas Eyre, Adam Teffont, Stephen Edyngdon, Henry Suthewyk, William Hull, William Doudyng, William Bysshop, Walter Nandre, Reginald Drewery, John Gylberd, Roger Stapelford, Robert Curtlyngstoke, Thomas Felde, John Lytle, William Woderove, Richard Weston.

[f. 3v. *blank*]

[f. 4; *badly faded, the upper half mutilated*]

9. Richard Spencer mayor (. . .; Account of the mayor:) William Furbour and others for rent of (. . .), paying 2s. a year; Philip Goldsmyth for rent of a solar above the wardrobe held from the mayor and commonalty, paying 10s. 4d. a year. [*Struck through for deletion*: the said Philip Goldsmyth owed to the mayor and commonalty £3 on a bond in the keeping of Richard Spencer mayor and it was paid to him.] John Crabelane owed the mayor and commonalty for arrears of rent for the house between the common wardrobe and 'dygyngs hous' £1, and for wasted timber (*meremio vastato*) from the bars 2s. [*Struck through for deletion*: Robert Seider is owed by the mayor and commonalty £5 on a bond of £45, also for the bars across Winchester Street for 4s. which were sold by John Nyweman, John Forest, and John Nedlere, which sum was accounted and allowed to him when John Nedlere was mayor; it was paid to him (*eidem Roberto satisfactum est*) by the mayor and commonalty for the payment [which] was from George's inn]. Edmund Enefeld and Thomas Blechere, executors of Robert Play's will, gave to the mayor and commonalty (. . .) which Thomas Boreford owed to them for various persons at (. . .) for the soul of the said Robert. [*Cf. below, no. 16.*]

[f. 4v.; *badly faded, the upper half mutilated*]

10. (. . .) Present: Richard Spencer (. . .)

11. [Assembly:] Wednesday (. . .) 21 Ric. II [*1397–8*]

Present: (. . .) John Walters, (. . .) [*the following names in column*] Reginald Drewery, John Judde, John Gylberd, Adam Morys, Adam Waryn, John Kynyton, Ralph atte Wode 'glover', Reginald Grenhull glover, John Knyht, Nicholas West dubber, Thomas Cake, John Yongge. (. . .) Which citizens on Wednesday after (. . .) 21 Ric. II were appointed to the court of Richard Spencer [mayor] (. . .).

[*The foregoing entry overlaps, apparently as the result of the damage to the MS. and its repair, a distinct entry, of which the purport is obscure. It mentions an earl, said not to be the earl of Kent, and ends*] wherefore on the consideration of the mayor, bailiffs, and citizens the said John (. . .) was placed in safe and secure custody until they see better what should be done with him.

In that connection [*Et circa hoc*] William Salle and John Dogton were bound to the mayor by a written bond under certain conditions.

John Wayte 'hosyer' and John Swyft, collectors of the tallage of John Moner when he was mayor, owed to the mayor and commonalty £2 11s. 6d. [Quit. John Forest senior owed to the mayor and commonalty £2 11s. 8d. which he received from the said collectors during Richard Spence's mayoralty; accounted by William Hull and his associate for expenses in parliament. *The entry has been struck through obliquely, and parts have been crossed out, for deletion.*]

John Drewery and John Judde owed 15s. remaining from a larger sum contained in a bond.

Robert Blake owed £50 as appears in his account made when John Cammel was mayor, of which he paid to Richard Spencer then mayor 10 marks for which Richard accounted.

[*Hatched for deletion:*] Thomas Castelton owed £20 for a charter under the seal of the mayor and commonalty releasing him from the office of mayor for life, and so that he should not be elected to that office there should be a bond to John Moner, Richard Spencer, and Edmund Enfeld, the bond to remain in the common chest. [*Added:*] Afterwards when Adam Teffonte was mayor the £20 was placed in the common chest.

[f. 5; *badly faded, the upper half mutilated, the lower half apparently blank*]

12. (. . .) Robert Curtlyngstoke and Thomas Boreford, over and above their receipts, have not accounted (. . .).

Elected as collectors: Thomas Pal(. . .), Walter (Salle?), Henry (. . .), and John Gilberd. On Saturday after the said feast they paid John Moner mayor 15s. (. . .) and are quit.

(Account of the mayor:) Robert (. . .) the bridge at Fissherton (. . . [*c. 7 lines illegible*]) (. . .) accounted for 13s. 4d. for the timber retained; allowed to the mayor and commonalty £2 (. . . [*c. 3 lines illegible*]).

[f. 5v.; *badly faded, the upper half mutilated, the lower half apparently blank*]

13. Saturday after (Michaelmas?) 21 Ric. II [*6 Oct. 1397?*]

[*The entry apparently relates to a dispute about the assessment to a subsidy, between the citizens and William Raynald, the king's assessor, who seems to have rejected the assessment of the artificers and labourers by Lawrence Druwery with the help of John Moner.*] Adam Teffonte, John Dogton, William Walters, John Barbour [*the assessors?*]; Richard Spencer [mayor].

[f. 6; *faded, the upper third mutilated*]

14. [*In the top margin:*] collectors William Walter and William Doudyng.

21 Ric. II [*1397–8*]. Money presented to the king in the mayoralty of Richard Spencer by the citizens below written.

[*In two columns*] John Cammel £40, Walter Nandre (£3?), Reginald Gloster (£2?), Richard Harlewyne (£3?), John Salesbury 'grocer' £12 6s., Richard Oward (. . .), John Eceshale (. . .), [John *crossed out*] Stoke excused the office of alderman (. . .), Thomas Sexton £3, Robert Curlyngstoke £2, W(illiam) Doudyng £2, Richard Bertoville £1, William Pycard £3, William Busshop £2, Thomas Chyld £2, John Nyweman £6, Thomas atte Felde £2, Richard Juwel £2, William Baly £2, John Wychford £3, John Swyft £1, Thomas Bowyer £3, William Warmwell £6, John Dogton £2, John Wollop £5 by Spencer, John Drewery £1, William Bour £2, Roger Stapelford £1 10s., Alexander Cake £1, Ralph Styble £1, Nicholas Boklond £2, John Judde £2, John Lytle £2. Sum £109 6s. 8d.

[*Column 2*] Richard Weston £1, John (Haselbere?) £1, William Woderove £1, John Moner £13 6s. 8d., Robert (. . .)ton £1, John Whelere £2, John (. . .) £1, Thomas Farmbor 'glover' £1, Thomas Castelton £4, John Nedler £3, Richard la Leche £5, Richard Spencer £2, Nicholas Hardyng £2, William Walters £2, John Levesham £2, Robert Deverel £2, John Barbour £3 11s., John Pope £1, John Baret £2, John Forest £3 6s. 8d., William Stout £1, John Chaundeler senior £3, John Caundel clerk £3, William Hull £2, Thomas Eyr £2, Adam Teffonte £3, John Parch £1, John Langebrewere £2, Henry Suthewyk £2, Stephen Edyngdon £1, William Salle £1, Richard Sherman £2, Robert Durant £1, Edmund Enefeld and Thomas Bleche executors of Robert Play £20. Sum £96 13s. 4d.

Sum total £206

[f. 6v. *blank*]

[f. 7; *badly faded, the upper third mutilated*]

15. Wednesday before All Saints 22 Ric. II [*31 Oct. 1397*]. Account of John Moner, mayor, in full assembly.

Expenses: Paid (. . .) to Lord Lovel at Clarendon (*Claryngdon*). [*The rest of the entry is in French*] Expenses of John Moner, Richard Spencer, (. . .) at (Evesham?), Ramsbury, (...) [and] for one time at Ramesbury and Stourton, £(...) 17s. 4d.; expenses for (. . .) on two occasions, £9 17s. (. . .); for (. . .), £12 19s.; for cloth (*drap'*) at the (. . .) in Stourton to the lord bishop's steward and to other loyal men in the house in 'Wacfeld' of William Warmwell, clerk of the justices, £8 2s. 8d.; in expenses of 'Brenchesle' on two occasions, £11; in two pipes of wine to our steward, one pipe for the sheriff, one pipe for John Chytterne, £7 16s. 8d.; in various presents to the justices of assize on two occasions at Bedwyn (*Baudwyn*) [and] Barford (*Berford*) and at our lord bishop's £3 5s.; for the expenses of Richard Juwell and John Cary at the parliaments at Westminster and Shrewsbury (*Shrouesbury*) for 37 days, £7 8s.; for the fees of William Stourton, John Gowayn, Robert Fraunces, and William Lord for the [limepits ('lymputtes') *crossed out*] marl pits ('ertheputtes') [*interlined*] of the portreeves ('portreues')[1] and for the mounding [?] ('mundy') of William Wychford £9 15s. 8d.; also paid to William Salle and John Serjant for the messengers, couriers, and cryers of the Common Bench, and to Robert Horyng £1 18s. 2d.; for a pipe of wine for our lord bishop £1 13s. 4d.; for the heralds' official £3 17s. 2d.; in the expenses of our lord le Lovel when he was at the friars, in 'Brenchesle', Stourton, the earl of Salisbury [*the meaning is not clear*], and other small expenses £2 12s. 10d. Sum £85 4s.

[f. 7v.] For liveries for the 'Gullif' [?, *sic*] of John Wykyng, Robert (Forest?), Richard Clerk, and William Lord, £2 11s.; for expenses at Marlborough (. . .) received by the court and rent £4 15s. 7d.; for expenses at (. . .) to London, £2 2s.; (. . .). Sum £11 10s. 7d. Sum (. . .). Paid for a purse at (. . .) to S(tephen) Tannere 6 marks. (. . .), for John Nyweman (. . .). Sum £8.

Sum total £104 14s. 7d.

Received from William Busshop and William Waryn, collectors of Richard Spencer, £58 2s. 11d.; from William Baylly and Thomas Chyld, 15s.; in rent, £4 10s.; from the town for the past year, £5 16s. 1d.; from the common seal, £2 5s.

Sum of receipts £71 9s.

Issues remaining to be paid to the said John Moner mayor £33 5s. 7d., which the collectors and assessors Stephen Edyngdon, William Bally, John Gilberd, and Thomas Stabbere, with the king's collectors William Raynald and Henry Suthewyk, will pay to the said mayor. [f. 8; *badly faded, the upper half mutilated, the lower apparently blank*] Received from (Stephen?)(*Est*. . .), from John (. . .). Account of from Stephen (Edyngdon?) and John Gilberd (. . .).

[1] The only mention in the book of the officers by that name.

[f. 8v.; *badly faded, the upper half mutilated*]

16. (. . .) Inventory of the property of Thomas Play deceased made by the assembly according to custom. (. . .[7 *lines illegible, apparently mentioning a room, cloth, and bakeries*], alehouse [*pandoxat'*] valued at £31 7s. 4d. Sum total £62 5s., from which was due to Edward, John, and Robert, the said Thomas Play's orphans (*orfanis*) for their purparty, £20 15s., as is fully contained in the said inventory. In his will Thomas left to his wife Alice his tenement facing the Cross, where produce (*fructus*) and vegetables (*olera*) are sold, between a tenement of St. Mary's [*the cathedral?*] on the west and the tenement of John Baker 'grocer' on the east, to hold for her life with reversion to Edward, John, and Robert and their children and the heirs of their bodies, contingent remainder to Ibote, his daughter, and the heirs of her body, as is fully contained in his will. [*cf. below*, **168**.]

[f. 9; *badly faded, the upper third mutilated*]

17. 28 May 21 Ric. [II; *1398*]. Copy of the king's letters patent to William Raynald, Richard Fulham, Reginald Glover, and Henry Suthwyk for levying one and a half fifteenth and tenth on all movables, as granted by the parliament at Shrewsbury, to be paid in three instalments, the first half fifteenth and tenth at Michaelmas following, the second a fortnight [*21 April 1399*] from Easter then following, the third a fortnight [*13 Oct. 1399*] from Michaelmas then following. [*Cf.* Rolls of Parliament, *iii. 368*.] Witnessed by the king at Westminster.

18. 14 March 2 Henry [IV; *1401*]. Copy of the king's letters patent to John Dotton, George Joce junior, John Kyngbrygge, and Walter Drur(y?) for levying a fifteenth and tenth on all movables, payable in two halves at Trinity [*29 May*] and All Saints [*1 Nov.*] next following, to be levied also on movables arising from lands and tenements acquired by the clergy after 20 Edw. [I; *1291–2*]. [*Cf.* Rolls of Parliament, *iii. 455*.] Witnessed by the king at Westminster.

[f. 9v.; *badly faded and largely illegible, the upper third mutilated, all but the top quarter apparently blank*]

19. 21 Ric. [II; *1397–8*]. Letter patent from the king for the collection of (. . .).

[f. 10; *badly faded, the upper third mutilated*]

20. (. . .)after the Conception [*8 Dec.*] (. . .).

[*In two columns*] Robert (. . .), William (. . .), John (. . .), William Warmwell, John (Charlyng?), John (. . .), John Eceshale, William Busshop, William Doudyng, Henry Suthewyk, William Salle, John Barbour, John Levesham, Thomas Postel, Richard Weston, William Baly, Thomas Deverel, John Pope, John Gilberd, William Raynald, Walter Orm, Thomas Abbot, William Boure, Thomas Blechere, Simon Trevynek, Stephen Edyngdon, John Sydenham, Edward Fontaygne, Thomas Eyr, William Woderove, John Merlawe, John Botyler, Robert Body [*besides c. 10 illegible names*].

[*Column 2*] Elected as assessors: Adam Teffonte, John Forest senior, Thomas Eyre, Simon Tredynek; as collectors: William Fuystour, John Judde, John Botyler, John Spencer.

[f. 10v.; *badly faded, the upper third mutilated, the rest apparently blank*]

21. Michaelmas [*29 Sept.*](. . .; payments . . .) John S(pencer?), William Sw(yft?), Richard

Spencer, John Forest and William Buss(hop?). [*Amounts and sum illegible.*]

[f. 11; *badly faded, the upper half mutilated*]

22. 31 Jan. 22 [Ric. II; *1399*]. In a full assembly of citizens (. . . [*reference to excessive imposition*] . . .) [*In a single column; ten names entirely illegible*], John (. . .), John (. . .), John Forest, John (. . .), John Spencer, William Boure, Thomas Blechere, William Salle, William Baly, Thomas Feld, Thomas Postel, Henry Suthewyk, William Raynald, Thomas Eyr, Thomas Chyld, John Swyft, Thomas Sextayn, William Doudyng, John Eceshale, William Waryn, John Levesham, William Busshop, John Botyler, John Gilberd, Thomas (Stobbere?), Walter Shyrle, Richard Leche, William Warmwell, William Walters, Robert Body.

[f. 11v.; *badly faded, the upper half mutilated*]

23. Friday after the Purification [*7 Feb. 1399?*] (. . . [*reference to refusal to pay*] . . .). Elected as collectors: John Levesham, William W(. . .), William Doudyng, William Busshop.

[*In three columns*] William Gys, John Forest senior, John Nedler, William Warmwell, John Moner, John Salesbury, John Nyweman, Robert Deverel, Henry Suthewyk, William More, John Botyler, Stephen Edyngdon, William Waryn, John Levesham, Robert Body, Thomas Blechere, John Lytle, John Pope, John Barbour, William Whyte, John Gilberd, William Raynald, Thomas Postel, Richard Weston, John Eceshale, Walter Orm, John Spencer, William Fuystour, Thomas Eyr, William Doudyng, Thomas Byston, William Ysaak , Thomas Chyld, Thomas Deverel, John Merlawe.

[*Column 2; apparently a new entry*]

24 . (. . .) J(. . .), John Forest, John Nedlere, (. . .), Robert Salle, Adam T(effonte), Walter S(. . .), William Fuystour, John (. . .), William Boure, Thomas Blechere, William Salle, William Baly, Thomas Felde, Thomas Postel, Henry Suthewyk, William Raynald, Thomas Eyr, Thomas Chyld, John Swyft, Thomas Sextayn, William Doudyng, John Eceshale, William Waryn, John Levesham, William Busshop, John Botyler, John Gilberd, Thomas Stabbere, Walter Shirle, Richard Leche, William Warmwell, William Walters, Robert Body.

[*Column 3; apparently a new entry again*]

25. (. . . [*c. 7 lines illegible, with a reference to the end of Easter, then c. 7 names illegible*], Richard (. . .), John Fuystour, William Ca(. . .), Richard Spencer, John Salesbury, John Chaundeler senior, John Forest senior, Robert Body, William Waryn, Adam Teffonte, John Lytle, Thomas Blechere, William Boure, John Chaundeler junior, William Raynald, John Gilberd, Richard Oword, William Busshop, Thomas Felde, William Baly, John

Kynggesbrugge, John Levesham, William Doudyng, Thomas Rede, John Barbour, John Boteler, Henry Suthewyk, John Baret, Thomas Eyr.

[f. 12; *badly faded, the upper half mutilated*]

26. Friday after St. (. . .) the same year [*1399?*]. Agreement in full assembly that Nicholas Brem(le? . . .) the mayor's seal. William Warmwell, John (. . . [*three names illegible*] . . .).

[*In three columns*] John Nedler, John Moner, John Nyw(eman), John Ba(ly?), Robert (. . .), Stephen (. . .) Stephen Joce, John Barbour, John S(. . .), John P(arch?), John Blechere, John Baret, John Nyweman, Henry Suthewyk, Thomas Eyr(e), William Boure, Adam Whyte, [*ten others names illegible*].

27. (. . .) Names of the collectors of a tenth at Easter next, along with commissioners: William Raynald, Henry Suthewyk; Reginald Gloucestre, Thomas Rede, John Langebrewere, George Joce junior, Roger Wodeford.

Saturday before St. Gregory 22 [Ric. II; *8 March 1399*] in the mayoralty of Edmund Enefeld. Assembly of neighbours for an election: John Moner, John Salesbury 'grocer', Thomas Nyweman, William Warmwell, John Forest, Adam Teffonte, William Doudyng, William Busshop, William Waryn, William Hull, Stephen Edyngdon, Walter Baly, Robert Body, John Gilberd, John Barbour, Walter Orm, Walter Nandre, Thomas Felde, William Salle, Thomas Eyr, Thomas Chyld, Thomas Rede, Henry Suthewyk, Thomas Stabbere, John Pope, and William More.

On the eve [*11 March*] of St. Gregory in the said year all the collectors assembled in the hall at the court held there and after the meal were sworn faithfully to collect and account, there being then present the mayor E[dmund Enefeld], John Moner, the four aldermen and others: [*Column 2*] John Moner, John Salesbury, grocer, Thomas Nyweman, William Warmwell, John Forest, Adam Teffonte, William Doudyng, William Busshop, William Waryn, William Hull, Stephen Edyngdon, Walter Baly, Robert Body, John Gilberd, John Barbour, Walter Orm, Walter Nandre, Thomas Feld, William Salle, Thomas Eyr, Thomas Chyld, Thomas Rede, Henry Suthewyk, Thomas Stabbere, John Pope, William More.

28. [*A new entry*] (. . .) [*then about nine names illegible*], (Thomas) Eyr, Walter Salesbury, William Mercer, John Lytle, John Judde, Thomas Deverel, John Barbour, William Raynald, Henry Suthewyk, Stephen Edyngdon, Thomas Eyr [*repeated*], Richard Weston, William Salle, William Busshop, Thomas Felde, Adam Teffonte, Thomas Chyld, Richard Leche.

[*Column 3*]

29. Assembly: The next day of the above year.

(. . .) [*An agreement by the citizens evidently relating to the assessment or collection of the fifteenth.*] William Gys, John Nedler, George Joce, John Salesbury, John Moner, Richard Spencer, Robert Forest, William Walters, Robert Curtlyngstoke, John Sydenham, John Cammel, Thomas Felde, William Hull, Nicholas Hardyng, William More, John Lytle, Peter Uphavene, Thomas Stabbere, Richard Oword, Richard atte Mulle, John Gilberd, William Busshop, Thomas Deverel, Adam Teffonte, John Levesham, William Salle, Thomas Eyr, Thomas Blechere, John Swyft, William (. . .) [*and perhaps one further name illegible*].

[f. 12v.; *badly faded, the upper half mutilated*]

30. Assembly: Friday (. . .)[*1399?*].

[Present:] (. . .) William Gys, John Forest, Richard Juwel, William (Busshop?), William Br(emle?) John Nedler, William Waryn, John Sydenham, (John) Stabbe, John Lytle, William Fobour, Walter [Gyl *crossed out*] (Sleges?), John (. . .), Richard (Deverel?), Stephen Felde, Henry (. . .), (John?) Eceshale, John Eyr, Thomas Chyld, Richard (. . .), John (. . .), John Blechere, John Botyler, John (Orm?), John Br(emle?), (Richard?) Oward, Reginald Drewery, Nicholas (Bokland?), John Salesbury, John (Nedler?), Richard Leche, Nicholas Hardyng [*the full list contained more than ten further names*].

Elected as assessors of £40 on {?} [11 Sept.]: Walter (. . .), (. . .) Lavenham, John Chippenham, John (. . .).

31. Wednesday after the Exaltation of Holy Cross [*17 Sept. 1399?*].

John Forest, John Nyweman, John (. . .), William Wale, Adam Teffonte, John (. . .), John (. . .), William (. . .), (Stephen) Edyngton, Walter (Orm?), William (. . .), (. . .) Baly, John Merlawe and others [*the full list contained more than fifteen further names*].

32. Friday before Michaelmas (. . .) [*26 Sept. 1399?*].

John Moner, Richard Spencer, William Walters, William Warmwell, John Nyewman, William (. . .), John Chaundeler, Nicholas Hardyng, John Nedler, Walter (Orm?), William Baly, William Busshop, William Doudyng, John (. . .), John Botyler, John Sh(erman?), Robert Body.

Account of William Baly [and] William Waryn, proctors of the guild of St. George, 4s. 9½d. owed; ordered that 1s. a year for the chapel of St. George be collected by the proctors for the time being on the said first day [and] sealed with the common seal (. . .).

Memorandum that on the feast of St. Roman 1 Henry [IV; *23 Oct. 1399*] in the church of St. Thomas the martyr Thomas Knoyell acknowledged himself bound to Edmund

Enefeld then mayor or his attorney and to the commonalty in £3 payable at the Annunciation next [25 March 1400]; in the presence of John Neweman, William Bailly, and others.

[f. 13; *badly faded, the upper third mutilated*]

33. Friday before Michaelmas 23 [Ric. II; *26 Sept. 1399*]. Account of the mayor for the year from All Souls 22 to All Souls 23 [Ric. II; *2 Nov. 1398 to 2 Nov. 1399*]. (. . . [*c. 8 lines largely illegible*]; expenses . . .) 7d.; in red wax for the (market?) seal, 5s.; (. . .) money paid for repairing the (tressles?) of the bridge at William (Forest?) on two occasions by view of Walter Orme and others, 3s. 8d.; in wine (. . .) to the sheriff of Wiltshire (. . .) by William Warmwell, 4d.; for repairs to the sagging eaves ('sagene eves'), 6d. Sum 5s. 6d.

Payments to various officials, viz. four officials of the earl of Northumberland on the morrow [*29 Oct. 1399*] of St. Simon and St. Jude, 2s.; Guy and his fellow king's officials on the morrow of St. Lucy [*14 Dec. 1398*], 3s. 4d.; a pursuivant of the duke of Exeter coming to proclaim the king's tournament (*hastiludum*), 2s.; another official, of Brian Cornwaile, 6d.; five other foreign (*extraneis*) officials, 2s.; an official of the duke of Exeter and three of Thomas West knight coming at the same time, 3s. 4d.; James Claronet of the earl of Salisbury and another stranger coming with him, 2s. 6d.; three officials of the town of Southampton, 2s.; a herald called Nottingham, 3s. 4d.; a pursuivant of the duke of Exeter on Easter day, 1s. 8d.; Edmund Criour [*or the crier*] and his fellow serjeants of the king's bench, 1s. 8d. Henry one of the king's officials and two others coming with him, 3s. 4d.; an official of the lord chancellor of England as he said, 1s.; four officials of the duke of Exeter with two of their servants on route to Ireland, 6s. 8d.; Adam Roter, 6d.; an official of Winchester, 1s. 8d.; three other officials of the duke of Exeter and one servant of theirs, 3s. 4d.; William Wilton the king's official, 2s.; the Hause official [?] otherwise the king's official, 2s.; a king's herald called Faukon, 6s. 8d.; William Byngley an official of the duke of Lancaster, 6s. 8d. Sum £2 18s. 2d.

Expenses of Richard Spencere, William Hull, and William Walter going to and from Coventry for 10 days to be with the king with the common seal of the city to seal a certain form sworn in the name of the whole community of the city, £3; expenses of the same William and William at another time going to and from Lichfeld and staying there with £200 conferred by the city to the king, 34s. for 14 days; their expenses going to various parts of the realm to take to the duke of Lancaster letters of credit of the city, £1 12s. for 9 days; for three horses hired by them, 9s. Sum £6 15s.

[f. 13v.; *badly faded, the upper half mutilated*]

Account of E[dmund Enfeld] mayor. (Expenses . . .)

Receipts: sealing 6 charters of Sir Richard Postelle with the common seal, (. . .); John Judde for 2 charters, 2s.; (John?) Nyweman for 2 charters, 3s.; Walter Nandre for 2 charters, 2s.; John Bosham for 3 charters, 3s.; Sir John Harnham for 1 charter, 1s.; Sir

William (Vukke?), 2s.; Thomas Childe for 1 charter, 1s.; Nicholas Hardyng for 3 charters, 3s.; John Servast for a copy of a charter (in triplicate?), 3s. 4d.; William Waryn one of the collectors of the tallage (. . .) at Salisbury, £1 4s.; John Gilberd one of the collectors of the expenses of John Moner, £4 6s. 8d.; Stephen Edyngdon another collector of the expenses of John Moner, £2 13s. 4d.; William Whyte for rent received in Dragon Street ('Drakhalstrete') for (. . .) of William Buterley, £4 10s.; John Chippenham and Nicholas Laverane collectors this year of the said expenses, £2; John Noble and John Shadde the other collectors of the said expenses this year, £2; the same, 4 marks; Thomas Blechere for the pits ('les pyttes'), £2. Sum received, £22 13s. 8d.

[f. 14; *badly faded, the upper half mutilated*]

34. [*1399–1400?*]. (. . .) On Wednesday before (. . .) of St. Mary [1?] Hen. IV because the said William [Raynald] imputed to John Moner, John Bakere, and Richard Spencer concerning the plundering (. . .) on which John, John, and Richard found sureties, viz. William Warmwell, George Meriot, John Nyweman, Robert Deverel, William Walters, and John Nedler, for their appearance before the king or his council to answer the things imputed to them by William Raynald. So the said William was placed under arrest; his sureties, Thomas Northwodes, John Tudeworth, John Ruddok, John Merlawe.

[*English*] Petition to the king by William Raynald of Salisbury: he has been wrongfully imprisoned by John Bakere, 'grocer', and John Moner of Salisbury for certain words that were true, [namely] that when Sir John Salesbury knight was condemned in parliament and sent to the Tower for execution Baker and Moner sent to the Tower Sir John Dene, priest, who brought away from John Salesbury 'burdons of gold', as Dene has told Raynald. Baker and Moner then imprisoned Raynald, accusing him of being a traitor and stating that he would be imprisoned in perpetuity by the earl of Warwick. The earl, then travelling through Salisbury to London, freed Raynald, making him find four pledges for £4 that on his release he would bind himself by a statute merchant for that sum to Bakere and Moner never to say the words that he had said nor to pursue them for wrongful imprisonment. [f. 14v.; *badly faded, the middle mutilated, the lower half apparently largely blank with traces of writing at the foot*] (. . .) [*apparently continuing the petition and mentioning words spoken to Raynald at All Hallows' church in London*].

[*English*] Charges, phrased in the second person, against John Moner, that he knew that John Salesbury was proved in parliament to be a traitor, and rehearsing the statements made in William Raynald's petition. John Dean was the cousin of Baker's wife; Raynald entered into the bond out of fear ('for drede'). [f. 15; *badly faded, the upper half mutilated*] Further charges against Moner were that when he was mayor of Salisbury he rode to Marlborough and there made arrangements about craftsmen contrary to the statute and to the detriment of the city, and that he had sent the mayor's seal overseas 'to what harm no man can say'.

John Br(emle?) for release from the office of alderman, £5 (. . .) Thomas Felde, paid by [*or* to] Richard le Leche, mayor.

Received from Thomas Blechere for the lime pits ('lyme puttes'), £3. (. . .).

[f. 15v.; *badly faded, the upper half mutilated, the lower half blank*]

35. Monday the eve of St. Matthew [*20 Sept. 1400*].

Adam Teffonte mayor, (. . .), William Eyr, William Walters, John Moner, William Warmwell, Thomas (Durneford?), (Richard?) Spencer, John Salesbury, Edmund Enefeld, Thomas (. . .), John (. . .), William Salle, John Lytle, Richard atte Mulle, John Kynggesbrugge, William (Swyft?), John (. . .), (Henry?) Suthewyk, John Parche, William Pycard, John Judde, Robert Su(. . .), Stephen (Ed)yngdon, Robert Ha(. . .), John Pope, Robert Charles, John (Forest?) senior, William War(yn?), John (. . .) [*the full list contained a further seven names*].

Resolved that (. . .) £30 be delivered to Thomas (. . .).

[f. 16; *badly faded, the second quarter mutilated*]

36. Wednesday the eve of St. Simon and St. Jude 2 Henry IV [*27 Oct. 1400*]. Account of Adam Teffonte mayor for expenses from All Souls 1 to All Souls 2 Hen. IV [*2 Nov. 1399 to 2 Nov. 1400*] approved by the full assembly of citizens on Wednesday: a pipe of wine to (Thomas?) Felde, former collector of the former sheriff of Wiltshire, £2 3s. 4d.; a pipe of white wine to Robert W(odeford?), former collector (. . .), £1 16s. 8d.; a pipe of red wine to William (Hulton *or* Hulle?), former collector of the same (. . .); 29 gallons of red (wine?) and 2½ gallons of malmsey to John (. . .)leny and (. . .), 17s. 10d.; wine to the collector Peter of Croteulhaye, 4s.; wine to bishop's collector, (. . .)s. 6d.; to the bishop at his palace, 2s. 2d.; wine to the sheriff of Wiltshire's collector at (. . .), 1s.; wine to the collector Thomas Chalre paid to the bishop, 1s. 3d.; (. . .)s. 8d.; wine to Sir John L(ovel?)'s collector, 2s. Sum £8 2s. 7d.

Expenses for the king's justices: 20 bushels of oats, 5s. 5d.; bread, 2s. 3d.; 12 bushels of oats the second time, 4s.; to the justices' crier, 1s. 8d.; taking a horse to Stockbridge for 'Brenchesle', 4d. Sum 13s. 8d.

Expenses of William Stourton: the first time at George's inn, 6s. 4d.; another time, 4s. 6d.; to John Stone for proclaiming a royal commission throughout the city, 6s. 8d. Sum 17s. 6d.

Fees: William Stourton, £2; John Gowayn, £2; Robert Fraunses, £2; William Loord, £1 6s. 8d.; for the city's pits (*puteis*), £1; to the bishop's reeve for a waste tenement, 19s.; John Liwet, attorney versus Henry Popham for the said mayor, 3s. 4d. Sum £9 9s.

Liveries for William Stourton, Robert Fraunces, and William Loord, 25s. 6d.; to John Lambard for copying the commission of array, 1s. 8d.; to William Whyte, collector of the city's rent late of Robert Russel, 1s. 8d.; to Oliver Cervyngton, the king's coroner, for viewing the body of a man killed, 3s. 4d. Sum £1 12s. 2d.

To a king's messenger with a letter from the king for the arrest of traitors (*proditores*), 3s. 4d.; to another royal messenger with a warrant for inquiring about the traitors' goods and chattels, 3s. 4d.; to three officials of Lord Lovel, 6s. 8d.; to two king's officials, 2s.; to another king's official, 2s.; to a king's herald ('Kyngheraud'), 6s. 8d.; to his fellow at Burford, 1s. 8d.; to four officials of the earl of Northumberland, 2s.; to Adam Rotere, 1s.; to a king's pursuivant, 1s. 8d.; to the earl of Oxford's officials, 1s. 8d.; to Henry, the king's marshall, 8d.; to another official, 1s. 8d.; to two king's officials, 1s. 8d. To Godfrey Boton a messenger inquiring about the prince of Wales, 1s. Sum £1 17s.

[f. 16v.; *faded, the upper third mutilated, the lower half blank*]

Expenses at parliament: William Hull and William Walters for eight weeks, receiving for each of the seven days 4s.; sum £11. [*The sum is for one day less than eight weeks.*]

Sum £33 11s. 11d.

Approved by the assembly: William Walters, John Moner, William Warmwell, John Barbour, John Forest, John (. . .), Edmund Enefeld, John Nedler, John Parch, Walter Child (?), Walter Nandre, Robert Durant (?), John Judde, John Levesham, William Pycard, Thomas (Swa)yne (?), William More, Clement (. . .), (John?) Eceshale, John Lytle, Roger Wodeford, William Waryn, John Kyngesbrugge, John (Br)a(t)ele (?), John Chaundeler, John Sydenham, William Nedler, William Cakes (Pakkes?), Nicholas (H)a(r)dyn(g) (?), Thomas Felde, Henry S(uthewyk?) [*the full list contained three further names*].

Appointment of assessors for the four wards: New Street, (. . .); Market, (. . .) Marlburgh (?); St. Martin, John Pope; Meadow, Henry Suthewyk. Appointment of collectors: New Street, John Kynggesbrugge and Roger Wodeford; Market, Nicholas Bokland and John Durneford; St. Martin, William Slegge and William Nedler; Meadow, John Sydenham and Laurence Lane.

[f. 17; *faded and stained, the upper half holed*]

37. Wednesday before [St. Simon and St. Jude *crossed out*] St. Denis 3 Hen. IV [*5 Oct. 1401*]. Account of [Adam *crossed out*] Richard le Leche mayor for the period All Souls 2 Hen. IV [*2 Nov. 1400*] to the same feast a year later, in full assembly.

[Expenses] (. . .) 9s.; in food given to the same justices (. . .) at the same time, 2s. 4d.; for 14 bushels of oats (. . .) sacrist of the chapel and guildsmen, 6s. 9d.; (. . .); to Alan Wakfeld (. . .) and for a copy of the jury list (*cop' panell'*) for John Ingram (. . .); for bread and wine for a meal for (Thomas?) Felde, the bishop's steward, 3s. 6d.

Fees: (. . .) William Bowyer, £2; William Lord, 23s. 8d. To the bishop's reeve 19s.   For liveries (*vestur'*): for William Stourton for the year, 9s. 6d., and for the summer, 9s. 7d.; for Robert Fraunses, 9s. 6d.; for William Coventre, 9s. 6d.; for John Whytyng, 9s. 6d.; for

Thomas Mannyng, 9s. 6d.; for William Bowyer, 9s. 6d.; for William Loord, 9s. 6d. [For legal services:] to William Elisaundre for his advice about the tenement of George's inn (*Georgesin*), 6s. 8d.; to Oliver Harnham and [*blank*] for advice, 6s. 8d.; to Andrew Reed, 3s. 4d.; the said William Stourton's fee during the mayoralty of Adam Teffonte, £2; to the said Andrew [Reed] at another time versus the dean and another chapter, 6s. 8d.; to the said William Stourton at another time for advice, £1.; to Thomas Bonham for having a fine more quickly between S(tephen) Meriot and Robert Deverel and Robert Dogton, 13s. 4d.; to the said William Elysaundre at another time for advice versus the dean and chapter, 6s. 8d.; to W(illiam) Bowyer for (Robert?) Tirewhyt, 6s. 8d.

Memorandum that the mayor made an agreement (*pepigit*) with John Wancy about the tenement where John Gillyngham lives, which the same John Wauncy bought from John Ingram son of John Ingram son of Ingelram atte Broke for 25 marks, by which he [the mayor] paid to the said John Wauncy 20(s.?) and to him and to John Ingram 6s. 8d., and to the said John Wauncy another time for having John Ingram and for hiring a horse 1s.; for getting an assessment against the said John Gillyngham for costs of 4s. and for getting the work done 3s. 4d.; to William Upton for writing the assessment 1s. 8d.; to the said John Wauncy another time for bringing the said John Ingram from Andover (*Ondevere*) to Salisbury when justices were there 3s. 4d.

Expenses of William Lord riding first to Stourton with William Bowyer to the house of the same William Stourton, and [?] Devizes (*la vyse*), 3s. 4d., and for hiring three horses for two days, 2s. Expenses of the said William Lord [riding] to Stourton another time for two days, 1s. 4d., and for his horse, 6d. To the clerk writing the collectors' roll, 2s., and for the parchment, 4d. To John Taillor, clerk, at one time, 4d., and at another, 4d. To Peter Uphavene for his writing and work with collectors at various times, 2s. The [?] scribe Amerall (*script' amerall'*), 3s. 4d.

[f. 17v.; *faded and stained, the upper half holed*]

To officials, heralds, and messengers at Christmas, 3s. [*sic*] 2s. 8d.; to the minstrel king (*al kyng des minst'll'*) and his five fellows at Colere [?], 6s. 8d.; to the king's porter (*al porteur regis*), 3s. 4d.; to the lord of Berkeley's (*Berkele*) official, 1s., and to another two, 1s.; to four king's officials, 6s. 8d.; to three officials, 5s. For settling a dispute (*pacificand' lit'*) between officials (. . .), 3s. 4d.; to four officials of the lord of Percy, 1s.; to the king's [?] (*h'log*), 6s. 8d.; to serjeant Erpyngham, (. . .).; to the heralds of P(. . .), 5s.; to the king's serjeant riding to Romsey (*Ramesey*) with W(illiam?) Bowyer, John Gatecoumbe and his (servant?), 10s.; to the official (. . .) riding to the king, 16s.; to the [?] common trumpeter (*al trompet co'i)*(. . .); to the king's official another time, 3s. 4d.; to William Rof minister of the king, (. . .); to an official, 1s. 8d.

Expenses of Richard Spencer, William Lytle (and) William S(. . .)r, £1.; to Richard Spencer and John Pene(fote?) (. . .), 12s.; to the canons of New Salisbury (. . .) 18s.; to the porters one time, 6d.; to Walter Byere for the collectors at Cafford [?], 2s. 2d.

Sum total £43 11d.

[f. 18; *faded and stained*]

38. Account of the said Richard Leche for expenses, after the said account, in the lawsuit between the city and the dean and chapter: expenses at the quidene of Michaelmas beginning 3 Hen. IV [*13 Oct. 1401*] for himself and William Warmwell and five other men going to London, first at Overton, 4s. 2½d., to Hartford Bridge (*Herforbrygge*), 1s. 4d.; to Bagshot (*Baggeshute*), 6d.; to Staines, (£1 2s. 8d.?); London for 2 days and 2 nights, 10s. 10d. (. . .), 3s. 6d. [Lawyers' fees:] Robert (Tir)ewhit, 6s. 8d.; John Stren (. . .) 6s. 8d.; Ralph Jed, 6s. 8d. To Robert (Mason?) (. . .), 3s 4d.; (. . .) of the attorney (*del attorne*), 6d. (. . .) [Returning from London:] to Stanes, 2s.; (. . .) 8d.; to Basingstoke (*Basynestoke*)(. . .), 6d.; to Andover (*Andever*), 1s. (. . .) William Lord 7d., (. . .), 4d. To various officials, 1s. 11d.

Sum £3 13s. 6½d.

39. Expenses of the said William Warmwell in the lawsuit against the dean and chapter (. . .): with his servants and William Lord, John Gatecombe, and William Boyton first at Andover, 10d.; at Overton, 1s. 4d., at Basingstoke, 2d., another at Hartford Bridge, 3d.; to Bagshot, 2d.; to Staines, 7s. 7d.; to Hounslow (*Haundeslewe*), 9½d.; London to supper (*al soper*), 2s. 10d.; (. . .) 3s. 11d.; at Westminster 3s. 4d.; for horses, 1s. 6d. [Lawyers' fees:] H. Wet attorney in Common Bench, 3s. 4d.; Walter Byere, 3s. 4d.; Tyrewhite, serjeant, 6s. 8d.; Culpyper, 6s. 8d.; Stratton, apparitor, 6s. 8d.; Andrew Reed, 6s. 8d.; William Bowyer [*blank space*], 6s. 8d. [Miscellaneous expenses relating to the lawsuit:], for horses, 2s. 8½d.; supper (*sena*), 2s. 3d.; William Lord and John [*no surname*] and their expenses in London while the said mayor was in Canterbury, 2s. 2d.; a meal (*prandium*) on Wednesday, 1s. 7d.; for boat hire ('botchiure'), 2d.; for horses, 1s. 10d., on Wednesday, 7s. 9d. [*this amount marked with a cross at each end*], and on Thursday; on Saturday 1s. 5d.; for Tirewhit's livery, 10s. 8d.; for the account of the rolls of the tenth, 1s. 8d.; a meal on Sunday, 2s. 6d.; a meal on Monday, 1s. 6d.; for horses while the said mayor was in Canterbury, 9s. 1d.; John Staverton of the Exchequer (*de leschecour*), 6s. 8d.; to the auditor (*al auditour*) of the same place, 6s. 8d.; Sirstane [*a lawyer?*], 6s. 8d.; dinner, 2s. 9d.; for horses, £1 1s. 10d.; candles, 2d.; dinner on Tuesday at Westminster, 6d.; boat ('boot'), 2d.; for horses, 1s. 7d.; from Salisbury to Staines, 1s. 11d.; for horses, 2s. 3d.; Bagshot, 1d.; Hartfordbridge, 2s.; at Basingstoke, 6d.; Overton, 2s. 7d.; for horses, 1s. 1d.; to Andover, 3s. 4d.; horse-hire for William Warmwell, 4s. for 12 days; horse-hire for William Lord for the same time, 4s. [Other expenses:] Andrew Reed [*in French for the rest of the paragraph*] for advice touching George's inn (*Georgesin*), 13s. 4d.; William Bowyer, 6s. 8d.; for the pits (*les puttis*), £1.

Sum £10 16s. 7d.

Sum total £14 10s. 1½d.

[f. 18v. *blank*]

[f. 19; *faded and stained, the lower half blank*]

40. Memoranda. [1] Examination on Tuesday before the nativity of [St. John the Baptist *crossed out*] the Blessed Virgin Mary 2 Hen. IV [*6 Sept. 1401*] of the witnesses written below on the articles written below [*they are not*] whether in the mayoralty of William Warmwell, 12 Ric. II [*1388–9*] and with the assent of the citizens, namely John Byterle, John Wollop, Thomas Castelton, Nicholas Hardyng, Robert Deverel, Thomas Eyre, Robert Play, John atte Hether, Thomas Hyndon, Walter Asshton, John Nedler (and) John Gillyngham, it was adjudged that the house of Adam Teffonte extending from Broun Street to the common ditch carrying water to the same was built on land belonging to the same Adam. [Witnesses:] Robert Deverel, William Walters, John Gillyngham [*and two others, illegible*].

[2] Punishment of bakers for selling defective bread: Wednesday after St. Denis 3 Hen. IV [*12 Oct. 1401*], John Sadylere, baker, for bread under weight fined 4s. and put in the pillory for two nights; (Whitsun?) 2 [Hen. IV, *22 May 1401*], Roger Bratele fined 9s. 6d. and put in the pillory for one night; the Wednesday aforesaid, Thomas Blakehalle for bread under weight fined 2s. 7½d., excused the pillory because the first time.

[f. 19v. *blank*]

[f. 20; *faded and stained, the lower half blank*]

41. [*Heading:*] Third writ for contempt.

Westminster, 4 Feb. 3 Hen. IV [*1402*].

Royal writ to John Neweman, mayor: John Milborn, merchant of Wiltshire, complained that whereas he had, before John Moner, former mayor, and William Bredewardyn, clerk for the recognizance of debts, acknowledged a debt of £40 to Thomas Godefray and Godefray had remitted and quitclaimed the debt to Milborn, as John Milborn, 'mercer' of Salisbury, as shown by a writing exhibited in Chancery, but afterwards sued Milborn for the same and had him imprisoned by Neweman, then mayor, and the king has ordered the justices at Westminster to hear the case and has ordered the sheriff of Wiltshire to summon Godefray to come before the justices at Westminster at one month from Easter to answer on the above, and because Ralph Spaldyng and Henry fitz John, both of Southwark, John Dene of London, 'grocer', and John [*forename interlined*] Weston of Salisbury stood bail for Milborn, the king ordered his release from prison if he was held only for the above reason, now the mayor is to have him released and is to come before the justices at Westminster on the quindene of Easter to show why he did not obey the order. Witness, W. Thirnynge.

[f. 20v.; *faded and stained*]

42. [*Heading:*] In the mayoralty of John Salesbury, 5 Hen. IV [*1403–4*]

Friday in Easter week 5 Hen. IV [4 April 1404]. In full assembly it was agreed that all collectors of the tallage when required by the mayor to do so are to render their accounts of receipts of books of payments without delay. All those written below, assessed or to be assessed, submit to the collectors' coercion now and in future.

Robert Deverel, John Dogton, William Busshop, John Chaundeler, Adam Teffonte, Richard Spencer, John Moner, William Warmwell, Richard Leche, William Walters, William Baly, John Nedler, John Eceshale, Stephen Edyngdon, William Bowyer, William Hulle, William Waryn, Roger Wodeford, John Lytle, (. . .)ihte, Simon Tredynek, Richard atte Mulle, John Pope, John Judde, William Pycard, Henry Swythwyk, Walter Orm, George Joce, Thomas Byston, Thomas Mason, Laurence Lane, William Salle, William Doudyng, John G(. . .), Thomas Rede, John Swyft, Thomas Chyld, William Mercer, Robert Hasilbe, John Chamberlayn, John Shad, John Hogeman, John Brewer, John Swyft [again], Edward Dubbere, John Purdy, John Bowyer, Robert Bowyer, William White, Walter Shirle.

Elected unanimously to receive and audit the collectors' receipts: [in column] William Wermwell, John Moner, Richard Spencer, William Walters, William Pycard, William Waryn, William Busshop, William Doudyng, William Salle.

The mayor's costs and expenses in his second year: a pipe of wine sent to Walter Beauchamp, then sheriff of Wiltshire, given in the name of the city, 60s.; red malmsey wine and other gifts sent to William Cheyne and Henry Thorp, emissaries for the commission [?], (4s. 8d.?); on the city's officials and their horses hired from Salisbury to Southampton and back during the war, (5s.?); on a king's messenger coming one time, 1s. 8d.; on another messenger at another time, [1s. 8d., 11d. both crossed out] 1s.; on Clarence [herald?] of the duke of Lancaster, ½ mark; on two of the king's heralds, 13s. 4d.; on another of the king's officials, 6s. 8d.; on Sir Thomas West's official, 1s. 8d.; on a king's herald coming another time, 1s.; on the earl of Arundel's official, 2s.

Sum of payments: £5 3s. 8d. [exceeds by 6s. 8d. the sum of the items printed above, two of which are doubtful being very faint in the MS.]

He accounts also for the costs and expenses of William Waryn and John Levesham being at parliament in the above year, £15, and for the costs and expenses of John Levesham for writs, £1 10s.

[f. 21; two lines at the top and two half-way down, faded]

He received from Simon Tredynek £5 and from Robert Haselbe and his fellow collectors of a tallage £6 6s. 8d.

(. . .) made in the mayoralty of Nicholas Hardyng, 9 Sept. 8 Hen. IV [1407], John Nedlere owes in arrears on his account, after allowances to him, [£18 crossed out] £16 17s. [4d. crossed out] 5d.

[f. 21v.; faded and stained]

43. [*Heading:*] Assemblies in the mayoralty of William Waryn, 6 Hen. [IV, *1404–5*]

Assembly: Friday after St. Martin that year [*14 Nov. 1404*].

Present: the said mayor, John Moner, John Salesbury, Adam Teffonte, Nicholas Hardyng, William Hulle, Robert Body, Richard Spencer, Thomas Abbot, Richard Leche, William Walters, John Nedlere, John Forest, William Salle, Robert Deverel, John W(. . .), William Pikard, Edward Gilberd, Thomas Coffe, John Fraunc(. . .), John Pope, Thomas Rede, William Shirle, John Levesham, Stephen Edyngdon, William Bowier, Roger Wodeford, John Sidenham, John Dogod, William Fuystour, Richard B(. . .), Robert S(. . .), John (. . .), Walter Orm, William West', Nicholas Hayward, William Purchas, John Judde, John Brewer, John S(. . .), Simon Tredynek, William More, Robert Ha(. . .), Thomas Eyr, John Hogeman, John Parch, Thomas Child, Thomas (. . .), George (. . .), William Busshup, William Baly, John Shupton, John Swyft, John Deverell, William Woderove [*and 2 others, illegible*].

Elected as clerks of the city: Stephen Edyngdon and William Lord (. . .); as constables: William Salle and Thomas Child. Agreed that (. . .) [?the constables] should in the future have a pipe of wine.

Reported: the purchase of George's inn (. . .). [?Contributions to the cost:] William Warmwell £20 in the hands of William Hull, Adam Teffonte and John Chaundeler (as executors?) of a will £8, John Parch £2, William Waryn 5 marks, John Nedler £2, William Baly [*no amount*], John Moner £10, John Salesbury 5 marks, William Walters 5 marks, Nicholas Hardyng 5 marks, John Forest £2, William Salle £2, Roger Wodeford ½ mark, William Busshup 5 marks, William Bowier ½ mark, Stephen Edyngdon ½ mark, Walter S(hirle?) (. . .), John Spencer ½ mark, John Wotton ½ mark, William Doudyng £1, Thomas Eyr £1, Thomas Child £1, John Hogeman (. . .), John Shupton ½ mark, Edward Dubbere ½ mark, John Eceshale £1, John Swyft £1, Simon Tredynek £1, Thomas Rede 1 mark, George Joce ½ mark, William (Deer?) ½ mark, Pleasant Deye 1 mark, Laurence Lane ½ mark, Richard Oward [*no amount*], Walter Orm ½ mark, Robert Body ½ mark, John Pope £1, Thomas Ferant ½ mark, Henry Suthewyk ½ mark, W(illiam?) Woderove ½ mark, paid by the mayor, John Beket £1, William Dounyng [*sic*, Doudyng?] ½ mark, Richard Coof £1.

(. . .) for donors to the [cost of the] same tenement during the mayoralty of John Salesbury [*below, no. 45*].

Agreed that money remaining (. . .); elected: Walter Shirle and William Doudyng.

Agreed also that money remaining in the hands of the collectors who have already accounted be levied in the way in which (. . .). And that all other collectors who have not yet accounted be compelled to render account, for which the auditors [are to be] chosen by the mayor, John Moner, Richard Spencer, William Walter, William Busshup, William Salle, William (. . .), (. . .) Child, Walter Shirle, William Doudyng, with the power to audit and determine the accounts according to the form of the statute and the customs of London, whether paid in person (*ad p'sona'*) or in another way making payment (. . .).

[f. 22; *faded and   stained*]

44. During the mayoralty of William Waryn, 6 Hen. [IV, *1404–5*], various assemblies made many ordinances, which stand.

Assembly 10 Sept. The mayor' account, expenses:

A pipe of wine sent by agreement to John Lysle, knight, sheriff of Wiltshire, for his kindnesses to the city in various matters, £4.

To William Stourton retained for the year for his advice, for wages £2, for livery 10s. 6d.; to John Gowayn retained for his advice, £2, for livery, 10s. 6d.; in wages to William Lord, the city's attorney in the Common Bench and for searching the rolls to identify outlaws, £2, for livery, 10s. 6d.; in wages to Stephen Edyngdon, clerk of the city, £1 6s. 8d., for livery, 10s. 6d. Sum £9 8s. 8d.

In bread, wine, oats, and other gifts sent to the justices at the assizes after the feast of St. Matthew, 17s. 2d.

Sent to the justices of the peace, 1s. 8d.

In expenses of John Wollop and Richard Juwell being at the parliament of the king at Coventry for a long time, £10.

In wages of 20 archers sent to the king in Wales in November, £4 13s. 4d.

In costs and expenses of William Walter and William Bowier sent to the king by agreement to excuse the city from going to Wales with the king in August, £2 4s.

For mending the bridge [over] the common ditch next to the Ryole [*la Riole*], 5s.

In money given to various officials of the king and the prince and of other lords at many different times, £5 9s.

Sum total £36 18s. 10d. [*evidently excluding the £4 13s. 4d. for the archers' wages*], for which an aid is levied; agreed to levy an additional £13 and more, so that the total is £50.

[f. 22v. *blank*]

[f. 23; *faded and stained, the lower half apparently blank*]

45. [*Heading:*] Continuing the assemblies in the mayoralty of William Waryn.

List, presented in the preceding assembly, of donations during the mayoralty of John Salesbury towards buying George's Inn: Robert Deverel £1, John Forest senior £2,

Richard Spencer £5, John Moner £2, William Warmwell £20; William Hull (and) William Walters £2 1s. 8d., John Nedler £20, John Chaundiler £2, William Shirle £1, William Waryn £2, William Baly £2, Walter Busshup £2, Nicholas Hardyng £2, John atte Mulle £1, Thomas Biston ½ mark, William Fuystour ½ mark, Henry Suthewyk ½ mark, Laurence Lane ½ mark, George Joce ½ mark, Thomas Mason 1 mark, William Picard £1, William Salle £1, Robert Body ½ mark, Robert Haselbe £1, John Judde ½ mark, John Shad ½ mark, William Doudyng £1, Edward Dubbere ½ mark.

46. Assembly (. . .) after the Conception of the Blessed Virgin Mary [*8 Dec.*] 6 Hen. IV [*1404*].

Agreed to levy and pay, according to the list, the third [fifteenth?] demanded by the King, at Christmas next.

Elected as assessors: William Busshup, Thomas Child, John (. . .), Nicholas Hardyng; as collectors: New Street, John Spencer; Market, John Nouble; St. Martin, John Pope; Meadow, John Elys.

Agreed to move the butchers' stalls from opposite the (. . .) cross [to] Butcher Row (. . .).

47. Assembly, 16 Jan. the said year [*1405*].

Present: the mayor and many other citizens.

George Meriot submitted himself to judgement by his fellow citizens for his offence made to the mayor in laying hands on the mayor. Chosen for Meriot's part: Richard Spencer, William Warmwell, and John Wollop. The mayor likewise submitted to judgement and chose for his part: John Moner, William Walter, and William Salle. A writing under their seals to be placed in the mayor's custody.

[*six lines illegible*]

[*An entry, largely illegible, relating to a tenement late of John Salle.*]

[*An entry, largely illegible, relating to suit between Richard Spencer and John Stokes, mentioning a sum of 5 marks.*]

[f. 23v.; *faded and stained, the lower half blank*]

48. Assembly, Wednesday (. . .) Oct. (. . .)

Present: (not named)

[*An assessment, mostly illegible.*]

49. Assembly, Monday after Epiphany (. . .) Hen. IV [*11 Jan. 1406?*]

Contributions to the purchase of George's Inn: William (. . .). John M(oner?) (. . .), (. . .) £2, William Barbour £5, Nicholas Hardyng £5, William Walter £5, Adam Teffonte (. . .), [*and c. 3 other illegible names*].

[*A further list, perhaps of those who had not yet contributed;*] William Baly 'draper' 5 marks, Walter Shirle 5 (marks), Nicholas Hardyng 5 marks, Thomas Child (£2?), Walter Slegge (. . .), Thomas Mason 6 marks, John Judde 6 marks, William Waryng £2, William Doudyng (?) £2, William Salle £2, John Parche 6 marks, (Henry) Shad £1, John Swyft £1, John Pope £1, Pleasant Diere £1 [*and 4 illegible names and amounts*].

50. Assembly (. . .).

[ff. 24–25 *blank*; f. 25v. *completely illegible*].

[f. 26; *faded and   stained*]

51. [*Heading:*]Assemblies in the mayoralty of John Nedler [7 Hen. IV, *1405–6*]

Assembly, (. . .) [before, on, *or* after] St. Valentine [14 Feb. 7 Hen. IV, *1406*]

Present: the mayor, John (Juwell?), William Loord [*and c. 7 others illegible*] and the citizens below: [*c. 10 lines illegible*]

52. Assembly [*date illegible, 1406?*]

Present: the mayor, [*others illegible*].

Elected to attend the parliament at Westminster to be held Monday in the first week of [March] 1406: William Bayly and William Boyton.

53. Assembly, feast of St. Peter and St. Paul 7 Hen. IV [*29 June 1406*].

Present: the mayor, citizens, and many others.

The assembly was notified of the king's licence for the city to acquire rents of 100 marks a year, secured by Thomas Ryngwode for a fine of 100 marks, the cost to be met partly from obits, including £5 held by John Eceshale and owed to Buterlegh (. . .), £7 held by John Blake and owed to the commonalty, £5 paid by the mayor through John Moner, and £5 12s. paid by Moner to the mayor on the bond of Robert Haselbe and George Jocce, collectors of a tallage.

Agreed that the said Thomas Ryngwode should have for his labour in seeking (*perquisicionis*) licence (. . .) £20 to be levied (. . .) the mayor.

Sureties to an agreement between William Hull and Thomas Rede: for Hull, William Walters and William Doudyng; for Rede, William Busshop and John Forest.

54. Assembly, 10 Oct. the same year 7 [Hen. IV, *1406*].

The mayor presented a list of costs and payments, contained in his account [*which follows on f. 27*].

[f. 26v. *blank*]

[f. 27a, *a small sheet, inserted, containing a list of names without explanation, the verso blank*:]

William Wotton, John Wyse 'draper', William Hore senior, John Hylle, William Shyrwode, William Mariotte [*struck through*], Thomas Pury [*struck through*], Guy Rutter, Nicholas Mason brewer, Thomas Felde [*struck through*], John Chyppenham [*struck through*], William Pole tanner, Thomas Leker.

[f. 27; *faded and stained*]

The mayor's expenses [*in two columns*]: for three officials of Sir Thomas [*later duke of Clarence*] the king's son, 6s. 8d.; for three officials of the duke of York, 3s. 4d.; for three messengers of the king's chancellor, 3s. 4d.; for four officials of the earl (Shrewsbury?) (. . .), 6s. 8d.; for five officials of (. . .) lord, £1; for money given to N(. . .),6s. 8d.; for Leicester(. . .), 3s. 4d.; [*column 2*] to John Wayte, the king's official, 1s. 8d.; to Henry Messager and his fellows, 3s. 4d. to two under-arrayers [?] (*subaris*) of the king, 3s. 4d.; to a [?] (*Proshalmariste* or *Proshaltariste*) of the duke of York, 1s. 8d.; for four officials of the earl of Arundel, 6s. 8d. for an official of the duke of Lancaster, 1s. 8d. Sum of the above £3 8s. 4d.

(. . .) to Walter Hungerford, sheriff of Wiltshire, 16s. 8d.; for 20 gallons [*lageniis*] of red and white wine, (. . .); for 4 gallons of wine, malmsey and (red?, *Rou.* . .), £1 2s.; (. . .) white [wine?] for the (duke?) of York's messengers (. . .), £1; in wine sent to the same lord's wife, 2s.; for bread, [wine, and] oats sent to the justices at assizes, £1 7s. 4d.; for fish and wine for the bishop of Salisbury's officials (. . .), £1; for William (Stourton's?) expenses at one time, 3s. 8d.; to Walter, secretary of the duke of York, in delivering 200 marks to him, 6s. 8d.; paid on account of one dozen of motle cloths [?] (*propter j duod' motle*) given to Thomas Ryngwode, £2 1s.; to his (Ryngwode's) servant for the taking the licence from king for acquiring rents, 6s. 8d.; for the fee for the seal for the same licence, £1 10s. 8d.; for William Bowier's expenses staying in London for the same purpose, 17s. 4d. Sum of the above, £13 3s. 11d.

To William Stourton retained this year for [his] advice, for wages £2, for livery 11s. 6d.;

to John Gowayn for [his] advice, for wages £2, for livery 11s. 6d.; to William Loord, the city's attorney in Common Bench and elsewhere, for wages £2, for livery 11s. 6d.; to Stephen Edyngdon, the city's clerk, for wages £2, for livery 11s. 6d. Sum of the above £10 6s.

For William Wichford's obit held this year, 10s.; for a city rent paid to the reeves there for a tenement ruined by the ditch, 19s.; for the rent of the house where the accounts of the collectors of tallage are audited, 13s. 4d. Sum of the above £2 2s. 4d.

For the wages of William Baly and William Bowiere, elected to parliament, £15; for the money paid to Thomas Ryngwode granted in full assembly for the king's licence to acquire a rent of 100 marks, £20; to the king as a fine for having the said licence, £40. Sum of the above £75.

[f. 27v.; *faded and stained*]

Sum total £104 7d.

55. Assembly, 13 Oct. [*1406*]

Agreed: the sum in the mayor's account, and that assessment be made for the sum.

Elected as assessors: William Walters, John Forest, (. . .), William L(. . .); as collectors: [New Street ward] Pleasant Deye and Thomas Biston, [Market ward] Richard Gage and Robert Blake, [St. Martin's ward] William Hendy and William Stoute, [Meadow ward] John Sydenham and Laurence Lane.

[The mayor's] account [of receipts:] from the executor of John Buterlegh's will (. . .); from the same executor for John Eceshale's payment (. . .); from Robert Blake for a debt through William Waryn's bond (. . .); money from the chest by the auditors (. . .); from Robert Haselbe and George Jocce, collectors of the tallage, £5; from the city's rents for lands and tenements of Robert Russel, paid by W[illiam] Whyte, £4; from the tallage from William Picard [and] J[ohn] Eceshale, £1; from John Crablane and John Coupere for rent of the house near the common latrine, £1; from William Furbour for rent owed for his building above the ditch next to the Countewelle Inn, 2s. Sum received £60 5s. 4d.

[The mayor's] account for receipts from Pleasant Deye and Thomas Biston, collectors for New Street ward, £13 4s. 4d., besides 10s. allowed in the list of payments, 13s. 4d. respited to George Meriot, and 15s. 8d. held by the collectors, their rolls listing payments of £15 3s. 4d.; from Robert Blake and Richard Gage, collectors for Market ward, £18 5s. 11d., besides £3 (0s. 1d.?) held by the collectors, their rolls listing payments of £21 6s.; from William Haulton [*sic, recte* Hendy?] and William Stoute, collectors for St. Martin's ward, £20 6s. 8d., besides 7s. allowed for the poor and 5s. pardoned to the collectors, who are quit, their [rolls] listing payments of £20 18s. 8d.; from John Sydenham and Laurence Lane, collectors for Meadow ward, £4 8d., besides 4s. 4d. allowed for the poor, their rolls listing payments of £4 5s. Sum of receipts from the collectors £55 17s. 7d., besides £3 15s. 9d. held by the collectors for New Street [and Market] wards.

[f. 28; *also numbered 25 in ink, in an earlier hand. A pencilled note near the foot, 19th-century?: 'This probably belongs to Ledger B 36 H. VI p. 28/29'. The entry is misplaced but the folio is part of the original book, being half of the same double leaf as f. 13.*]

56. Names of the young men (*valett'*) paid wages (*vadiat'*) at Southampton in 36 H[en. VI, *1457*]:

[*In three columns:*] Edmund Asheley 3s. 4d., Richard Marchell 2s., Richard Huberd 1s. 4d., Richard Tailor 2s., John Cropper 1s. 4d., John Mason 1s. 4d., John Fuist' 1s. 4d., John Noke 1s. 4d., John Couper 8d., John Worcet' 1s. 4d., John Harper 1s. 4d., John Stevenes 1s. 4d., Richard Bakere 8d., William Gore 1s., John Style 1s. 4d., William Lyzt 1s. 4d., Thomas Brice 8d., John Brian 8d., William Hardyng 1s. 4d., Thomas Carter 1s. 4d., John Hoten(. . .) 1s. 4d., John Crand(. . .) 1s. 4d., Maurice Dyer 1s. 4d., John Hour(. . .) 1s. 4d., John (Raddynge?) 1s. 4d., John Yonge 1s. 4d., John Cherynge 1s. 4d., John Litell 1s. 4d., Richard Bakere 1s. 4d., William Martyn 1s. 4d., John Skutt 1s. 4d., Thomas Newe 1s. 4d., Richard Pynde 8d., Richard Hautyn 1s. 4d., John Formage 1s., Richard Wynde 8d., John Jakson 1s. 4d., Thomas Warman [*corrected from* Warmwell] 1s. 4d., William Piper [haymesman (?), *interlined*] 1s. 4d., John Meke 1s. 4d., John Goldesmyth 1s., John Brekerake 1s. 4d., Thomas Taverner 1s. 4d., Richard Marchall 'glover' 1s. 4d., [*in the margin:* John Calet 1s., (. . .)fencher 1s., (Pleasant?) Deye 1s.], Henry Skute [*blank*], Andrew Corne [*blank*], Roger Kerver [*blank*], John Stronge [*blank*], William Prydy [*blank*], David Moleyn [*blank*], William Wever [*blank*], Nicholas Wever [*blank*], William Dye 1s. 4d., Thomas Coppter 1s. 4d., Peter Gryffyn 1s. 4d., Richard Browdere 8d., William Brewderer 1s. 4d., William Parke 1s. 4d., Walter Wynne 1s. 4d., Thomas Calett 1s. 4d., John Sawnder 1s., Thomas Fletcher 8d., (. . .) Ethen 8d.

[*column 2:*] Roger Davy 8d., John Kynge 8d., Hugh de Ford 8d., Alexander Wyht 8d. The first week. Sum [*blank*].

[*column 3:*] Richard Marchalle 2s., Richard Tailor 2s., William Parke 1s. 4d., Edward Etton 1s. 4d., Hugh de Banco 1s. 4d., John Yonge 1s. 4d., Alex Howles 1s. 4d., John Foryster 1s. 4d., John Stevenes 1s. 4d., Morgan Davy 1s. 4d., Thomas Wodeward 1s. 4d., Morgain Dyere 1s. 4d., John Kynde 1s. 4d., William Cropper 1s. 4d., Thomas Calett 1s. 4d., John Mason 1s. 4d., William Ferrour 1s. 4d., John Brekerake [?] 1s. 4d., John Mason 'chepman' 1s. 4d., John Noke 1s. 4d., Richard Hakeston 1s. 4d., John Newe 1s. 2d., John Bryan 1s. 2d., Robert Helyere 1s. 4d., Thomas Warman 1s. 2d., William Lyht 1s. 4d., John Stevenes 1s. 4d., Richard Bakere 1s. 4d., John Stylle 1s. 4d., Roger Browderer 1s. 4d., William Martyn 1s. 4d., Richard Nowell 1s. 2d., Walter Wynn 1s. 4d., John Elyot 1s. 4d., Thomas Taverner 1s. 4d., three minstrels 4s., Wylliam Dyer 1s. 4d., Thomas Strynger 1s. 4d., John Goldesmyth 1s. 4d., Hugh de Forde 1s. 4d., John Kynge 1s. 4d., Roger Davy 1s. 4d., Thomas Fletcher 1s. 4d., John Sawnder 1s. 4d., Peter Gryffyn 1s. 4d., Thomas Copter 1s. 4d., Richard Hubert 1s. 4d., Thomas Newe 1s. 4d. The second week. Sum [*blank*].

[*At the foot, in English:*] For a dinner at Southampton (*Hampton*) upon the soldiers [being] there, in beef and mutton, 8s. 6d.; to the friars for wood and other things, 2s. Sum 10s. 6d.

For dinner for the mayor and his brethren there: a brace of capons 1s. 4d., a brace of ducks 7d., a pig and a goose 1s. 1d., three pigeons 4d. Sum 3s. 4d.

In ale at Romsey 7d., and at Lockerley (Lokerley) 5d., for various horse meat 5s. 6d., to our minstrel at Southampton 1s. 4d., to a merry friar there 8d. Sum 8s. 6d.

Sum [total] £1 2s. 4d.

Paid to the king's messenger bringing a privy seal [letter] to have men sent to the Isle of Wight 3s. 4d., for costs of a man and one horse to the Isle of Wight for five days 5s. 6d., for the commission of the muster 12s. 8d., for a commission to be justice of the peace £1 12s. 4d., for his [the mayor's] costs there to get it £2. Sum £4 13s. 10d.

[f. 28v. *blank, save at the foot either* 29 (*or* 39), *inverted, or* SE]

[f. 29; *badly faded*]

57. [*Heading:*] Assemblies in the mayoralty of Nicholas Hardyng [*1406–7*].

Assembly: [*virtually all illegible*]

58. Assembly: (. . .) June (. . .)

[*Largely illegible; references to debts and the collection of tallage.*]

Elected as auditors: (. . .), John Moner, Richard Spencer, and William Waryn.

59. Assembly: Friday after St. Andrew the said 8th year [Hen. IV, *2 Dec. 1406*].

Present: the mayor, John Moner, Richard Spencer, William Waryn, William W(. . .), Walter (Sherman?), John Sydenham, and others. Business [*partly legible*] concerning the will of Thomas Gilbert: John Nedlere presented himself as executor of John Nedlere the elder, Gilbert's executor, and Robert (Culle?) presented himself as Gilbert's kinsman and heir; references to Gilbert's holding in Castle Street (. . .*stelstret*) and to St. Edmund's church.

60. Assembly: 7 Jan. [*1407*].

Present: the mayor, John Moner, Richard Spencer, William Waryn, William W(. . .),

[William] Walter, Richard Leche, John (. . .), William Ba(ly?), Robert Deverel, William Busshup, William Shadde, Thomas Child, William Doudyng, Laurence Lane, John (. . .), Thomas Feld, Walter Shirle, John (Dubbere?), William Toyl, Thomas (. . .), (. . .) Blecher, John Lake, Thomas Biston, Pleasant Deye, William D(. . .), (Edward?) O(. . .), (John?) Crablane, Richard Oward, John Judde, William B(. . .)re, William Whyte, William Brante, Robert Blake, Stephen (. . .), (Edward?) Bradele, William Fuyste, Edmund Prydy, John Lytle, Richard Gage, Adam Teffonte, and others.

[f. 29v.; *faded*]

John Lake, Pleasant Deye, Thomas Biston, and William Dounyng [*sic*] produced the king's letters patent directed to them for paying the fifteenth granted to the king in the first week of Lent next, and sought help in that. Elected as assessors: Robert Deverel, William Doudyng, John Judde, William Stoute: as collectors: for Market ward, George Jocce and Edward Dubbere; for Meadow ward, John Ruddok and John (Unfray?); for New Street ward, Walter Orm and John Spencer; for St. Martin's ward, John Pyl and another.

61. Assembly: 11 Feb. (. . .)[*1407.*]

Present: (. . .), Richard Spencer, William Warmwell, William Walter, John Forest, William Salle, William (. . .), William Mercer, Henry (. . .), John Purdy, Pleasant Deye, Edward Purdy, George Joce, Edward Dubber, Robert (Marchall?), John (. . .), John Cockes, William (Stoute?), Nicholas Melbury, Robert Haselbe, John Swyft, Robert Deverel, Thomas Messager, Adam Teffonte and others [*and eight others illegible*].

Henry Chubbe (. . .) [raised the question] of remunerating the collectors of assessments. Agreed that 6s. 8d. [should be paid to]: John (. . .), Edward Clerk, Richard (Pay?), Robert (. . .)olfel, Richard (. . .)erde, Henry Chubbe, Richard Spencer, Walter (. . .), [Thomas] Ryngwode, Robert Pottreffeld, William Wriche, Thomas Foul, John Sades, John Billyngshawe, John Mercer [*and six others illegible*], for whom there would be a tallage in the common form at the next assessment. Afterwards all were paid through Nicholas Hardyng, mayor.

62. Assembly: 19 March in the said 8th year [of Hen. IV, *1407*].

Present: the said mayor and the balliffs in the court sitting there. Account of Thomas [Biston] and Pleasant Deye, collectors of the tallage, concerning which they appeared before the auditors (. . .) arrears of £5 13s. 2d. committed to the care of Roger Enterbussh, the city's serjeant (. . .), to find pledges for the arrears. Walter Shirle and John Lake undertook faithfully to pay through a reasonable allowance made to them.

63. Assembly: eve of Michaelmas in the said 8th year [*28 Sept. 1407*].

Present: the mayor and many other citizens. Elected to attend the parliament at Gloucester on 20 Oct. next: Thomas Child and John Beckot.

64. Assembly: eve of the Nativity of the Blessed [Virgin] Mary in the said 8th year [*7 Sept. 1407*].

Present: the said mayor, John Moner, Richard Spencer, William Warmwell, John Nedlere, Adam Teffonte, William Waryn, William Walter, William Salle, Thomas Child, Walter Nandre, Thomas Eir, Thomas Felde, William Stoute, John Eceshale, George Jocee, William Toyl, John Pope, Richard Oword, Walter Orm, Laurence Lane, Pleasant Deye, Edward Gilbert, John Spencer, Robert Blake, William Loord, William Purchas, John Forest, Robert Haselbe, William Busshup, William Baly, William Doudyng, Thomas Riede, and many others.

The said Nicholas Hardyng mayor accounted for his receipts and expenses, as in his detailed account, the sum of which, with £6 paid to the city's men in Wales, was £25 8s. 8d., which it was agreed to levy by a common tallage. Elected as assessors: John Parch, William Tuyl, Richard atte Mulle, Richard Oword; as collectors: Walter Shirle, John Ruddok, Thomas Eir, Thomas Riede.

Thomas Ferant seeks the favour (*po[nit] se in g[raci]a*) of the mayor and his fellow citizens for the violence and scandal done to him against Robert Blake, collector of tallage in the mayoralty of John Nedler.

[f. 30; *faded and stained*]

Account of the mayor, Nicholas Hardyng, for his receipts and payments 8 Hen. IV [*1406–7*].

[Receipts:] (. . .) of Robert Russel for some years £4 (12s.?), city rents (. . .) above the bridge at Fissherton 8s., rent of another house (. . .) 10s., (. . .) from the tallage granted for his expenses £23 5s. [*or* £26 5s.], Thomas Riede and John Ruddok's by whose account it appears elsewhere in the list, (. . .), (. . .) the common ditch in Pynnoke's inn paid by William Furbour, (. . .) 13s., [£1 *crossed out*] by John Pope (. . .). Sum total [£32 17s. 4d. *crossed out*] £32 [9s. 10d. *crossed out*] 6s. 2d.

[Expenses:] (. . .) bread, wine, and oats for William Hungerford and his fellow justices of the king (. . .) at the Lent assizes £1 7s. 10d., paid to various officials of the king and other lords £3 19s. 8d., [bread,] wine, and oats for the justices at their second visit at the feast of St. Margaret £11s., paid to William Stourton, John Gowayn, William Loord attorney, [and] Stephen Edyngton clerk for their wages £8, viz. to each £2, and for their liveries £2 5s. 10d., to the city reeves and tenants of the city for the expenses of digging and demolition (*per fossat' su'pt' et devast'*) 19s., for the obit of William Wichford held annually at the church of St. Edmund 10s., paid for the house where advice and the accounts are received opposite the 'Gildhall' 13s. 4d., for repairing and mending the common bridge [over] the ditch in the high street 8s. 8d., to William Loord the city attorney for prosecuting and sustaining a writ against Thomas Biston and Pleasant Deye collectors of the tallage during John Nedler's mayoralty to render their accounts 3s. 4d., for the wages of eighteen men waged in Wales for their remuneration beyond the £20 given to them on their return because they were compelled to remain there for a long time by the king's command, as at last allowed to them in the last assembly after [discussion in] various assemblies, £6. Sum total £25 8s. 8d.

The mayor asked for allowances of 7s. allowed by the auditors to Walter Shirle, Thomas Eir, John Ruddok and Thomas Riede collectors of the tallage, as previously discussed, for various poor fugitives having nothing (*fugi's et nich' h'ent'*), of 1s. 10d. allowed to the same another time, of £3 6s. 8d. paid to Walter Shirle on behalf of William Bowiere for arrears of his wages at parliament, of £1 paid to Richard Spencer on behalf of William [Bowiere] in wages for his advice, of 3s. 4d. allowed by the assembly paid to the [same *crossed out*] clerk for compiling and writing the rolls, and of 12s. held by Thomas Riede and John Ruddok collectors of the tallage as arrears.

[*Crossed out and marked* vacat: Sum of money paid above [£5 5s. *crossed out*] £5 10s. 10d. Remaining in the said mayor's hands £2 17s. 10d. net From this he sought an allowance of £2 given to the men going to Wales; request respited. A repayment of £5 to be made to him for a payment for George's inn. 3s. 4d. in revenue of the market in green wax for the same. The said Thomas Rede and John Ruddok, then collectors, [held?] of the said debt on his net account 12s. and more.]

The extents of the collectors of the fifteenth in the said mayoralty follow.

[f. 30v.; *faded and stained, the lower half blank*]

Stephen [*recte* Walter; *cf. no. 60*] Orme and John Spencer collectors of the fifteenth for the king during Nicholas Hardyng's mayoralty as contained in roll of the aldermanry of New Street in that year's list, £19 7s. 10d. (. . .). Edward (Dubbere?) and Edward (. . .) collectors for Market ward [during] Walter Shirle's mayoralty paid (. . .)£ 14s. 3d. which is accounted. (. . .) paid afterwards to W[illiam] Busshup by John Stoute [placed?] in the chest. (. . .). John Pope and John (. . .) collectors for Meadow ward (. . .) William Bowier, and (. . .) Spencer (. . .). Stephen (. . .) and (. . .) collectors from St. Martin's ward (. . .). Held by the collectors of the fifteenth for Market ward £1 3s. (. . .)d., for St. Martin's ward 12s. 4d. (. . .).

[f. 31; *faded and stained*]

65. [*Heading:*] Assemblies in the mayoralty of William Busshup 9 Hen. [IV, *1407–8*].

Assembly, 10 Nov. [*1407*]. (. . .)

66. Assembly: (. . .).

Present: (. . .) Waryn, William (. . .).

[*Largely illegible, names include*] George Jocee, (. . .) Wodegrove.

67. Assembly: 2 Jan. [*1408*].

Present: the mayor, fellow citizens, and others.

The assembly was shown the king's letter patent to Richard Weston, John Noble, John Ruddok, and Richard Oward concerning the levy of a whole and a half fifteenth granted by the parliament held 2 Oct. [1407], a half to be collected on the Purification [*2 Feb.*], another half on 1 May following, and another on the Purification following [*2 Feb. 1409*].

Thomas Child and John Bakot citizens elected to parliament presented their expenses of £9 12s., to be levied with the first [half] fifteenth.

Elected as [assessors] for the first levy: Thomas Mason, Nicholas Melbury, William Doudyng, and Robert Blake; as collectors: John Durneford, (. . .), John Corscombe, and Nicholas Southam.

68. Assembly: 13 March [*1408*]

Present: the mayor and many citizens and others named in the list.

The collectors account in part for the payment of the first half of a fifteenth. Thomas Child and John Beckot, citizens for parliament, were paid fully for in the sums as above collected. The full account follows. The collectors pay on their account to the said mayor [41s. 8d. *crossed out*] 38s. 4d. as appears in the list.

69. Assembly: the feast of St. Alban [*22 June 1408*].

Present: the said mayor and many other citizens named in the list.

Agreed that all money owed to the light of St. George or to the fraternity of the same be promptly levied by the elders of the same, who render the accounts, to advance the building of the house next St. Thomas's cemetery.

70. Assembly: 8 Aug. [*1408*].

Present: the said mayor and many others named in the list.

Agreed that common livery be worn for the arrival and installation of the bishop [*Robert Hallum, who received the temporalities of the see 1 Dec. 1407*], and that 40 marks in money or wine be given to the bishop in the name of the city. To make the payment, William Doudyng gave the mayor £13 which he had his keeping, of which £10 was from John Forest's fine for being excused the office of mayor and £3 was from Thomas Knoyel senior for being excused from the office of alderman; Stephen Edyngdon gave to the mayor £5 acquired by him for the commonalty [for] praying for [the soul from the executors of *crossed out*] William Hykedon; John Nedler gave to the mayor £8 which he held.

[f. 31v.; *faded and stained*]

71. Assembly: 20 Sept. [*1408*]

Present: the mayor and many other citizens.

Agreed that Richard Spencer and his heirs should have by grant of John Moner, William Salle, and other feoffees a tenement with racks which Margaret Godmanston, widow, gave to the same feoffees (. . .) a cottage opposite St. Edmund's church, paying to the city £1 6s. 8d. a year for ever.

The mayor presents an account of £22 12s. (. . .). [Elected] as assessors: John Swyft and John Sydenham; as collectors: John (. . .) and John (. . .).

Accounts of Nicholas Southam, John Corscombe, and their fellow collectors of the grant to be paid at Purification. Nicholas Southam and John Corscombe, collectors for Meadow ward, account for £12 (. . .) as appears in the list. They account in full and are quit. John Durneford and William Brante, collectors for Market ward, accounted in full to the mayor and auditors on 14 Mar. [1408] for the [roll] given to them containing £15 15s. 2d., from which various payments and petitions were allowed to them such that they owed 7s. 6d. net. Thomas Boner and William Penyton, collectors for St. Martin's ward, accounted by the roll given to them containing £18 19s. for the year, from which various payments and petitions were allowed to them as appears in the list, and so they owed 10d. net. Sum above owed from the first tallage by these collectors, 8s. 4d. The mayor, according to this account, was answerable for £1 18s. 4d. received from the said collectors as appears below.

The collectors were to account before Walter Shirle mayor and the other auditors on 8 Mar. 10 [Hen. IV, *1409*] for the second tallage granted for payment on 1 May; as appears in the rolls given to them, £38 14s. The same collectors paid £37 10s. 1d. and so they owed £1 3s. 11d. They had not yet accounted for the third [half of a fifteenth], amounting to £39 19s. 8d. because the collection was to be made in the next mayoralty.

[f. 32; *faded and stained, the lower half blank*]

Accounts of John Beckot, Henry Suthewyk, and their fellow collectors of the tallage of £50 for the business of the city during the mayoralty of William Busshup. Beckot and Suthewyk, collectors for New Street and Meadow wards, accounted for £13 8s. 2d. With allowances for various payments (. . .), [they owe] £3 5s. 10d. net. These payments

(. . .) John Parche and Robert Deverel promised [to] Henry [Suthewyk]. John [Sampson] and [John Dounton], collectors for Market and St. Martin's wards, accounted for £33 11s. 6d. [With allowances, they owe] net £6 11s. 6d. For this payment (. . .) Dounton and Stephen (. . .) promised Sampson £3 [owed by] Dounton and Sampson. Sum owed by the collectors, £9 18s. 4d. The mayor was answerable for these in his account. He [received] from Beckot and Suthewyk £2 [and is] owed by them £1 5s. 10d.; from Dounton and Sampson, £3, and they owe £3 12s. 6d.; total owed by the collectors, £4 18s. 4d.

[f. 32v. *blank*]

[f. 33; *faded and stained*]

Account of William Busshup for receipts and payments during his mayoralty, 9 Hen. IV [*1407–8*].

[Receipts:] £10 held by the mayor from the sale of the tenement late John Wheoler's given to the commonalty for the soul of Wheoler, Alice his wife, and William Woderove (. . .), £10 received from William Doudyng from the fine of John Forest for being excused the office of mayor, £3 received from [William Doudyng] from the fine of Thomas Knoyel for being excused the office of alderman, (£5?) from John Nedler [and another?] for their arrears, (. . .) from the tenement of William Hyke [given] to the commonalty for commending his soul, (. . .) from the fine of John Honython for being excused the office of alderman, £4 (. . .) from the tenement late of Robert Russel's within the city, (. . .) from William D(. . .) from the rent of a house of the commonalty above the bridge next to the latrine, 7s. from the rent of another house late held by John Crablane, 2s. annual rent from the building above the common ditch next to Pynnoke's inn which William Furbor paid, £47 8d. from the last tallage for his costs and expenses assessed in his mayoralty. Total £93 10s. 8d.

[Payments:] £8 paid to William Stourton, John Gowayn, retained by the city for [their] advice, William Loord attorney and Stephen Edyngdon clerk of the city this year (£2 each), for their liveries this year 11s. 4d., 6s. 8d. paid H[enry?] Notyngham the king's herald, £1 1s. for the liveries of the city officials this year, 19s. for bread, wine, and oats for the royal justices at the Lent assizes, 12s. for similar gifts to the same justices at the assizes at the feast of St. Margaret, £2 13s. 4d. for a pipe of wine given to Walter Beauchamp sheriff of Wiltshire for his friendship this year, 8s. 5d. for wine sent to Lord Lovell at the said assizes, and for the costs of the watch for preserving the peace [*blank*], 6s. 6d. for the obit of Alice late wife of George Meriot held this year, 10s. for the obit of William Wichford held annually in St. Edmund's church, 1s. 6d. for making and mending the bridge above the common ditch in the high street, 19s. paid to Nicholas Belle and William Tuyl, reeves of the city this year, for the tenement in the city damaged by digging (*pro ten' in civit' per fossat' devast'*), 13s. 4d. paid for rent of the house where advice and accounts are heard, £26 13s. 4d. presented to the bishop at his installation in the name of the whole commonalty of the city and 1s. 8d. of a purse for putting the money in. Total £45 11s. 1d. [*evidently including an item or items amounting to £1 14s. omitted from the preceding list*].

[f. 33v.; *faded and stained, the lower half blank*]

Sums granted from the receipts of £93 10s. 8d. and from the charge as appears at the foot of the account of the first tallage of a half of a fifteenth below, £1 18s. 4d. Total sum of receipts is £95 [9s.]. Allowed to the mayor for his expenses and payments, £45 11s. 1d., and he asked for the further allowance of £10 which he held for carrying forward the building of the house next to St. Thomas's cemetery, £3 which he held from John Pa(. . .), 8s. from the rent of the house late John Crablane's owing (. . .) allowed by the auditors for the poor, sum total £62 9s. 2d. He therefore owed £32 19s. 11d. net (. . .). On 4 Aug. 1 Hen. V [*1413*] in the mayoralty of John Beckot mayor William Busshup accounted before the mayor, Richard Spencer, Walter Shirle, William Walter, William Doudyng, Nicholas Belle, Thomas Child, Robert Warmwell, and others for all arrears of the said debt at the foot of the above account and likewise for building the house next to St. Thomas's cemetery, to the effect that with all the allowances the city remained indebted to him in £4 15s. 4d., provided that debts of Beckot and Suthewyk and other collectors as appear in another earlier part of this folio remain due to the said William, which money is to be raised for William's use. Remaining with the mayor and commonalty are the arrears of rent of Thomas Steor and other tenants.

[f. 34; *faded and   stained*]

72. [*Heading:*] Assemblies held in the mayoralty of Walter Shirle 10 Hen. [IV, *1408–9*].

Assembly: 26 Nov. [*1408*].

Present: the mayor and many others.

Ordered that for paying the debts owed to the commonalty by the collectors John Moner, Richard Spencer, William S(alle?), [William?] Walters, (. . .) G(. . .), (. . .), and the mayor should have full power to hear and determine their accounts for payment according to the force of the law (. . .).

73. Assembly: (. . .) [*1408–9*].

Present: the mayor (. . .).

Agreed that the payment of (. . .) 12s. 3d. by Thomas (. . .) is sufficient, and he is therefore quit. (. . .) [William] Waryn, William Salle, William Doudyng, Nicholas Belle and John Forest. (. . .).

74. Assembly: 18 May [*1409*].

Present: the mayor and others named in the list.

William Waryn appeared to account for his mayoralty. Likewise William Walter for his mayoralty. Deferred to another time.

75. Assembly: 24 May [*1409*].

Present: the mayor, Richard Spencer, William Warmwell, Adam Teffonte, Richard Leche, John Nedlere, William Salle, Thomas Mason, William Baly, William Doudyng, Nicholas Melbury, John Swyft, John Levesham, John Judde, John Shad, Thomas Ferant, Richard Bristowe, John Lytle, Henry Preterjon, Walter Orm, William Slegg, Richard Oword, William Fuyst', John Beckot, Thomas Riede, Laurence Lane, Henry Suthwyk, William Loord, and others.

William Walter appeared to account for his receipts, expenses, and payments during his mayoralty. He said that he had received £14 0s. 10d. after his account made in various allowances. Because it seemed to the auditors that the allowances asked for were unreasonable as they were shown in his list, the requests were deferred to another assembly of which he was to be given reasonable notice.

76. Assembly: 18 Aug. [*1409*].

Present: the mayor, Richard Spencer, William Warmwell, John Moner, William Waryn, William Walter, Nicholas Hardyng, John Nedler, William Salle, Walter Nandre, William Busshup, Thomas Child, Nicholas Melbury, Simon Tredynek, John Sydenham, Thomas Rede, Richard Oword, Thomas Blechere, John Nouble, Pleasant Deye, Laurence Lane, William Tuyl, Walter Orm, Nicholas Belle, William Fuystour, John Becket, Thomas Eir, Edward Dubbere, John Lytle, Richard Gage, Thomas Boner, George Jocee, and others.

At the commonalty's request Nicholas Hardyng granted to the commonalty, for prayers for the soul of John Nyweman in perpetuity in the fraternity of St. George, a tenement late John Nyweman's next to the tenement late William Hull's. To discharge the tenement from a bond by which Nyweman and Hulle owed certain sums to William Warmwell, on the gift Warmwell granted a general acquittance which was made and sealed.

Agreed by all to support the mayor against John Corscombe the aulnager [?] (*vlnat'*) if he should intend anything by reason of the arrest [of John] at the Annunciation last [*25 Mar. 1409*] for his wrong done to various strangers.

77. Assembly: Friday before Michaelmas [*27 Sept. 1409*].

Present: the mayor, John Moner, William Warmwell, Richard Spencer, William Walter, Adam Teffonte, John Nedlere, William Busshup, Nicholas Hardyng, William Salle, Thomas Child, William Doudyng, Nicholas Melbury, John Judde, William More, Richard Oword, John Lytle, Pleasant Deye, John Ruddok, William Doudyng, John Parche, George Jocee, Henry Chubbe, John Sampson, Henry Suthwyk, William Stoute, William Fuystour,

William Bowier, John Castelton, Richard Cristchurche, John Dounton, Walter Orm, Robert Wolf, John Swyft, William Purchas, Simon Bradele, Thomas Blechere, William Mede, Richard Juwell, Thomas Messager, John Hogeman, William Barbour, and others.

Agreed by all the £26 2s. 9d. which the mayor accounted for as having paid and expended on the city's business during his mayoralty, besides the 40 marks given as a present to the king and other secular lords who were with him [f. 34v.; *faded, stained, and damaged, the lower half blank*] at Clarendon and Salisbury at the Annunciation [*25 Mar.*] this year. With the said 40 marks (. . .) the total sum to be levied by a tallage on the city was £52 15s. 1d. Elected as assessors: John Beckot, John Parche, John Judde, and John Hogemann; as collectors: John Castelton, Richard Crischurche, Robert Wolf, and John Boteller.

Granted that William Penyton (?) have a place (*statum*) in the shops late of John Prentis, feoffees having had that place by grant of Richard Pate and Joan his wife, daughter of the said John Prentez by indenture paying yearly to the commonalty of the city 2 marks over and above the 2 marks to Pate and his wife for arrears in rent for the annual obits of John Prentiz, Katherine his wife, Thomas (. . .), and Alice his wife (. . .); and that Thomas Ar(. . .) skinner (. . .) above the latrine (. . .) friars preachers at Fisherton for the term of the indenture, paying yearly to the mayor and commonalty (. . .) at the Nativity of St John the Baptist [*24 June*] next to come, maintaining and repairing (. . . .).

78. Assembly: 3 Jan. [*1409*].

Present: the mayor and many others.

Elected as one of the city coroners: Robert Deverel (. . .); as supervisors of George's inn: Walter Shirle, William Warmwell, William Salle, William Doudyng, Nicholas Hardyng, and John Bekot (. . .).

79. Assembly: 4 Feb. [*1409; cf. no. 419*]

Present: the mayor, William Salle deputy (*subrog'*) mayor, John Moner, Adam Teffonte, William Walter, William Waryn, Nicholas Hardyng, William Busshup, William Doudyng, Nicholas Deverel, (John?) (. . .), Robert Deverel, Thomas Child, John Levesham, John Judde, John Boteller, Richard Oword, William Stoute, John Hogemann, Thomas (. . .), (. . .), Edward Dubbere, Henry Suthwyk, Thomas Riede, (Stephen?) Bowier, William Fuystour, Thomas Messager, John Castelton, (Richard Wayte?), John Ruddok, William Mede, Robert Bowier, John Forest, John Shute, William Barbour, Stephen Lythenard, William More, William Tuyl, William (Slegge?), Thomas (Corscombe?), Walter Nandre, John Lytle, John Lympner, John (Parch?), Robert Wolf, Thomas Slegg, William Penyton, Edward Bremore, Thomas Warlond, William Purchas and others.

Decided and agreed that henceforth there should be two city chamberlains; elected: John Beckot and John Judde, and against them to keep a counter-roll (*contrarotuland'*) was nominated comptroller Thomas Rede. These three sworn to levy and receive all and everything owed to the commonalty when and where debts to the commonalty were required to be paid, to find out what was due from tenements and persons, and when given notice to account faithfully in the presence of the mayor and the appointed auditors.

[f. 35; *badly faded and stained*]

80. Account of the mayor, Walter Shirle, for his receipts and payments 10 Hen. IV [*1408–9*].

[Receipts:] 6s. 8d. net from William Penyton in rent of cottages which he held at the Nativity of St. John the Baptist [*24 June*] from Richard Pate and Joan his wife as in the indenture, 6s. 8d. in rent from the same cottages from Michaelmas term last, 2s. from the tenement which William Furbour held at Pynnoke's inn for the building above the common ditch, £4 10s. annual rent from the tenement late of Robert Russel 'chivaler' and granted to the commonalty, the rent being [payable] to the mayor himself (. . .), £52 16s. 1d. from John Castelton, Richard Crischurche, Robert Wolf, and John Boteller. Sum total (. . .).

[Payments:] a pipe of wine sent to Sir Robert (. . .), 53s. (. . .)d., 12s. 8d. paid to Richard Patte (. . .), £2 2s. (for timbers?) (. . .), 19s. 8d. (. . .) from tenements (. . .) 3s. 4d. for (. . .) to John Pate (. . .), 22s. 4d. (. . .) to officials (. . .), 13s. (. . .)d. (. . .), gifts (. . .) at Clarendon, (. . .) to the king's officials (. . .), for John Mande (. . .), to [various other] officials (. . .), 19s. for a penalty (. . .). Sum, £12 0s. 6d.

[f. 35v.; *badly faded and stained, the lower half blank*]

[*Only fragments legible and intelligible*]. The mayor asked for allowances of £4 10s. for the yearly rent late of Robert Russel by reason of the election of the chamberlains, and of 6s. 8d. for the rent of William Penyton for Michelmas term for the said reason.

[f. 36 and v. *blank*]

[f. 37; *badly faded and stained*]

81. [*Heading:*] Assemblies in the mayoralty of William Salle 11 Hen. IV [*1409–10*].

Assembly: (. . .).

Present: the mayor, (. . .), Richard Spencer, William Waryn, (. . .), Robert Deverel, John (. . .), William Doudyng, (. . .), John (. . .) [*and about five illegible lines*].

Elected to (. . .): [Robert?] Juwell and Robert Deverel [*and others? illegible*]; as constable, with Thomas Child: John Beckot (. . .).

Walter Warmwell promised to deliver a bond (. . .) at Christmas in the future. Paid. And it remains in the [common?] chest (. . .).

82. Assembly: 10 Jan. [*1413. For the date cf. History of Parliament. The entry is evidently a later insertion on a folio used, apparently, for entries relating to 1409-10.*]

Present: the mayor and many [others].

Read: the king's letter for holding a parliament (. . .). Elected to attend it: Walter Shirle and William Waryn.

83. Assembly: 30 June [?*1410*].

Present: the mayor and many other of his fellow citizens.

Read: the king's letter under privy seal to the mayor, bailiffs, and good men of the city for a loan to the king in return for [sureties] agreed to by the bishop of Winchester. Agreed: a sum of 100 marks [or £100 *crossed out*] to be paid at the feast of St. Martin [*11 Nov.*], for the security of which John Blake of Winchester and Thomas Abingdon of the soke there made a bond to William Salle and Richard Spencer.

84. Assembly: 11 Sept. [?*1410*].

Present: the mayor and many others of his fellow citizens named in the list.

The mayor's account of his expenses and payments as in the detailed list (*per parcell'*) amounting to £25 8s. 9d. He asked for an allowance for expenses, costs, and gifts given and sent to officials of the prince at his visit, for expenses sent and given to officials of the queen coming afterwards, for expenses of the bishop of Winchester coming for the money to be lent to the king, for other expenses made and sent to the bishop of Salisbury at various times and especially on his arrival from foreign parts for making peace (*pro unitate facienda*), and for other expenses made and sent to knights from Brittany at the queen's request by letter. For these said costs it was allowed that the tallage should amount to £40. The mayor pardoned and released to the commonalty a large sum such that his tallage should not exceed £34 10s. for which thanks (. . .). Elected as assessors of that amount: John Hathewey, George Jocee, Richard Deverel, Stephen Edyngdon; as collectors: John Durneford, John Nouble merchant, John Shirle, John Chippenham.

[f. 37v.; *badly faded and stained*]

85. Assembly: (. . .) Feb. [?*1410*]

Present: the mayor and [many] other fellow citizens named in the list.

(. . .) [*The business evidently related to an obit, with mention of William Warmwell and Thomas Hardyng, and, after mention of (John?) Corscombe and William Waryn, to an almshouse.*]

86. Assembly: Friday (before?) St. Matthew [?*19 Sept. 1410*]

Present: the mayor and many [others].

[*Largely illegible, referring to a lodging or hospital (*hospit'*), the Friday [19 Sept.] before St. Matthew, the sum of 40 marks, and John Becket.*]

87. Assembly: 27 Sept. [?*1410*]

Present: the mayor and many of his fellow citizens named [in the list].

It was seen that the commonalty as a whole had no right in the tenement called Georges inn except by grace of the feoffees. Ordered that the feoffees should have entire possession and they might demise it at farm to whomsoever they thought fit, and that they should have the management of it; they joined with themselves (*affirmant sibi*) William Waryn, William Busshup, William Doudyng, John Levesham, William Tuyl.

88. Assembly: 6 Oct. in the same year [*evidently 1410; 6 Oct. 11 Hen. IV was 1409, and a later hand corrected the error, replacing* supradicto *with* xij].

Present: the mayor and other citizens named in the list of the assembly.

The king's letters patent were shown for the levy of a tenth and a half a tenth, a half to be collected on (. . .) next, another half on the same feast following, and the third on the feast of St. Martin [*11 Nov.*] following, as granted by parliament and allowed by the aldermen. Elected as assessors: Pleasant Deye, Thomas (. . .), William Tuyl, John Messager; as collectors: [William Depedan *crossed out*] John Heliere 'irmanger' [*interlined*], Robert Warmwell, William Cokkis, Henry Suthwyk.

[f. 38 and v.; *badly faded and stained, apparently blank*]

[f. 39; *badly faded and stained*]

89. Account of William Salle, mayor, for his expenses before the assembly of citizens.

[Expenses: *Twelve lines illegible except*] Sum £2 13s. 8d. (. . .) Sum (. . .). William Loord, Stephen [Edyngdon] (. . .) a similar livery given to William W(. . .), 11s. 10d.

(. . .) in bread allowed to the city officials this year, £1; given to the Nottingham herald, 3s. 4d. [Sum] (. . .)s. 4d.

In bread, wine, and oats sent to the royal justices for four days, £1 6s. 5d. For bread and wine to the king's justices (. . .) William Cheyne, Wa(. . .)yng, Robert Chippenham, William Elisaundre, and others, (. . .) to William Restyng (. . .), 5s. Sum £1 11s. 5d.

For two writs to choose two new coroners for the city to replace Robert Curtlyngstoke and William Bally, 4s.; for the expenses of a man sent to Winchester to obtain sureties for the 100 marks loaned to the king through the mediation of the bishop of Winchester, and for other expenses in London to obtain a bond from the bishop for that payment, 2s. 3d.

Paid to John Brid, the queen's receiver, by virtue of a writ of *fieri facias* on the goods, chattels, and lands of the mayor and commonalty in the matter of the fine with the king of 100 marks for licence to acquire lands and tenements within the city, 10 marks. Sum £6 13s. 4d.

Paid by the reeves this year for the rents belonging to the bishop of Salisbury for lands and tenements within the city, 19s.; paid by the reeves for rent to the bishop this year for the cottage late of John Prentis, 11½d. Sum 19s. 11½d.

For the obit of John Prentis held in St. Edmund's church, 5s.; for the obit of John Wallop held in the same church, 5s.; allowed annually for the obit of William Wichford held there, 10s.; for the obit of William Teyntorer and Alice his wife held in St. Thomas's church, 12s. 4d. Sum £1 12s. 4d.

For the year's rent of the house called 'Counseilhous', 13s. 4d. Sum 13s. 4d.

Sum total £26 7s. 9½d.

[f. 39v.; *badly faded and stained, largely illegible*]

(. . .) for the obit of (. . .). [*Nine lines illegible except*] John (. . .) £8 2s. 3d. (. . .) 2s. 3d. (. . .) [Sum?] £37 10s. (. . .)d.

[Receipts:] (. . .) John Clerk alderman of New Street (. . .) Hungerford (. . .) Richard Walter (. . .) of Joan late wife of Robert Arnald concerning the sale (. . .) John Forest (. . .) Thomas Randolf (. . .) hiring a store-room (*conducendo celer'*) at George's inn (. . .) from John Durcheward for the shop now held by him beside George's inn (. . .); from the sale of a 'fornace' to John Swift 'irmonger', £1, spent on the house next to the latrine above Fisherton bridge; from broken gold (*auro fracto*) [?] and scots from John Sampson, Edward Purdy, Peter Barbour and John Clyve, commissioners of the half of a fifteenth, and from William Depedene, Robert Warmwell and Henry Southwyk joined with them by the assembly to assist them in part payment of the arrears of their account as appears in the list of accounts this year, 17s.

[f. 40; *badly faded and stained, the lower half blank*]

90. Assembly: Saturday (. . .).

[*An entry largely illegible but concerning vacant properties and the appointment of individuals to collect rents and debts resulting from the comptroller's examination of the list. It mentions the vacant tenement next to that late William Knolle's given to the community; a sum of £6 8s. 8d.; the rent of an empty tenement by 'le Coldecorner' granted to the mayor and commonalty by Nicholas Hardyng for commending the soul of the late John Nyweman.*]

[f. 40v. *blank*]

[f. 41; *faded and stained*]

91. [*Heading:*] Assemblies in the mayoralty of Walter Nandre 12 Hen. IV [*1410–11*].

First assembly: 8 Nov. [*1410*].

Present: the mayor, John Moner, William Warmwell, William Salle, William Waryn, Walter Shirle, William Busshup, William Walter, Adam Teffonte, Richard Leche, Nicholas Hardyng, Robert Deverel, William Doudyng, Thomas Child, John Beckot, William Tuyl, Thomas Boner, John Gilbert, John Ruddok, Richard Oword, Pleasant Deye, John Forest, Thomas Riede, William Slegge, Edward Gilbert, John Clerk, Thomas Durneford, Henry Suthewyk.

Agreed unanimously that William Stourton and John Gowayn be retained to advise the city, that William Loord attorney in Common Bench and elsewhere be retained, and that Stephen Edyngdon be continued as city clerk, for the wages and liveries as before. Likewise William Westbury, reeve, to have the silk livery (*vestur' de setta*) of the citizens. The sheriff henceforth to have a pipe of wine for his friendship in his office, in the usual way, and to have the livery of the citizens, receiving one of silk at Christmas.

92. Assembly: 14 Jan. [*1411*].

Present: the mayor, John Moner, Richard Spencer, William Walter, William Waryn, William Busshup, Walter Shirle, Adam Teffonte, William Walter, Robert Deverel, John Beckot, Thomas Child, Thomas Mason, Nicholas Belle, Nicholas Melbury, William Doudyng, Edward Dubbere, William Tuyl, Thomas Blechere and John Chippenham.

Walter Shirle, William Waryn, and Richard Cristchurch were chosen to represent the city in the king's court and elsewhere in resisting the injuries done by the mayor and burgesses of Southampton to the mayor and city of Salisbury and of Winchester concerning unjust customs, expenses, and regulations contrary to the freedom of this city and the agreement made between Southampton and this city. They may act in the matter at the expense of the whole commonalty.

93. Assembly: Friday after the Annunciation [*27 March 1411*].

Present: the mayor, John Moner, Richard Spencer, Walter Shirle, William Walter, William Waryn, William Salle, William Busshup, William Doudyng, John Beckot, Thomas Child, Nicholas Melbury, Robert Deverel, William Tuyl, Thomas Riede, John Judde, John Forest, and Pleasant Deye.

John Moner, Richard Spencer, Walter Shirle, William Waryn, William Walter, William Lord, and many other citizens agreed to exert themselves outside the city to hold a discussion with the burgesses of Southampton on the grievance between that town and this city and Winchester, on Thursday before Palm Sunday [*2 April*].

94. Assembly: 2 May [*1411*]

Present: the mayor, Richard Spencer, William Waryn, William Busshup, William Sall, William Doudyng, Nicholas Melbury, Richard Leche, Adam Teffonte, Thomas Mason, John Judde, George Jocee, John Lytle, Thomas Blechere, Thomas Boner, Walter Orm, John Bottenham, Robert Bowiere, William Slegge, John Lake, John Clerk, John Forest, Edward Dubbere.

In the dispute between Southampton and Salisbury and Winchester about the unjust customs proposed, because a day has been set in London for Mr. John Chyterne chosen for this city and William Esturmy for Southampton. Richard Spencer and William Waryn were chosen to be present at the discussion. And for them to have their expenses with them, all those in the assembly who had a title over their heads [?] (*qui titulum habeant super capita*) agreed to acquit William Salle late mayor of their loans of nobles for the fund for buying George's inn. Moreover John Lake, Thomas Boner, Adam Teffonte, Richard Leche each lent 1 noble and Thomas Blechere lent 3s. 4d., towards the £5, together with £3 10s. spent from the common purse attached with the city's seal, which £5 was given to Richard Spencer and William Waryn on 4 May for their expenses and costs in the matter until it can be levied on the city.

[f. 41v.; *faded and stained, the lower half blank*]

95. Assembly: Wednesday after the Exaltation of Holy Cross [*16 Sept. 1411*].

Present: the mayor, John Moner, Richard Spencer, Walter Shirle, William Salle, William Waryn, William Busshup, Nicholas Hardyng, Thomas Mason, Nicholas Belle, John Levesham, John Judde, John Bottenham, Thomas Child, Thomas Riede, Thomas Durneford, Edward Frith, John Gilbert, Thomas Abbot, Richard atte Mulle, William Dounyng, John Hogeman, Thomas Boner, Walter Orm, Henry Southwyk, John Clerk,

John Forest, John Sydenham, John Brewer, Thomas Messager, John Parch, John Swyft, John Beckot, William Tuyl, William Lord, William Fuystour, William More, Edward Dubbere, John (. . .).

The mayor's account of expenses and payments, of which the sum granted together with £10 loaned for his dealings (. . .) is £35 6s. 1d. Elected as assessors: John (. . .), John (Chrischur)ch, John Forest, John Ruddock; as collectors: Thomas Biston, Edward (. . .), Thomas Boner, John Nedlere.

96. Assembly: 16 Oct. 13 [Hen. IV, *1411*].

Present: the mayor and many others (. . .).

[Read,] a commission for levying and paying a half of a fifteenth to the king at Michaelmas. Assessors: Pleasant Deye, George Jocce, Thomas Rede, Thomas Messanger; collectors: (. . .), Robert Warmwell, Thomas (. . .), Henry Suthwyk.

97. Assembly: Friday after St. Luke 13 [Hen. IV, *23 Oct. 1411*].

Present: the mayor, Richard Spencer, William Waryn, Walter Shirle, William Salle, William Walters, William Busshup, William Doudyng, Nicholas Belle, Robert Deverel, John Levesham, John Beckot, William More, John Sydenham, William Tuyl, John Bottell', Thomas Blech', John Chippenham, John Lytle, Thomas Messager, Peter Dawe, Robert Warmwell, Thomas Biston, John Gilbert, Richard Oword, William Fuystour, Thomas Riede, Edward Dubbere, Thomas Boner, Richard Cone, Thomas Durneford.

Read: a writ to the mayor and bailiffs for a parliament at Westminster on the morrow of All Souls [*3 Nov. 1411*]. Elected: Richard Spencer and Walter Shirle.

[f. 42; *faded and stained*]

98. Account of Walter Nandre, mayor, for his costs, expenses, and payments, 12 Hen. IV[*1410–11*].

For a pipe of wine sent to John Berkele, treasurer of the sheriff of Wiltshire, with the assent of his fellow citizens for the business of the assembly [and] for his friendship in his office, £3; in bread, 2s.; in wine, 10s.; for 20 letters sent to the royal justices coming for the assizes at Salisbury on the feast of St. Matthew [*21 Sept.*], 7s. 6d.; given to an official of the king's son Sir Thomas, 3s. 4d.; given to two heralds of another lord, 3s. 4d.; given to the king's Nottingham herald, 3s. 4d.; given to the king's messenger Muriel, 4d.; for the expenses of William Lord being with the mayor and fellow citizens at Winchester with a letter sent there, 1s.; for bread, 2s.; for wine 5s.; for 20 bushels of oats sent to the king's justices coming for the assizes the second time on the feast of St. Margaret [*20 July*], 8s. 4d. Sum £5 6s. 2d.

For the wages of William Stourton retained by the city for his advice, £2; of John Gowayn for his advice, £2; of William Lord attorney for the city in Common Bench and elsewhere, £2; of Stephen Edyndon, city clerk, £2. Sum £8.

For liveries for the said William Stourton, John Gowayn, William Lord and Stephen [Edyndon], viz. for each 10s. [10d. *crossed out*], [£2 3s. 4d. *crossed out*] £2; for a livery for William Westbury, the city reeve, 10s.; for coloured and striped (*strag'*) cloth for the city officials, £1. Sum £3 10s.

Paid on the obit of William Wichford held at Michaelmas, 10s. as fixed; not accounted for: the obits of John Wollop and John Prentiz held at the same time in the second week of Lent, or the obit of William Teynturer and Alice his wife held in St. Thomas's church, because they are charged to the chamberlains. Sum 10s.

Account also for the rent of the house called 'Counseilhous' this year, 13s. 4d.; paid by the city reeves this year for rent to the bishop owed for a (. . .) ruined by digging, 19s.; for the rent paid to the bishop by the same reeves for the rent of Richard Pate's cottage late John Prentiz's, 11½d. Sum £1 13s. 3½d.

Sum total £18 19s. 5½d.

[*Crossed out, unfinished*: For which the said late mayor received from the collectors assigned to levy the tallage, whose names appear in the [record of the] preceding assembly.]

The mayor also accounted for £5 from William Salle late mayor from the loan of money in his hands from certain persons, each of them lending 1 noble towards the fund (*stauro*) for buying George's inn [and] for advancing the business between Salisbury and Southampton regarding the bad new customs newly started by them against the city; also for £5 of which £3 10s. was spent from the common purse when the common seal was affixed and of which £1 10s. was from other persons as appeared in the last assembly accountig for similar business; and for £6 6s. 8d. [paid *crossed out*] for the costs of Walter Shirle and William Waryn prosecuting the same business in London and elsewhere, as in a pipe of wine for drink given to a worthy (*cuidam probo*) and for other expenses of the kind. Sum of the above £16 6s. 8d.

Sum total £35 6s. 1½d. of expenses and payments made. [*It is not clear why the first two amounts in the preceding paragraph were reckoned as payments rather than as receipts.*]

[f. 42v. *blank*]

[f. 42a (*insert*); *the right-hand edge torn away*]

99. 16 Feb. 13 Hen. IV [*1412*].

Writ of *venire facias* from Thomas Denham, sheriff of Wiltshire, to the mayor and constables to summon twelve men to appear on Wednesday (. . .) at Salisbury before

[William de Beauchamp and the other] commissioners appointed by the king to inquire into tenements worth £20 or more.

[*Endorsed with the certificate of*] William Doudyng, mayor, and Thomas Child and John Beckot constables, who had complied with the writ. [*The certificate names William de Beauchamp.*]

[f. 43; *faded and stained*]

100. [*Heading*: Assemblies of citizens held in the mayoralty of William Doudyng, 13 Henry [IV, *1411–12*].

Assembly: 6 Nov. [*1411*].

Present: the mayor and many other citizens etc.

Agreed by all: the sheriff henceforth to have a pipe of wine as other sheriffs have had for their friendship, and to have a common livery of silk (*setta*) [as] among the good citizens at Christmas.

101. Assembly: 13 Jan. [*1412*].

Present: the mayor, Richard Spencer, Walter Shirle, William Salle, Walter Nandre, Nicholas Hardyng, William Busshup, Adam Teffonte, William Waryn, William Walter, Thomas Mason, Thomas Child, William Tuyl, John Swyft, Thomas Riede, William Slegge, William Phebis, Thomas Messagere, William Dounyng, William Baskot, John Chippenham, Edward Purdy, Richard Coof, John Shute, John Ruddok, Thomas Frogge, John Parche, William Stoute, John Hogeman, Robert Bowiere, Edward Dubbere, Stephen Lychenard, George Jocee, William Fuystour, John Corscombe, Richard Sherman and very many other clothmakers in the city.

Moved: the grave damage to the community in that striped cloths (*panni strag'*) in the hands of clothiers at the last Westminster fair were seized because they were not 6 quarters [sc. of a yard] wide, according to the old statutes. Because of this the striped cloths still in the city cannot be sealed with aulnager's mark. To provide a remedy Walter Shirle and William Walter were chosen for making suit to the king etc. at the common cost of the whole city.

102. Assembly: the feast of the conversion of St. Paul [*25 Jan. 1412*].

Present: the mayor, Richard Spencer, Walter Shirle, William Waryn, William Walter, William Salle, William Busshup, Walter Nandre, Nicholas Belle, Thomas Mason, John Beckot, John Levesham, Thomas Riede, John Forest, John Boteller, Thomas Frogge, Stephen Lythenard, William Phebis, Laurence Lane, John Shad, John Ruddok, William

Slegg, Robert Warmwell, John Spencer, Thomas Boner, William Barbour, Richard Weston, John Parch, Richard Oword, Edward Dubbere, William Tuyl, John Swyft, John Hogeman, Richard atte Mulle, Robert Wolf, John Castelton, John Lake, Thomas Child, Richard Gage, John Corscombe, Richard Sherman, John Cornyssh, Edward Passewell, William Willy, and John Bythewode and many others of the commonalty.

Noted: the grave damage as in the preceding assembly and the common damage through the new custom levied at Southampton (*Hampton*) against the citizens and other inhabitants of this city. Agreed by all: Walter Shirle, William Waryn, and William Walter to pursue the matter for a remedy, etc., [for which the said mayor and William Waryn put up and brought £5 *crossed out*] in aid of which the stewards of the weavers' guild put up £5 and the stewards of the fullers' guild [£3 *crossed out*] £2, until it can be levied in common through the city, to which assessment of one penny all agreed.

103. [the mayor's court]: 8 Feb. [*1412*].

Present: the mayor and others his fellow citizens.

John Fissher, weaver, was arraigned for certain articles started by him to the opprobrium and destruction of the whole guild of weavers. So arraigned, he sought the indulgence (*ponit se in gracia*) of the mayor and masters of the guild, and swore to follow his craft faithfully.

104. Assembly: Monday the feast of St. Peter in Cathedra [*22 Feb. 1412*].

Present: the mayor and many others, both his fellow citizens and from the commons of the various guilds.

Walter Shirle, William Waryn and William Walter, sent to London for business as appears above reported that by the will of the king and other lords of the realm every striped cloth made falling short of 28 yards in length and 6 in width folded and tacked (*takkat'*) should be penalized. Agreed that three striped cloths be shown to the king in council, one unfinished ('rawe'), one partly fulled, and the third completely fulled and stretched, to show that cloth of this kind could not be made of that width.

[f. 43v.; *faded and stained*]

105. Assembly: Thursday in Easter week [*7 April 1412*].

Present: the mayor and many other of his fellow citizens.

Richard Spencer, Walter Shirle, Walter Salle and William Waryn were chosen to discuss with the bishop and with the dean and chapter of Salisbury the acquisition under the king's licence of 100 marks in rent, to which those present promised to give their support.

106. Assembly: 8 June [*1412*].

Present: the mayor, John Moner, Richard Spencer, Walter Shirle, William Waryn, Walter Nandre, William Walter, William Salle, Adam Teffonte, William Busshup, Thomas Child, John Levesham, John Judde, William Tuyl, John Skot, John Shute, John Hogeman, Richard Gage, William Mede, John Gilbert, John Spencer, Robert Warmwell, Thomas Boner, William Barbour, Edward Dubbere.

Elected as the king's coroners for the city by virtue of two royal writs: Nicholas Melbury and John Judde, in place of the deceased Richard Juwell and William Baly.

Elected as assessors: Thomas Child, John Parch, Thomas Masone, John Corscombe; as collectors: William Slegge, Stephen Lythenard, William Stoute, George Jocee.

Richard Spencer and Walter Shirle presented the king's writ close, addressed to the mayor and bailiffs, for paying them £11 for [attending] the parliament held on the morrow of All Souls [*3 Nov.*]. Sent to London on the city's business as appears in preceding assemblies, they accounted for their expenses as appears in the list of this assembly, which were paid with their expenses in parliament, £38 11s. 4d. as above. Elected as assessors: Thomas Child, John Parch, Thomas Mason, John Corscombe; as collectors: William Slegge, Stephen Lythenard, William Stoute, George Jocee.

107. Assembly: 9 June [*1412*].

Present: the mayor and many other of his fellow citizens.

Presented: the king's privy seal letter to the mayor, bailiffs, and good men of the city for an aid of £1,000 for his voyage into France. After deliberation, Walter Shirle and William Walter were appointed to discuss with the king's council the reduction of the sum to 100 marks, which sum it was agreed to levy among the citizens at large according to their present status. Among whom Thomas Biston, assessed at 6s. 8d., refused to pay and would not appear before the mayor although often summoned by the city serjeant. For this presumption William Doudyng, mayor, John Moner, Richard Spencer, William Waryn, Walter Nandre, John Beckot, and many other reputable citizens personally went to Biston's house and put their seals on it because he was not found. After they had left his door, Thomas contemptuously appeared and broke the seals. For this contempt he was arrested by common consent and committed to the custody of Walter Short, the city serjeant. It was proposed to send a petition (*billa*) to the king's council in these words: [*The petition, in French, is set out in full, reciting the events and requesting exemplary punishment for Thomas.*] When the petition was made known to Thomas he submitted himself to the mercy and indulgence of the mayor and citizens and found as surety for his good behaviour Walter Nandr', who entered a bond of £40 with the mayor for Thomas, which bond remains in the [common] chest.

[*The passage above was clearly written some time after the meeting which it purports to record.*]

108. Assembly: morrow of the nativity of the Blessed Virgin Mary [*9 Sept. 1412*].

Shown: a letter confirming the king's licence to the mayor and citizens for acquiring £40 [in rents], under the seal of the bishop of Salisbury and of the dean and chapter. The letter is in the mayor's keeping. [*Added later:* Afterwards, as appears in later entries, the letter, along with many other memoranda, was placed in the common chest in St. Thomas's church.]

[f. 44; *faded and stained, the lower half blank*]

109. Assembly: morrow of St. Matthew [*23 Sept. 1412*].

Present: the mayor, John Moner, Richard Spencer, Walter Shirle, William Walter, William Salle, Walter Nandre, John Levesham, Robert Deverel, John Beckot, Thomas Mason, John Judde, William Lord, Thomas Riede, William Fuystour, Thomas Blechere, William Dounyng, William Slegge, Laurence Lane, Thomas Boner, John Swyft, William Barbour, Edward Dubbere, George Jocee.

The mayor accounted for keeping the expenses and fees of the city (apart from the account of other expenses as appeared in the preceding assembly of 8 June), which as shown in the list amounted to £19 11s. 8d. Agreed: the sum to be assessed and levied with the half of a tenth to be paid to the king on the morrow [*12 Nov.*] of St. Martin. Elected to help the assessors: John Noble, Laurence Lane, William Penyton, Richard atte Mulle; as collectors, [William Depedene *crossed out*] John Helier, 'irmonger' [*interlined*], Robert Warmwell, William Cokkes, Henry Suthewyk.

110. Assembly: morrow of Michaelmas 13 [*recte* 14 Hen. IV, *30 Sept. 1412*].

Present: the mayor and very many other fellow citizens.

[*The following entry is doubtful, being faint, heavily abbreviated, and much amended.*] Moved: payments (. . .) [for the purchase of?] George's inn, concerning which William Harnhull, barbour, voluntarily granted to the mayor and commonalty after the death of himself and his wife Alice for prayers for their souls a cottage, at an annual rent of 16s., towards St. Martin's (church?), and he added from a gift of 10s. paid to the house (called?) 'almeshous' 6s. 8d. for prayers for their souls. Other contributions towards the same business [of buying George's inn] Richard Gage £1, Thomas Boner £1, John Gilbert 3s. 4d., William Stoute [*blank*], Stephen Lythenard £1, John Cornyssh 1 mark,

Robert Stonard 1 mark, Thomas Yevele 3s. 4d., William Penston 1 mark, Thomas Blechere 1 mark, Edward Purdy 1 mark, William Phebis ½ mark, John Castelton 1 mark, John Sampson 10s., William Grante 1 mark, John Ruddok 1 mark, John Dounton 2 marks, John Corscombe 10s., Simon Bakere 1 mark, John Clyve 1 mark, Richard Chesham ½ mark, Robert Gilbert 'tannere' £1, Edward [no surname] 1 mark, Reginald Glovere gave a cuirass (*loricam*), a gold ingot (?, *palat'*), and a pair of apothecary's scales (?, *par botecarum de plates*) jointly with (*in c'*) W. Furbour. {?}

111. Assembly: 7 Oct. 14 [Hen. IV, *1412*].

Present: the mayor and many other fellow citizens.

Agreed by all: John Moner and Richard Spencer to be fully enfeoffed of all lands, tenements, and rents to be given to the mayor and commonalty, so that when the time should come they may be granted to the mayor and commonalty according to the king's and the bishop and chapter of Salisbury's licence, which was afterwards done [? *i.e. the enfeoffment*] and in the following year in the mayoralty of John Beckot was in part completed [? *i.e. the grant to the mayor and commonalty*].

[f. 44v. *blank*]

[f. 45; *faded and stained, the lower half missing*]

112. Account of William Doudyng then mayor accounted of his receipts and payments with the agreement of the neighbours as appears in the assemblies on the feast of the conversion of St. Paul [*25 Jan.*] and 8 June 13 [Hen. IV, *1412*].

From the tallage assessed by virtue of the said assemblies, £42 16s., for which the collectors for New Street and Market were William Stoute [and] George Jocee, for St. Martin and Meadow, William Slegge and Stephen Lynthenard. From which he paid to William Stoute and Walter Shirle citizens for their expenses and wages at the last parliament held on the morrow of All Souls [*3 Nov. 1411*] at Westminster according to the writ to the mayor and bailiffs £11, and to Walter Shirle for various other expenses in London on the city's business (. . .) and to Richard Spencer likewise (. . .).

To John Hemyngby and other clerks going with the said collectors, 3s. 4d.; allowed to the same collectors for eleven men each assessed at 4d. but fugitives and having nothing, 3s. 8d.; allowed to the collectors for full payment to the masters of the guild of weavers of the £5 advanced by them, and to the masters of the guild of fullers for the £2 advanced by them, as appears in the preceding assembly in said mayoralty.

[f. 45v. *blank*]

[f. 46, *also numbered 47 and 41; stained*]

113. [*Heading:*] Assemblies of citizens held in the mayoralty of John Beckot from the feast of St. Martin 14 Hen. IV [*11 Nov. 1412*] to the same feast 1 Hen. V [*11 Nov. 1413*].

First assembly: Friday the eve of St. Katherine the virgin [*25 Nov. 1412; Friday 25 Nov. was the feast, not the eve, of St. Katherine*].

Present: the mayor, John Moner, Richard Spencer, Walter Shirle, William Waryn, William Doudyng, Adam Teffonte, William Walter, William Busshup, Walter Nandre, John Levesham, Thomas Child, Nicholas Belle, John Judde, Thomas Mason, Robert Warmwell, Richard Oword, Robert Tannere, Robert Stonard, William West, William Nedler, Henry Southwyk, William Barbour, Richard atte Mulle, Richard Gage, Thomas Rede, Edward Frith [*named twice*], Edward Dubbere, George Jocee, and others.

Agreed: the reeves' rolls to be supervised and corrected carefully (*bona examinacione*), and the next sheriff (*futurus*) to have [a] pipe of wine presented in the city's name of the city for his friendship and the common livery of the good citizens (*inter probos cives*) at Christmas. William Sturton and John Gowayn, and William Lord attorney for the city [and] Stephen Edyngdon city clerk to continue at the wages and liveries earlier agreed and granted.

Walter Shirle, William Doudyng, Nicholas Belle, Thomas Rede, Robert Warmwell, and Richard Gage were appointed to procure and carry forward the city's business with competent men in aid of the licence granted (*in auxil' licenc' concesse*).

Elected as a constable: Thomas Mason draper, to fill that office with Thomas Child, already sworn.

William Doudyng and Robert Warmwell, as the named executors of William Warmwell, declared his will that after his death the mayor and commonalty should have all his cottages opposite the Friars Minor and also £1 annual rent from Stephen Lythenard's curtilage with a rack (*reck'*) in Freren Street and 10s. annual rent from the tenement and shop late John Thorbourne's opposite 'le Bolehall', to pray for his soul and hold his obit yearly in the church of the Friars Minor of Salisbury.

Henry Southwyk, called to account for wrongly wearing (*contrafecit*) the livery of the good citizens when he was not one of the number of those ordained for that livery, was fined £2.

114. Assembly: feast of St. Hilary [*13 Jan. 1413*].

Present: the mayor, John Moner, Richard Spencer, Walter Shirle, and many other citizens named in the list.

Exhibited: a writ for two citizens for the king's parliament to be held at Westminster on the morrow [*3 Feb.*] of the Purification. Elected: Walter Shirle and William Waryn.

William Doudyng enrolls the fact that £4 remains [owed] to the mayor and commonalty from the sale of the tenement of John Seevyne according to the tenour of his will, the money remaining in William's own hands until etc. [*sic*].

115. Assembly: Friday after ther conversion of St. Paul [*27 Jan. 1413*].

Present: the mayor, Richard Spencer, Walter Shirle, William Walter, William Busshup, William Salle, William Doudyng, Nicholas Hardyng, Nicholas Belle, John Levesham, Thomas Child, John Judde, John Chippenham, Laurence Lane, Richard Oword, John Hogeman, William Slegge, Edward Purdy, Robert Warmwell, Richard Gage, William Fuystour, William Penyton, John Shupton, and others.

Moved: that the citizens attending parliament in future do all that they can for a remedy for the assize of cloth. The king's licence and that of the bishop and the dean and chapter of Salisbury for acquiring lands and tenements for the work of the mayor and commonalty were delivered to Walter Shirle, one of those elected to parliament, for acquiring a writ *ad quod dampnum*. On the Tuesday following [31 Jan.] Robert Warmwell and Richard Gage paid Walter Shirle 100s. from the common pyx in their keeping for carrying out the said business, in the presence of the mayor, William Waryn, Thomas Child, S[tephen] Edyngdon, and others.

116. Assembly: the eve of the Annunciation 1 Hen.V [*24 March 1413*].

Present: the mayor and many other fellow citizens whose names appear in the list.

Walter Shirle and William Waryn, elected to parliament, exhibited the king's licence addressed to John Moner and Richard Spencer for appropriating and amortising to the mayor and commonalty four messuages and 4 marks rent within the city. And with it they proffered the king's old licence together with the said licence of the dean and chapter which had earlier been delivered to them for acquiring the present licence. (Continued overleaf.)

117. Memorandum [*inserted later*] that on the eve of St. Simon and St. Jude 1 Hen. V [*27 Oct. 1413*] Thomas Russel, cousin and heir of Robert Russel 'chivaler', before John Beckot then mayor, William Waryn, William Busshup, William Doudyng, Walter Nandre, John Park, Stephen Edyngdon, Roger Enterbisshe, and many other citizens present in the church of St. Thomas, Salisbury, undertook to pay and satisfy the mayor and commonalty of all the arrears of the annual rent of £4 10s. issuing from his lands and tenements and owed to the mayor and the commonalty from Michaelmas in the mayoralty of William Busshup to Michaelmas in the mayoralty of William Doudyng, viz. in the mayoralties of Walter Shirle, William Salle, Walter Nandre, and William Doudyng, in whose time at the said Michaelmas term the rents granted by indenture were etc. [*sic*].

[f. 46v.]

118. Assembly: 27 March 1 Hen.V [*1413*].

Present: the mayor and many other fellow citizens whose names appear in the list of the assembly.

Walter Shirle and William Waryn, elected to parliament, brought back an ordinance made there that rayed and motled (*stragul' et motle*) cloths are to contain in length in the flat before fulling and shearing (*in playto ante lotu' et tonsur'*) 28 yards and in width 5 quarters on pain of forfeiture of all cloths of this kind of smaller measure (*minor' assise*).

119. Assembly: 1 April [*1413*].

Present: the mayor, Richard Spencer, Walter Shirle, William Waryn, William Busshup, William Doudyng, William Walter, John Levesham, Nicholas Belle, Thomas Child, Thomas Mason, John Judde, William Salle, Walter Nandre, Nicholas Hardyng, John Swyft, and others.

Agreed: John son of John Bottenham hereafter to be excused the office of alderman by reason of the promise made to the mayor and commonalty to pay the £25 ordered in his father's will.

120. Assembly: 5 April [1413]

Present: the mayor and many other fellow citizens whose names appear in the list of the assembly.

Exhibited and read: a writ for a parliament at Westminster three weeks [14 May] from Easter; elected: Walter Shirle and William Waryn.

121. Assembly: 19 April [*1413*].

Present: the mayor and many other fellow citizens.

John Moner was paid £4, besides all his receipts from the rent of George's inn, from the common money of the community remaining in the coffer in the keeping of Robert Warmwell and Richard Gage; Richard Spencer was likewise paid £12 0s. 7d., besides his receipts from the same rent; in full satisfaction of all payments owed to the said John and Richard for their payments for George's inn. The coffer with the money in it was delivered to Walter Shirle. All the muniments touching George's inn remaining in Richard Spencer's keeping and all the charters and muniments touching the mayor and the commonalty remaining in the keeping of S[tephen] Edyngdon, the clerk, were placed in a small chest under two locks and delivered to the mayor's keeping etc.

122. Assembly: 4 Aug. [*1413*]

Present: the mayor and many other fellow citizens.

William Busshup undertook to indemnify John Moner and Richard Spencer concerning a bond in his keeping which bound them to someone whose name was now not known for certain.

William Doudyng accounted for his receipts and payments during his mayoralty as appears in the list of this assembly. Remaining in his hand, £15 4s. 1d.; allowed for a repayment to Finiane, wife of John Sheppere mercer, of her first payment (*de pristino prestito*) of 13s. 4d. So he paid £14 10s. 9d., which money was delivered to Robert Warmwell for placing in the coffer. So he [William] is quit, saving better information (*mel' avisamento*).

123. Assembly: 25 Sept. [*1413*].

Present: the mayor and many fellow citizens whose names appear in the list.

Elected as coroners for the city by virtue of the king's writ: John Judde and John Swyft.

124. Assembly: 16 Oct. [*1413*].

Present: the mayor and many other fellow citizens whose names appear in the list.

Exhibited: the king's commission addressed to Laurence Lane, Henry Southwyk, John Leokere, and Robert Gilbert tanner for the half of a tenth granted by parliament to the king to be paid on the feast of St. Martin next [11 Nov. 1413], and likewise for the other half to be paid at Easter then next following [8 April 1414]. Elected as assessors: William Walter, Walter Shirle, William Doudyng, and William Fuystour, Thomas Rede and Richard Coof; as collectors: Nicholas Southham, John Nouble, John Pope, and John Chippenham.

Granted: the £18 for the expenses of citizens elected to parliament to be added and levied with the £27 10s. 1d. to be levied in the city for the half of a tenth.

125. Assembly: 8 Nov. [*1413*].

Present: the mayor, Richard Spencer, Walter Shirle, William Busshup, William Salle, Walter Nandre, John Levesham, Nicholas Belle, and others.

William Walter openly declared that it would be his last will that the tenement newly built by him, where Richard Coofe draper lives, opposite the market, will, after the death of William and Petronilla his wife, remain in perpetuity to the mayor and commonalty for holding their obits in the church of St. Edmund, Salisbury, in perpetuity.

[f. 47; *faded and stained*] [*Heading:*] Beket

Receipts of William Walter and Robert Warmwell, elected chamberlains, during the mayoralty of John Beckot, 1 Hen.V [*1413–4*].

[From William Doudyng on his account during his mayoralty, £14 10s. 9d. *crossed out.*] From the same Wiliam Doudyng from the sale of the tenement late John Seewayne's, £4; from John Bottenham junior in part payment of £25 ordered by John Bottenham his father to the mayor and community for commending his soul, £10; put in the coffer from the payment made by Walter Shirle and various other persons as appears in the first assembly held in the time of Thomas Mason draper in all accounts (up to?) the Conception of the Blessed Virgin Mary 1 Hen. IV [*9 Dec. 1413*], £45 2s. 8d.; from the rent of the hospice in George's inn from Christmas 14 Hen. IV [*1412*], [*no amount entered*]; from the rent of a tenement and rooms by the cemetery of St. Thomas's church [*interlined*: of which part appears in an earlier folio], the first term being Michaelmas 1 Hen.V [*29 Sept. 1413*]; from Thomas Steor's tenement in Castle Street [*crossed out*: from Christmas 13 Henr. IV [*1411*]; *interlined*: viz. 4 marks a year] for which Thomas's arrears of rent after the account of William Busshup, made on 4 Aug. 1 Hen.V, for the term from then to the following Michaelmas; from the rent of a cottage granted to William Penyton at £2 per year according to the indenture, the first term being Michaelmas in the said year, but arrears remain; from the rent of a tenement granted to Richard Spencer from the feast [*incomplete*]; from the rent of Thomas Artour, for the arrears assigned to the chamberlains by John Beckot, 6s. 8d. from £1 a year, the rent beginning on the said feast; from the whole rent of 2s. a year for the building above the ditch by Pynnoke's inn; from the rent a corner tenement late John Thorbourne's from the feast [*incomplete*]; from the rent of a cottage in Nuggeston (*Nhuggeston*) [*interlined*: after the death of John Scot junior kinsman of John Baker] before Michaelmas 1 Hen.V [*29 Sept. 1413*], the rent of which appears in a part of a following folio.

[f. 47v. *blank*]

[f. 48] [*Heading:*] Beket

126. Rents and tenements in the city of Salisbury appropriated to the mayor and commonalty in the mayoralty of John Beckot, 14 Hen. IV [*1412–13*].

The hospice called George's inn which Thomas Randolf holds with a laundry (*lavandria*), solar, cellar, shop, houses, and its appurtenances pays yearly at farm [besides *crossed out,* with *inserted*] repairs £20.

The capital tenement which John More baker holds by St. Thomas's cemetery pays yearly at farm [besides *crossed out,* with *inserted*] repairs £4.

Another room there, next to the said tenement, which Thomas Baker chaplain holds pays yearly at farm [besides *crossed out,* with *inserted*] repairs 10s.

Another room there, with a solar, which James Grene chaplain holds pays yearly 10s.

Another shop there, with a solar, which Nicholas Wight chaplain holds pays yearly 10s.

Another shop there, with a solar, which two chaplains hold pays yearly 10s.

Another shop there by the entry through the cemetery, with a solar upstairs (*supra scalar'*), which John Sherman holds pays yearly £1.

A tenement in Castle Street which Thomas Steor holds, with a shop, garden and appurtenances, pays yearly with repairs £2 13s. 4d., for which John Wollop's obit will be held in perpetuity in St. Edmund's church in the first week of Lent.

Three cottages which William Penyton holds in Wyneman Street, with a garden adjacent, pays yearly in quit-rent [*inserted*: from the legacy of John Prentis] £2, for which John Prentis's obit will be held in perpetuity in St. Edmund's church in the second week of Lent for the souls of him and Joan and Katherine his wives and of Thomas Thursteyn, Joan his wife, and William their son.

The whole of the newly built messuage which Richard Spencer holds towards St. Edmund's church in Gigant Street pays yearly in quit-rent by the charter granted to the same Richard £1 6s. 8d.

A tenement by the corner tenement late William Hull's in Winchester Street ('Wynchestret') is now empty [*Added*] afterwards demised to John Parch by indenture who pays yearly for the same £1.

A building above Fisherton bridge which Thomas Artour 'skynner' holds by indenture, to be repaired at his expense, pays yearly £1.

A building above the common ditch adjacent to a shop at Pynnoke's inn, which John Noble holds, pays yearly in quit rent 2s.

A corner tenement late John Thorbourne's and previously John Shouve's opposite 'le Bolehall' pays yearly in quit-rent, from the legacy of William Warmwell, 10s.

[f. 48v.; *faded and stained*]

A corner shop or cottage which Thomas Rede 'taillor' and Joan his wife hold by indenture made by grant of John Bakere grocer, in Nuggeston towards St. Edmund's church, pays yearly, with a garden and another house adjacent at the end of the garden, 16s.

Another cottage there by the same cottage, which John Hayward 'webbe' holds, with a garden adjacent, pays yearly 10s., the term of payment beginning at Michaelmas 1Hen. V [*29 Sept. 1413*].

Another cottage there which Nicholas Shawe weaver holds, with a garden adjacent, pays yearly 10s.

Another cottage there which John Lord weaver holds, with a garden adjacent, pays yearly 10s.

Another cottage which Robert Peteresfeld and Juliana his wife hold by indenture, with a garden adjacent, pays yearly £1, but according to the indenture it pays £1 4s.

Another cottage there which John Cappe holds, without a garden, pays yearly 7s.

Another cottage there by John Lake's cottage, with houses adjacent, pays yearly 15s., but is now empty and used to pay £1.

127. Rental of the mayor and commonalty of the city of New Salisbury made the 10th day of the month [*blank*] 6 Hen.V [*1418–19*].

The hospice called George's inn pays yearly at farm by the indenture granted to John Burton, with the laundry adjacent, £20, from which hospice there goes yearly to the scholars of De Vaux College (*domus de Valle*) of Salisbury 19s., and for which the obit of William Teynterer junior and Alice his wife will be held annually in perpetuity in St. Thomas's church of Salisbury on the feast [*unfinished*] and John Becket's similarly at the Exaltation of Holy Cross [*14 Sept.*].

The capital tenement which John More baker [holds] by indenture by St. Thomas's cemetery pays yearly, with the shop immediately adjacent, in free and quit-rent £4.

Another shop there with a room which a parish chaplain holds pays yearly, with a solar, 10s.

Another shop there which two chaplains hold by the same shop pays yearly, with a solar, 10s.

Another shop there which Nicholas Wight chaplain holds. with a solar, pays yearly 10s.

Another shop, with a solar upstairs, which John Sherman holds pays yearly £1.

A tenement which Thomas Steor holds in Castle Street with appurtenances pays yearly £2, for which tenement the obits of John Moner and John Wollop draper will be held annually in perpetuity at the same time in St. Edmund's on the Sunday before Christmas.

A tenement and three cottages which William Penyton holds at the corner of Wyneman Street pays yearly in free and quit-rent besides all charges £2, for which tenement and cottages the obits of John Prentis, Joan and Catherine his wives, Thomas Thursteyn, Joan his wife, and William their son will be held annually in perpetuity in St. Edmund's church in the second week in Lent at the expense of William Penyton and his heirs.

A tenement in Gigant Street (*Gigorstret*) towards St. Edmund's church lately Richard Spencer's pays yearly in quit-rent freely £1 6s. 8d.

[f. 49; *faded and stained*] [*Heading*:] Beket.

A tenement by the cottage late John Buterlegh's towards St. Edmund's church in Gigant Street is now empty but used to pay yearly 15[s.].

Another small cottage there which John Cappere held 7s.

Another tenement there which Robert Peteresfeld and his wife hold by indenture, with a garden adjacent, pays yearly 24s.

Another cottage there which John Lord held pays yearly at will 10s.

Another cottage there which Nicholas Shawe lately held pays yearly 10s.

Another cottage there which Thomas [*blank*] held there pays yearly 10s.

Another cottage there which John Haiward 'webbe' holds pays yearly at will 10s.

Another corner cottage there which Thomas Rede 'taillor' holds by indenture pays yearly 16s.

A tenement in Winchester Street (*Wynchestret*) which John Parch holds by indenture by William Cok's tenement pays yearly in free and quit-rent £1.

A separate tenement with adjacent cottages late of William Asshle chaplain which now Thomas Messager holds by an indenture pays yearly in free and quit-rent 5 marks besides all charges, for which tenement the said William's obit will be held annually in St. Thomas's church at Thomas Messager's expense on the feast of St. Peter in Cathedra [*22 Feb.*].

A tenement by the same tenement, late the said William's, in which Robert Hyndon lately lived pays yearly during the life of Edith, wife of John Vincent 'webbe', kinsman of the said William Asshele, whose obit as above, £1 4s.

10s. a year rent from two cottages late John Thorbourne's in Brown Street next to the corner there, from the legacy of William Warmwell.

2s. a year from a building above the common ditch by Pynnoke's inn, by an old ordinance.

A building by the common latrine above Fissherton bridge, which Thomas Artour 'skynner' holds by indenture, pays yearly in free and quit-rent besides all charges £1.

A tenement which Richard Coof holds in the market, late William Walter's, pays yearly
£5, for which tenement the said William's obit will be held in perpetuity in St. Edmund's
church [on the feast *crossed out*; on the morrow *inserted*] of Ascension and at the same
time William Wichford's obit. [*A marginal note, crossed out and marked* vacat, *gives
the date of William Wichford's obit as the Tuesday after Michaelmas.*] At which obits, it
was ordained in full assembly held 31 March 7 Hen. V [*1419*] in the mayoralty of
Robert Puynant, in the presence also of Walter Shirle, William Waryn, William Busshup,
Thomas Mason, Walter Nandre, John Judde, John Swyft, Thomas Boner, John Bremle,
Robert Warmwell, Henry Man, John Wichford, Richard Oword, Richard Gage, Edward
Dubbere, John Parch, John Everhard, and others, that all citizens of the Twenty-Four
present in the town should come to the mass at the offertory on pain of 2 lb. of wax,
and similarly those of the other Twenty-Four (*xxiiii al' prob' magis civibus*) should also
come at the offertory on pain of 1 lb. of wax, unless they have a reasonable excuse.

[*Above the last entry is a pencilled note in an ? 18th-century hand*: inserted at y place
for (post?).]

[f. 49v *blank*]

[f. 50; *faded*]

128. [*Heading*:] Assemblies held during the mayoralty of Thomas Mason draper, from
the feast of St. Martin 1 Hen. V [*11 Nov. 1413*] for the following year.

The first assembly, 1 Dec. [*1413*]

Present: the mayor, John Moner, Richard Spencer, Walter Shirle, William Waryn, John
Becket, Walter Nandre, William Salle, William Doudyng, William Busshup, Nicholas
Hardyng, John Levesham, John Judde, William Fuystour, William Tuyl, Richard Oword,
Thomas Boner, Robert Warmwell, Robert Gilbert, Thomas Rede, John Clyve, William
Barbour, William Nedlere, John Shute, John Cornyssh, Laurence Lane, John Chippenham,
William Slegge, John Noble, John Durneford, William West, George Jocee, Richard
Gage, William Walter and others.

Ordered: the Twenty-Four and six others retained for their advice to the city to be
clothed in silk (*de una setta vestiantur*). Moved: the pipe of wine customarily presented
to the county sheriff to be respited until (. . .). Elected as city coroners: William Tuyl
and William Fuystour, in place of Thomas (. . .) and Thomas Child (. . .).

On Saturday (. . .)[? following, *i.e. 2 Dec.*] the coffer was opened, containing £55 16s.,
from which was paid to Walter Shirle for his old advance for the work of George's inn
(. . .) [*the amount illegible, but from what follows can be calculated as* £1 13s. 4d.] and
5 marks besides the allowance in place of his promise; paid to Thomas Mason for a
similar advance £2 besides the 2 marks which he promised; paid to John Judde £1
besides (. . .) which he promised; paid to William Busshup for his last advance [to the
king *interlined*] £1 besides (. . .) which he promised (. . .); paid to William Walter for

a similar advance for George's inn £1 13s. 4d. besides (. . .) of his promise for the same work. [The sums expended amounted to £10 13s. 4d., so that there remained £45 2s. 8d. put in the coffer and delivered to the chamberlains, in the presence of the mayor, Richard Spencer, Walter Shirle, William Waryn, William Walter, William Busshup, William Doudyng, John Beckot, John Judde, Robert Warmwell, and others.

129. Assembly: Friday the morrow of St. Thomas the apostle [*22 Dec. 1413*].

Present: the mayor and many other citizens named in the list of the assembly.

Agreed by all: John Bottenham junior be excused the office of alderman on condition of his paying £15 to the mayor and commonalty ordered by his father from a larger sum.

130. Assembly: 1 Feb. [*1414*].

Present: the mayor and many other fellow citizens.

By common assent all the muniments concerning George's inn and other muniments in the small chest which were in the keeping of John Beckot together with the common seal were put in the common chest in St. Thomas's church.

131. Assembly: 20 March [*1414*].

Present: the mayor and many other fellow citizens.

Agreed by all: the same assessors and collectors for the half of a tenth to be levied for the king at Easter next as were appointed collectors for the feast of St. Martin last [*11 Nov. 1413*], except that George Jocee was appointed in place of John Noble.

Elected to attend the parliament at Leicester 30 April: Walter Shirle and John Beckot.

Ordered: the broken bridge in High Street outside John Spencer's tenement to be repaired at the common expense.

132. Assembly: 13 June 2 [*Hen. V, 1414*].

Present: the mayor and many other fellow citizens.

The mayor with John Moner, Richard Spencer, William [*sic, recte* Walter] Shirle, William Waryn, William Walter, and William Doudyng and with Edward Frith, Richard Gage, Thomas Boner, Thomas Reede, John Bottenham, and John Parch were elected to examine (*sciend'*) and oversee the the expenses and payments on George's inn, to know how much has been paid for the hospice by the Twenty-Four and how much by others of the commonalty.

Agreed by all: John Parch to have the tenement late John Nyweman's in Winchester Street by the corner tenement late William Hull's for a term of 98 years for a rent of £1 a year paid to the mayor and commonalty, repairs and maintenance at John's expense, by an indenture to be drawn up, the payment to begin at Christmas next.

133. Assembly: St. Matthew's day 2 [*Hen. V, 21 Sept. 1414*]

Present: Thomas Mason, mayor, John Moner, Richard Spencer, Walter Shirle, William Walter, William Busshup, William Doudyng, Walter Nandr', John Becket, John Levesham, Nicholas Belle, Robert Warmwell, and others and William Fuystour, Richard Oword, Henry Man, Thomas Rede, Thomas Blechere, John Cornyssh', Robert Gilbert, Laurence Lane, John Spencer, William atte Lee, William Barbour, Thomas Boner, Edward Dubbere, William West, William Purchas, and many others.

The mayor accounted for his payments and expenses, of which details are in the following folio.

William Walter and Robert Warmwell, city chamberlains, accounted for their receipts, both from the city rents and from other money, and for their payments as appears in the following folio. They were appointed to fill the same office for the year to come, and they (. . .) to make their account, to each of them £2.

Ordered that the expenses of Walter Shirle and John Beckot, the citizens elected to the last parliament held at Leicester (. . .) to be assessed and levied in common by the king's writ. Elected as assessors: William Fuystour, John Swyft, Thomas Boner, and Edward Dubbere; as collectors: John Ruddok, William Cokkes, John Heliere 'irmonger', and Richard Chesham. The sum was neither assessed not levied, and nothing was done [?] (Continued overleaf.)

[f. 50v.; *faded and stained, the lower part blank*]

134. Assembly: 3 Nov. 2 [Hen. V, *1414*].

Present: Thomas Mason, mayor, John Levesham his successor elect, John Moner, Walter Shirle, Walter Nandre, John Beckot, William Waryn, William Doudyng, William Walter, William Busshup, Nicholas Hardyng, John Swyft, Thomas Boner, William Fuystour, Robert Warmwell, Richard Oword, Henry Man, Thomas Durneford, John Sydenham, Thomas Blechere, Nicholas Hardyng [*repeated*], William atte Lee, John Clyve, Edward Dubbere, John Durneford, Richard Cristchurche, William West, John Bremle, John Noble, Richard Coof, and others.

Exhibited: the king's writ addressed to the mayor and bailiffs for a parliament at

Westminster on Monday after the octave of St. Martin [*19 Nov. 1414*]. Elected: Walter Shirle and John Ruddok.

[f. 51; *badly faded and stained*]

135. Account of Thomas Mason draper mayor of his payments during his year of office from the feast of St. Martin 1 Hen. V [*11 Nov. 1413*] for the year following.

For two gallon tuns of Malmesey (. . .) 2s. 8d. [*Nine lines largely illegible, including* 4s. 4d. . . . 4s. 4d. . . . for the justices . . . coming to Wiltshire . . . £3 9s. 8d. . . . to William Elisaundre . . . for livery 12s. 6d. Sum £3 2s. 6d. . . . £1 2s.] Sum of the above £4 5s. 2d.

Sum total of all payments £7 14s. 10d.

Receipts: nothing accounted because all received by the chamberlains in rents and other income. The mayor was paid for his sum by William Walter and Robert Warmwell, city chamberlains, on Michaelmas day 2 Hen. V [*29 Sept. 1414*].

136. Account of William Walter and Robert Warmwell, city chamberlains, of their receipts and payments both in rents and in other income, made for the mayor and community on St. Matthew's day 2 Hen. V [*21 Sept. 1414*] in the presence of the mayor, John Moner, Richard Spencer, Walter Shirle, William Busshup, [William Walter *crossed out*], William Doudyng, John Beckot, Walter Nandre, John Levesham, Nicholas Belle, [Robert Warmwell *crossed out*], and Thomas Rede.

Receipts: put in the coffer after payments to various persons as appears in the first assembly of the said mayor [*no. 128*], £45 2s. 8d. ; from William Doudyng, proceeds of the mayor and community from the sale of the tenement late John Seewyne's, £4. Sum, £49 2s. 8d.

From Thomas Randolf for the rent of the hospice of George's inn for the terms of Christmas 14 Hen. IV [*1412*] and Easter, St. John the Baptist, Michaelmas, Christmas, Easter, and the Nativity of St. John the Baptist 1 and 2 Hen. V [*1413–14*], from £20 annual rent according to the indenture, £30, and he owes £10 at Michaelmas next;. from John More, baker, at Michaelmas, Christmas, Easter, and St. John the Baptist 1 and 2 Hen. V [*1413–14*] for the annual rent of the capital tenement where he lives by St. Thomas's cemetery, from £4 annual rent, £4, and he owes £1 in arrears at Michaelmas next; [f. 51v.; *stained*] from Thomas Bakere, chaplain, at the said terms for a shop with a solar by St. Thomas's cemetery, from 10s. annual rent, 7s. 6d., and he owes 7s. 6d. at Michaelmas next; from James Grene, chaplain, at the said terms for two lower rooms with a solar, from 15s. annual rent, 10s. and he owes 7s. 6d. at Michaelmas next; from Nicholas Wight, chaplain, at the said terms for another shop there with a solar, from 10s. annual rent, 12s., and he owes 2s. 6d. at Michaelmas next; from a chaplain for another lower room at the tenement there at the said terms for one of which it was empty, from 5s. annual rent, 2s. 6d., and he owes (. . .) at Michaelmas next; from the tenement in

William Doudyng's hand for the rent of John Thornton, shearman ('sh'man'), for a shop (. . .) and another room, from £1 annual rent, 10s., and he owes with arrears £1 at Michaelmas next; from Thomas Steor at the said terms for a tenement where he lives in Castle Street, late John Wollop's, from £2 13s. 4d. annual rent, 16s. 8d. (. . .) earlier arrears from William Busshup's mayoralty; from Richard Spencer at the said terms for a tenement which he took in Gigand Street towards St. Edmund's church, from £1 6s. 8d. annual quit-rent, 10s., and he owes 16s. 8d. at Michaelmas next; from William Penyton, 'digher', at the said terms for a cottage next to the corner tenement where he lives in Wyneman Street, from (. . .) annual rent, £2, and he owes £1 10s. at Michaelmas next; from Thomas Rede, 'taillor', at the said terms for a corner shop, late John Bakere's, in Nhuggeston, from 16s. annual rent, 8s., and he owes 12s. at Michaelmas next; from John Haiward at the same terms for another cottage which he holds there, from 10s. annual rent, 6s. 8d., and he owes 5s. 10d. at Michaelmas next; from Nicholas Shawe at the same terms for another cottage which he holds there, from 10s. annual rent, 7s. 6d., and he owes 5s. at Michaelmas next; from John Lord at the same terms for another cottage there, from 10s. annual rent, 3s. 4d., and he owes 8s. 10d. at Michaelmas next. Nothing received in rent from Robert Peteresfeld at the said terms for another cottage there which he holds by indenture for £1 annual rent; nor from John Cappe at the said terms for another cottage there without a garden for 7s. annual rent; nor for another messuage there at the said terms because it was empty through all those terms, usually 16s. annual rent; nor from Thomas Artour at the said terms for houses above Fisherton latrine, demised by indenture at £1 (annual rent), and he owes £2 6s. 8d. at Michaelmas next in arrears together with arrears from John Beckot's mayoralty; nor from William Walter at the said terms from 10s. annual quit-rent for a corner tenement in Winchester Street, late John Shouve's, from the legacy of William Warmwell, and he owes [blank] at Michaelmas next; nor from William Furbour from 2s. annual quit-rent for the building above the ditch by Pynnokes inn, and he owes arrears for the past ten years; nor from the tenement, late John Nyweman's, given by Nicholas Hardyng, at the said terms, because it was empty through all those terms, but it has now been demised to John Parch by indenture for a terms of years, at £1 annual rent, payable for the first term beginning at the Christmas next.

Sum of all the above annual rents [blank]. Sum of receipts in this account, both from rents and from other issues [blank]. Sum of arrears [blank].

[Added later at the foot: £3 18s. 8d. in arrears besides the collectors' account in Thomas Mason's mayoralty.]

[The chamberlains' account is continued in no. 140.]

[f. 52; faded and stained. The folio, written in a markedly different hand from those which precede and follow it, is not in its original place: cf. note on the collation of the MS.]

137. 8 Feb. 1399. Copy of a writ from Richard II to Edmund Enefeld, requiring an oath of loyalty from the citizens of Salisbury and others.

138. 22 Ric. II [1399]. *Copy of a loyal address, in French, in response to the above writ. The document is printed in translation, without the names of the citizens, in H.M.C. Var. Coll. IV, p. 192.*]

The citizens of Salisbury write that they have bound themselves and their heirs by oath upon the gospels to observe the statutes, ordinances, and constitutions made in the parliament held at Westminster and continued at Shrewsbury and Coventry and have put their seals to the letter, namely Esmond [*sic, recte* Edmund] Enefeld mayor, William Warmwell, John Moner, Thomas Bowier, George Joce, John Wallop, John Salesbury, Richard Spencere, Thomas Boreford, Richard Jewell, Richard Leche, John Newman, John Forest, John Nedlere, Robert Deverell, William Walter, Thomas Castelton, Robert Curtlyngstoke, John Chaundler, William Gys, Adam Teffont, William Baylly, Thomas Postel, Richard Weston, Thomas Deverell, George Meriot, John Cammell, John Levesham, Nicholas Hardyng, William Picard, William Doudyng, William Busshop, Thomas Chyld, William Waryn, Thomas Feeld, Walter Nandre, Thomas Gerveys, John Ecyshale, Walter Orm, Robert Wodeford, John Kyngesbrugge, Reginald Glovere, Simond Tredynek, John Spencere, Philip Goldsmyth, Robert Weye, George Tangle, Thomas Sextayn, John Merlawe, William Plomere, John Swyfte, Richard Oword, Robert Blake, Edward Bremmore, Reginald Druerye, John Gylberd, John Noble, John Drywery, William Boure, Richard Pridye, George Joce junior (*le Joefne*), John Colier', John Canyng, Robert Charles, John Stabber', Stephen Thernbourne, John Gillyngham, Stephen Bullok, William Purchas, John Lytle, William Woderove, John Stagard, Adam Morys, John Newman 'hattere', John Waite, Thomas Blechere, Robert Body, William Salle, John Grendon, William White, John Brewer', John Botyler', Robert Bowier', Gilbert Oword, Robert Goylyn, William Stoute, John Barbour, Adam White, John Parche, John Baret, John Wutton, John Bosham, Thomas Rede, Stephen Broun, Thomas Hamme, William Hore, William More, William Wilton, Henry Wynpeny, Thomas Eyre, William Reignold, William West, William Isaac', Robert Nywport, Richard atte Mulle, William Godale, William Slegge, Nicholas Combe, Henry Suthwyke, Stephen Edyngdon, John Caundel, John Sidenham, John Frankelayn 'welere', William Syre, Robert Redyng, John Harnham, Gilbert atte Broke, Thomas Byston, John Merlawe, John Corscombe, John Judde, John Schadde, Richard Coffe, Simon Blund, William Waterlane, John Hogman, John Ferour, Richard Gage, Edmund Purdy, John Chypenham, John Forest junior (*le jofene*), John Moule, William Fulham, William Reignold, John Reignold, Thomas Stere, William Schirwold, William Hanley, Hugh Braban, Walter atte Mulle, John Skympayn, John Bridde, John Lange, John Mury, John Leker', Thomas Radenham, John Bovedon, Thomas Pides, John Hathwey, John Butte, John Horsmul, and George London. Dated at Salisbury.

[f. 52v.; *most of the verso is modern repair material*]

139. 31 August [*1399. Copy of a letter, in French, headed* 'Second letter of the said duke (*of Lancaster*) addressed to the mayor, bailiffs, and community of Salisbury'. *It is printed, in translation in* H.M.C. Var Coll. IV, pp. 192–3.]

Acknowledging a letter brought by William Hulle and William Waltier, burgesses of

Salisbury, thanking for the city's good disposition and loyalty, and undertaking to preserve its liberties and franchises. Dated at St. Albans.

[f. 53; *badly faded and stained*]

140. [*Continuation of the chamberlains' account, 21 Sept. 1414, from no. 136.*]

[*Payments:*] Out of the said receipts, for a pipe of wine sent to Walter Therbourne, sheriff of Wiltshire, in John Beckot's mayoralty, £2 13s. 4d.; paid for (. . .) at George's inn (. . .), £3 17s. 2d.; for repairing two rooms (. . .), 8s. 2½d.; (. . .) a great room (. . .) John Bakere, £2 19s.; (. . .) £1 1s. 6d.; (. . .) 19s. 4d. [*Three lines illegible.*] (. . .) £2; (. . .) in John Beckot's mayoralty, with arrears (. . .); (. . .) the Council House the same year (13s.?); for the obit of William Teyntourer by John Wollop the same year, 7s. 8d.; for (. . .) for bread, wine, and oats to the royal justices coming to hold the assizes at the feast of St. Peter in Cathedra [*22 Feb.*] (. . .) Mason's mayoralty (. . .); for buying planks to keep in stock, (£1 2s. 7d.?); for buying fifteen dozen studs (*stodes*) for the same, 3s. 2d.; for laths likewise (. . .); for a new house in the tenement of John Moner, baker; in all repairs (. . .), £1 8s. 5d; for repairing a room in George's inn, 2s. 11d.; to John Goudchild, 'carpenter', in inclusive payment (*in grosso conduct'*) for building with timber and other work and for carpentry on the bridge in High Street newly made this year, £5 0s. 8d.; for hiring labourers to move the ovens (*fornos*) before the same repair, 7s. 6d.; for freestone and masonry on the same bridge, 11s. 8d.; for other labourers for diverting the privies (*neccessaria*) in John Parch's tenement, 5d.; for scaffolding (*tabul' calcate*) and having other necessary things for making the said bridge, accounted for in detail, 5s. 11d.; for (. . .) detailed by the chamberlains in writing, 2s.; given to William Lord, city attorney, for advice (in a dispute with?) Reginald Kyngbrigge about a tenement in Nuggeston, 8s. 11d.; to Thomas Boner and Robert Warmwell, city reeves, for the bishop of Salisbury's rent at Easter last, 10s. 9d.; to the scholars of De Vaux College, Salisbury, from the bishop's rent (. . .) in part payment of his [*or their*] annual rent, 3s. 6½d.; for bread and fish sent to the bishop of Salisbury at Woodford in Thomas Mason's mayoralty during Lent, 4s. 6d.; to John More for bread sent to the duke of York coming to Clarendon in autumn this year, 3s.; for making and improving a (. . .) between the tenements of Pecket [*recte* Becket?] and George's inn, £4 0s. 8d. Sum [*blank; added later at the edge of the folio*] £49 11s. 1d.

[f. 53v.; *most of the verso is modern repair material*]

Note that on the above day and year [*21 Sept. 1414?*] John Noble and John Griffith, stewards of the fraternity of St. George, accounted in the last preceding assembly for newly arrived brothers, namely Walter Hungerford 'chivaler', William Pakyn, William Warwyk 'mercer', Stephen Mercer living in Market [*ward?*], John Gilberd, Edward Dubbere, John Pole 'taillour', Guy Miles.

[f. 53a, *an insert, stained, the verso blank*]

141. [*An unexplained list, in column*] Edmund Penston, William Hore, John Hony(ssorne?), Thomas Whytynge, John Otto(. . .), Thomas Cokes, Andrew Brent, John Parche, Harry Schadde, John Hamsmyth, John Slyghe, Thomas Glover, John Belherst, John Gylbert, John Clyffe 'tanner', Thomas Leker, John Hert 'carpynter', John Wylly, John Baton 'smythe', John Cokelett, Walter Byrde, Thomas Copter, John Large, John Cryckmore, John Chynthyn, William Chylde, John Doogodee, William Ceckespyller.

[f.54]

142. Assemblies held in the mayoralty of John Levesham 2 Hen. V [*1414–15*].

First assembly: 17 Dec. 2 Hen. V [*1414*].

Present: the mayor, Walter Shirle, William Walter, William Waryn, William Busshup, Walter Nandre, William Doudyng, Thomas Mason, John Beckot, John Bottenham, (. . .), John Swyft, Richard Oword, William atte Lee, Thomas Boner, William Fuystour, Thomas Stabbere, Henry Man, Richard Christchurch, William Slegge, Thomas Blecher, John Cornyssh, Robert Tannere, Edward Dubbere, John Spencer, Richard Coof, John Noble, Richard atte Mulle, John Parch, William Barber, John Ruddock, John Durneford, George Jocee, Stephen Lythenard, Thomas Reede, John Clyve, Thomas Ferant [?], Robert (Stonard, and others?).

Agreed by all: a pipe of wine to be given to Henry (. . .). Also that William Elisaundre (. . .).

143. Assembly: 11 Jan. [*1415*].

Present: (the mayor), William (Shirle), William Walter, William Busshup, [*and c. six names illegible*] and many other citizens named in the list.

Exhibited: the king's letters patent addressed to William Po(. . .) 'dyere', John Heliere 'irmonger', [*and c. two others illegible*] to levy within the city the whole (tenth?) granted in the last parliament, (half) payable at the Purification next [*2 Feb. 1415*] and (half) at the Purification then following. The Assembly therefore elects assessors and commissioners [*sic*]. Elected as assessors: Robert Warmwell, Richard Gage, John Swyft, Edward Dubbere; as commissioners [*i.e. collectors*]: John Everhard for Market ward, Pleasant Deyer for New Street, William Basket for St. Martin's, and John Sydenham for Meadow. To the sum [*sc. to be levied*] £13 to be added for the expenses of Walter Shirle and John Beckot, elected to two parliaments as appears in the preceding year.

144. Assembly (*Convocacio proborum*): 15 Feb. [*1415*].

Present: the mayor, Walter Shirle, William Waryn, William Walter, William Busshup, William Doudyng, and others named in the list.

Agreed by all: to discuss with Richard Spencer's wife the recovery of records in her hands concerning the city (*quod communicacio habeatur pro uxore Ricardi Spencer ut munimenta de potestate et manubus [sic] suis habeantur civitatem tangencia*). Also that bread, wine, and oats be given to the king's justices of assize at their coming at the feast of St. Mathias [*24 Feb.*] in the usual way. And that the collectors of the last tallage be given notice to account for the citizens' expenses at the said (term?).

145. Assembly: the morrow of St. Mathias [*25 Feb. 1415*].

Present: the mayor, William Waryn, William Walter, William Busshup, Walter Nandre, William Doudyng, John Beckot, and others named in the list.

Discussed: the arrival of the duke of York and the bishop of Winchester, Chancellor of England, for the money to be advanced to the king. Similarly, the effect of moving the outside (*extranei*) butchers from their places and having their stall by the ditch behind Butcher Row ('le Bochrewe')so that by them that road can better be finished and improved, but the materials were not yet (. . .).

146. Assembly: 2 March [*1415*].

Present: the mayor, Walter Shirle, William Waryn, William Walter, William Busshup, William Doudyng, Walter Nandre, John Beckot, and others named in the list.

Exhibited: the king's letter addressed to the mayor and fellow citizens, which was delivered to the mayor in the presence of his fellows by the said duke [of York] and chancellor, for an advance of money to the king. After discussion the mayor and his fellows agreed with the duke and the chancellor on a loan of £100 to be raised by the citizens and other competent inhabitants of the city, the sum assessed as follows:

[*in four columns*] John Moner £10, Walter Shirle £2, William Waryn £2, William Walter £2, William Busshup £2, William Doudyng £2, Walter Nandre £2, John Beckot [*blank*], Thomas Mason £2, Nicholas Hardyng £2, Nicholas Belle 2½ marks, John Swyft 2½ marks, William atte Lee 2½ marks, Richard Oword £1, Robert Warmwell 2½ marks, John Judde £2, [*col. 2*] William Fuystour 2½ marks, William Tuyl 2½ marks, Thomas Castelton £2, Thomas Bouer 2½ mark, Robert Deverell 13s. 4d., John Bottenham £2, John Wichford £2, Henry Man £1, John Clerk 'lympner' 13s. 4d., John Haster £1, John Spencer 1 mark, Thomas Stabbere 1 mark, John Heliere 'irmonger' £1, John Broun 'boucher' £1, Richard Boteller 1 mark, Thomas Randolf 1 mark, [*col. 3*] Gonora Bower 1 mark, Robert Gilbert £1, Richard Gage £1, John Dounton £1, Richard Coof £1, Edward Frith £1, Peter Dawe £1, John Parch £1, Gilbert Tannere £1, Edward Dubbere 1 mark, John Darcy 'webber' 1 mark, John Everhard 1 mark, John Lake £1, William Charlyng 1 mark, William Chepman 'touker' 1 mark, William Ponyten [*recte* Penyton] 1 mark, [*col. 4*] Richard Crischurche 1 mark, John Scoppe £1, John Hampton 'brewer' 1 mark, Robert Barbour 2½ marks, Richard Sherman £1, John Corscombe £1, Edith Spencer £5, Thomas Rede 1 mark, William Halstede 1 mark,

John Bremley £1, John Teffonte £1, John Griffith £1, William Slegge £1, Richard Herberd 1 mark, William Febis £1, John Ruddok 1 mark, [f. 54v.; *faded and stained*] [*in three columns*] John Hogeman 1 mark, Henry Southwyk 1 mark, Geoffrey Goldsmyth 1 mark, Thomas Danyel 1 mark, John Wellis senior 1 mark, John Cornyssh 1 mark, Richard Gates 1 mark, George Jocee 1 mark, [*col. 2*] William Shupton 'corvecor' [*i.e. corduuainer*] 1 mark, Robert Pottere 1 mark, Thomas Frogge £1, Stephen Mercer £1, John Sibely 1 mark, John Shad 1 mark, John Park 1 mark, John (Hayne?) £1, [*col. 3*] William Nedlere 1 mark, John Dale 1 mark, William Cokkes 1 mark, William West 1 mark, Thomas Nedlere 1 mark, Stephen Lythenard 1 mark. [*The sum is £102 13s. 4d.*]

147. Assembly: 11 April 3 Hen.V [*1415*].

Present: the mayor, John Moner, Walter Shirle, William Waryn, William Walter, William Busshup, William Doudyng, Walter Nandre, John Beckot and many others named in the list.

Walter Shirle was chosen to (. . .) to the king (. . .) of the loan made to him to have sufficient sureties for repayment.

148. Assembly: 27 May [*1415*].

Present: the mayor, John Moner, Walter Shirle, William Waryn, William Walters, William (Doudyng?), Thomas Mason, John Beckot, Walter Nandre, and others named in the list.

The mayor with Walter Shirle and W(. . .) Danyel went to William Cambrigge [*MS. Mainbrigge*] and his wife, being in Salisbury, showing them lists containing £19 13s. 4d. which (. . .[William of London]) in his lifetime owed to the community in various amounts. In the presence of the mayor and his fellow citizens, William Cambrig (. . .) in the presence of John Walpoll', John Brenchesle, William Vale, and others neighbours of William of London, declared and acknowledged that he [*sc.* William of London] would pay the said sum within a short time. The mayor with his fellow citizens referred [*or* returned (*retulit*)] the acknowledgement to the said neighbours. And with this he [*sc.* William Cambrigge] paid to Walter Shirle the £5 5s. for which the said Willliam Cambrig's wife was assessed to the said loan while she was unmarried [*sola*], in addition to the £100 paid earlier.

149. Assembly: 17 June [*1415*].

Present: the mayor, John Moner, Walter Shirle, William Waryn, William Busshup, Walter Nandre, William Walter, John Beckot and others named in the list.

Walter Shirle, coming from the king, reported to the mayor and his fellow citizens that he could not obtain a surety or pledge for the said loan until the king's arrival in these parts. So by agreement of the mayor and fellow citizens the money was entrusted to Walter until it should be known what was to be done with it.

150. Assembly: 3 July [*1415*]. [*The entry begins not in the usual way, but with* Et postea in alia convocacione.]

The said Walter [Shirle], coming from the king's council at Winchester, reported that if he had not there paid the said sum the community would have incurred the king and council's grave indignation. For the payment of the £100, the chancellor promised repayment by assigning the customs on wool at Southampton at a certain time.

151. Memorandum that on 4 Aug., the Sunday after St. Peter in Chains [*1415*], a crowd of the duke of Lancaster's men (as it was said), lodged at Fisherton by Salisbury, whose leader was James Haryndon, and engaged to set out with the king overseas, attacked many of the city's men on Fisherton bridge, driving them off with arrows and swords and killing four of them with arrows, viz. John Baker 'laborer', William Hore 'touker', Henry his servant, [and John Tannere, *cf. no.* **153**]. To consider: what to do about the deaths and the terrible affray, with bells rung all around (*campanis undique pulsatis*).

152. Assembly: 9 Oct. [*1415*].

Present: the mayor and many fellow citizens named in the list of the assembly.

Exhibited: the king's writ addressed to the mayor and bailiffs for a parliament to be held at Westminster on Monday after St. Luke the Evangelist [*21 Oct.*]. Elected: Walter Shirle, Henry Man.

Elected anew as city chamberlains to levy the rents belonging to the community, to receive the income, and to do other things belonging to their office; John Swyft, John Parch. Elected to keep one key of the common chest: Richard Coof.

John Levesham mayor accounted for his payments during his mayoralty, amounting to £1 8s. 5d., which was paid to him by William Walter and Robert Warmwell, chamberlains for the preceding year, the particulars as follows.

[f. 55; *faded, torn, and holed*]

153. Account of John Levesham for his payment during his mayoralty:

To a king's messenger bringing a [letter] patent for a levy of two tenths, 1s.; to Nottingham herald, 3s. 4d; to a king's purveyor (*provisori*) for sparing the malt (*verbrasium*) in the city when providing oats for the king's journey, 6s. 8d.; in bread given to him and his clerk for taking measurements, 5s. 2d.; (…) given to the chancellor of England's official,

1s. 8d.; to an official at Winchester, 1s. 2d.; to an official from Wales for bread and oats when taking measurements (. . .) in the city's defence at the time of the attack at Fisherton bridge by the earl of Lancaster's men, 1s. 6d.; in drink given to another official (. . .), 8d.; for having a watch at St. Edmund's gate against hostile strangers at the time of the great watch, (1s. 1d?); for expenses in burying John Tannere, killed by those attacking the city at Fisherton bridge, 11d.; for bread sent by the city chamberlains to Walter Hungerford, knight, and for two crossbowmen sent to him [2s. 8d. *crossed out*]; to the diggers of earth to form the barrier at Wyneman Street, [*blank*]. Sum £1 3s. 9d.

154. Read: a letter patent under the great seal, to John Levesham mayor, Walter Shirle, William Charlyng, and (. . .) for the arraying of light horsemen, bowmen, and other fencibles within the city. (. . .) the chancellor of England by way of advice to the mayor and fellow citizens for fortifying the city and for keeping the peace. In accordance with the patent a muster was held in the city.

[*There follows an account of the king's expedition to Harfleur, of his victory at Agincourt, and of his return to Westminster. It is printed in translation in* H.M.C. Var. Coll. IV, *pp. 195–7*.] Be it known that our lord the king of England, Henry V, passed with his great army overseas towards Harfleur (*Harfler*), and made the said port on the vigil of the Assumption of the blessed Mary [*8 May*] in the third year of his reign [*1415*], where he laid seige to the town with the dukes of York, Clarence and Gloucester, and various others, earls, barons and lords. Afterwards, on Sunday 22 Sept., the town surrendered and so the king valiantly took it. The town thus taken, he made arrangements for its safe keeping, appointing the earl of Dorset captain thereof. This done, the king himself with his army withdrew towards Calais (*Calesia*) by reason of the grievous pestilence that was prevalent at Harfleur. And while he was thus on the march a great French army, some 100,000 strong, offered him battle, he having with him no more than 10,000. Which said two armies valiantly joined battle, and therein were slain of the French on the field of Agincourt (*Argencort*) on Friday, the feasts of SS. Crispin and Crispinian, 25 Oct., in the year of our Lord 1415 and the third year of the said King Henry V, to wit [*there follows a list of 91 names, in which the document lapses into French*] and 4,000 valiant knights and squires without counting the rest. [*The language reverts to Latin*.] And in like manner were taken prisoners of our lord the king [*7 names*] and other gentlemen. And on the side of our lord the king were slain the duke of York, the young earl of Suffolk ('Southfolk') and of lords no more, but of their varlets about fifteen. Thus on that day did our lord the king overcome all his enemies, giving thanks to the most high God, and His mother the Virgin Mary, and St. George and all the saints of God. And being come with his army to Calais, he there rested and refreshed himself, and sent whom he would of his said army to England there to refresh themselves. After which rest our said lord the king, being cumbered with various affairs of his realm, returned to England, making Dover (*Dovoria*) on Saturday 23 Nov. in the third year of his reign [*1415*], bringing with him the said French lords his prisoners and captives. And as he approached London he was met by an immense multitude of folk of that city wearing red garments with white capuches, who attended him on either hand into the city on the following Saturday, to wit, the last day of the said month, being the feast of St. Andrew. And so great was the multitude of both men and women who stood in the streets from the corner by St. George's church in Southwark (*Suthray*) as far as Westminster, that starting at ten o'clock the king with the said lords his captives was scarce able to reach Westminster by three in the afternoon, which delay was also in part occasioned by the presentation to him of various ordinances and gifts by the said city upon his arrival. A great victory: glory to God in the highest.

[f. 55v. *blank*]

[f. 56; *faded, stained, and holed*]]

155. City officials elected on All Souls day 3 Hen.V [*2 Nov. 1415*]

Mayor: William Waryn. Reeves: Edward Frith, Henry Man. Aldermen: New Street ward, John Wichford; Market, Robert Gilberd; St. Martin's, William Cok; Meadow, John Shad. Serjeants: Walter Short, Roger (Qutkin ?).

Among various persons for their benefits, Edward Frith by unanimous assent was dispensed from election to the office of alderman, and for this dispensation he gave £4, but he was elected to the office of reeve, as appears above, in place of Nicholas Melbury. Henry Man was likewise dispensed by the mediation of various of the good men of the city from election to the office of alderman, and for this dispensation he promised (. . .) elected to the office of reeve, as appears above, and was bound by the said promise. (. . .) Thomas Cardmaker of Warminster an outsider (*forincecus*) citizen of Salisbury (. . .) by his friends the good men of the city was dispensed from all office of alderman (. . .) and for this dispensation he promised £3, for which William Doudyng was his surety (. . .).

(. . .) charter of William Asshlegh, chaplain, to Nicholas Hardyng, Walter Shirle, and Stephen Edyngdon, citizens, and their heirs and assigns in perpetuity of tenements, shops, and a cottage in Salisbury in St. Martin's Street, Brown Street, and Castle Street as appears in the enrolment of the same in the book called Domesday, the charter being in Nicholas Hardyng's keeping by the donor's wish and assignment, with attached to it a schedule of the donor's intention declared publicly before the mayor and feoffees, namely that he should have all the things contained in the charter freely and quit during his life and that after his death the said feoffees should make the tenement named in the charter in which Thomas Messagier dwells in St. Martin's Street and all the shops and the cottage to be appropriated to the mayor and community of Salisbury and their successors in perpetuity so that they be put to no other use but only in aid of their charges and in mitigation of the tallage and to the honour of God and the support of the chapel of the fraternity of St. George, for the prayers and other dispensations of the poor in the city's almshouse, and for other prayers of the community for benefaction made and to be made, and for the souls of the donor, of (William?) Asshlegh his father, of Joan his mother, and of all the faithful departed for ever.

After the donor's death the feoffees gave to his cousin Edith, daughter of the late Robert Blake, an estate for term of her life in the tenement named in the charter, which was formerly John Gatecombe's, after Edith should be married to some honest man. After her death the tenement was to be sold by the feoffeees and the money forthcoming to be paid to the donor's executors to be disposed of for his soul.

Also after his death the feoffees gave to John Heliere and Margaret his wife and to the longer living of either of them an estate for term of life in the part which was late their mother's of the tenement in Castle Street, after their deaths that part of the tenement to remain to the feoffees for appropriation in perpetuity to the mayor and community for prayers for the souls as above.

Because William the donor died within a month of making the charter and after making the feoffment, the tenements and cottage with their annual rent were viewed by the feoffees, having been conferred and after it had been enfeoffed. The rents as to the tenement in St. Martin's Street and the cottage in Brown Street were granted to the donor's executors, to pay his debts and carry out his legacies, for the Easter payment following the date of the charter, as follows:

Thomas Messager pays yearly for the tenement which he holds by indenture 4 marks for all services, so for the term 13s. 4d.; Walter Haudlo pays for a corner shop which he holds there yearly 12s. for all services, so for the term 3s.; Edith Westmor for a small shop there pays yearly 4s. 6d., so for the term 1s. 1½d.; Edith Brian for another shop there yearly 4s. 6d., so for the term 1s. 1½d.; Ysaac Howtoon for another shop there yearly 4s. 6d., so for the term 1s. 1½d.;. William Byde for a cottage there pays yearly 7s., so for the term 1s. 9d.; John Sende for another cottage there pays yearly 7s. 4d., so for the term 1s. 10d.; John Pariclet for another cottage there yearly 6s. 8d., so for the term 1s. 8d.

[f. 56v.; *faded, stained, and holed*]

156. First assembly in the mayoralty of William Waryn: 15 Nov. 3 Hen.V [*1415*].

Present: the mayor, John Moner, John Levesham, William Busshup, Walter Nandre, William Doudyng, John Beckot, William Tuyl, Edward Frith, Robert Warmwell, Walter Fuystour, Richard Oword, John Swyft, William Walter, Nicholas Belle, Thomas Bouer, William atte Lee, John Bottenham, Thomas Reede, John Sampson, Edward Gilbert, John Parch, John Hogeman, Richard Coof, Robert Gilbert, William Cok, John Shad, John Shute, Richad atte Mulle, William Febis, John Ruddok, William Purchase, Thomas Messager, and others.

[*An entry largely illegible, including*] Stephen Edyngdon as [city] clerk to have his livery at the community's expense. (. . . the Twenty-Four to have robes?) at Christmas (. . .) in default 6d.

(Elected as auditors?): Walter (Shirle?), William Walter, Walter Busshup, William Doudyng, Thomas Mason, Walter Nandre, William [Tu]yll, Thomas (. . .) [*and another illegible name*].

157. Assembly: 16 Nov. [*1415*].

Present: the mayor, Walter Shirle, William Walter, (. . .), William Doudyng, William Busshup, John Beckot, Walter Nandre, and many other neighbours greater and lesser.

Exhibited and read: the king's writ for a whole tenth payable to the king (half at the Purification next [*2 Feb. 1416*] and half) at the Purification following, as granted at the parliament at Westminster in the mayoralty of Thomas Mason. Elected as assessors: John Swyft, Robert Warmwell, (Richard?) Gage, Edward Dubbere; as collectors: John Ruddok, John Heliere 'irmongere', John Cornyssh, and William (. . .); assigned [to help them?]: John Spencer, John Everhard, William Besket, and John Sydenham.

158. Assembly: 22 Jan. [*1416*].

Present: the mayor, Walter Shirle, William Doudyng, William Busshup, Thomas (Mason?), Thomas Bouer, Thomas Rede, William Walter, John Swyft, John Parch, Robert Warmwell, Walter Sergeant, Stephen (Edyngdon?).

Robert Warmwell and William Walter [past chamberlains] offered £43 10s. in gold (*de auro*) remaining in their keeping from the time of their predecessors as city chamberlains, and the money was placed in the common chest in St. Thomas's church until etc.

William Doudyng paid to John Swyft and John Parch, city chamberlains elect, £3 for Thomas Cardmaker's fine for being excused the office of alderman, as appears above [*no. 155*].

159. Assembly: 20 Feb. [*1416*].

Present: the mayor and many others his fellow citizens named in the list of the assembly.

Read: the king's writ addressed to the mayor and bailiffs for a parliament to be held at Westminster on 16 March. Elected: Walter Shirle and Henry Man.

160. Council [*sic*] of neighbours held at the 'Counseilhous' 9 March [*1416*].

Present: the mayor, Walter Shirle, William Walter, William Busshup, William Doudyng, John Beckot, John Swyft, Henry Man, Thomas Bouer, Robert Warmwell, William atte Lee, Thomas Rede, John Shute, and others.

Read: an indenture made by the mayor and warden of the hospital (*domus pauperum*) of Holy Trinity that Robert Chirche, rector of the church of Minterne, Dorset, should have the nomination during his life of seven of the poor in the said hospital, and after his death the nomination of the same number of poor should belong to the abbot of Cerne and his successors in perpetuity, the rector procuring for the grant both the mayor's and the warden's seal. Because John Chaundeler, dean of Salisbury, advised that the grant be made the citizens agreed unanimously. On this Walter Seriant having discourse with the rector received from him 100 marks and left the indenture with him. The money was afterwards put in the common chest of the hospital for its support.

Walter Shirle was paid the full sum of £1 16s. for his wages at the parliament summoned for the morrow of All Souls [*3 Nov.*] last past. Henry Man his fellow citizen was paid £1 10s.; 6s. remained payable to him [*added later*, and was afterwards paid to him].

161. Thursday the morrow of the Annunciation [*26 March 1416*].

In the presence of the mayor, Walter Shirle, William Walter, and many other fellow citizens, William Reynald was arraigned for his wicked words and the scandal uttered against John Moner, for which he did penance, promising that he would not further offend against him.

[f. 57; *faded and stained*]

162. Assembly: 3 June [*1416*].

Present: the mayor, William Walter, William Busshup, William Doudyng, and many other citizens both greater and lesser.

John Goudman 'webbere' appeared saying that one John Harry 'webbere' said in the presence of various men of the city that the mayor was a traitor to the king in that he was not seen nor present with the city's men at Southampton. He denied the words. John Goudman confirmed the accusation, which was to be verified. John Harries was committed, and afterwards bailed.

163. Assembly: 4 June [*1416*].

Present: the mayor and many other fellow citizens named in the list of the assembly.

John Bottenham and William Tuyl, elected as constables, were excused the office. Appointed in their place to keep the watch: Richard Oword and William Fuystour.

164. Assembly: 8 June 1416

Present: the mayor and many fellow citizens and others named elsewhere.

(. . .) Exhibited: the king's commission for the levy of a tenth, payable at the feast of St. Martin [*11 Nov.*]. Elected as assessors: William Walter, William Doudyng, John (. . .), and Walter Nandre; to assist them: John Everhard, Richard Coof, John Parch, and John

Noble: as collectors: Thomas Felde, John Boteller, Henry Blakemore, and Thomas
Durneford. The amount with (the usual?) expenses, £80.

165. Assembly: (seventh day?) of Whitsun [*14 June?, 1416*].

Present: the mayor, Walter Shirle, William Walter, and many other fellow citizens.

John Wichford was arraigned for saying that William Doudyng and all his fellows were
falsely and manifestly perjured in that they had assessed him in the tallage at £1. He
denied the words, and the matter was to be considered.

166. [Assembly]: 26 Aug. [*1416*].

Present: the mayor and many others of his fellow citizens.

William Fuystour was arraigned before the community for uttering scandalous words
about the mayor in saying to Robert Tannere, alderman of Market ward, that he did not
care for him or for the mayor and that he would not give them a halfpenny even
though the alderman constrained him to observe the mayor's precepts. William denied
the words, but so that the mayor should not be troubled on his account he asked the
mayor's pardon (*ponit se in gracia eiusdem*) which was respited.

167. Assembly: 2 Oct. [*1416*].

Present: the mayor, Walter Shirle, William Walter, William Busshup, William Doudyng,
John Levesham, Walter Nandre, Thomas Mason, John Judde, Thomas Bouer, Richard
Oword, Edward Frith, John Swyft, Thomas Rede, John Noble, John Griffith, John
Bremle, Richard Sherman, Thomas Messager, William Penyton, John Cornyssh, John
Sampson, John Parch, William Stoute, Edward Dubbere, Robert Tannere, William Cok,
John Shad, Richard Gage, Richard Coof, William Febis, John Shute, William Warwyk,
Richard Crischurche, Thomas Slegge, John Dounton, Stephen Lythenard, William
Dounyng, John Clyve, Robert Stonard, William Brante, John Durneford, William Slegge,
Edward Purdy, William Fuystour, and others.

Exhibited and read: the king's writ for a parliament at Westminster on 19 Oct. Elected
for the city: Walter Shirle and Thomas Mason 'draper'.

Account of William Waryn, mayor, for his expenses and payments:

A pipe of wine given to Thomas Calston sheriff of Wiltshire with the assent of his
fellow citizens, £3; for the liveries of three city officials, £1 5s.; given to a herald and to
other officials of various lords and for wine sent to Sir Walter Hungerford and to other
at various times, £1 6s. 4d. Sum total £5 11s. 4d. Agreed: that he be paid by the
chamberlains should pay him.

Agreed by all present that because the mayor had performed the office well and with honour he should have in remuneration £10, besides his said payments, considering that he had performed the office well and honestly twice. It was further ordained that any future mayor who held the office twice, governing well and honestly for a second year, should have as large a sum besides his reasonable payments as accounted.

[f. 57v.; *faded and stained; the lower half blank*]

Likewise they agreed in that assembly that the ordinances drawn up by the mayor be henceforth observed, namely:

that victuallers bringing food to the city for sale do not sell in secret or before full daylight, but only in the places prescribed for them;

that horses coming to the city with victuals, after unloading are not to be allowed to stand in the market or in the streets because of the hindrance to passers-by and the damage to the city's (. . .);

that victuallers with cheese, milk, grapes, plums, apples, pears and other fruit should keep to the place assigned to them in the market opposite Richard Oword's tenement;

that outsider (*extranei*) butchers (. . .) in the place prescribed opposite the market in 'Whelerardrowe';

that the common ditches running through the middle of the city are to be kept clean and without obstruction under pain of (. . .);

that secret tenures (*possessiones*) and feoffments are henceforth invalid and void.

In the same assembly it was announced that Nicholas Hardyng had given to the mayor and community £2 in aid of the city (. . .) John Swyft and John (Ruddok?) by (the chamberlains?) (. . .).

[f. 58; *a modern leaf containing only a fragment of an earlier folio*]

There was a very great crowd [*or* disturbance] (*Maxima turba fuit*). William Boucher. [*The significance is not clear; the hand appears to be seventeenth-century.*]

[f. 58v., *blank*]

[f. 59 and v. *blank*]

[f. 59a; *a small inserted piece of parchment, the verso blank; illegible except for*] Robert Poynant and John Forest, chamberlains, and William Parch and (. . .) collectors.

[f. 59c; *an inserted strip of parchment, in two pieces sewn together, indented on the left and bound in at its head; partly illegible through heating (?) and creasing*]

168. Inventory of all utensils, goods and other things which were Thomas Play's, made 23 March in the said year 21 [Ric. II ?, *1398; cf. above* **16**].

In the hall: a dosser ('dorser') 6d.; two benches ('bankres') 8d.; twelve cushions ('quyssons') (. . .)d.; a table (*tabila*) 6d.; three 'trestells' (. . .)4d.; four 'pelues' [pillows?] with wool (. . .)1s.; an ewer [?] (*lavat' de pl. . . .)*6d. An iron 'hebbroud' [?] (. . .). Sum £1 (17s. 4d. ?)

In the chamber: six covers with (. . .); five blankets (*lodicos*) (. . .); twenty pairs of (L. . .); three 'quiltes' (. . .); eight chests (. . .); a [?] habergeon (*hob'ion*) 1s.; a silver belt [?] (*sona arg'*) (. . .); a [?] dagger (*baselard*) (. . .); a sword (. . .). Sum £10 17s. 11d.

In the pantry: four table cloths (*mapp' mensal'*) (. . .); four towels (. . .); four 'savernapes' (. . .)8d.; five latten candelabras 1s. 8d.; two pewter salts 4d.; sixteen silver spoons £1 6s. 8d.; five bowls bound with silver £1; three pieces of silver with covers £10; a flat piece of silver 6s. 8d.; a bread box 8d.; four pewter 'pottes' 2s.; four vessels for ale 2s.; three empty pipes 1s. 6d. Sum £14 8s. 11d.

In the kitchen: six brass pots £2; five maslin pans 18s.; a dozen and a half of pewter vessels £1; four iron vessels 1s. 4d.; a pair of andirons 1s.; an iron rack ('rekke') 1s.; two iron pans 10d.; a knife 2d.; two mortars 8d.; two tripods 6d. Sum £4 3s. 6d.

In the alehouse: two ovens £5; six vats ('fates') 13s. 4d.; twenty 'trendels' [little wheels or disks] 16s.; three tubs (*couvell'*) 1s.; four pails 8d.; a 'boket' 1s.; an oven (*focal'*) £1 6s. 8d.; four horses £2; a cart with apparatus £1; two bins for grain (*siste pro molend'*) 2s.; ten sacks 6s. 8d.; six score and fifteen sheep £8; a sack of wool 6 marks; a 'mill' and the house [called] 'le Stuyh' £5; twelve quarters of malt £3. Sum £31 7s. 4d.

Sum total £62 5s. from which is due to the said Thomas Play's boys for their share in common £20 15s.

[f. 60; *faded, stained, and holed*]

169. [*Heading*:] Walter Shirle.

Election of the mayor and other city officials on All Souls' day 4 Hen.V [*2 Nov. 1416*].

[*An entry, largely illegible, of two lines apparently relating to a payment for being excused the office of alderman.*] Robert Fuystor (. . .) alderman (. . .) £4.

Walter Shirle, mayor, Thomas Yevele, William Pakyn, John Pope, Thomas Brighampton [*aldermen*], Walter Shere', Roger Burdbusshe, serjeants, Robert Pyndone, Walter (. . .), reeves.

[*An entry, only partly legible, relating to a loan to the king, to an earlier loan made in the mayoralty of John Levesham (above, no. 146), and to their repayment.*] (. . .) loan to the king in the mayoralty of Walter Shirle in 4 [Hen.V, *1416–17*] (. . .) at the instance and request of the bishop [of Winchester, the lord chancellor] (. . .) addressed to the earl of Salisbury and Walter Hungerford knight. The bishop, then chancellor of England, promised in good faith that (. . .) repayment would be made both of that sum and of the other £100 advanced to the king in the mayoralty of John Levesham, and granted on sufficient security. Recorded that the loan was repaid in January 5 [Hen.V, 1418], as appears below:

[In the list which follows, in three columns on the recto and verso, each name is preceded by quit, *the forename has been crossed through, and the amount after the name is followed by* repaid *(resol'), the exceptions being that the names John Moner, William Walter, John Clerk 'lympner', and John Spencer do not have* quit *or the forename crossed through, and the amounts after the names John Moner, John Bottenham, John Clerk 'lympner', and John Spencer are not followed by* repaid. *The entry for Walter Shirle stands on a line by itself.]*

Walter Shirle, mayor £1; [*column one:*] John Moner £2; William Waryn £1; William Walter £1; William Busshup £1; William Doudyng £1; Thomas Mason £1; John Levesham £1; Walter Nandre £1; Nicholas Hardyng 1 mark; Nicholas Belle £1; William atte Lee £1; John Swyft £1; John Judde £1; Henry Man £1; William Tuyl £1; Edward Frith £1; William Fuystour £1; Thomas Castelton £1; Thomas Bouer £1; Robert Pynant £1; John Bottenham £1; Robert Warmwell £1; Richard Oword ½ mark; John Clerk 'lympner' ½ mark; John Barbour ½ mark; John Bower 'curreour' ½ mark; [*column two*] William Depedene ½ mark; John Warham clerk ½ mark; Agnes Eceshale ½ mark; John Furbour 'armerer', 10s.; Richard Harlewyn, 10s.; John Spencer ½ mark; Geoffrey Goldsmyth, 10s.; John Wynchestre 'barbour', 10s.; Thomas Randolf 1 mark; Robert Pynnere ½ mark; John Smyth 'chandler', 10s.; John Heliere 'irmongere' 1 mark; John Huchon 'bocher' ½ mark; Henry Trowne 'baker' ½ mark; Richard Milis 'baker' ½ mark; Richard Boteller, 10s.; John Stok 'sadler' ½ mark; John Broun 'bocher', 10s.; William Chaundeller, 10s.; Thomas Danyel 'taillour', 10s.; Alice Becket ½ mark; John Thornton 'spicer' ½ mark; William Avene 'skynnere' ½ mark; John Swyft 'digher' ½ mark; Thomas Artour 'skynnere' ½ mark; [*column three*] John More 'baker' 1 mark; Gonora Bowier, 10s.; John Weller senior ½ mark; John Wychewode 'touker' ½ mark; Richard Gater 'fuller', 10s.; William Chepman 'fuller' ½ mark; John Cornyssh 'fuller' 10s.; Henry Hame ½ mark; Robert Gilbert 'tanner' 10s.; Richard Gage 1 mark; Edward Gilbert 'dubbere' 10s.; John Chippenham ½ mark; Robert Stonard ½ mark; George Jocee 10s.; William Gloucestre ½ mark; William Shupton 'corvicor' 10s.; Robert Pottere ½ mark; Richard Chesham ½ mark; Thomas Frogge ½ mark; John Dounton 'draper' 1 mark; Stephen Mercer 1 mark; John Sybely 'taillour' ½ mark; John Shad 'draper' ½ mark; Richard Coof 'draper' 1 mark; Richard Coupere ½ mark; John de Park 'helier' ½ mark; [f. 60v.; *badly faded, stained, and holed*] [*column one*] John Everhard clerk ½ mark; William Charlyng (½ mark?); Thomas (. . .); John (. . .); (. . . [*three names illegible*]); John (. . .); (. . .); (. . .) 1 mark; (. . .) 1 mark; (Thom)as (Cobbe?) 1 mark; (. . .)tinley 'draper' ½ mark; Nicholas Pyle 'webbe' 10s.; John Scoppe 'chepman' 1 mark; John Hayne 'loder' 10s.; William Stoute 'webbe' ½ mark; John Hampton 'brewer' 10s.; [*column two*] William Warmwell 'mercer' 1 mark; John Dale 'draper' ½ mark; Nicholas Charlyng ('draper'?) ½ mark; (. . .) ½ mark; (. . .) 1 mark; (. . .) ½ mark; [*c. eleven entries illegible*]; (Margaret?) Black (. . .); Thomas Rede (. . .); John Pope (. . .); William

Halstede 'helier' (. . .); William Reynald 'webbe' 10s.; John Pope junior ½ mark; William Basket 'webbe' 1 mark; [*column three*] Walter Cok 'mercer' ½ mark; John Bremle 1 mark; John Teffonte 10s.; John Griffith 1 mark; (. . .) 10s.; (. . . H)ogeman 'webbe' (. . .); [*c. twelve lines illegible*].

170. First assembly in the mayoralty of Walter Shirle, from the feast of All Souls 4 Hen. V [*2 Nov. 1416*] to the same feast next following. 22 Nov. 4 Hen. V [*1416*].

Present: the mayor, William Waryn, William Busshup, William Walter, William Dowdyng, Thomas Mason, John Levesham, Walter Nandre, John Swyft, Richard Oword, Robert Poynant, Henry Man, William Fuystour, Robert Warmwell, John Bottenham, Thomas Rede, John Bremle, William Cok, George Jocee, William Barbour, John Shad, John Nouble, Thomas Yevele, Robert Gilbert, John Wichford, Richard Gage, Edward Dubbere, Richard atte Mulle, Thomas Felde, Richard Coof, John Botiller, William Nedler, William Febis, John Ruddok, Henry Southwyk, Thomas Randolf.

Agreed by all: the sheriff of the county in future to have a pipe of wine for his friendship and favour to the city; all those who have been retained with the city counsel henceforth to be retained for their present wages and liveries; the common livery of the Twenty-Four of silk to be worn at Christmas; and the mayor this present year to have John Boteller as a third city serjeant because of the visit to the city of the king and other lords at the mayor's expense.

171. [Note]: on 4 Dec. [*1416*] in the presence of W[illiam] Waryn [deputy] mayor [*cf. no. 172*], John Swyft chamberlain and the others, Walter Shirle, elected and being at the parliament held at Westminster which was continued from 16 March 3 Hen. V [*1416*] until the Whitsun following [*7 June*] was paid £6 6s. for his wages there. Likewise Henry Man, his fellow, was paid the same sum. After which the mayor paid to John Swyft, one of the chamberlains, the money remaining £4 15s. 8d.

172. Assembly: 18 Dec. [*1416*].

Present: William Waryn the mayor's deputy [*locum ten'*], William Walter, William Busshup, William Doudyng, Henry Man, W[illiam] Tuyl, Robert Poynant, R[obert] Warmwell, J[ohn] Judde, John Swyft, R[ichard] Coof, R[ichard] Gage, William Fuystour, Thomas Bouer, W[alter] Nandre, Edward Dubbere, J[ohn] Shad, R[obert] Tannere, Thomas Rede, John Bremle, and others.

William Waryn, William Walter, W[illiam] Doudyng, W[illiam] Busshup and W[illiam] Tuyl were appointed to negotiate with the chancellor and others being sureties if a loan is requested for the king or for anyone else.

173. Assembly: 31 Dec. [*1416*].

Present: the mayor, William Waryn, William Doudyng, Thomas Mason, William Busshup, Walter Nandre, John Swyft, and many others, both citizens and other neighbours.

A warning from Walter Shirle and Thomas Mason, citizens at the parliament, of the tenth and half a tenth [granted] by the parliament held at Westminster from 19 Oct. to a week [*19 Nov.*] from St. Martin, payable at the Purification next [*2 Feb. 1417*]. Named as commissioners: John Clerk 'lympner', John Spencer, Thomas Frogge, and William Halstede; as their fellows: John Teffonte, Thomas Slegg, Robert Pynnere, and John Wynchestr' 'irmongere'; as assessors: John Judde, Robert Warmwell, Thomas Bouer, Robert Tannere, William Febes, and John Shad.

[f. 61; *faded and stained*]

174. [*Heading:*] W[alter] Shirle.

Assembly: eve of the Purification [*1 Feb. 1417*].

Present: the mayor, William Waryn, William Busshup, William Doudyng, William Walter, Walter Nandre, Thomas Mason and many others named in the list of the assembly.

Discussed: the king's letter about the sureties both for the 100 marks to be advanced to the king and loan of £100 in the mayoralty of John Levesham. All wished that the half of a tenth payable at the feast of St. Martin [*11 Nov.*] (. . .) and the rest to be had from the king's customs at Easter if possible (. . .).

175. Assembly: 1 April 5 [Hen. V, *1417*].

Present: Walter Shirle mayor, William Warmwell, William Doudyng, William Busshup, (Walter) Nandre, Thomas Mason, and many others.

Agreed that the seal of the aulnager's deputy for the city and the county of Wiltshire be held by the mayor and community by the grant and wish of John Harlestone, farmer. John Noble, (. . .) was chosen to hold the office.

Agreed that Thomas Messagier should hold the corner shop with annexe late of Sir William Asshele, previously held by Robert Hyndon, for fifty years, rent £3 13s. 4d.

176. Assembly: 19 (April?) [*1417*].

(Present: . . .), William Buss(hup), John (Levesham?), Thomas Mason, Walter Nandre (. . ., and others) named in the list.

[*The remaining line and a half illegible except* sexta ordo (restitutione?).]

177. Assembly: 4 May [*1417*].

Present: the mayor, William Waryn, William Busshup, William Doudyng, and many (others and the city) officials in the guildhall, before whom appeared John Barham of Nether Wallop (to answer a charge that ?) on 1 May he bought in the market malt that had been regrated for resale (. . .) to the earl of Warwick's use. Afterwards he admitted that he had sold it to one John Hele of Wallop and he was committed to prison until etc. And afterwards he was delivered by the court.

178. [Assembly]: 17 May [*1417*].

Present: the mayor, William Waryn, William Busshup, William (Edyngdon?) clerk, Thomas Mason, John Judde, William Bowier and many others.

On an accusation of treason, Richard Shapewyk 'webbe' [and] William Biston clerk of St. Martin's church appeared and were sworn on the book to tell the truth. William Biston said that he heard on the preceding day William Reynald 'webbe' saying openly and *viva voce* in his own home that there were fifteen false traitors to the king in this city, of whom the first was William Febis, who knew all the others. On the order of the mayor and other neighbours present William Reynald was [brought] by Walter Serjant, the city serjant, and was interrogated and called to account for those words. He did not deny saying certain words, but said that he was ready to say before the king the words which he had spoken. Then John Judde the king's coroner came and asked if he would say anything to him as counsel for the king, and William was silent, saying as before that what he had said he would say before the king. On this he was placed in custody. The mayor and some of his fellow citizens discussed with some of the king's council what should be done, and on their advice William Reynald was asked about the said words, whether he would avow them, and he then said that he would not. Then by favour he was pledged by John Bremle and Richard Gage to good behaviour and peace to the king and the people and all inhabitants of the city.

179. Assembly: 6 June [*1417*].

Present: the mayor, William Busshup, William Doudyng, Walter Nandre, John Swyft, John Judde, William Tuyl and many others whose names appear in the list.

Agreed by all: the seizure of the goods and chattels for arrears of £18 rent which Thomas Russel esquire owed for his tenement in the city of Salisbury, as appears in an assembly in the mayoralty of John Becket, to be taken to the 'Counseilhous' and there be appraised and sold, after which if they do not reach the said value John Becket, John Judde, and Thomas Rede are to answer now for then to the chamberlains and the comptroller.

Also, if anyone receives wages from the city and is counsel for another impleading someone from the city about free tenements, he is to lose his wages unless he has a reasonable excuse.

Also, that the mayor, William Doudyng, Robert Warmwell, and Richard Gage, previously elected, should strive to levy and collect money from those who pledged various sums for the city's use and for George's inn.

180. Assembly: 12 July [*1417*].

Present: the mayor, William Waryn, William Busshup, William Doudyng, Thomas Mason, Walter Nandre, John Swyft, John Judde, and many others.

Exhibited: a dozen [cloths] of white motley ('motle'), and there in the presence of Walter Mede, John Machyn, and John Pridy, stewards of the weavers' guild, and for their lesser width they were adjudged to be forfeit; to remain at the 'Counseilhous' until [*unfinished*].

181. Assembly: Monday the morrow of the Assumption [*16 Aug. 1417*].

Present: the mayor, William Waryn, William Busshup, William Doudyng, John Swyft, William Tuyl, and many others at the 'Gildhall'.

Before the mayor and bailiffs and other officials there was surrendered, produced, and exhibited a cloth part woven but for most part not woven, found in the keeping of John Lauerence 'webbe'. And because the thread of the warp ('werp') was black mixed with thread of a green colour in deception and against the city's ordinance, it will be considered what is to be done, whether it should be burnt or otherwise.

(Continued overleaf).

[f. 61v.; *badly faded, stained, and holed, the lower half wholly illegible or blank*]

182. Memorandum that on 6 Oct. 5 Hen.V [*1417*] Mr. Henry Harburgh, precentor of the cathedral church of Salisbury, Mr. Simon Sydenham, archdeacon, and John Frank, canon of the same church, came to the 'Gildhall' and in the presence of Walter Shirle mayor, William Waryn, William Doudyng, John Swyft, John Judde and other fellow citizens on behalf of the dean and chapter announced the death of the bishop, Robert Hallum, on 4 Sep [*1417*]. [*The rest of the entry is largely illegible but relates to chaplains holding tenements in the city.*]

183. Assembly: 10 Oct [*1417*].

Walter Shirle, William Waryn, William Doudyng, John Levesham, John Judde, John Swyft. [*The rest of the entry is largely illegible; it relates to the payment of a tenth on 19 (Oct.?) and mentions the chamberlains.*]

184. Assembly: 1 [?] Nov [*1417*].

John Judde, mayor elect, William Waryn, Walter Busshup, William Doudyng, Walter Nandre, John Swyft, Robert Poynant (. . .) [*The rest of the entry is largely illegible; it appears to include an election to the parliament to be held at Westminster on 16 Nov. 1417, which Walter Shirle and William Waryn attended.*]

[f. 62; *badly faded and stained*]

185. [*Heading:*] John Judde

Election of the mayor and other city officials: All Souls' day 5 Hen. V [*2 Nov. 1417*].

Elected to the Twenty-Four: Richard Coof and William Nedlere, in place of Nicholas Bell and William Walter, deceased; sworn; as mayor: John Judde; as bailiffs: John Bromle and William Febis; as alderman of New Street ward: Robert Asshlegh; of Market: John Cornyssh; of St. Martin: Thomas Randolf; of Meadow: John of Jivichirche; as serjeants: W. Short and R. Enterbussh.

[*Three lines illegible*].

(. . .) Retained by the council as attorney of the city: William Alisaundre, (for his wages and livery?) as in earlier years.

The pipe of wine for the sheriff respited. Likewise the common livery for the good men (. . .).

186. [Assembly]: morrow of St. Thomas the apostle [*22 Dec. 1417*].

Present: the mayor, Walter Shirle, William Doudyng, Thomas Mason, Henry (Man?), Thomas Bouer, Richard Gage, and many others.

Adjudged that a cloth of John Lauerenz 'webbe' in part woven with the wrong warp (*de Bosud'* [?] *Warp falsitate*) should be burnt publicly in the market place.

187. Assembly: on the feast of St. Silvester [*31 Dec. 1417*].

Present: the mayor, Walter Shirle, William Waryn, Walter Nandre, Thomas Mason, John Swyft, Henry Man, Robert Puynant, Edward Frith, Robert Warmwell, and many others named in the list.

Exhibited: the king's commission addressed to John Hampton, Gilbert Tannere, Robert Grene, and John Furbour for two whole tenths and granted in the parliament held 16 Nov. last, one to be paid at the Purification next [*2 Feb. 1418*], the other at the Purification following, which parliament was held at Westminster before the duke of Bedford in place of the king who was in Normandy. Elected assessors: William Nedler, Henry Man, John Bromle, and Edward Dubbere; as collectors, together with the commissioners: for New Street aldermanry: John Wynchestr' 'barbour'; Henry Hamme for Market; Richard Nedlere for St. Martin; John Mulle for Meadow.

188. Assembly: 15 Jan. [*1418*].

Present: the mayor, Walter Shirle, William Waryn, Walter Nandre, William Doudyng, Thomas Mason, John Puynant, William Tuyl, Robert Warmwell, and many others named in the list of the assembly.

Ordered: the chamberlains, collectors of tallage, and all others owing money to the city to account without delay. Elected as auditors: the mayor for the time being and Walter Shirle, William Waryn, Richard Gage, and John Everard. Those auditors and all others in future to have a day every year on the feast of St. Luke [*18 Oct.*] for certifying to the mayor and community in an assembly held for the said auditors, and for receipts etc.

The coffer which was kept in the common chest was opened, and found in it was £43 6s. 8d. From this sum Walter Shirle was paid £12 for his expenses and payments during his mayoralty in the preceding year. At the same time the said Walter paid to the mayor £28 3s. 4d. which he received in London to satisfy those who advanced money for the next loan to the king, viz. 100 marks, whose names are listed in [the record of] Walter's mayoralty.

189. Assembly at the 'Counseilhous': 11 March [*1418*].

Present: the mayor, William Waryn, William Busshup, William Doudyng, Walter Nandr', John Swyft, Henry Man, and many others.

Exhibited: a letter addressed to the mayor and his fellow citizens from John [*Chandler*], bishop of Salisbury, giving notice of his installation three weeks after Easter [*17 April*], the service beginning with 'Jubilate', and asking them all to attend the service and a dinner (*prandio*).

190. In the next assembly [*no date given*] John Corscombe of New Salisbury was arraigned before the said John, mayor, and Walter Shirle, William Waryn, William Busshup, William Doudyng, Thomas Mason, Walter Nandre, John Puynant, and many others, and before John Harleston, the king's aulnager in Wiltshire and in the said city, for the fact that John Noble, the aulnager's deputy (*substitutus*) in the city, found in John Corscombe's possession in his house twenty-one rayed (*straguil'*) cloths sealed with a seal counterfeiting the king's seal and that ordained for the city. On which it was to be decided what should be done. Agreed by all: the deputy aulnager to visit all houses every Monday for sealing cloths.

Ordered by common consent: the bishop to have as the city's gift at his installation 40 marks. Elected to provide that sum: William Shirle, William Waryn, William Doudyng, Richard Gage, John Bremle, and William Warwyk, to assess it at their discretion and to be repaid next Whitsun [*15 May 1418*]. The names of those paying appear below [*no. 193*].

[f. 62v.; *faded and stained*]

191. [*Heading*: John Judde mayor].

Assembly: eve of Whitsun 6 Hen.V [*14 May 1418*].

Present: the mayor, William Waryn, William Doudyng, Thomas Mason, Robert Puynant, and many others.

Elected as city constables: Thomas Bouer and William [*surname omitted*], in place of William Fuystour and Richard [*surname omitted*] who were removed and excused from that office.

192. Assembly: 28 May [*1418*].

Present: (. . .) Walter Shirle deputy mayor (*locum tenente maioris*), William Waryn, William Doudyng, Walter Nandre, Robert Poynant, (William) Fuystour, (. . .), John Sydenham, Richard (Chesh)am, and many others from the city.

[*An entry largely illegible, apparently relating to the sale of cloth at fairs and to rayed (stragul') cloth.*]

193. Assembly: 7 Nov. [1418]

Present: the mayor, Walter Shirle, William Waryn, William Bishyp, William (. . .), Robert Poynant, Walter Nandre, John Swyft.

John Judde, mayor, accounted for his expenses and payments (. . .): (. . .) £40 (. . .) of the king and to the auditors, 10s.; for liveries for the city officials, 18s.; (. . .).

William Depeden appeared and paid 19s. (. . .) money paid to [*or* by] S. Edyngd'. Paid to [*or* by] Richard Gage (. . .), 10s.; (for the wages and expenses of?) Walter Shirle and William Waryn, citizens elected to the parliament, (. . .).

The names of those contributing sums to the 40 marks presented to John Chaundiler, bishop of Salisbury, at his installation: [*in column, with 'repaid' (*resol'*) to the left of each name*] John Judde mayor £1, Walter Shirle £1, William Waryn £2, William Busshup £2, William Doudyng £1, Thomas Mason £2, John Swyft £1, Thomas Bouer £2,

William Fuystour £1, Richard Coof £5, William atte Lee £2, Richard Gage £1, William Febis £1, John Bremley £1, Thomas Randolf £2, Robert Tannere £2, Stephen Mercer £1, William Warwyk £1.

[*To the right of the column*] They were all repaid their said sums before All Souls in the mayoralty of Robert Puynant 7 [Hen.V, *2 Nov. 1419*], from the money arising from the account of John Swyft and John Parch, city chamberlains, viz. 40 marks paid by them in part payment of their arrears. The residue of the money of the said advance remaining in the hands of John Judde, then mayor, was also repaid, and so [all is] equal. [*The sum of the contributions listed above is £29, or 43½ marks.*]

[f. 63; *stained and apparently blank*]

[f. 63v.; *faded and stained*]

194. [*Heading*:] Salesbury.

Assembly: 11 July 17 Ric. II [*1393*].

Present [*in column*]: John Salesbury, mayor, John Cammel, Thomas Boreford, John atte Hethe, John Moner, William Warmwell, John Buterleygh, Robert Play, John Nedlere, Thomas Bowyere, William Gys, William Ashton, John Niweman, John Nedlere junior, Robert Deverel, Richard Spencer, Robert Bowyere, Thomas Eyre, John Dunyton, Adam Teffonte, John Eceshale, William White, John Gillyngham, John Chaundeler senior, Robert Body, John Barbour 'brasiere', John Lytle, Reginald Drewery, John Sompnour, Thomas Teyntourer, John Cary, Adam Countewell, Thomas Ferant, John Swyft, John Wayte 'hosiere', Thomas Play, Philip Goldsmyth, Nicholas Hardyng, and others.

[*To the right of the column*:] Agreed by all: against the king's arrival the Sixty to be dressed in cloth of the same silk (*de una setta*) and three casks of wine (to be provided?), two for the king and one for (. . .) the royal (?) street Minster Street to be repaired and improved at the common expense, and all broken streets to be mended by view of twelve (. . .). Elected to the office of clerk and steward (. . .).

[f. 64; *faded and stained*]

11 July 17 Ric. II [*1393*]. [*The following notes of debts, the nature of which is obscure, are arranged in the MS. as each a separate paragraph widely spaced from the next.*] John atte Hethe and Thomas Castelton owe John Buterleygh, William Warmwell, and Robert Play £60, so that they are owed net £45 [*struck through and marked in the margin* quit]. John Nedelere owes the said John, William, and Robert Play £20, so that they are owed net £10, of which paid by Robert Play (. . .) [*struck through and marked in the margin* quit]. John Franklayn owes the said John, William, and Robert £3, so that they are owed net £2 5s. [*struck through and marked in the margin* quit]. John Thorbourne and John Drewery owe the said John, William, and Robert on a bond £40; they received 15s. as appears earlier in Richard Spencer's account [*struck through and marked in the*

margin quit]. Philip Goldsmyth owes the said John Wollop and Robert £3 [*marked in the margin* owed.] [f. 64v.; *faded and stained*] Robert Deverel and William Loord owe the said John, William, and Robert Play £60, so that they are owed net £45; quit £5. Thomas Chapelayn, John Chaundeler, and William Loord (owe) the said John, William, and Robert £60, so that they are owed net £45, of which the mayor received £10 from Robert Play [*marked in the margin* quit]. John atte Hethe owes the said John, William, and Robert £60, so that they are owed net £15. Those bonds were delivered to John Cammel, mayor, Friday the morrow of the Circumcision 17 Ric. II [3 Jan. 1394]. A gilt cup worth £3 11s. 8d., delivered to John Cammel, mayor, on Friday the morrow of the Circumcision the same year 17 [Ric. II; *unfinished?*].

[f. 65; *faded and stained*]

195. [*Heading:*] Salesbury.

Assembly: the eve of St. James the apostle 17 Ric. II [*24 July 1393*].

Present: [*in column*] John Salesbury, grocer, mayor, John Cammel, Thomas Boreford, John Hethe, John Mor(. . .), John (. . .), Richard (. . .), John (. . .), Thomas (. . .), [*two names illegible*], John D(ounton?), John (Eceshale?), William Whyte, (John?) Gillyngham, John Chaundeler, John Chaundeler junior, Robert Body, John Sompnour, John Cary, John Swyft, Philip Goldsmyth, Nicholas Hardyng, John Thorbourne, Walter Orm, Henry Suthewyk, William Walter, Robert Sexhampcote, Thomas Sexhampcote, Simon Tredynek, Edmund Enfeld, William Wilton, Richard Juwel, Stephen Edyngdon, John Gatecombe, Robert Blake, Roger Wodeford, William More.

[*An entry to the right of the column of names is largely illegible, but relates to a gift to the king on his arrival, to the queen, and to the bishop on his arrival. In the left-hand margin of the folio are noted*] Gifts [to King H. V of 100 marks *crossed out*], to King Richard of 100 marks and to the queen of 50 marks; to the bishop £20.]

196. [*Also to the right of the column of names in no. 195*] Assembly: Friday before the nativity of the Blessed Virgin Mary 17 Ric. II [*5 Sept. 1393*].

Agreed: John Gowayn, the bishop of Salisbury's steward, for his friendship and his diligence towards the bishop and other magnates, to have £5, which was paid to him, viz. [*the contributors, in two columns*] William Gys, T. Bowyere, R. Play, John Buterleygh, John Salesbury, mayor, W. Warmwell, John Moner, Edmund Enefeld, John Chaundler senior, W. Asshton, John Cammel 'grocer', Robert Body, R. Deverel, T. Castelton, John Kyngesbrugge, T. Sexteyn, J. Sompnour, J. Franklayn, William White, [*column two*] John Nedlere junior, Nicholas Hardyng, John Lymyngton, Adam Teffonte, Simon Drapere, William More, Philip Goldsmyth, W. Wilton 'bocher', and others.

[f. 65v.; *faded and stained*]

197. Assembly: Friday after St. Matthew 17 Ric. II [*26 Sept. 1393*].

Present: John Salesbury 'grocer', mayor, John Buterleygh, John Moner, Robert Play, John atte Hethe, Thomas Bowyere, Edward Enefeld, John Chaundeler senior, John Cammel, John Thorbourne, Richard Spencer, Robert Deverel, Richard Juwel, William Gys, Robert Body, Simon Tredynek, John Lytle, Richard Oward, John Kynggesbrugge, William White, Thomas Eyre, Adam Teffonte, Thomas Sextayn, Robert Stapelford, Walter Orm, Nicholas Hardyng, John Nedlere junior, John Eceshale, and others.

John Salesbury accounted for his receipts and expenses during his mayoralty: received from John Forest, collector of the king's subsidy of cloth sold in Salisbury during the year, £20; (. . .) to be levied by John Moner and John (. . .) For various expenses at the arrival of the king's justices (. . .); to officials of various lords (. . .); for a pipe of wine given to the sheriff (. . .) as in the said assembly (. . .) £9 1s. 8d. (. . .). From which are accounted for his receipts as appears above £20, and so there remain of arrears £4 3s. (. . .). Agreed: the said £69 1s. 8d. to be levied on the community of the city. Elected as assessors: Hugh Hore, Walter Nandre, Richard Oward, William Busshop; as collectors William Fuystour, John Mury, John Poleyn, and Richard Weston. Agreed also: to levy the £3 given to the mayor and community by John Franklayn wheeler and remaining in the hands of Philip Goldsmyth.

198. Election of the mayor: Sunday the feast of All Souls 17 Ric. II [*2 Nov. 1393*]. Assembled in the church of St. Edmund: the mayor and his fellow citizens, sc. John Salesbury, mayor, William Warmwell, John Nywan [*sic*], Robert Deverel, John Nedlere junior, Thomas Boreford, George Joce, John Moner, John Chaundeler senior, Thomas Castelton, William Asshton, William Gys, Richard Leche, John Cammel, Thomas Bowyer. [*The name of the new mayor is not given.*]

199. Assembly: Friday after St. Leonard 17 Ric. II [*7 Nov. 1393*].

Present: the mayor and his fellow citizens, viz. John Salesbury 'grocere', John Nedler junior, Hugh Hore, Robert Deverel, John Cammel, Robert Play, William Warmwell, Thomas Bowyere, William Gys, John Niwman, John Wollop, John Merlawe, Gilbert Oward, John Barbour 'brasier', Adam White, John Gilberd 'sompnour', Henry Suthewik, Nicholas Hardyng, William Wilton, William Walters, Walter Orm, William Raynald, William Woderove, William White, William Salle, John Drewery, Adam Teffonte, Richard Swift, John Chaundeler senior, Thomas Eyr, Robert Bowyere, Thomas Sexhamcote, William More, John Thorbourne, and others.

Agreed: the mayor to be allowed all his expenses made for the common good after the feast of All Souls last [*2 Nov. 1393*] for the whole time for which he held the office of mayor after the said feast.

[f. 66; *faded and stained*]

200. [*Heading:*] John Camel mayor.

Assembly: 5 Dec. 17 Ric. II [*1393*].

Present: John Cammel 'grocer', mayor, and other citizens, viz. John Buterleigh, Thomas (. . .), Edmund Enfeld, William Gys, Hugh Hore, William Asshton, William Warmwell, (. . .), John Ch(aundeler?), Robert Deverel, John Nedlere junior, (John?) Ga(. . .), John (. . .), (Thomas Eyr?), Thomas E(. . .), (Robert?) Full(. . .), [*two names illegible*].

[*Several illegible lines, but including, apparently, a note of the ratification of John Cammel's election as mayor and ending, apparently, with an entry about the collection of rents.*] (. . .) Buterleigh and William Warmwell for the use of the city at Christmas.

(. . .) on their arrival with the mayor at the common expense of the community.

201. Rental of the mayor and community made 12 Aug. 7 Hen.V [*1419*] in the time of John Bromley and Robert Gilbert, elected chamberlains. [*The rents given below are specified in the MS. as annual rent, and are followed, except for the last item, by the quarterly rent.*]

John Bourton innkeeper (*ostell'*) for the hospice of George's inn £15. John Bofer 'bocher' for a tenement late John Moner's by Fisherton bridge [*blank*]. John More 'baker' for a tenement by St. Thomas's cemetery £4. A room with a fireplace (*camena*) by the cemetery there 10s. Another room there by the same room 10s. Another room there of Nicholas Wight chaplain 10s. Another shop of John Sherman by the cemetery with a room upstairs £1. A tenement late Thomas Stoor's in Castle Street ('Castelstret') [*blank*]. Richard Coof 'draper' for a tenement facing the market £5. [f. 66v.; *faded and stained*] William Penyton 'dighere' [*i.e. dyer*] for three cottages by his corner tenement late John Prentiz's in Wyneman Street ('Wynmanstret') £2, with which rent the same tenement is charged. A tenement in Gigant Street ('Gigorstret') late Richard Spencer's by Richard Weston's cottage £1 6s. 8d. quit rent. John Parch for all the cottages late of John Baker 'grocer' in Nuggeston ('Nhuggeston') towards St. Edmund's church £2 6s. 8d. quit rent. The same John for a tenement late Nicholas Hardyng's in Winchester Street ('Wynchestrestret') and previously John Nyweman's £1 quit rent. A tenement late John Becket's in Winchester Street by the ditch £2 13s. 4d. quit rent [*For this item the annual and quarterly rent, 13s. 4d., are transposed in the MS.*]. Thomas Messagier for a chief tenement and cottage late Sir William Asshle's in St. Martin's Street (*vico Sancti Martini*) and Brown Street ('Brounstret'), £3 6s. 8d. quit rent. Another tenement late the same William's and previously Robert Hyndon's in the same street £1 4s. Cottages which W. Waryn now holds, late John Thorbourne's, in Brown Street ('Brounstret') by the chief tenement there late the same John's 10s. The building above the ditch by Pynnoke's inn ('Pynnokes in') in Minster Street ('Minstrestret') 2s. quit rent.

[f. 67; *faded, stained, and holed*]

202. [*Heading*:] Robert Poynant.

Election of the mayor and other officers: All Souls' day 6 Hen.V [*2 Nov. 1418*].

John Wichford and John Bremle elected and sworn to the number of the Twenty-Four good men, in place of John Moner and John Levesham deceased.

Richard Coof 'draper', for £3 to be paid for the city's use, was excused the office of reeve and from election to lower office. Likewise John Wichford gave to the community (. . .) to be excused henceforth from filling the office of reeve.

Elected as mayor, Robert Poynant; as reeves, Edward (. . .) and Robert Gilberd; as alderman of New Street ward, John P(. . .); of Market, Thomas Stallbrigge; of St. Martin's, John Deverel; of Meadow, Robert Grene; as serjeants, Robert E(. . .) and Walter Short.

203. First assembly: 11 Nov. [*1418*].

Present: the mayor, Walter Shirle, William Waryn, William Busshup, William Doudyng, Walter Nandre, John Swyft, Edward Frith, Richard Coof, John Bremley, William atte Lee, William Fuystour, Richard Oword, William Tuyl, Robert Tannere, Edward Gilbert, Richard atte Mulle, John Shad, John Marshel, John [Botenham *crossed out*; Chippenham *interlined*], John Cornysshe, John Furbour, Thomas (Ch)arlyng, John Deverel, Robert Grene, William Cok, George Jocee, Thomas Randolf, John Parch, Thomas Messager, and others.

Agreed by all: William Alisaundre for advice, William Lord as attorney, and Stephen Edyngdon as city clerk, [to be retained] for the wages and liveries as before. As to the livery of William Westbury, bailiff, respited until etc. The common livery to be worn by the good men this year. Anyone summoned to the assembly and absent without reasonable excuse to pay 6d. according to the preordained custom. The incoming (*futurus*) sheriff of Wiltshire to have a pipe of wine as a gift from the city for his friendship.

All outside (*extranei*) victuallers, both butchers and fishmongers, to be separated in their standings from the victuallers of the city. No one living in the city to take in grain after the ninth hour under penalty of ½ mark, or fish or meat or any food under the same penalty. Those having pigs, geese, or ducks are altogether prohibited from putting them out (*exire*).

Because lately the auditors elected for the accounts of the collectors and others, both the chamberlains and the stewards of the fraternity of St. George, did not carry out (*continuarunt*) their office assiduously, there are joined with them William Doudyng, John Judde, William Tuyl or another whom they may wish to call on for help. Renewed and named as auditors: the mayor for the time being, Walter Shirle, William Waryn, William Doudyng, and William Tuyl.

204. Assembly: 16 Dec. [*1418*].

Present: the mayor and many fellow citizens named in the list.

Agreed by all: after Thomas Rede merchant has been removed from the office of subwarden of the 'almeshous', William Panter to replace him if he is willing, but if not William More to be subwarden for the usual and preordained wages.

Elected to hold one of the keys of the common chest: John Swyft.

Robert Warmwell, late a city chamberlain with William Walter deceased, accounted fully for his time. Before the auditors, he [*sc.* William Walter?] was said to owe net £1 19s. 4d., which the chamberlains are charged with levying.

205. Assembly at the 'Counseilhous': 6 Feb. [*1419*].

Present: the mayor and many fellow citizens named in the list.

By grant of all then present John Parch took [a lease of] all the cottages with curtilages and other appurtenances which the mayor and community lately had by grant of John Baker 'grocer' in Nuggeston ('Nhuggeston') from Easter next for 20 years, paying £2 6s. 8d. a year to the chamberlains and the rent and charges due to the bishop and anyone else, and maintaining and repairing the cottages, the chamberlains having the right to repair them if he does not and to repossess them if the rent is in arrears for one month.

It was attested and proved by John Wotton and Walter Gilmyn [and by John Cammel *interlined*] that William Reynald in the presence of some people of the city spoke odious and scandalous words, which appear in the list of the assembly and for which he was committed into the custody of Walter Short the city serjeant. He was afterwards freed by sureties.

[f. 67v.; *faded, stained, and holed*]

206. Assembly: 31 March 7 [Hen.V, *1419*].

Present: the mayor with other fellow citizens named in the list of the assembly.

Alice late the wife of John Becket appeared and publicly granted to the mayor and community her life estate in the tenement late her husband's in Winchester Street ('Wynchestrestret') by the ditch of running water, the reversion of which belonged to the mayor and community by virtue of the said John's legacy for holding his obit annually in St. Thomas's church. That obit is ordered to be held with that of William Walter and his wife Alice on the feast of the Exaltation of Holy Cross [*14 Sept.*] at the community's expense.

The executors of John Moner's will unanimously grant to the mayor and community the tenement with its appurtenances by the bridge, which John Crablane 'digher' [*i.e.*

dyer] lately held, for holding annually the said John [Moner's] obit in St. Edmund's church. That obit is ordered to be held.

The obit of John Wallop 'draper' (on Sunday next after the feast of . . .).

Ordered: the obits of William Walter and William Wichford in St. Edmund's church on the morrow of Ascension for ever at the community's expense.

Ordered: the obit of William Asshle chaplain and the obit of William Asshle his father to be held for ever in St. Thomas's church on the feast of St. Peter in cathedra [*22 Feb.*] at the community's expense.

The obit of John Bridel called Prentiz and of Katherine his late wife, also of Thomas Thursteyn and Joan his wife, to be held annually for ever in St. Edmund's church in the second week of Lent at the expense of William Penyton and his heirs by reason of the farm granted to him in perpetuity of the cottages (adjoining?) his tenement in Wineman Street ('Wynmanstret').

Ordered: all the good men of the Twenty-Four to attend all those obits at the mass, under penalty of 2 lb. of wax, unless they have a reasonable excuse. Likewise the [second] Twenty-Four of the city's good men to be there also under penalty of 1 lb. of wax, unless they have a reasonable excuse.

207. Assembly: 22 May [*1419*].

Present: the mayor with others his fellow citizens named in the list of the assembly.

Elected constable: Henry Man, with Thomas Bouer, in place of William Nedler deceased.

208. Assembly: eve of St. Peter and St. Paul [*28 June 1419*].

Present: the mayor with others his fellow citizens named in the list of the assembly.

John Swyft and John Parch were removed from the office of chamberlain. Elected in their place: John Bremley and Robert Gilbert 'tannere'.

William Panter was removed altogether from the office of subwarden of the 'almeshous'. Appointed in his place: William More.

209. Assembly: 8 July [*1419*].

Present: the mayor with other fellow citizens named in the list of the assembly.

Agreed by all: the whole tenement or hospice called George's inn ('Georgesyn') to be committed at farm to John Bourton innkeeper (*ostellar'*). The said John received the said hospice with certain necessaries and other appurtenances, to hold to him and his assigns from the nativity of St. John the Baptist last [*24 June 1419*] for ten years, paying £15 a year to the mayor and community for all other rents and services, saving that he and his assigns maintain and repair the said hospice in all its necessaries at their own expense, together with all the necessaries committed to him, and at the end of the term to demise them so repaired.

John Bofer 'bocher' received the tenement late John Moner's by Fisherton ('Fissherton') bridge, which John Crablane 'digher' [*i.e. dyer*] lately held, to hold to him and his assigns for a term of [*blank*] years, paying £3 a year, beginning on the feast of [*blank*] next, and maintaining and repairing the premises at their own expense, and receiving for maintenance and repair four cartloads of timber. Also granted to the same John that he should have all the tenure and the houses which Thomas Artour holds there when Thomas's term is finished, paying then both for the said tenement granted above and for what Thomas Artour now holds £4 in all at the four terms. Granted also that John have there a 'scaldynghous' to be maintained in all things at his own expense.

210. Assembly: eve of the Assumption [*14 Aug. 1419*].

Present: the mayor with other fellow citizens named in the list of the assembly.

Exhibited: the king's privy seal letter addressed to the mayor and citizens for ordering an aid to the king in Normandy either in men or in money for wages. To be considered: what should be done.

[f. 67a, *an inserted sheet of paper, badly faded and stained, the lettering trimmed away at the top, the right-hand side mutilated*]

[*A fragmentary draft letter in French, much amended and largely illegible, in which the mayor and commons plead with the king to relax his demands on the city, which has been assessed for payment of the fifteenth at £75 0s. 2½d. The reason given appears to be a decline in the weaving industry, in which most of the population is employed, and which in the time of Richard II had 500 looms ('lomes') at work.*]

[f. 67a verso, *faded, stained, and mutilated*]

[*A list of men, possibly those who might go to serve with the king, in three columns.*] (. . .), Robert S(. . .), John Wynchestre, Gover Bocher, John Chaundeler, John Bochere, John Yrmonger, Stephen Waryn 'sadiler', John Pakker, Nicholas Brounyng, John Caryour, Anselm Graunt, William Hore, Anselm Skynnere, Peter de Varw, John Sower, William Charlyng, Richard (Slaitler?), Walter Carogan, (. . .), [*column two*] John (Deverel?), (William Waryn?), William Prangnel, John Morys, John Chippenham, John Gilberd, John Alisaundre, Thomas Durneford, William Wrythe, Robert Portere, [John Motte touker, Thomas Malrbr' *crossed out*], John Androw 'mercer', John Asshford, John Wyot 'brewer', John Purdy, John (Everard?), Nicholas Shute, John Gerveys, John Houchyn 'bocher', Thomas Brasyer, [John Tyssebury *crossed out*], William Knoll, Roger Brounyng, Thomas Whityng, Philip Ger(ard?), John Clyve 'tannere', Richard Gage, [*column three*] William Hals(tede?), John Neue, John Bornyng, Walter Short, Nicholas (Whyte?), John Grysoins, Richard Balfot, William Prydy, John Gy, William Gloucestr', John Colyngbourne, Thomas Androw, John Clyve 'brewer', John Sulyth.

[f. 68; *faded and stained*]

211. [*Heading:*] Robert Warmwell.

Election of the mayor and other officers: All Souls' day 7 Hen. V [*2 Nov. 1419*].

Before the officers were elected, there was discussed the dispute and disagreement (*contradictio*) of John Wichford, elected the year before to make up the number of the Twenty-Four, in that he refused [*dedicit*] to pay the £3 imposed on him by his own consent for being excused the office of city reeve in the presence of Robert Puynant, mayor, Walter Shirle, William Busshup, Nicholas Hardyng, Walter Nandre, John Judde, Thomas Castelton, Robert Warmwell, Henry Man, John Swyft, (Thomas Androw?), Richard Coof, John Bremle, John Bottenham, and John Wichford, who then all agreed that in the next assembly the disagreement (. . .), unless John Wichford makes satisfaction before that assembly, should be discussed as to what should be done, particularly in that William Waryn, Thomas Mason, Edward Frith, William Tuyl, and Richard Oward (. . .[were not present?]).

Discussed: the death of William Doudyng, William atte Lee, William Fuystour, and William Nedlere of the number of the Twenty-Four. Elected in their place: William Alisaundre, Richard Gage, John Noble, and Robert Gilberd 'tannere'.

Because the said John Noble (. . .) did not appear having been elected as reeve, he gave to the community (. . .) that he henceforth be excused election to that office.

Afterwards they proceeded to the election: as mayor, Robert Warmwell; as reeves, Thomas Randolf, John Pape junior; as alderman of New Street ward, John Wodehay; as alderman of Market, William Shupton; of St. Martin's, Richard Nedlere; of Meadow, Thomas Hankyn; as serjeants: Walter Short, John Boteller.

212. First assembly: morrow of St. Andrew 7 Hen. V [*1 Dec 1419*].

Present: the mayor, Walter Shirle, William Waryn, William Busshup, Walter Nandre, John Judde, Henry Man, John Swyft, John Bromley, John Bottenham, John Wichford, Robert Gilbert, Thomas Bouer, John Noble, John Sydenham, William Cok, Thomas Reeded, Thomas Blechere, William Barbour, John Cornyssh, John Wodehay, John Chippenham, George Jocee, John Ruddok, John Shad, Richard Nedlere, Roger Serjant, John Marchel, Thomas Messager, Edward Dubbere, Thomas Randolf, William Halstede, John Shute, Richard Coofe, Thomas Durneford.

Stephen Edyngdon openly offered £2 from William Doudyng's legacy to the city, which John Bromley one of the city chamberlains took for the city's use and accounted for. [*Added*:] Nothing here because charged in the account of the mayoralty of Robert Warmwell by the said John Bremle and Robert Gilberd then chamberlains.

[f. 68v.; *faded and stained*]

Discussed: the recompense and repayment that future mayors should have while in office. Because it could not be fully agreed through the absence of many fellow citizens, adjourned until the next assembly.

Agreed: those retained by the council for their advice to be retained this year at the same wages and liveries as in the preceding year. The incoming (*futurus*) sheriff to have a pipe of wine from the community's goods for his friendship.

On the day of the assembly, before the mayor and many other citizens, the coffer that was kept in the chest at the 'Counseilhous' was opened and the money in it was viewed and replaced (. . .) with the community's seal (. . .) the chamberlains in safe keeping until etc.

213. Assembly: 10 Jan. [*1420*].

Present: the mayor, Walter Shirle, William Waryn, William Busshup, Thomas Mason, Walter Nandre, John Judde, and many other fellow citizens.

Exhibited and read: the king's letter patent addressed to John F(. . .), John (. . .), Thomas (. . .) for levying and paying a tenth and fifteenth granted to the king in the last parliament. A third part of the tenth is to be paid on the feast of St. Martin next [*11 Nov.*]. Elected as assessors: John Swyft, John Furbour, John Shad, John Chippenham; as collectors, together with the commissioners: John Parch, Geoffrey Goldsmyth, John (Charlyng 'currier'?), and Robert Pottere 'corvysor'.

Exhibited: the king's letters patent addressed to the mayor for repaying the loan or money to the mayor and his fellow citizens lending it on the feast of St. Martin next from the third part of the tenth then payable to the king, as above. The citizens and neighbours of the city were assessed for various sums according to their status [*the significance of the abbreviations following six of the amounts is obscure*]:

[*in two columns*] Robert Warmwell mayor 10s. Walter Shirle 10s. [?] of broken gold (*fr'c*), William Waryn 10s., Thomas Mason 10s., John Judde 10s., Robert Puynant 10s., William Busshup ½ mark, Walter Nandre ½ mark, William Alisaundre 10s., John Swyft 10s., John Bremle 10s. [?] counterfeit (*co'fr*), Richard Coofe 10s. *fr'c* [?], Thomas Bouer 10s., Richard Gage 10s., Robert Gilbert 10s., Henry Man ½ mark, Thomas Castelton ½ mark, Edward Frith ½ mark, John Noble ½ mark, John Curteis 'taillour' ½ mark, John More 'baker' ½ mark, John Welles senior 5s., William Chepman 'touker' 3s. 4d., John Cornyssh 'touker' 3s. 4d., John Marchal 'dyer' 5s., Henry Hamme ½ mark, Edward

Dubbere ½ mark, [*column two*] John Morys 10s., Stephen Lythenard 3s. 4d., William Shupton 'corvysor' ½ mark, Robert Potter 'corvysor' 3s. 4d., Stephen Mercer 13s. 4d., Nicholas Jogen ½ mark, John Shad 5s., William Child 'hosier' 5s., William Warwyk 10s., John Park 5s., Richard Coupe ½ mark, John Everard 3s. 4d., John Clyve 'tannere' 3s. 4d., Peter Dawe ½ mark [?] of broken and defective gold (*fr'c et defec*), Richard Gater ½ mark, John Charlyng 3s. 4d., John Colyngbourne 3s. 4d., John Hampton 'brewer' ½ mark, William Penyton 3s. 4d., John Hayne 'loder' ½ mark, John Corscombe ½ mark *f'c & loc'* [?], John Griffith ½ mark, John Hogeman 3s. 4d., William Cok 3s. 4d., John Pope senior 3s. 4d., William Reynald ½ mark, John Pope junior 3s. 4d., John Teffonte 3s. 4d., [f. 69; *faded, stained, and holed*; *heading*: Robert Warmwell] John Clyve 'brewer' ½ mark, Gilbert Tannere ½ mark, Hugh Tannere 5s., Richard Sherman ½ mark, John Motiffonte 3s. 4d., John Clerk 'lympner' 3s. 4d., John Paule 'furbour' ½ mark, Geoffrey Goldsmyth ½ mark, John Wynchestre 3s. 4d., Thomas Randolf ½ mark, John Helier 'irmonger' 10s., William Halstede 5s., John Anthon 'bocher' ½ mark, William Charlyng 3s. 4d., John Wyot 3s. 4d., (. . .) ½ mark, [*column two*] John Willy 'mercer' 3s. 4d., John Bracy 'webbe' ½ mark, William Avene ½ mark, John Sydenham 5s., Robert Grene 3s. 4d., John Ruddok 3s. 4d., John (. . .) 3s. 4d., Richard H(. . .) 5s. *fr'c* [?], William Arp(. . .) 3s. 4d., Robert Pyle ½ mark, John (Chew?) 'drovere' 3s. 4d., (. . .) Danyel ½ mark, Robert Rede 'draper' ½ mark, William Vialfot 5s., William Vefer 'corvysor' 3s. 4d. Sum £25. [*The actual total is £26 10s.*]

214. Wednesday after Epiphany in the year of the preceding assembly [*10 Jan. 1420, i.e. the same day as that assembly though the date is differently expressed, and those named as present are not all the same*].

John Clerk 'lympner' presented before the mayor, Walter Shirle, William Waryn, John Judde, Robert Puynant, Henry Man, Thomas Bouer, and Robert Gilbert being present in 'la Counseilhous' two bonds by one of which Reginald Kyngbrigge chaplain [was bound] to Thomas Biston in £100 and by the other the same Thomas [was bound] to the said Reginald in a like sum, with a defect in the indenture, and delivered them to the mayor, and for that delivery those present promised to indemnify John by reason of the delivery.

215. Assembly at the 'Counseilhous': the feast of St. Fabian and St. Sebastian [*20 Jan. 1420*].

Present: the mayor, Walter Shirle, William Waryn, Henry Man, John Swyft, John Bromley, and Robert Gilberd.

Before them the sealed purse, as mentioned in the first assembly of this year, which remained in the keeping of the two chamberlains, was opened and in it was £3 1s. 2d. of good money. From that £1 11s. 8d. was paid to William Lord the city's attorney to sustain the pleas against Thomas Biston for the costs of the last and the coming term, and 3s. 4d. was paid to John Clerk 'lympner' for the fee or payment to the bailiff for taking possession by writ [?] (*pro feodo sive soluc' Ballivo capti per breve*). There then remained £1 6s. 2d., which was paid to the chamberlains to render their account for it.

Delivered to Henry Man, broken gold weighing $1^3/8$ oz. to be exchanged in London, and to him also 10s. in false gold and to John Bromley 10s. to get what they could for it in London; if they get anything it is to be turned to the community's profit. [*Added later, partly interlined*] John Bremley paid the 10s. as 1 noble and 2 quarters of silver-gilt which he had received earlier; the payment was made before W. Waryn mayor, Walter Shirle, Robert Warmwell, John Everard, William Lord on Wednesday after St. Peter and St. Paul 1 Hen. VI [*30 June 1423*].

On St. Vincent's day following [*22 Jan. 1420*] the mayor paid to Henry Man £25 in gold to take to London and pay to the treasurer of England, raised by way of a loan from the citizens by virtue of letters patent addressed to the mayor, from the persons written above, on receiving from the treasurer sufficient security for repayment on the feast of St. Martin next [*11 Nov. 1420*] from the third part of the tenth granted to the king and then payable according to the form of the said letters patent.

[f. 69v.; *faded, stained, and holed*]

216. [*Heading:*] Robert Warmwel mayor.

Assembly, for urgent business concerning the city and for finding a suitable remedy: Monday after St. Michael [*30 Sept. 1420*].

Present [*in column*]: Robert Warmwell mayor, Walter Sherle, William Waryn, Thomas Mason, Walter Nandre, Robert Puynant, Henry Man, [*in paragraph to the right of the column*] John Swyft, John Bremle, William Warwyk, Thomas Bouer, Richard Gage, Thomas Durneford, John Wodehay, William Penyton, John Colyngbourne, Thomas Freman, John Marchal, Thomas Mass(. . .), Henry Hamme, William Cokkys, Thomas Massinger, (. . .), George Joce, John Deverel, Richard Gatour, John Willy, John (Boly?), Henry More, Edward Gilberd, John Shad, John Machyn, William (. . .), John Noble.

Ordered and constituted: henceforth no deed to be sealed under the seal of the mayoralty except by the city clerk deputed for this.

Elected as chamberlain from the feast of the nativity of St. John the Baptist [*24 June*] until etc.: John Bremle and Richard Gatour.

Ordered: John Marchal to have the keeping of one key of the common chest.

Elected and deputed as city clerk: William Lord.

Ordered: the chaplain of St. George for the time being to be attendant at convenient and necessary times on the mayor for the time being. [*Added later:*] This ordinance to be inserted in the little black book of paper (*nig^o pp^iro parvo*) of the fraternity of St. George.

Allowed to Gilbert Marchal, the bishop of Salisbury's clerk, for various orders by William

Waryn and William Busshop against Thomas Byston, sued by the chamberlains for paying [*incomplete*].

[f. 70; *faded, stained, and holed*] Robert Poynant came and asked for an allowance in the following particulars paid by him during his mayoralty, and they were allowed to him by the chamberlains: for the officials' liveries, £1 1s.; paid for a messenger of the duke of Bedford, 3s. 4d.; given to the Nottingham ('Notyngham') herald, 3s. 4d.; to a messenger bringing privy seal letters, 3s. 4d.; for the costs of the said Robert, W. Shirle, H. Man, (. . .)ton, 10s.; (. . .). Allowed.

217. Account of John Bremle and Robert Gilberd, made on the feast of St. Luke 8 Hen. V [*18 Oct. 1420*] of various receipts and payments by them in the time when they were city chamberlains, viz. from the nativity of St. John 7 Hen. V [*24 June 1419*] to the same feast then following.

First, an account of the city rents: from John Burton innkeeper (*ostiler*) for the tenement called George's inn ('Georgesin') held from the mayor and community per year, £15; from John Bower for the tenement at Fisherton ('Fissherton') bridge held as above per year, £3; from Thomas Artour 'skynnere' for the rooms at the common latrine at the said bridge held as above per year, £1; from John More 'baker' for the tenement by the cemetery granted for the use of the fraternity of St. George per year, £4; from the chaplains for four rooms by the said tenement granted under the same form per year, £2 10s.; from Walter Cok for a tenement in Castle Street ('Castelstret') granted to the mayor and community by John Wollop per year, £1 6s. 8d.; from Richard Cove for a tenement facing the market granted to the same by William Walter per year, £5; from William Penyton for a tenement in Wineman Street ('Wynemanstret') granted to the same by [*blank*] Prentys per year, £2; from William Caumbrigge for two tenements in Gigant Street ('Gigorestret') the rent of which was granted to the same by Richard Spencer, £1 6s. 8d.; from John Parch for a tenement by William Cokk's in Winchester Street ('Wynchestrestret') granted to the same by [*blank*], £1; [f. 70v.; *faded, stained, and holed*] from the same John Parch for a cottage in Nuggeston granted to the same by Nicholas Hardyng, £2 6s. 8d.; (. . .) with shops [and] cottages facing St. Martin's church in Brown Street ('Brounstret') granted by W. Asshele, 5 marks; from (. . .) in New Street (*novo vico*] (. . .) by William Asshele, £1 4s.; from (. . .) for the rent from (. . .) by Warmwell, 10s.; from William (. . .) in High Street (*alto vico*) Richard Py(. . .), 2s.; from William Short (. . .) inn ('ynn'), 10s. Sum £44 2s. 8d.

[Other] receipts: from William Doudyng in money given to the mayor and community, £2; from Robert Warmwell mayor and others, £1 6s. 2d.; from a brass pot sold, 4s. 4½d.; from a basin with ewer, 4s.; from two brass pots, 3s. 4d.; from a saddletree ('sadeltre'), 1s. 8d.; from a basin with ewer, 1s. 4d. Sum £4 0s. 10½d.

Sum total £48 3s. 6½d.

[f. 71; *faded and stained*]

[*Heading:*] Robert Warmwell.

The said chamberlains ask for allowances as detailed below.

For tenements empty for some of the time: for the tenement which John (. . .), £1 10s.; for the cottage by (. . .), 5s.; for the tenement which Thomas (. . .), 13s. 4d.; for the tenement which Roger S(. . .) worth for half (. . .), 12s.; for the assised rent (. . .) of John (. . .), 10s.; for the tenement (which) Walter Shott in Winchester Street ('Wynchestrestret') (. . .) held for the whole year, 10s. Sum £4 0s. 4d.

For fees: for a gown given to each of Thomas Ryngwode, William Westbury, William Alysaundre, William Lord, and Stephen Edyngdon, £3 6s. 10d.; for William Alysaundre's fee, £2; for William Lord's fee, £2; for a cask of wine given in place of the tenants at the corner [?] (*collat' loco tenent' ang'l'*), £6 6s. 8d.; for a pipe of wine given to the sheriff, £3; for the said chamberlains' fee, £2; for the fee of the chaplain of St. George, £5 6s. 8d.; for Robert Poynant's expenses during his mayoralty, £2 1s. Sum £26 1s. 2d.

[f. 71v.; *faded and stained*]

[*Heading:*] Robert Warmwell.

For the money allowed to Robert Warmwell: for timber, lathes, 'bords', studs and 'tilpynnes', £5 7s. 9d.; for the head of the solar, £5 1s.; for lime ('lym') (. . .) the tilers' wages, £4 19s. 6d.; for the assised rent to (. . .), 19s. 4d.; for the rent (. . .) given from (. . .) by W(. . .), 15s.; for rent to the bishop for waste spaces in the city given in perpetuity to the community, £1 5s.; for the rent of the community's 'counselhous' [held] from the dean and chapter, 12s. 2d.; for timber given for the house which John Bouer holds (. . .), £1; for ironwork ('yregar') for the repair of various tenements (9s. 4½d.). Sum £20 9s. 1½d.

They also ask for allowances for anniversaries: of John Beket and William Teynturer and Alice his wife, 2s. 8d.; for William Asshele chaplain, 3s. 6d.; for William Walters and William Wichford, 9s. 1d. [*apparently written as* 11s. 1d. *and poorly corrected*]; for the order against Byston for Gilbert, the bishop of Salisbury's clerk, 4s. Sum 19s. 3d.

For the suit against Reginald Kyngbrigge at various times and the carriage of muniments to London, £3.

Sum total £54 9s. 10½d.; deducted from that £48 3s. 6½d., there remained £6 6s. 4d. owed.

[f. 70a, *inserted before f. 71, a strip of parchment 360 mm. long by 25 mm. wide, in two pieces sown together, unnumbered in the principal enumeration but numbered 78, as is also the preceding folio, in the enumeration added at the foot. The parchment is so worn as to be not easily legible, and the right-hand end may have been cut off.*]

218. [*The nature and meaning of the document are not clear.*] John Judde, mayor, 5 and 6 Hen.V [*1417–1418*]. Parliament 16 Nov., 5 Hen.V at the beginning of the mayoral year. Elected to the parliament, Walter Shirle and William Waryn, as appears at the end of the said mayor's account 6 Hen.V. For the collector John Wynchestr' for [*two words illegible*]. Sum in the coffer £43 6s. 8d. There was paid to the mayor £24 3s. 4d. to pay to those contributing to the loan of 100 marks in Shirle's mayoralty; from 10s. arising from the goods of John Nyweman [in] broken [or] counterfeit [money] delivered to the mayor of another town or towns or of other lords [?] (*fract' contrafact' liberate maior' vel alterius vel aliarum villarum vel dominorum*). [*On the second piece of parchment, not running on from the foregoing*] Returned at All Souls as citizens at the parliament one week [*18 Nov.*] from St. Martin and at another on the Monday [*5 May?*] before Whitsun, Walter Shirle and Robert Poynant, who each as mayor is henceforth to have £10 paid at the end (. . .). And the chamberlains made a loan to the king, for repaying which the tallage [is] in Walter Shirle's keeping. Payment made to the said citizens for parliament by the chamberlains. Fines £15 as appears by the rolls of the chamberlains' account. (*Ret(. . .) Animarum cives ad parliamentum in octabo Sancti Martini et aliud die Lune proximo ante festum Pentecostes, Walter Shirle, Robertus Poynant, qui quiscumque maior decetero habeat x solidos in fine (. . .). Et camerarii p'st domino regi unde pro resolucione tall' in cus' Walteri Shirle. Sol' fact' civibus predictis pro parliamento per camer'. Fines xv li' prout patet per rotulos comp' camer'.*)

[*No.* **193** *records the election to the parliament of 1417. No.* **188** *records the sum found in the coffer, but gives the payment to the mayor on that occasion as £28 3s. 4d., which might conceivably be the figure in the document above, if the v of xxviii has been worn away to look like i. Walter Shirle and Robert Poynant represented the city in the parliament which was summoned for 2 Dec. (not 18 Nov.) 1420 and was adjourned to 2 May (not 5 May) 1421: cf. no.* **220**.]

[f. 72 and v. *blank*]

[f. 72a *blank. The folio is not an insert, and the number was given perhaps because the preceding folio had earlier not been numbered because it is blank. Although the folio is not numbered at the foot, it falls between the folios numbered at the foot 80 and 82.*]

[f. 72a verso; *faded and stained*]

219. [*Heading:*] Henry Man. [*The name is repeated, sometimes as H. Man or Henry Man mayor, at the head of ff. 73, 73v., 74, 74v., 75, 75v., 76, 77, 78, 78v., and 79v. and at the foot of f. 74; at the foot of f. 76v. and of f. 77v. is In the time of Henry Man mayor.*]

Assembly of Henry Man, mayor: Friday after the Purification of the Blessed Virgin Mary 8 Hen.V [*7 Feb. 1421*] for urgent business concerning the city and finding a suitable remedy, especially concerning the fairs, as appears in a later folio.

219A. [*Written at the foot of the folio in a formal hand, on two lines:*]

Here are contained the names of the citizens of New Salisbury.

Here begins [the mayoralty of] Henry Man.

[*The list is arranged in two columns, in each of which the names are two to a line.*]
John Bottenham John Bremle, John Swyft John Judde, Thomas Mason Walter Nandre,
Walter Shirle William Waryn, Robert Poynant Thomas Bouer, John Noble Richard
Gage, Robert Tannere John Shad, Edward Dubbere Thomas Rede, Robert Rede John
Sampson, William Arnhull John Marchal, John Hogeman John Cornyssh, John
Chippenham Richard Gatour, Henry Hamme John Morys, John Deverel Gilbert Tannere,
Geoffrey Goldsmyth George Joce, John Shute John Parch, John Machyn Thomas
Massinger, Richard Mille Thomas Durneford, John Coscombe Robert Chynchon, John
Hampton 'mercer' John Clerk 'mercer', Edward Gudyer John Park 'hosyer', Thomas
Danyel Henry Elyot, John Purdy John Dale, [*column two*] Robert Warmwell Thomas
Chalsey, William Touker John Colyngbourne, Robert Pyl Nicholas Shute junior, Richard
(Gys?) John Wantynch, Stephen Hert John Smyth, John More H. Kyngton, Thomas
Broun John Mason, John Bourne John Dier 'webbe', Philip Grym William Well, John
Helier John Kyng, Thomas Pencrich [*corrected from* Pentrich] Thomas Whityng,
Nicholas Pyl John Daubeney, Edmund Wytteney John Berton, Walter Mede William
Pridy, John Godde William Gudyer, John Bradle Richard Hamersmyth, Thomas Payn
Stephen Rede, John Sele Thomas Hele John Hele [*three names on the line, the last with
a mark, perhaps* d, *above it*], John By þe Wode [*with a mark, perhaps* d, *above the name*]
Richard Herberd, Joyhn Weyse John Bosampton, Richard Lauerans John Farle Robert
Grym [*three names on the line*], John Furmage Thomas Pentrich, William Broun John
Dunnyng, Thomas Mog William Chyld [*the last two names added later*].

[f. 73; *faded and stained*]

219B. Stewards of the weavers: Richard Gore [*recte* Gage?], Thomas Broun; Nicholas
Shute, John Mason.

[*Written at the foot of the folio in a formal hand:*] Names of the masters.

[*The list is arranged in three columns, the first containing a pair of names on each line,
the second and third relatively close together.*] William Slegge William Stout, John
Parch William Dunnyng, William Basket John Stour(ton?), William By þe Wode Edward
Gudyer, William Hasilber John Stork, Ralph Defnyssh William Higon, John Ferys William
Pouke, Richard Herbert Laurence Dryw, Walter Sawyer Nicholas Neue, Roger Fader
John Durneford, William Hosbrygge Roger Taillor, William Palycer Robert Pleyer,
John Joop John Lylye, John Kymerych Robert Wroxale, Roger By þe Wode John Neel,
John Okford Patrick Gray, John Bulmere Richard Cokelot, John Franklayn William
Frere, John Weston John Pygon, Warin Bronham William Bylk, James Hamme John
Crystel, John Harries William Crede, Thomas Wayte Walter Pynkebrygge, Nicholas Dol
Robert Gelde, Thomas Breinton Thomas Hayne, Robert Lord John Russhton, John
Wayte Nicholas Norys, [*column two*] Thomas Pymperne, John Holwey, Thomas Ferour,
John Hayward, John Gryffyn, William Compton, William Hardyng, William Mede,

Thomas Wyot, Thomas Grene, William Turnour junior, John Lord junior, Thomas Fyryng, Nicholas Rychard, William Smyth, Richard Page, Nicholas Bray, John Lombe, Nicholas Hardyng, Thomas Frogge, Thomas Fadyr senior, Nicholas a Neve, John Kymton, Robert Tonnere, John Franklayn, Edward Gudyere, William Fulham, [*column three*] Thomas Carysbrouk, George Clatford, Richard Whyte, John Wykham senior, Robert Sharp, William Chapyr, John Spragey, William More, Peter Styward, John Wykham junior, John Hardyng junior, John Anketill junior, Robert Ramville, Thomas Pytton, Richard Dyere, John Colynes, Nicholas Alrigge, John Wattys, John Gauge, Edward Clerk, William Mede, Thomas Penn, William Brian, William Purmour, William Teone, John Shyfford, William Fowke.

[f. 73v.; *faded and stained*]

219C. [*Written at the foot of the folio in a formal hand*:] Names of the weavers.

[*The list is arranged in four columns, with the title and names of the stewards of the journeymen weavers across the top of columns three and four and of all four columns of folio 74.*]

Stewards of the journeymen (*vallettorum*) weavers: John Lylye senior, John Wayte, William Grove, Robert Pyper.

[*Column one*] William Hugon, John (Wayte?) junior, Laurence (Bore?), John (Duyk?), Peter Forstere, John Hulle, Thomas Penne, Richard Page, John Cristel, Stephen (Entesborne?), Walter Parche, Thomas Dyryton, Philip Gyffard, William Horwode, William Whitlok, John Fyssh junior, Edward Dyere, Richard Tolly, John Person, John Aunsel, Averay Morgan, Philip Grene, Robert Asshton, Robert Frye, Thomas Pese, John Asselyn, John Sextayn, Robert Asselyn, Ralph Burgeys, John Bakke, [*column two*] Nicholas Steor, John Golyn, Robert Lombe, John Tutsay, John Cranbourne, William (No?), William Yorke, John Lord Thomas Farley, Nicholas Bere, Robert Wrygel, John Tannere, John Symond, William Bryan, Paul (*Poule*) Smyth, John Glastyngbury, John Tolly, Richard Shapewyke, Roger Moule, William Mortemer, John Lauerans, John Godfray, John atte Wylle, Walter Harryes, Thomas Neraforyd, Richard Forster, William Bole, William Phelpys, William Lowte, John Trilly, [*column three*] William (Becket?), John Dogood, William [*blank*], Thomas Burgeys, John (Fymen?), Richard (Chambere?), Roger Rolf, John Gentel, William Symond, John Curteys, Thomas Fouler, William Fys, Walter Boly, John Godfray, John Spencer, Nicholas Pokelchourche, Thomas Penne, William London, Stephen Wylmyngton, Henry Whitby, John Vyncent, Henry Shapwyk, Richard Medmower, John Bacheler, William Crane, Philip Chalke, [*column four*] John Wattys, William Grene, Thomas Cros, William Edyngdon, William Wynde, John Lond(on?), John Hulle, Richard Thychy (Chychia?), William Norys, Philip Kyrchyl, John Verle, Thomas Kyngton, John Ailward, John Chitterne, John Albon, John Skotte, William Yorke, John Charlton, John Porton, John Kyngton, William Langbrygge, John Portour, John Purdy, Robert Stedham, John Myllere, [f. 74; *faded and stained*] [*column one*] Richard Page, John Fontel, John Kyng, John Mylton, Richard Dol, John F(. . .)age, John Cosyn, John Babbestoke, Robert Haywarde, Hugh Diere, William Pouk, Richard Kyngston, Thomas Fader senior, John Godard, Edward Phelps, John Byke, Richard

Coty, Robert Dawe, Thomas Moweyese, Edward Clerk, John Sende, John Mylde, Walter Bryd, John Golfynch, [*column two*] John (Speygey?) junior, John Wilkyns, Edward Mede, John Pry, Edward (. . .), Thomas (. . .)agge, Robert Babbestoke, Richard Pyeres, John Person, Henry Wylteshire, John Besant, John Farley, Thomas Fader junior, Henry Wodeward, John Payse, Thomas London, John Chaunceler, John Baudray, John Thomsone, Henry Mast, John Herte, John Harnham, Thomas Waget, John Yrych, [*column three*] (. . .)rone, (. . .), Thomas Warwyk, Robert (Fryok?), Henry Wheler, John Godwyne, John Gyfford, Nicholas Poure, Richard Kokelot, Robert Tonnere, Thomas Kynton, John Noke, Walter Forde, John Brytford, Richard Bypewode, John Sherle, John Waleys, John Symond, John Wodeyate, John Tannere, John Eustas, William Raulynes, Thomas Pyllyng, John Wynterbourne, George Cerle, [*column four*] Thomas Hayward, John Wheler, William Kymerych, Henry Cornysshe, John Kyngston, John Crestel, Nicholas Bere, Richard Pymperne, John Ballard, Thomas Norton, Walter Parche, John Chapman, Robert Yonge, John Kempe, Hugh Cappys, John Stagard, Edward Pynte, Thomas Dyryton, Peter Pyse, Philip Gyffard, Thomas Burgeys, Richard Hygon, Thomas Lauende, Roger Blake, John Chapyr.

[*Written at the foot of the folio in a formal hand*: Names] of the journeymen weavers.

[f. 74v., *badly faded and stained*]

219D. [*Written at the foot of the folio in a formal hand*:] Names of the masters.

Stewards of the fullers: (. . .), John (Lynchwode?), (. . .).

[*The list is arranged in four columns*] William Peny (Penyton?), John (Danberry?), John Swyft, Thomas (Strinble?), Thomas Forster, Richard Durneford, William Turrok, John Cloterych, Richard Rounde, William Broun, [*column two*] (. . .), Philip P(. . .), Walter P(. . .), John Raynald, John Wexey, John Bemond, William Sawyere, [*column three*] [*three names illegible*], John Helier, John Beshampton, John Waryn, John Moner, William Gelde, Edward Passewell, William Wryche, Richard Marchal, Richard Chesham, John Rowe, Thomas Wake, John Nasshe, Richard Sherman, William Sherman, Thomas Portour, John (Jouster?), Thomas Evesham, [*column four*] (. . .), Walter (. . .), John Br(. . .), William Chepman, John Waryn, Henry Colyngbourne, William (Grye?), John Pynch, Roger Waleys, John Wilton, Oliver Touker, William Chamberlyn, Thomas Lantesdale, John Sprot, Hugh Touker, Nicholas Whibete.

[f. 75; *badly faded, stained, and holed*]

219E. [*Written at the foot of the folio in a formal hand*:] Names of the journeymen [fullers].

Stewards of the journeymen fullers: John Salot and Robert (. . .)ora(. . .).

[*The list is arranged in a single column*]: John (Soph?), Henry (. . .), [*six names illegible*], John (Waltham?), (Walter?) Ferour, Richard Wallop, Adam Furlang, John Blaunchard,

Peter Trweman, Nicholas Honyballek, John Vyncent, John Wroxale, John Taillour, Richard Godfray, Henry Perkyn, Bartholomew Cok, John Mathew, Richard Tygyl, John Hulle, William Bampton, Robert Spakman, Robert Mille.

[f. 75v.; *faded, stained, and holed*]

219F. [*The next four paragraphs are written in majuscule, with the initial letters of each omitted presumably for a decorated capital.*] Of inspections (*examinibus*) at the fair or market outside the city of New Salisbury [*four lines largely illegible*] in the form noted above, it was thus ordered (. . .).

No citizen nor any craftsman or resident is by any craft of artifice to carry or have carried any rayed or motley (*motle*) cloths or cloth or any part for sale at a fair or market or any place whatsoever outside the city, only St. Edward's fair which happens once a year being excepted.

Nor may any of the said people sell by sample or by letter bearing a specimen (*intersignum*) between the parties any rayed or motley cloth or any part of the same to anyone outside the city, under penalty of forfeiture of the same and under penalty of £20 to be raised from the goods of the offender for each offence (*tociens quociens in hace parte contrarie contigerit*) for the use of the city at the discretion of the mayor for the time being and his fellow citizens.

[f. 76; *faded, stained, and badly holed*] And if [*seven lines largely illegible, referring to* rayed or motley cloth *and the said fair*] under penalty of £20 to be raised from the chattels of the owners for the community's use at the discretion of the mayor for the time being and his fellow citizens.

[*In ordinary script.*] Afterwards within a fortnight came William Pridy and declared upon oath that on the feast of St. Kalixtus [*14 Oct.*] before the said constitution he had sold to John Drapere of Shrewsbury six dozen white rayed cloths, and asked for licence to take them out of the city and deliver them, and it was granted to him. It was likewise granted to John Gage for taking out of the city twenty-two cloths sold earlier, and to William Chepman for a cloth of white motley and 3 yards sold to Mr. Richard Harwill canon of Wells before the said constitution.

[f. 76v.; *faded, stained, and badly holed, the lower half blank except for the note of Henry Man's mayoralty*]

219G. The names of those who made fine for (being excused) the office of alderman: [*seven lines illegible*].

[Other income:] W(. . .). Richard E(. . .). William Halstede (. . .). John Hunte from the legacy of Nicholas Belle (. . .). John Shad for a fine (. . . £2?). John Noble for a fine (. . . £2?).

[f. 77; *faded, stained, and badly holed*]

[*Heading in majuscule:*] Commendations to be made in the assembly for the souls written below, (who during their?) life gave goods or tenements to the community (. . .).

First for the tranquillity of the whole church (. . .) and all heresy [?] (*herises universe*). For the peace of the whole realm of England (. . .), the estate of the king of England and the queen and all his brothers and their good (. . .). (. . .) of the mayor and community of the city of New Salisbury (. . .). (For the soul?) of the most (. . .) prince, King Henry IV, who gave the licence to the mayor and community to acquire tenements to the value of 100 marks a year. For the soul of Robert Halom, late bishop of Salisbury, who with the assent of the dean and chapter of Salisbury confirmed the licence up to the sum of £40. For the souls of William Wychford, Nicholas Taillour, John Upton, William Teynturer senior, William Teynturer junior and Alice his wife, John Bytterleye, John Wollop, John Nyweman, John Prentys, John Baker 'grocere', Margaret Godmanston, William Salle, William Warmwell, William Asshele chaplain, William Walters, John Moner, John Beket, John [blank], who gave various lands and tenements to the said mayor and community. For the souls of John Talbot who gave the reversion of tenement now Edmund Assheley's and of John Pynnok who also gave to the same various reversions. For the soul of Thomas Yeuvele for £1. For the soul of Thomas Belle for 8 marks. For the souls of Walter Shirle, Joan his wife, and Richard their son. For the souls of Henry Baron and Christina his wife [*added later:* and Christina Chapman and of all her husbands [?] (*omium maritorum suorum*) who gave to the mayor and community a messuage called 'Otemelcorner']. For the good estate and prosperity of the mayor and community of the city of New Salisbury. For the soul of William Warwik and of Joan his wife who gave to the mayor and community, after her death, four cottages and the racks with their appurtenances standing in Endless Street ('Endelestrete').

[f. 77v.; *faded, stained, and badly holed*]

220. Assembly: Friday after the Assumption of the Blessed Virgin Mary (9) Hen. V [*22 Aug. 1421*].

(Present: . . .), Thomas Mason, Robert (. . .), John Sydenham, John Swyft, Robert (. . .), (John?) Noble, Edward Dubbere, John Bottenham, (. . .), William Cok, Richard Gatur, John Bremle, John Clerk, Thomas Rede, (. . .)yng, John Cornyssh, William Harnhull, Thomas Gryffyn, Thomas Gry(. . .), (. . .) Randolf, John Chippenham, John Morys [*about sixteen names in all illegible*].

Ordered: Walter Shirle and Robert Poynant being at the parliament held at Westminster a week from St. Martin 8 Hen. V [*18 Nov. 1420; but the parliament was summoned for 2 Dec. 1420*] for twenty-eight days and at the parliament held there on the Monday before Whitsun 9 Hen. V [*5 May 1421; but it was summoned for 2 May*] for thirty days to be paid their wages by the chamberlains.

Also, William Lord to be allowed £1 6s. 8d. for his labour and costs about the king's letters patent under the great seal concerning the liberties of the city acquired for the citizens of the same city.

[f. 78; *faded, stained, and holed*]

221. Assembly: Monday the feast of St. Giles 9 Hen.V [*1 Sept. 1421*].

Present: Henry Man mayor, William Waryn, Walter Nandre, Robert Poynant, Robert Warmwell, John Bromle, John Noble, John Swyft, (Walter?) Cofe, William (. . .), John B(otten?)ham, John Shad, Richard Gatour, John Hunte, Henry (. . .), Thomas D(. . .), (. . . Gilberd?), (. . .), John Hayne, John Everard, Thomas Massinger, William (. . .), Thomas Yevele, Robert Rede, John Marchal, George Joce, John C(. . .), John Deverel, Gilbert Tannere, Geoffrey Goldsmyth, John Hampton, John (Colyngbourne?), Stephen Lythenard, John Griffyn, Thomas Freman, John More, (. . .) Clerk 'touker', William Arnhull, William Dunnyng, William Basket, (. . .).

Ordered: the mayor for the time being to choose at his pleasing two of his fellow citizens to audit with him the accounts of those holding the community's goods.

Also, whoever shall henceforth be mayor to be allowed for all charges and expenses during the year of his mayoralty £10 to be paid by the chamberlains, half at Easter and the other half at the end of his term. And if he dies after Easter, the [second] half then to remain in the chamberlains' hands for the use of the city, excepting for the expenses of officials who are to have them paid. The mayor for the time being to have an allowance for the board of the chaplain of St. George who is ordered to be at home (*domesticus*) with the mayor. If the king or another secular lord or prelate comes to the city, nothing is to be given to him [*sc. the mayor*] except by the assembly's order. Further, the said chaplain, for his good diligence and because he is attending on the mayor for the time being [*unfinished*].

[f. 78v.; *faded, stained, and holed*]

222. Account of John Bremle [and] Richard Gatour, city chamberlains, from the nativity of St. John the Baptist 8 Hen.V [*24 June 1420*] until the same feast next following for various receipts and payments (. . .), before Henry Man then mayor, Walter Shirle, William (. . .), (. . .) Gage, John Everard, and John Marchal, the city auditors, on the feast of St. Luke [*18 Oct. 1421*].

City rents (. . .), £42 9s. 4d. From fines for the offices of city reeve [and] city alderman (. . .), £15. From recognizances of the fraternity of St. George in the city, £5 5s. 6d. From various sales of timber, 8s. Sum total received, £63 2s. 10d.

[f. 79; *faded, stained, and holed*]

[*Heading:*] Account of John Bromle and Richard Gatour.

For fees and other payments of the city's counsel (. . .), £(53) 2s. 8d. For gifts (. . .), £1 4s. 9d. For various particulars of the city(. . .), 16s. 0½d. For rents to the office (. . .), £2 12s. 4d. For John Beket' obit, 6s. 8d. For John Moner's obit, 15s. 11d. For William Walters's obit, 10s. 4d. Sum total of payments, £59 8s. 8½d. They owe net £3 14s. 1½d., which they paid on the account. Afterwards it was delivered to John Bremle for safe keeping etc. And so they are quit as appears by the roll of the account, on the back.

223. [*Between ff. 78 and 79 is inserted a gathering of 5 leaves of paper, smaller than the leaves of the book, containing part of an assessment of the inhabitants of Market and St. Martin's wards, of uncertain date and character, arranged in two columns. Some of the forenames are unusual.*]

[f. 78a]

223A. Market ward.

John Swyft 'deiher' [*i.e. dyer*] 3s. 4d., John But 'corveser' 6d., William Bowier 6d., Katherine Peyntour [1s. 4d. *crossed out*] 4d., John Launge 'fleccher' 1s., John Couper 1s., John Halle 6d., John Junour 1s., John Clitour 'mullward' 3s., Robert Bowier 4d., Robert Arthour 2d., William Goldsmyth 8d., Walter Elsabeth 'corveser' 1s., Geoffrey Peuterer 4d., John Arnold 'corvesor' 4s., Thomas Arthour 5s., Richard Wytele 1s. 6d., John Pynner 8d., John Bryd 'sadeler' 1s., John Drw 'boucher' 2d., Robert Cok 'skynner' 8d., Robert Wite 'corveser' 2s., John Cariour 'corveser' 1s., Agnes Coupere 4d., Allen Goldsmyth 4d., John Ferour 4d., John Smalbothe 8d., Geoffrey Taillour and Tanner [?] 4d., Ralph Cardmakier 1s. 4d., John Smythes 6d., Thomas Yonge 'touker' 4d., John Scherman 8d., John More 'baker' 5s., Gonnora Bowier 8s., Richard Oword 8s., John Tysbury 'mercer' 1s., Robert Taillour 4d., John Tysbury 'barbour' 6d., John Clerke 6d., John Fadeur 'corveser' 16d., John Irlound 'taillour' 4d., [*column two*] John Cortais 'taillour' 1s. 8d., John Well 'boucher' 5s., Nicholas Forns' 3s. 4d., Thomas Taillour 6d., Jokyn Cornysch 2s., Thomas Forster 'deiher' 1s. 8d., John Riuby 4d., John Rovere 1s. 8d., John Smyth 2d., John Hor' 2d., William Jonus 'corveser' 2d., Walter Cok' 1s. 4d., John Wode 2s., Alson Bottenham 3s. 4d., Joan Warmwell 2s., Robert Warmwell 5s., [Bartelot Cok' *crossed out*], John Joc' 6d., Nicholas Abyngdon 4d., John Wynterslewe 2d., John Resyngton 1s., William Lyshog' 6d., Roger Waleis 2s., Hugh Touker 4d., John Bruton 4d., Thomas Chalsey 1s. 8d., Robert Pleier 6d., Thomas Pyllyng' 2d., John Colas 2d., Thomas Yevele 2s., John Hele 4d., John [Hungeford *crossed out*] Daubeney 2s., Richard Gratour [2s. 6d. *crossed out*] 3s. 4d., John Webber 4d., William Bowier 3s. 4d., William Chepman 3s. 4d., John Cornysch 2s., Robert Yong 2d., Edward Passewyll 2s. 6d., Thomas Chedford 6d., John Cosse 'touker' 8d., John Wilkes 8d., Agnes Collville 4d., Thomas Dyrneford 4d., John Roddon 4d., John Marchall 2s. 6d., John Holwey 6d.

223B. [f. 78a verso] Walter Schirle 13s. 4d., Robert ate Walle 4d., John Colepyn 1s. 4d., John Perkewyn 8d., Henry Ham 3s. 4d., Thomas Brempton 4d., John Dyraint 2d., Roger Taillour [8d. *crossed out*] 1s., Richard Stokbrigg' 4d., [John Caise *crossed out*],

Edward Bremmer 4d., John Dirneford 3s. 4d., Robert Gylberd 6s. 8d., Ricard Gage 4s., Edward Dubbere 3s., John Dyrneford 'webber' 4d., Thomas Boton 8d., John Smythes 'tanner' 4d., John Tanner 1s., John Numan 1s., William Bythewode 1s., William Loord 2s. 6d., William Fustour 10s., Thomas Cake 6d., Margaret Gylberd 1s., John Smythes 'dubber' 1s., John Pykard 3s. [6d. *crossed out*], Thomas Smythes 6d., William Pragnail 1s., John Stagard 4d., [William *crossed out*] John Nouble 3s. 4d., Adam Glover 1s., Edmund Purdy 2s., John Schupton 1s. 4d., Henry Adam 8d., Robert Glover Rydon [? *for* Robert Rydon 'glover'] 8d., Henry Maritfeis 3s. [6d. *crossed out*], Ralph atte Wode 4d., William Cake 2d., Robert Tarent 4d., John Crocker 6d., John Schupton 6d., William Stonynge 2d., John Schyppenham 3s. 4d., [*column two*] [Nicholas Lamwell *and* William Taillour *crossed out*], Thomas Nordwode 8d., Walter Glouc' 4d., William Smythes 4d., Stephen Hert 4d., John Baron 2d., Robert Aston 4d., [John Sterr *crossed out*], John Kempe 2d., Guy Glover 2d., Robert Nouble 4d., Thomas Watts 4d., [Mant' Pynts (*sic*) *crossed out*], John Hese 'parchmenter' 2d., Nicholas Tutsy 2d., John Weler 1s., Robert Grene [1s. 8d. *crossed out*] 2s., John Strete 4d., [Robert Lansiner *crossed out*], Thomas Baron 8d., Thomas Gor' 8d., John Mason 2s. 6d., William Bakere 'stonher' [? *i.e. stonehewer*] 8d., Richard Growe 2d., William Brante 2s., Walter Tytelynge 2d., Robert Stonnard [5s. *crossed out*] 4s., John Crappe 4d., Edward Clerk 4d., Thomas Weler 2d., Robert Chynchon 8d., John Houpere 4d., Thomas Dyrneford 8d., Robert Spakman 2d., William Wriche 1s., John Waryn 'touker' 8d., William Belde 4d., George Joc' 4d., William Hasylbere 4d., Thomas Ster 1s., William Glouc' 2s., Thomas Masson 13s. 4d., Roger atte brigg 8d., Stephen Edyngdon [3s. 4d. *crossed out*, 4s. *crossed out*] 3s. 4d., John Eustas 4d., William Grym 8d., John Mone 6d., Nicholas Boukelond 8d., John Schirle 'touker' 4d., William Chamberlayn 1s. 4d., John Schupton 'corveser' 5s., Alson Noteky' 6d., Robert Potte 3s.

223C. [f. 78b] Richard Schesham 3s., Nicholas Touker 8d., Joan atte Will 4d., Thomas Hele 8d., [John Tanner *crossed out*], Edmund (*Ed's*) Schuppist' 2s. 6d., William Ferour 10d., Palton [?] Barbour 2d., Walter Ryngwode 2d., Thomas Frogge 4s. 6d., Richard Hen 6d., Agnes Gneis 1s., John Stoure 18d., Robert Chamberlayn 2s., John Dounton 6s. 8d., John Judde 13s. 4d., Stephen Mercer 6s. 8d., William Webb' John Susetere and William Stobb' 1s. 8d., John Sibiles [3s. 4d. *crossed out*] 4s., William Tull' 10s., Nicholas Lyndraper 2s. 6d., Peter Prentis 1s. 4d., Makerell' [?] de Schaftebury 4d., Richard Berde 1s., Joan Sergantes 3s. 4d., Thomas Mounk 1s., Hankoc Lyndraper [? *i.e. — Hancok linendraper*] 5s., Thomas Schephurd 5s., Thomas Cardmakier 3s. 4d., Nicholas Ingel 3s. [6d. *crossed out*], Henry Schadde 4d., 'le fitz' Hankoc 8d., Thomas Dale 4d., John Schadde 5s., Richard Cof' 6s. 8d., William Childe [1s. 4d. *crossed out*] 2s., Roger de Wythes 4d., John Danbury 1s., John Instour 1s., Bon Jon [*sic*] 1s., John Thorndon de forde 1s., Stephen Roberd 4d., Richard Coupere 2s. 6d., John de Parke 3s. 4d., Will Catteron 4d., Walter Russell 1s., [*column two*] Thomas Combe 'hosier' 1s., Nicholas Taillour 8d., Geoffrey Sergant 6d., John Glouchestre 6d., John Tytfeld 4d., Thomas Dawy 2d., Robert Asman 1s. 4d., Richard Loundon 1s., Thomas Feraund 2s., Thomas Mil' 6d., John Still' 4d., John Lily 2d., William Purchas 8d., Edward Goudesire 8d., John Estbury 3s. 4d., Roger Bythewode 8d., John Okford 1s., Robert Deiher 2d., Thomas Duke 4d., John Everard 3s. 4d., John Stork' 6d., William Skynner 8d., William Fywyan 2s., Nicholas Schute 2s., Thomas Stull' 8d., William Charlyng' 3s. 4d., William Dounnyng' 3s., Edmund (*Ed's*) Barbour 2d., John Chalk' 4d., Thomas Casbrok' 2d., John Gordon

2d., Simon [?] (*Sy'me*) Bradele 5s., John Helier 3s., John Wybet 4d., John Smythes 4d., William Deiher 4d., Richard Wite 4d., John Nell' 8d., John Schyfford 6d., Adam Moris 4d., Christian Duyn 2d., Richard Goldynge 4d., Reynold Wicford 1s. 4d., William Hosbrig' 6d., John Bradele 6d., John Wilkes 1s. 4d.

223D. [f. 78b verso] John Gay 6d., Thomas Warlond 4d., Nicholas Swyndron 1s., Richard Tanner Swyndron [? *for* Richard Swyndon 'tanner'] 1s., Edmund Wytteney 6d., John Kyng' 1s., John Rainwile 4d., Richard Dorset 6d., Richard Wode 2d., John Clywe 4s., William Hugon 6d., Richard Seger 2s., John Manyford 2d., Robert Pyle 1s. 6d., Purs Puse 6d., John Machon 1s. 4d., John Schute 4d., John Rap 2d., Purs Coppe 4d., William Goudesire 1s. 8d., John Sexteyn 1s. 6d., John Tomsyn 4d., Ralph Lokier 1s. 6d., Edward (*Ed'us*) Bryt 2d., Stephen Ride 4d., Edward Frithes 12s., William Fulham 4d., Richard Houpere 1s. 4d., Purs Dawe 6s. 8d., John Fraunkeleyn 4d., John Hamby 'wemakier' [? *i.e. roadmaker*] 4d., John Monour £1 6s. 8d., Thomas Blechere [3s. 4d. *crossed out*, 5s. *crossed out*] 4s., John Bampton 4d., John Mergo 4d., Richard Spenser 6d., John Smythes 4d., William Weler 4d., Thomas Abbot 4d., William Smythes 'wolmonger' 8d., John Momfort 1s., John Hor' 1s. 4d., William Kyttes 1s. 4d., William Osteler 4s., Andrew Plomer 18d., Thomas Scherman 4d., William Bevere 3s. 4d., [*column two*] John Ryngwode 8d., Agnes Martyn 4d., William Grene 1s., John Asford 1s. 4d., Thomas Sadeler 6d., Roger Laungerygg' 1s., Richard Nedler 4s., Sybon [?] Tannere 6s. 8d., William Well' 1s., John Berton [1s. 6d.] 1s., Thomas Norton 4d., William Vyntenere 2d., John Parch' 6s. 8d., William Pouke 4d., John Tyrres 4d., Robert Wrygyl 4d., William Pagton 3s. 4d., Thomas Moris 6d., John Wauntyng 2s., John Watte 4d., Edmund (*Ed's*) Pope 4d., Thomas Notyngham 6d., John Lake [9s. *crossed out*] 8s., Henry Cokour 6d., John Litle 6d., George Corveser 1s. 4d., John Fysche 4d., Thomas Cooke [8d. *crossed out*] 1s., Robert Masson 4d., Thomas Childe's wife 6d., Robert Juwel 4d., William Dynton 4d., John Well' junior 4s., John Barnabe 2d., William Dainton 6d., John Mannyerg' 1s., Agnes Aleyn 4d., Maud Wynpeny 2s., Frie [*sic*] Bouchorcus (*Boucho'9*) [8d. *crossed out*] 1s., Nicholas Dovere 8d., Jakes [*sic*] 1s., William Ropere 8d., Thomas Roukbrigg' 2s. 6d., Thomas Chaundeler [5 *crossed out*] 1s., Dalewode [*sic*] 1s., John Bracy 8s., Harold [*sic*] 4d., Edward Chaundeler 4d., [f. 78c; *a narrower leaf, with a single short column*] Laurence Chaundeler 4d., John Bryd junior 1s. 4d., John Foxham 1s., Adam Spisour 1s., John Wynch 1s., John Bate 4d., Houchon Irmonger [*sic*] 1s. 4d., John Fox 1s. 8d., John Knoll' 2s. 6d., Maud Mates 4d., John Barneis 6d., William Chepman [3s. 4d. *crossed out*] 3s.

Sum £30 [2s. *crossed out*] 16s.

[f. 78c verso, *blank*]

[f. 78d]

223E. St. Martin's ward.

John Masson 'webber' 2s. 6d., John Deiher 8d., Roger Fadour 2s. 6d., Nicholas Pile 3s., Thomas Doly 4d., Thomas Deiher 4d., William Frer' 1s. 6d., Richard Hakeleston 4d.,

Richard Cristechurche 8s., John Stoppe 5s., John Par' 4d., William Sywyer 4d., Walter Pynkebrygg' 6d., John Toly 4d., John Hayne 6s. 8d., William Clerk' 1s., John Forest 4s., John Broneston 4s., William Penyton 2s., Richard Weston 8d., [John Hampton 'brewer' 5s. *crossed out; see below*], Robert Deiher 6d., John Besaunt 2d., John Forest 2d., John Schute 2s. 6d., John Brewer 1s. 8d., Simon Lawyngton 4d., Robert Belde 4d., Richard Deiher 2d., John Hert 4d., Richard Taillour 4d., William Asselyn 1s., Thomas Wytynge 4d., Robert Pettisfeld 4d., Nicholas Schawe 4d., Haiward Webb' 4d., Thomas Riede 'taillour' 6d., Robert Loord 4d., Thomas Hayne 6d., John Formage 4d., Richard Gor' 1s., John Lord 4d., [*column two*] Thomas Viryng' 1s. 4d., William Chapour 1s., John Blaneford 6d., John Wykeham 1s., Thomas Farle 4d., John Charlton 2d., Richard Touk' 2d., John Snow 2d., Thomas Pentrygge 1s., William Stoute 3s. 4d., Walter Mede 2s. 4d., John Deiher 3s. 4d., John Grym 4d., Robert of Willam 2d., John Fysch' 2d., John Hardynge 4d., Laurence Role 1s., Roger Bevez 2d., Robert Forest 3s., John Boteler 6d., William Chepman 6d., John Hampton 'brewer' 6s. 8d., Thomas Chepman 4d., Hugh Cappe 4d., Edward Edolfe 4d., Henry Taillour 6d., John Kymrygg' 4d., Richard Colier 2d., John Porton 2d., John Huwysche 2s. 6d., John Wykam 4d., Richard Kynggeston 2d., John Cofe 4d., John Mulward 4d., Thomas Attemull' 4d., Edward Mede 2d., William Mede 2s., Thomas Wiot 1s., George Clatford 3s., Walter Averyll' 2d., John Swaulclyf' 1s., Thomas Bouer 12s.

223F. [f. 78d verso] Robert Pynard 1s., Henry Westbury 4d., John Doget 4d., Thomas Dancastr' 1s., John Crac 2d., Eustace Taillour 6d., Walter Orcoppe 6d., William Deller 2s., Thomas Coupere 8d., John Todeworthe 6d., William Taillour 4d., John Wilton 4d., John Cristechurche 4d., Robert Launge 1s. 8d., Robert Pomfray 1s., John Raundolf and Cat [*sic*] 1s., Malyn Tylt' 6d., William Hor' 6d., John Wroxale 4d., John Wymbourne 4d., Thomas Barbour 6d., Saundr' [? *i.e. Alexander*] Taverner 4d., John Lycfeld 6d., Henry Helier 1s., Nicholas Brynkenham 6d., John Brynkenham 4d., Cristian Pynnok' 4d., James [*sic*] Mabour 1s., John Warwik' 5s., William Mor' 1s. 4d., John Dale 3s. 4d., John Charlyng' 3s. 4d., William Wolmonger and his brother John 1s., Nicholas Babbe 1s., Thomas Swayn 1s., Laurence Gogayn and Pudyl [?] 1s. 4d., Henry Caym 1s., John Grene 4d., John Nony 6d., [*column two*] Bossam Wolmonger 6d., Thomas Ropere 6d., Rainold Loder 8d., John Pollard 4d., John Sopere 1s. 4d., Walter Carpenter 4d., Penyton de Wynch' 1s., James [*sic*] Carpenter 2d., Richard Ston' 6d., Thomas Castelton [16s. 8d. *crossed out*] £1, Edward Goudesire 4d., Hor' [*sic*] Wolmonger 1s. 4d., William Barbour [3s. 4d. *crossed out*] 4s., William Rygenham 1s., Robert Ferour [5 *crossed out*] 1s., William White 'taillour' 6d., Thomas Plomer 1s., Robert Vale 4d., John Bottenham 13s. 4d., William Mottellemakier 4d., Purs Skynner 2d., John Peyneoc (*Peyneo'*) 4d., John Taillour 2d., William Compton 2s., John Holl' 1s., John Beauchir 4d., John Kyng' 4d., Hugh Scrywayn 4d. , John Beauchurche 6d., Philip Harrys 8d., Nicholas Alrygg' 8d., William Saundres 4d., Robert Edmond 4d., John Portour 4d., John Coppe 4d., John Hamersmythes 1s., Grete [?] Morwemasse 4d., William Hogyn 4d., John Waram 4d., Alson Alysby 6d., John Baker 6d., John Clerk' 'tannere' 1s. 8d.

223G. [f. 78e] Patrick ('Patrok') Taillour 2d., Nicholas Norys 3s., Alice Coriour 2d., John Riede 'taillour' 2d., Isabel Schuppyst 2d., John atte Mulle 3s. 4d., Roger [Taillour *crossed out*] Staynour 6d., John Broun 'corveser' 6d., Richard atte Mull' 3s. 4d., Purs Taillour 4d., Robert Fysche 4d., Thomas Nasch' 1s. Alson Spenser 4d., Roger Carpenter 6d., William Nedler 6s. 8d., John Cardmakier 6d., John Nettone 6d., John Sampson 5s., William Gevais 1s., Richard Scherman 6s. 8d., John Motesound 3s. 4d., John Chaundeler 1s., John Diker 2s. 6d., John Corskombe 6s., Stephen Touker 6s., Thomas Androw 1s. 8d., Nicholas Hardyng' 10s., William Walter [15s. *crossed out*] 13s. 4d., Henry Colbround' 8d., John Hampton 5s., John Waryn 'touker' 6d., Oliver Touker 4d., John Rowe 1s. 4d., Henry Ston' 6d., John Lauer' 6s., John Colyngbourne 3s., William Gylmyn 1s. 4d., John Pynch' 3s., Henry Wroxhale 6d., [*column two*] Alson Leche 6s. 8d., William Goudale 6d., Robert Stedham 6d., Richard Deiher 6d., John Wattes 4d., John Lomb 1s., Alson Taillour 1s., Thomas Aversham 8d., John Levesham 8s., Edmund (*Ed's*) Mercer 6s. 8d., John Broun 1s., Robert Bowier 4d., John Golyn 6d., Thomas Putton 6d., Richard Page 6d., William Averyll' 4d., John Strode 1s., John Symond [10 *crossed out*] 8d., Robert Deverel 6s. 8d., Robert Cokelot 1s., John Pentrych' 1s., John Momfort 2d., Joan Schuppyster 2d., Thomas Riede 6s. 8d., John Loundon 8d., John Pope 5s., John Wotton 1s., John Hemmyngby 6d., Purs Barbour 2s., John Wite 'touker' 1s. 4d., Thomas Duramton 4d., William Halstede 4s., Adam Douly 4d., Thomas Waget 2d., John Nortfolk' 4d., William Cok' 4d., John Wareyn 4d., John Soper 4d., Stephen Touker 6d., John Martyn 2d.

223H. [f. 78e verso] William Raynold 4s., Henry Sopere 2d., Richard Schapwike 4d., Thomas Bekamdon 6d., Thomas Coppe 4d., Mortemer [*sic*] 2d., Nicholas Bray 1s., John Glastyngbury 4d., Purs Stuward 4d., William Broun 1s., Thomas Masson 6d., John Pope junior 4s., John Combe 4d., Robert Tannere 4d., Robert Fereis 2d., John Dawy 4d., John Chapour 1s., John Horn 6d., John Leche 4d., William Harpour 2d., William Smythes 3s., John Kynggesbury 1s., Thomas Broun 1s., William Basket 3s., John Clerk' 1s. 8d., Thomas Slegg' 2s. 6d., Nicholas Blaunchard 1s., John Hogeman 5s., Kyng' Bakere 1s., William Cockes 6s. 8d., John Cortais 2d., William Purdy 1s. 8d., John Berford 2d., Henry Blakemour 1s. 8d., John Dawe 4d., Richard Medemower 4d., Agnes Lord 8d., Nicholas Lord 1s., John Ferour 2d., [*column two*] Robert Michel 2d., Philip Carpenter 3s. 4d., John Hulle 4d., John Route 4d., Simon Canyng' 2d., Richard Curchill' 4d., John Parson 2d., John Dorset 8d., John Bromle 8s. [8d. *crossed out*], Richard Balfot 8d., Roger Tornour 4d., John Hulle 4d., John Herwy 3s. 4d., Bennet Webb' 1s. 4d., John Truman 1s. 4d., Hugh Tannere 3s. 4d., Walter Gylmyn 8d., John Galoun 8d., John Absolon 1s., John Tenant with his mother 10s., Henry Leker 2s., John Walisman 6s. 8d., William Crede 1s., William Godde 1s. 8d., John Borne 1s., John Patrek' 6d., William Slegg' 6s. 8d., John Clywe 1s. 4d.

Sum £23 9s. 2d.

[f. 79v.; *faded, stained, and holed*]

224. List of persons assessed to the sum of 100 marks procured (*attornod'*) for the king from the city of Salisbury, to be repaid on the feast of St. Martin [*11 Nov.*] from the half of a tenth and fifteenth granted to the king, for which the tallage of the sum is in Walter Shirle's keeping for the use of the lenders (. . .).

[*In two columns. The abbreviation for* quit, *against most of the names, is added to the left of the name. At the bottom edge of ff.* 79v. *and* 80 *are scribbled figures below each of the first four columns,* £25 3s. 4d., (. . .) 10s., £19 13s. 4d., *and* £11 15s., *which are not the totals for those columns.*]

224A. Henry Man mayor £1, Walter Shirle £1 6s. 8d., William Waryn £1 6s. 8d. quit, Thomas Mason £1, John Judde £1 , Robert Poynant £1, Robert Warmwell £1, John Bromle £1, Thomas Castelton 6s. 8d. , Robert Gilberd £1, Edward Gilberd £1, John Swyft £1, William Warwyk £1 6s. 8d., Richard Coofe £1, John Noble £1, John Shadde 13s. 4d. quit, Thomas Bouer £1, [John Sydenham 13s. 4d. *added and crossed out; see below*], William Shipton 13s. 4d. quit, John Everard 10s. quit, John Machon 13s. 4d. quit, Stephen Lythenard 3s. 4d., John Gage 6s. 8d. quit, John Corscombe 6s. 8d. quit, John Hampton 'grocer' 13s. 4d. quit, William Halstede 10s. quit, John Pope senior 3s. 4d. quit, John Pope junior 3s. 4d. quit, William Cokkes 3s. 4d. quit, Hugh Holurst 6s. 8d. quit, William Clerk 'touker' 3s. 4d. quit, Roger Waleys 3s. 4d., Juliana Webb' 6s. 8d. quit, Thomas Randolf 13s. 4d. quit, Thomas Broun 3s. 4d. quit, John Sydenham 13s. 4d., Stephen Mercer £1 quit, John Hunte £1, John Willy 10s., [*column two*] [*about six lines illegible*], (Thomas?) Freman 10s. quit, William Chyld 10s. quit, John Wyot 6s. 8d. quit, John [Parch *crossed out;* Park *interlined*] £1 quit, Richard Coupere 10s. quit, John Asshford 10s. quit, William Charlyng 10s. quit, Robert Pottere 10s. quit, Thomas Frogge 6s. 8d. quit, John Hampton 'brewer' 6s. 8d., Simon Westby 3s. 4d. quit, John Cammel 6s. 8d., John Colyngbourne 6s. 8d. quit, Edith Mercer 6s. 8d. quit, Thomas Andrew 3s. 4d. quit, Thomas Rede 6s. 8d. quit, Henry Blakemour 6s. 8d. quit, John Hogeman [5s. *crossed out*] 3s. 4d. quit, John Clyve ['brewer' *added*] 6s. 8d. quit, John Griffyth 13s. 4d. quit, William Slegge 6s. 8d. quit, John Teffonte 6s. 8d., Patrick Wefer 3s. 4d. quit, John Hervy 5s. quit, William Prydy 5s. quit, [Roger Waleys *crossed out*] 3s. 4d., John Rede 'brewere' 6s. 8d. quit, Thomas Forster 3s. 4d. quit, Stephen Garveseye 3s. 4d. quit, Gunnora Bowyere 6s. 8d. quit, John Curteys 6s. 8d. quit,

224B. [f. 80; *faded, stained, and holed*] Thomas Wilteshire 3s. 4d., Robert White 5s. quit, Thomas Artour 'skynnere' 5s. quit, John Duychesman 6s. 8d. quit, Walter Elisabeth 6s. 8d. quit, John Clyter 6s. 8d., John Fletchere [*added later between the lines*: sol' h'berd, *the meaning obscure*] 6s. 8d. quit, John Swyft 'diere' 6s. 8d. quit, John Wynchestr' 13s. 4d. quit, John Dale 3s. 4d. quit, Geoffrey Goldsmyth 10s. quit, Robert Culk(. . .) 6s. 8d. quit, John Spencer 6s. 8d., Henry Swyft 13s. 4d. quit, Robert Levyng 6s. 8d. quit, John Poule 6s. 8d. quit, Agnes Eceshale 6s. 8d. quit, John Warham 3s. 4d., Robert Glover 3s. 4d., John Lymner 6s. 8d. quit, William Basket 6s. 8d. quit, William Avene 13s. 4d. quit, Richard Thornton 3s. 4d. quit, Gervase Galochemaker 3s. 4d., John Gower 5s. quit, William Geveys 3s. 4d. quit, William Chaundeler 6s. 8d., John Stokke 6s. 8d. quit, Richard Boteler 6s. 8d. quit, Richard Mylys 6s. 8d. quit, George Westby 3s. 4d., Richard Artour ['skynnere' *crossed out,* 'corviser' *added*] 5s. quit, John Hunte 'taverner' 6s. 8d. quit, Henry Troune 6s. 8d., Roger Brounyng 5s. quit, William Brounyng 5s. quit, John Helyere 13s. 4d. quit, John Chaundeler 6s. 8d. quit, Robert Pynnere 5s. quit, Thomas Yevele 3s. 4d. quit, William Mercer [3s. 4d. *crossed out*] 6s. 8d. quit, Thomas Bugbrigge 3s. 4d. quit, [*column two*] John Bracy 13s. 4d. quit, John Tissebury 'grocer' 3s. 4d. quit,

John Stork 6s. 8d., Thomas Beton 3s. 4d. quit, Joan Knoll(. . .) 6s. 8d. quit, Thomas Cardmaker 3s. 4d. quit, John Broun 'bocher' 6s. 8d., John Webbe 3s. 4d. quit, John Houchyn 10s. quit, John Charlyng 6s. 8d. quit, William Harnhull' 5s. quit, Nicholas Ingoll' 6s. 8d. quit, Robert Longe 3s. 4d. quit, Richard Gage 13s. 4d. quit, Richard Gatour 6s. 8d. quit, Gilbert Tannere [13s. 4d. *crossed out*] 6s. 8d. quit, William Grym 3s. 4d., Henry Hamme 10s. quit, William Bever 5s., William Gloucestre 6s. 8d. quit, Peter Dawe 6s. 8d. quit, Robert Rede 13s. 4d., Thomas Payn 6s. 8d. quit, John Clyve 6s. 8d. quit, William Godezer [5s. *crossed out*] 3s. 4d. quit, John Brewere 5s. quit, John Mason 'webber' 5s., Nicholas Pyl 6s. 8d., John Hayne 13s. 4d., William Penyton 5s. quit, Walter Mede 6s. 8d., Richard Gore 3s. 4d. quit, Richard Sherman 10s., Thomas Foul 3s. 4d. quit, Christina Doudyng 6s. 8d., Nicholas Shute 5s. quit, Simon Bradele 10s. quit, John Helier' 6s. 8d. quit, William Writhe 6s. 8d. quit, George Joce 3s. 4d. quit, William Chaumb' 6s. 8d. quit, John Bradele 3s. 4d. quit,

224C. [f. 80v.; *faded, stained, and holed*] [*a single column*] Robert Chynchon 3s. 4d., Thomas Danyel 10s. quit, John Chippenham 6s. 8d. quit, Henry Mautravers 6s. 8d. quit, John Pycard 3s. 4d. quit, William Prangnel 3s. 4d. quit, John Marchal 6s. 8d. quit, John Daubeney 10s. quit, John Cornyssh 6s. 8d. quit, William Chepman 6s. 8d. quit, [John Hampton 'brewer' *crossed out*] 6s. 8d., John More 13s. 4d. quit, Thomas Chalsey 6s. 8d. quit, Henry Loweyn 3s. 4d. quit, William Preston, John Motesfonte, Richard Balfot, John Hobbes [*no amounts entered for the last four*].

[f. 80b, *an inserted strip of parchment, numbered* 80b *on the recto,* 80a *on the verso*]

225. [*Miscellaneous notes.*] The collectors of one tenth paid on the feast of the Purification [*2 Feb.*] the year within written and of another tenth on the feast of St. Martin [*11 Nov.*]. The same collectors' account. From arrears of William Basket £1 19s. 0½d. Parliament on Monday next before St. Martin 1 Hen. VI [*9 Nov. 1422*]. Citizens at the said parliament: Walter Shirle, Henry Man. Chamberlains: John Noble, Richard Gage. Collectors, with the commissioners: Thomas Freeman 'mercer', John Hunte, and others.

[f. 80a, *verso of the above*]

226. [*Note of elections.*] John Swyft mayor 9 and 10 Hen. V and 1 Hen. VI [*1421–2*]. Chamberlains: John Bremle, Henry Hamme. Auditors: Walter Shirle, William Waryn, John Everard, John Marchal. Fines: £9. Citizens for the parliament held at Westminster 1 Dec. 9 Hen. V [*1421*]: Walter Shirle, Thomas Bouer.

[f. 81; *faded, stained, and holed*]

227. [*Heading:*] John Swyft mayor.

Assembly: Friday after All Saints 9 Hen. V [*7 Nov. 1421*].

Present: John Swyft mayor, [*then in three columns*] Walter Shirle, William Waryn, Walter Nandre, Robert Poynant, Robert Warmwell, John Judde, Henry Man, John Bromle, Thomas Bouer, Richard Gatour, Thomas Rede, John Shad, [*column two*] John Everard, Thomas Massager, Robert Durneford, John Hamme, John (Everard?), John Morys, Gilbert Tannere, John Chippenham, John Marchal, Henry Hamme, William Halstede, [*column three*] John Shute, William Penyton, John Hampton, Thomas Beton, John More, William Phebus, John Poule, Geoffrey Goldsmyth.

Nominated and elected as chamberlains: John Bromle and Henry Hamme, who under the supervision of the mayor and certain other citizens will order the clothing of the Twenty-Four, of the bailiff, and of William Alisaundr' and William Lord at Christmas.

Elected as city auditors of common goods: Walter Sherle, William Waryn, John Everard, John Marchal. Nothing was done about the pipe of wine for the sheriff.

Fined on election day for the office of alderman: John Willy 60s. quit, John Hunt 60s. quit, John Clyve 60s.; John Willy and John Hunte paid the 60s. to the chamberlains on that day. John Clive is to pay at the Annunciation next [*25 March 1422*] by pledge of Robert Gilberd.

[f. 81v.; *stained and holed*]

The key of the common chest which was in the keeping of John Swyft mayor was delivered to Robert Warmwell for safe keeping.

Received: the mandate of William Darell', sheriff of Wiltshire, containing the king's mandate dated 20 Oct. by John, duke of Bedford, Lieutenant (*custod'*) of England, to elect two citizens to attend parliament at Westminster 1 Dec. next. Elected: Walter Sherle, Thomas Bouer.

228. Assembly: Saturday after the conversion of St. Paul 9 Hen. V [*1 Feb. 1422*].

William Darel, sheriff of Wiltshire, has sent to the mayor and citizen's the king's writ for the election of another county coroner in place of John Swyft, who, as the king has heard, is unable to carry out the duties of the office. Elected, to take his oath at the next county court, viz. on Tuesday the feast of St. Scholastica next [*10 Feb.*]: John Bremle.

[f. 82; *faded and stained*]

229. [*Heading:*] John Swyft mayor.

Assembly: Friday after All Saints 9 Hen. V [*6 Nov. 1421*].

Exhibited: the king's letter patent [*reproduced in the entry*] addressed to Stephen Mercer, Henry Hamme, John Hayne and William Basket of New Salisbury for the collection of a tenth and fifteenth granted in the last parliament at Westminster, half to be levied at the Purification next [*2 Feb. 1423*] on the following conditions: [*in English, at verbose length, and with little abbreviation of the words*] those who pay in gold coin, in the form of a noble [*a gold coin of the value of 6s. 8d.*], half noble, or quarter noble ('othir ferthyng') that amounts to the value of 5s. 8d. by weight for a noble, to be allowed an abatement, counting a noble as full payment of 6s. 8d.; if payment in gold coin exceeds the value by weight of 5s. 8d. for a noble, the excess to be credited to the payer; if it falls short the collectors are not to refuse it provided that the payer makes up the value. [f. 82v.; *worn and stained*] [*Continuing in Latin:*] The other half of the fifteenth and tenth to be paid on the feast of St. Martin following [*11 Nov. 1423*], to be levied on the men of the city and its suburbs, from all secular lords and laymen great and small having goods and possessions in the city and suburbs, and also on ecclesiastics with goods arising from lands and tenements acquired after 20 Edward I [*1292*].

Commissioners by virtue of these letters: Stephen Mercer, Henry Hamme, John Hayne, William Basket. Assessors for a whole fifteenth: Edward Dubbere, Thomas Rede, Richard Gage, John Chippenham, John Shute. Collectors of the fifteenth: Thomas Freman, John Hunte, Henry Blakemour, John More. Sum of the whole tenth within the city, from an ancient assessment: £75 0s. 2d.

[f. 83; *faded and stained*]

230. [*Heading:*] John Swyft mayor.

Accounts of Stephen Mercer, Henry Hamme, John Hayne and William Basket, made separately for themselves and for John Hunte, John More, Thomas Freman, Henry Blakemour, collectors of the half of a fifteenth, before John Swyft mayor, Walter Shirle, William Waryn, and others on Friday after Trinity 10 Hen. V [*12 June 1422*].

New Street ward: the said Stephen accounted for £11 19s. 10d. as contained in his rolls: paid to the king £9 4s. 8d., there remaining owed £2 15s. 2d. which he paid on the day of the account to the said mayor in nobles and half nobles of less weight [than 6s. 8d.] by 7s. 1d., which were accepted according to the said commission, and so he was quit.

Market: Henry Hamme accounted for £16 17s. as contained in his rolls and paid (*satisfact'*) to the king, and he was quit.

Meadow: John Hayne accounted for £2 10s. 2d. as contained in his rolls and paid to the king, and he was quit.

St. Martin's: William Basket accounted for £10 13s. 2d. as contained in his rolls, and he was found to be £1 19s. 0½d. in arrears, to be paid a week after the nativity of St. John the Baptist [*1 July 1422*] by pledge of Walter Shirle and William Waryn.

[f. 83v.; *faded and stained*]

231. William Darel, sheriff of Wiltshire, sent the king's summons for two citizens to attend the parliament to be held at Westminster on Monday next before St. Martin 1 Hen.VI [*9 Nov. 1422*] to the mayor and citizens, who in the assembly at the Guildhall (*Guildaula*) elected in the usual way Walter Shirle and Henry Man. Henceforth they were to elect to parliament one old man and one young one.

Assembly at the 'Gildhall': Monday next after St. Luke the said year [*19 Oct. 1422*].

On the said day, with the citizens attending as named below, elections was made in the usual way as below. [*In column on the left, the last three names in a second column*] John Swyft mayor, Walter Shirle, William Waryn, William Alisaundr', Walter Nandre, Thomas Mason, Robert Warmwell, Henry Man, John Noble, Richard Gatour, John Bottenham, Richard Coof, John Bremle, Edward Gilberd, Robert Gilberd, John Shad, John Willyes, Robert Rede, John Sydenham, Richard Gage, John Wodehay, John Hunte, John More, John Motesfont, John Hampton, Stephen Mercer, Heny Hamme, William Chaundeler, John Chippenham, John Morys, Thomas Durneford, John Marchal, William Cokkes, Thomas Massager, William Child, Thomas Freman 'mercer'.

[*To the right of the page*] Elected as chamberlains: John Noble, Richard Gage; as constables: John Noble, Thomas Rede.

[f. 84a, *an inserted strip of parchment, the verso blank and obscured by its mount*]

232. The king's writ, dated Westminster 19 Dec. 1 Hen. [VI, *1422*], to the mayor and bailiffs of the town [*sic*] of New Salisbury for the payment to Walter Shirle and Henry Man, burgesses of the said town at the parliament summoned at Westminster last Monday [*sic*], of £9 4s. for their expenses in coming, staying for 46 days, and returning, each receiving 2s. a day.

[f. 84; *faded and stained*]

233. [*Heading:*] William Waryn mayor.

Assemblies in the Guildhall (*Guildaula*): Monday next before St. Martin 1 Hen.VI [*9 Nov. 1422*] and another Wednesday next after St Gregory that year [*17 March 1423*]. [*It is not clear to which assembly each part of the record relates.*]

[*In column on the left-hand side of the page*] [Present:] William Waryn mayor, Walter Nandre, Robert Warmwell, Henry Man, John Swyft, Richard Cofe, William Warwyk, John Bottenham, Robert Gilberd, Edward Gilberd, John Noble, Thomas Rede, John Shad, Thomas Randolf, William Cok, Richard Gatour, John Hunte, John More, John Clyve, George Joce, John Teffonte, Henry Hamme, John Chippenham, Thomas Danyel, John Hayne, John Shute, William Harnhull, William Child, John Port, Thomas Yevele, Thomas Durneford, John Marchal, Robert Rede.

[*On the right-hand side of the page*] [Agreed:] that in every future election both for the mayor and for other officers and for citizens to parliament, or for any other election, it should not be done by the nomination of any single distinct person (*per denominationem alicuius singularis persone difinitive*).

Also, that the mayor's livery (*liberata*) for the Twenty-Four and the city's counsel each year be henceforth ordered within the fortnight from the nativity of St. John the Baptist [*24 June*].

Elected as assessors of the expenses of the knights or citizens attending parliament by virtue of the writ included herein: Edward Gilberd, Thomas Rede, John Chippenham, John Shute.

A copy of the writ [*above, no.* **232**; *not a literal copy, beginning* Rex maiori *instead of the king's full title, using different abbreviations, and having* burgencibus *for* burgensibus *and* summoniri *for* summoneri.]

The collectors at the next assembly, as contained in another part of the folio, paid the £9 4s. to the said Walter and Henry Man, and they were quit.

[f. 84v.; *faded and stained*]

234. Assembly: Monday the eve of St. Peter and St. Paul [*28 June 1423*]. [*The caption for the assembly comes after the next two paragraphs in the MS., but the dates given show that it should precede at least the second of them, which begins with* Item.]

Collectors for the expenses of the knights [*sc.* citizens at parliament] in the city: Thomas Durneford, William Child for Market and Meadow wards; John Hunte, John Teffonte for New Street and St. Martin's.

William Darell, sheriff of Wiltshire, ordered the mayor and citizens to act on the king's writ, dated Westminster 7 May 1 Hen. VI [*1423*] [*which is quoted at length*]: Because the authority of the coroners appointed by Henry V ceased at his death, the sheriff was by the community's consent to have two coroners elected and sworn, and was to return their names.

Present [*in column on the left-hand side of the page*]: William Waryn mayor, Walter Shirle, Henry Man, Robert Warmwell, John Bremle, William Warwyk, John Swyft, Richard Coof, John Noble, Edward Gilberd, John Willies, William Cokkes, Richard Gatour, John Bottenham, Thomas Randolf, Robert Gilberd, Richard Gage, John Sydenham, John Shute, John Morys, Hugh Androw, John Wantynch', William Clerk, Thomas Massag', William Child, George Joce, Thomas Durneford, John Chippenham, John Marchal, Henry Hamme, John Teffonte, John Hunte, William Ovyng, and others.

[*On the right-hand side of the page*] Elected as coroners: Edward Gilberd, Richard Gatour.

[f. 85; *faded, stained, and holed*]

235. [*Heading:*] W. Waryn.

Assembly: Monday the eve of St. Bartholomew 1 Hen.VI [*23 Aug. 1423*].

Present: Thomas Mason, John Swyft, [*then in a single column*] William Warwyk, John Bremle, Richard Gatour, John Willy, Robert Gilberd, Thomas Randolf, Thomas Rede, John Shad, William Cokkes, John Everard, John Shute , John Teffonte, Thomas Durneford, William Ovyng, John (. . .)al, William Pridy, John Helyer', William Clerk 'touker', Thomas Massyng', Thomas Payn.

By virtue of the writ for electing coroners, because Edward Gilberd, one of the coroners elected, died before the return of the writ, another was elected in his place, to be joined with the other coroner as associate coroner, viz. Richard Gatour and William Cokkes, and the reply of their election was to be delivered to the sheriff.

236. Assembly: Friday next after St. Matthew 2 Hen.V[I] [*24 Sept. 1423*].

Present: William Waryn mayor, Richard Gatour, John Bottenham, Robert Gilberd, William Warwyk, Thomas Mason, Walter Shirle, Robert Warmwell, Henry Man, John Cofe, John Bremle, Thomas Rede, John Noble, William Cokkes, John Chippenham, William Well', William Stout, John Freman, Ralph Somer, John Wantynch, Hugh Androw, John Hampton, John Morys, John Everard, Henry Hamme, Robert Wolf, John Teffonte, George Joce, John Machyn, William Penyton, John Daubeneye, Walter Mede, Thomas Randolf, John More, John Durneford, John Wodhay, Edward Passewell.

Elected, by virtue of the king's writ, dated 1 Sept., for the election of citizens to attend the parliament to be held at Westminster on 20 Oct.: William Alisaundr', Walter Shirle. [*The official return published in* Members of Parliament, *pt. I, p. 307, names Thomas Husee and John Everard as the city's members for that parliament and William Alisaundre and Walter Shirle as members for Old Sarum, a mistake noted in* History of Parliament, House of Commons, 1386–1421, *ii. 24 n..*]

[Ordered:] that the horses of outsiders [*extraneorum*] coming with their cattle to the fair or market within the city be not permitted to stand outside the stable in the oat market (*otu' mercato*) because of the danger which could arise therefrom.

That city butchers should not slaughter their animals in front of Butcher Row ('Bochelrewe') in the common street, but behind Butcher Row, because of the foulness of the rotting remains (*propter abhominationem, turbitudinem, et viliditatem putredorum dictorum animalium*); that they should not render (*liquescent*) [*blank, sc.* fat] by day but in the night; and that they should not remove (*asportent*) the filth or intestines of their animals by day but in the night.

[f. 85v.; *faded, stained, and holed*]

That poulterers and all others carrying or driving their goods (*res*) or victuals to the city for sale (. . .); that the poulterers should not sell their poultry (. . .). [*cf. no.* **419B**.]

Account of William Waryn mayor (. . .) to officials (. . .); for a gift to Walter Hungerford (. . .), 40s.; (. . .), 7s. 8d.; (. . .).

[*An entry, largely illegible, mentioning* Walter (. . .)igle *and* John Botteler *and an arrest.*]

237. Assembly: Monday next before St. Andrew 2 Hen. VI [*29 Nov. 1423*].

Present: the mayor, Thomas Freman, John Bottenham, John Shad, William Cokk', John Bremle, John Swyft, Henry Man, John Noble, Robert Gilberd, Richard Gatour, John Hunte, John Chippenham, John Marchal, Thomas Yevele, John White, John Fobour, John Sampson, William Chepman, John Cotoreys, Robert Pottere, Hugh Androw, William Clerk, Stephen Lythenard, John Machyn, Richard Nedler', George Joce, William Halstede, John Clyve, Gilbert Tannere, Thomas Freman, John Morys, William Penyton, Henry Hamme, Thomas Durneford, John Deverel, William Harnhull, William More.

Ordered: William Alisaundre and William Lord to have their fees and livery from the city, and William Westbury to have his livery, as they used to. And the officers to be retained by the city and to have their liveries for the year.

238. Assembly: Wednesday next after St. Hilary 2 Hen. VI [*19 Jan. 1424*].

Present: the mayor, Henry Man, William Cokk', John Willi, John Bremle, Thomas Mason, Walter Shirle, John Swyft, William Warwyk, Richard Coof, John Noble, Robert Gilberd, Robert Warmwell, Richard Gatour, Thomas Randolf, John Shad, John Hunte, Thomas Freman 'yeman', John Sydenham, John Morys, Richard Gage, John Hampton, William Penyton, Richard Nedler, Stephen Coupere, William Chaundeler, John More, John Chippenham, John Port, John Sampson, William Child, John Shute, William Pakyn, John Marchal, George Joce, William Halstede, Geoffrey Goldsmyth, Thomas Durneford, John Wantynch, William Clerk, Stephen Lytenard, William Knoll, John White, Hugh Androw, John Clyve, John Motefonte, Laurence Drew, William Chepman, John Fourbour, John Hobbes, and Gilbert Tannere.

Ordered: 7 marks and 4s. 6d. which was with the common seal in the common purse, and which came from [fees for] sealing with the common seal, to be looked after by William Waryn mayor. Afterwards on Tuesday next after St. Valentine then next following [*15 Feb.*] in the presence of Thomas Mason, Robert Warmwell, Henry Man, John Swyft, Richard Gatour, Richard Gage, and others the money was placed in the common chest, and so he [the mayor] was discharged.

[f. 85a, *an inserted parchment strip, the dorse being blank*]

239. The king's writ, dated Westminster 22 Nov. 2 Hen. [VI, *1423*] and signed Frank', to the mayor, aldermen, and community of New Salisbury, on behalf of John Becclys, chaplain and parson of the church of Stanton Harcourt, in Lincoln diocese, who has complained that, though a clerk in holy orders, he was elected, contrary to law and custom, to the office of alderman or bedel of the city by reason of his free tenement there: if he is in holy orders, the mayor, aldermen, and community are to desist from compelling him to perform the office and to reimburse any amercements levied from him for that cause. [*The writ is briefly noted in* H.M.C. Var. Coll. IV, *p. 197, which gives it the date 19 Nov.*]

[f. 85b, *an inserted piece of parchment*]

240. The king's second writ, dated Westminster 8 Dec. 2 Hen. [VI, *1423*], to the same on behalf of John Becclis, repeating the the substance of the earlier writ and requiring a reply one week [*20 Jan.*] from St. Hilary, which would also show why they had failed to answer to the earlier writ.

[f. 85b verso, *the dorse of the above writ*]

241. [*Written at right angles to the writing on the front*] Draft certificate by William Waryn mayor, Richard Nedelere, Stephen Coupere, and Walter Ovyng aldermen, and the community to the second writ: no other writ for John Beccles had been delivered to them, they had not compelled John to take the office of alderman or bedel and had not levied money from him as an amercement for that cause; they could not discharge him from the office, but later, by the lord [bishop?]'s favour, he, having willingly sworn to perform the office, appointed Robert Canne as his deputy in the office.

[f. 86; *badly faded, stained, and holed*]

242. [*Heading:*]: W. Waryn mayor.

Elected as constables: John Noble, John Hunte 'mercer'; as chamberlains: John (Swyft?), Thomas Freman (. . .).

[*Several lines that are largely illegible appear to record fines for being excused office, and mention a* payment of 10 marks and (. . . a payment half at) Easter next and half (. . .)].

Afterwards William Alisaundre and Walter Shirle, elected for parliament as appears in another part of an earlier folio [*above, no.* **236**], brought the king's writ for their wages in the usual form. Elected as assessors for the £22 12s.: William Warwyk, Robert Gilberd, Henry Hamme, John Marchal; and as collectors for St. Martin's and Meadow aldermanries: John Pope and John More who answered for £6 11s. 8d. which they paid to William Waryn mayor on Monday 3 July 2 Hen. VI [*1424*], and so they were quit; as collectors for New Street and Market aldermanries: Ralph Pakkere and John Moreys.

243. Assembly: Friday next after St. Matthew 3 Hen.VI [*22 Sept. 1424*].

Present: William Waryn mayor, Walter Shirle, Thomas Mason, Henry Man, John Swyft, Richard Coof, John Nobul, John Hunt 'mercer', John Bromle, William Warwyke, Thomas Randolf, John Bottenham, William Cokkys, John Shad, Robert Gylberd, John Marchel, John Hampton, John More, Stephen Mercer, Richard Nedeler, John Morys, William Amelyn, John Port, William Clerk 'tanner', John Clyve 'tanner', Robert Chynchon. ¶ Walter Shyrle, John Shad, William Cokkys, John Nobul, Thomas Mason, Robert Warmewell, Robert Gylberd, John Wylly, Richard Gage, Gilbert Tannere, George Joce, Henry Hame, Richard Nedeler, Thomas Yevel, John Port, John Sampson, William Chepman, William Knoll, John Clyve, Robert Pyl, Robert Potter, John Morys, John Wodhay, John More, Henry Man. [*The relationship of the two lists, separated by a paragraph mark and having many names in common, is not clear.*]

[f. 86v.; *faded, stained, and holed*]

Particulars allowed to the mayor on his account: [*Largely illegible*] for fifteen yards [of cloth] for the officers at 1s. 8d. a yard, £1 5s.; for (wine for?) for William Fyne, 2s.; for the board (*tab'*) of the chaplain of St. George for this year and a quarter and five weeks (. . .), 5s. S(um?) (. . .) 6d.

244. Assembly: Friday the eve of St. Simon and St. Jude 3 Hen.VI [*27 Oct. 1424*].

[Present:] William Waryn mayor, William Cokk', Richard Cofe, John Bremle, John Swyft, Robert Warmwell, Robert Gylberd, John More, John Nobul, John Clyfe, George Joce, Thomas Danyel, John Everad [*sic*], John Marchal, Henry Hamme, John Chippenham, Richard Nedeler', Hugh Androw, William Chepman, Laurence Drw [*sic*], John Shuth', Richard Gatour, Thomas Randolfe, Thomas Androw.

[Agreed:] William Lord to ride to London to deal with the matter of William Fyns with wise counsel for the lands and tenements of the mill in West Harnham and New Salisbury.

If the chaplain of St. George should happen to be ill so that he cannot be at home with the mayor (*quod non sit domesticus maioris*), the mayor to pay him for each week that he is ill 1s.

To be allowed to the said mayor, for his good diligence during his time of office, £5 for his reward besides his fee.

And for the chamberlains: Thomas Randolf, John Hampton [*unfinished*].

[f. 86a, *an inserted strip of parchment, badly faded and stained, its verso blank and obscured by the mount*]

245. The king's writ, dated Westminster 28 Feb. [*1424*] and signed Haseley, to the mayor and bailiffs of the city of New Salisbury for the payment to William Alisaundre and Walter Shirle, attending the parliament summoned at Westminster on 20 Oct. last, £22 (12s.) [*cf. no.* **242**] for their expenses in coming, staying for (one hundred and thirteen) days [*calculated from the sums involved*], and returning, each receiving 2s. a day.

[f. 87; *badly faded, stained, and holed*]

246. [*Heading:*] W. Warwyk 3 Hen. VI [*1424–5*].

Assembly: Friday a week from St. Martin in the mayoralty of William Warwyk [*17 Nov. 1424*].

[*Much of the upper part of the page is illegible, starting with a list of payments in column on the right-hand side*] (. . .) £2 Robert Warmwell, (. . .) £2 Walter Shirle, (. . .), (. . .) £2 John Bromle, (. . .) John Port, (. . .) John Noble.

Present [*besides about ten names illegible*]: William Waryn, John Waryn, Robert (Basket?), John (Purdy?), George Joce, Stephen (. . .), Walter (. . .), Richard (Nedler?), John Hampton, William Chyld, John (. . .), John Forbour, William Clerk 'touker', Ralph Pakkere, William Harnhull, Stephen (Eyr?), Thomas Durneford, John Chippenham, William Ovyng, John Moreys, Robert (. . .), John Clife, William Loord, Walter Short, Robert Wolf, William Chepman.

Agreed: William Alisaundre, William Loord to receive fees from the city (*sint ad feoda civitatis*), and the officers to have liveries from the city (*sint de vestura civitatis*).

The pipe of wine for William Fynderne, sheriff of Wiltshire, to be respited. Afterwards, on consideration by the mayor, William Waryn, Thomas Mason, Robert Warmwell, Henry Man, John Swyft, it was ordered: because the said sheriff promised before them that neither he nor his servants would try to do anything relating to his office within the city without the consent of the mayor for the time being, except where the mayor or his servants failed to act (*nisi in defectu predicti maioris vel servientum suorum*), Thomas Randolf to pay to the said sheriff 40s.; which he later paid on the said condition.

[f. 87v.; *faded, stained, and holed*]

247. Assembly: Friday next before St. Gregory 3 Hen. VI [*9 March 1425*], in the mayoralty of William Warwyk.

Present [*in a column on the left-hand side of the page, the last three names in a second column at the foot of the right-hand side, most of the names being followed by the amount of a contribution for the purpose mentioned below*]: William Cokkes 4d., John Shadde (. . .), Richard Coofe 8d., John Swyft (8d. ?), Thomas Masey, William Waryn 8d., Robert Warmwell 8d., Henry Man (. . .), Richard Gatour (. . .), John Bremle (. . .), Robert Gilberd 8d., Thomas Randolf 8d., Johnes Morys 4d., John Marchal 8d.,

John Machyn, John Hampton 8d., William Child 4d., John More 4d., John Gauge, William Chepman, Stephen Mercer 4d., William Dunnyng, John Paule furbisher ('forbour') 4d., William Barbour, John Clyve 4d., Hugh Androw, Thomas Yevele, John Noble 8d., John Willy 8d., George Joce 4d., William Amelyn 4d., Henry Hamme 4d., John Boteler 4d., Richard Nedler 4d., John Walisshman 4d., William Clerk 'touker' 4d., Radulf Pakker 4d., William Arnhull 4d., Stephen Hert 4d., Thomas Durneford 4d., John Chippenham 8d., William Ovyng 8d., Walter Short 4d., Robert Wolf 4d.

All those written above agreed to be brethren of the hospital or fraternity of the Holy Trinity in New Salisbury; for which William Cokkes undertook to pay 4d. a year for the support and relief of the poor and debilitated of the said hospital [and the others accordingly].

[*On the right-hand side of the page*] Agreed: William Wa(. . .), Henry Man, Robert Warmwell, Thomas Randolf, William Lord to deal with (*communicent*) (. . .) David Cervyngton for his estate which he claims in the lands and tenements in West Harnham late John Pynnok's.

[f. 88a, *an inserted strip of parchment, the verso blank and obscured by its mount*]

248. The king's writ, dated Westminster 20 Nov. 4 Hen. VI [*1425*] and signed Haseley, to the mayor and bailiffs of the town [*sic*] of New Salisbury for the payment to William Alisaundre and Henry Man, burgesses at the parliament summoned at Westminster on 30 April last, of £16 for their expenses in coming, staying, and returning, viz. for eighty days, each receiving 2s. a day.

[f. 88; *badly faded, stained, and holed*]

249. [*Heading*;] W. Warwyk.

Assembly: Friday next after Easter 3 Hen. VI [*13 April 1425*].

Present [*in four columns, nearly all of the first lost because of a large hole*]: W(. . .) (William?) Alisaundre, (. . .), [*column two*] John Moreys, Laurence Drewery, Thomas Durneford, John Hampton, John Bottler, William Knoll, John (Port?), William Chyld, Thomas Freeman, William (. . .), Robert (Pesor?), [*column three*] John Willy, John Co(. . .), Thomas (Shadde?), John Charlyng, John Everard, Henry Hamme, John (Marchal?), George Joce, John Wodhay, John Griffith, [*column four*] Nicholas Ha(rdyng?), William Ovyng.

William Fynderne, sheriff of Wiltshire, sent to the mayor and citizens a writ, dated at his exchequer at Fisherton 4 April 3 Hen. VI [*1425*], quoting the king's writ for elections to a parliament to be held at Westminster on 30 April next. [*The entry begins as a report, but quotes the wording of the king's writ, without the date at the end, and continues with the final wording of the sheriff's writ.*]

Elected by virtue of this writ: William Alisaundre and Henry Man. To whom was paid by virtue of the writ below, £16. [*Cf. no. 248, bound in before no. 249 but at the bottom of the book, so that it appears below.*]

[f. 88v.; *faded, stained, and holed*]

250. Assembly: Friday next before St. Simon and St. Jude 4 Hen. VI [*26 Oct. 1425*] in the mayoralty of William Warwyk.

Present: William Cokkes, John Swyft, Thomas Mason, Robert Warmwell, John Bremle, John Noble, (. . .) Randolf, Robert Gilberd, John Morys, John More, John Everard, Thomas Hamme, John (. . .), John Wodehay, Richard Gage, John Chippenham, Richard Gatour, Henry Man, Richard Cofe.

Elected as assessors of the expenses of the knights [*sc.* citizens at parliament] for eighty days, which [expenses] extend (. . .): John Bremle, John More, John Noble, John Chippenham; as collectors: Geoffrey (. . .)[Goldsmyth?], Peter (Gys?), Henry All(. . .).

Elected as constables: John Noble, John Cammel.

Allowed to the mayor for his expenses, besides the £10 of his fee, £1.

Settlement of a dispute between the mayor and William Waryn on the one part and John Hunte, a governor (*presidem*) of the Twenty-Four on the other. In Whitsun week 3 Hen. VI [*27 May–2 June 1425*] at the time of the market the said John had an outsider to run a stall there, contrary to the mayor's limitation and will, to his detriment, and challenging his authority (*in derogationem et status sui reprobationem*). When William Waryn supported the mayor in this matter, as he was bound to do (just as John Hunte and all others of the Twenty-Four were obliged to assist the mayor for the time being in what he did), John scurrilously and falsely challenged William, using improper and unfitting words in the presence of the crowd, contrary to his oath. It was decided by Robert Warmwell, Henry Man, John Swyft, Thomas Mason, John Bremle, John Noble, Thomas Randolf, and Richard Gatour, to whose correction John Hunte had submitted himself, that he be discharged from the office of city constable, that as an example to others henceforth he no longer attend meetings [?] (*in nullo modo decetero se intromittat*), and that he feast all the citizens or pay £1 for a banquet.

[f. 88a [*bis*], *an inserted piece of parchment, the dorse blank*]

251. Writ from Walter Pauncefot, sheriff of Wiltshire, dated at his exchequer at Fisherton 31 Jan. 4 Hen. VI [*1426*] to the mayor and bailiffs of the liberty of the bishop of Salisbury of the city of New Salisbury, quoting in full the king's writ, dated Westminster 7 Jan. 4 Hen. VI, for a parliament to be held at Leicester on 18 Feb. next. The sheriff required a reply a week before the date of the parliament. [*The king's writ is printed in full in Report on the Dignity of a Peer, iv. 863.*]

[f. 89; *faded, stained, and holed*]

252. [*Heading:*] In the mayoralty of William Warwyk.

Assembly: Friday after the Purification 4 Hen.VI [*8 Feb. 1426*].

Present [*in three columns, much of the first lost because of a large hole*]: (. . .)John (. . .)el , W(. . .), John (. . .), R(. . .), (Robert Warm?)well, (William Wa?)ryn, [*three names wholly lost*], (Thomas Ran?)dolf, (. . .), [*column two*] Robert Gilberd, Richard Gatour, John Marchall, John Scha(dd)e, John Willyes, John Bottenham, John Boteler, Henry Hamme, William Chepman, Laurence Drewe, William Amelyn, [*column three*] Simon Paye, William Arnold, Thomas (Freman?), John Chippenham, Thomas (Feraunt?), Hugh Androw, John Sampson, John Moor, John Moreys, Thomas Davy, William Halstede, William [*blank*].

From fines in William Warwyk's mayoralty 4 Hen.VI: Laurence Grome chaplain £3, Robert Chynchon £3, [William *crossed out*, John *interlined*] Wyot £2 10s., John Helier £2, and Thomas Frogge £3, pledge John Bremle.

Elected, by virtue of the said writ [*above, no. 251*], to the parliament at Leicester: Henry Man, John Bremle.

[f. 89v.; *badly faded, stained, and holed*]

Fines: John Everard £3, John Wyot £3, Laurence Grome £3, Robert (C)hynchon £3; John Heliere £3, (Thomas Frogge?) £3; (. . .). [*The list overlaps with that in the penultimate paragraph above.*]

253. Assembly: (. . .) St. Barnabas 4 Hen.VI [*before or after 11 June 1426*].

(. . .) [*The illegible part evidently included a record of the king's writ for the payment of the expenses of Henry Man and John Bromley in attending the parliament at Leicester on 18 Feb. 1426.*]

Elected by virtue of the above writ as assessors of the wages of the citizens [in parliament] written on the other part [of the folio]: John Noble, Thomas Randolf, John Chippenham, John More; as collectors: for New Street aldermanry, John Wexchaundeler; for Market, William Jones; for St. Martin's, Richard Thornton; for Meadow, Richard Walker.

[f. 90; *badly faded, stained, and holed*]

[*Heading:*] W. Warwyk.

[Agreed:] The livery for [the visit of] the duke of Gloucester to be motley green with contrasting green with a red hood (*motle virid' separatim cum virid' cum rub' cap'*), to be chosen by Richard Gage, Robert Warmwell, John Hunte, and John More.

(. . .) to Walter Hungerford, sheriff of Wiltshire, (. . .).

(. . .)

(. . .) by virtue of the said writ (. . .) Warwyk mayor.

(. . .)

254. The king sent his privy seal writ as follows: [*in French, quoted verbatim*] dated Westminster 8 July 4 Hen.VI [*1426*]. The king requires for the defence of the realm a large sum of money and has commissioned the Lord Hungerford, the dean of Salisbury, John Beaucham knight, and Robert Andreau esquire to treat with the city for a loan.

Assessed, by virtue of the above letter, for the sum of 100 marks [*most of the names have* quit *written to the left, indicating payment or repayment of the loan*]: William Warwyk mayor £1, William Waryn £1 11s. 8d. quit, Thomas Mason 13s. 4d., [Robert *crossed out*, William *interlined*] Warmwell £1 quit, Henry Man 13s. 4d. quit, [John Swyft 13s. 4d. *crossed out*] quit, [Richard Gatour 10s. *crossed out*] quit, John Bromle 13s. 4d. quit, John Noble 10s., Thomas Randolf 13s. 4d., Thomas Freman 13s. 4d. quit, Robert Gilberd 13s. 4d., Richard Coof 13s. 4d. quit, John Hunte 'mercer' 13s. 4d. quit, Richard Ecton 6s. 8d., John Marchal 6s. 8d., [William Cokk' 10s. *crossed out*] quit, Joan Shirle 13s. 4d. quit, John Willy 10s. quit, John Bottenham [*blank*], John Cammel 6s. 8d.quit, John Shad 6s. 8d., [*then in three columns*] John White 'mercer' 6s. 8d. quit, Robert Levyng 'sadiler' 6s. 8d. quit, Geoffrey Goldsmyth 6s. 8d., Richard Boteler 6s. 8d. quit, William Avene 'skynnere' 6s. 8d., John Talwchaundeler 6s. 8d., John Helyer 'yrmonger' 6s. 8d., John More 'baker' 6s. 8d. quit, William Charlyng 6s. 8d. quit, John Charlyng 6s. 8d. quit, John Hampton 6s. 8d., John Teffont 6s. 8d. quit, John Colyngbourne 6s. 8d., [*column two*] Nicholas Pyl 6s. 8d. quit, Gilbert Tannere 6s. 8d., Thomas Davy 6s. 8d., John Pope 6s. 8d. quit, John Boteler 'mercer' 6s. 8d. quit, Robert Chynchon 6s. 8d., William Halstede 6s. 8d. quit, John Griffith 6s. 8d., John Hayne 6s. 8d., John of Port 6s. 8d., William Chapman 6s. 8d. quit, Thomas Danyel 6s. 8d. quit, John Morys 6s. 8d. quit, [*column three*] John Chippenham 6s. 8d., John Helier 6s. 8d. quit, Robert Pottere 6s. 8d. quit, Nicholas Shute 6s. 8d. quit, William Shipton 6s. 8d. quit, Stephen Mercer 6s. 8d. quit, Richard Payn 6s. 8d., William Jonys 6s. 8d. quit, John Wyot 6s. 8d., Richard Gage 6s. 8d., John Houchyn 6s. 8d. quit, John Gerveys 6s. 8d., William Brounyng 6s. 8d. quit, [f. 90v.; *faded, stained, and holed*] [*in a single column*] Thomas Freman 'yeman' H [?], William Phebys 6s. 8d. quit, Robert Watercombe 6s. 8d., Peter (. . .) 6s. 8d. quit, Richard Sherman 6s. 8d. quit.

255. [Assembly?]: (. . .) Sept. (. . .).

Present [*in two or more columns*]: Thomas Mason, Robert [?] Warmwell, John Swyft, John Noble, Richard Ecton, Thomas Randolf, Richard Gatour, Thomas Freman, John Willy, Robert Gilberd, [*column two*] Stephen (. . .), John Carpenter, John B(. . .), John

Paule, William Knoll, John Port, Richard Payn, William Cokkes, William Brounyng, Roger Brounyng. [*There were possibly two more columns, no longer legible.*]

Afterwards, on the following Tuesday, Roger Trubody, undersheriff of Wiltshire and servant of the Lord Hungerford, treasurer of England, [came] bringing with him a tally from the king's Exchequer for the said 100 marks to be repaid to the mayor and citizens, endorsed thus: from John Foxhol' and William Sopere, collectors of the subsidy of 3s. on a cask [of wine] and 1s. on a pound [of wool] in the port of the town of Southampton, arising from the same subsidy after the feast of St. Martin next to come, for the men of the town of Salisbury for the money loaned. *Pasch'* [?] 29 Aug. 4 Hen.VI [*1426*].

256. [*In red ink.*] Arbitration made at New Salisbury on Monday next after St. Matthew 5 Hen.VI [*23 Sept. 1426*] between William Warwyk mayor on the one part and Thomas Freman 'mercer', one of the Twenty-Four, on the other, about certain controversies and falsehoods (*inhonestis oblequiis*) touching the said mayor and perpetrated by the said Thomas, by virtue and authority given by the parties to the arbitrators below, viz. [*in three columns*] William Waryn, Thomas Mason, Robert Warmwell, Henry Man, John Swyft, [*column two*] John Noble, John Bremle, Richard Cofe, Thomas Randolf, John Huntte, [*column three*] John Wylly, Richard Gatour, Robert Gilberd, John Bottenham, William Cokkis, Richard Ecton, John Schadde: the said Thomas to pay as reprisal (*vadiet*) a pipe of red wine to the said mayor, for his forgiveness, and to pay 20s. for a breakfast for twenty-four of the city's good men. Further, ordered by the agreement of all the said arbitrators and of the said good men and of John Cammel and John Marchel, two of the Twenty-Four: anyone of the said men who maliciously utters scandalous or false words against the mayor for the time being, on its being proved in due form, to incur a penalty of a cask of wine to the value of £5 to be given to the mayor for the use of the said Twenty-Four.

[f. 91; *faded and stained*]

257. [*Heading:*] John Bremle then mayor.

Assembly: Friday next after one week from Easter 6 Hen.VI [*16 April 1428*].

[Present, *in three columns*:] John Cammel, John Swyft, William Warmwell, Thomas Mason, John Waryn, William Alisaundr', John Noble, John Willy, William Mohun, John Frend, Hugh Androw, Roger Balfot, Robert Chynchon, John Pakkere, [*column two*] John Knoll, John Aport, Henry Hamme, William Dunnyng, Stephen Hert, Richard Wyse, Geoffrey Goldsmyth, John Clyve, John More, John Moris, Elias Plomer, Walter Short, John Crykmour, [*column three*] John Hampton, Robert Warmwell, John Franklayn, William Chaundeler, William Chepman, Thomas Randolf, John Skot, William Clerk 'toukere', Robert Chamberlayn, John Boteler, Henry Man.

Assessors for the expenses of the citizens [at parliament]: Robert Warmwell, Henry Man, Henry Hamme, John More; collectors: John Wyte, William Knoll, Richard Balfot, [*a name erased and illegible*], William Brounyng [*all five names struck through*]. Constables: William Pakyn, John Bottenham. Collectors [*perhaps in place of those struck through above*]: New Street ward, William Brownyng; Market, Robert Canne; St. Martin's, William Wrythe; Meadow, Stephen Catelyn.

258. Assembly, at the 'Counseilhous' because the king's *Vet'r Est* [?] occupied the guildhall (*Gildaulam*): Tuesday the morrow of St. Luke 7 Hen. VI [*19 Oct. 1428*].

Present: John B. mayor, [*then in five columns*] William Waryn, William Alisaundr', Robert Warmwell, Henry Man, John Noble, William Warwyk, Richard Gatour, Thomas Freman, John Marchal, John Bottenham, Thomas Randolf, [*column two*] John Cammel, John Shad, William Cokk', Stephen Coupere, Henry Hamme, Richard Gage, Thomas Freman 'yeman', Richard Ecton, John Chippenham, John More, Elias Plomer, John Deverel, [*column three*] John Everard, John Machyn, Henry Frend, Ralph Pakker', George Joce, Walter Short, Thomas Durneford, John Moris, Robert Gilberd, Robert Ferour, John Boteler, John Teffonte, John Hampton, [*column four*] William Clerk, John Pope, John Colyngbourne, John Gage, William Chepman, John Griffith, William Phebys, John Paule 'fourbour' [*i.e. furbisher*], John Clerk 'lymnour' [*i.e. illuminator*], John Wyot, William Charlyng, William Halstede, [*column five*] Peter Barbour, Hugh Androw, William Gloucestr', John Payn, William Koull [*sc.* Knoll?], John Wantynch', William Ovyng, William Mouhn, John Wodehay, Robert Watercombe.

Agreed: anyone who has been mayor to be quit of that office for the five years immediately following, provided always that three other suitable men of the Twenty-Four are written down and their names sent to the commons of the city at All Souls on the day of election. Later on the same day by common consent of the commons it [*sc.* the decision] was confirmed by protestation.

[*In the narrow space between that and the following entry* Let him be elected mayor etc. (*eligatur maior &c.*) *has been added; it is not clear to what the words relate.*]

Walter Short to hold his tenement for term of his life and his wife Margaret's from the mayor and community without any rent except a red rose at the nativity of St. John the Baptist [*24 June*], so that they maintain the said tenement in all things, etc.; and he was to hand over an indenture by which it was granted to him for a term of sixty years for 10s. a year rent.

[f. 91v.; *badly faded and stained*]

259. [*Heading:*] John Bremle [*though he was presumably not mayor for the first assembly below*].

Assembly: Friday next after St. Matthew 6 Hen. VI [*26 Sept. 1427*].

John (Stourton), sheriff [of Wiltshire], sent the king's mandate for electing citizens to the parliament to be held two weeks from Michaelmas next [*13 Oct.*], by virtue of which writ the undermentioned citizens [*the list, mostly illegible, is apparently in four or five columns*] H(. . .), (. . .), John (. . .), John (Danyel?), William Massenger, John (Marchal?), John Bremle, Robert Tannere, John Bottler, (. . .), [*column two*] William (Pakkere?), John Swyft, William (Purdy?), Henry Man, Thomas Randolf, John Freman, Stephen Mercer, (. . .), [*column three*] (. . .), [*column four*] (. . .), Henry Hamme, Stephen (. . .), (John?) Wyot, (. . .) Ferant, (. . .).

Elected to parliament: William Alisaundre, William Warwyk, to ride to parliament on the Friday before. The parliament was adjourned until two weeks from Hilary [*27 Jan. 1428*].

260. John Bromley mayor.

Assembly: Friday the eve of St. Nicholas 6 Hen. VI [*5 Dec. 1427*].

Present [*in four columns*]: John Hunte, John Shad, William Cokk', John Swyft, Thomas Mason, William Waryn, John Noble, Thomas Randolf, [*column two*] John Willy, Richard Gage, John Hampton, William Penyton, George Joce, John Morys, John More, [*column three*] John Griffith, Henry Hamme, Simon Poy, William Clerk, Robert Chynchon, John Machyn, [*column four*] William Mohune, John Paule, Walter Short, William Dunnyng, Robert Warmwell, William Lord.

Ordered: outside fishmongers (*piscatores extranii*) to be separated from the city's (*indiginis*) fishmongers and their place (*stacio'*) to be above the common ditch behind the place of the city fishmongers (*piscatorum civitatis*).

All those having beasts put out for sale to keep to their place at Barnwell Cross ('Bernewell Cros') and Culver Street ('Colverstret') to sell them there.

Walter Short to have and hold the tenement which he holds from the mayor and community quit for term of his life, maintaining that tenement and bearing other charges according to the form of his indenture, paying no rent.

[*f. 92; faded and stained, the lower half of the folio replaced by repair material*]

The city's debtors:

John Swyft [*struck through*] on his account is pardoned for 10 marks; quit because in the common chest. John Hunte [*struck through*] for Nicholas Belle, 8 marks; quit because paid to W. Alisaundre. Thomas Randolf and John Hampton on their account £15 0s. 8¾d.; the same on their other account 1s. 11¾d. Richard Gage on his account £4 17s. 3d. Thomas Frogge for a fine £3; of which he is pardoned by his auditors for £1 10s. William Warwyk for the surplus on a dozen of cloth given to the duke of [Clarence *crossed out,* Gloucester *interlined*] 6s.; the same for the remainder of the wages of the knights [*i.e. citizens at parliament*] in his time 5s. 6d. (. . .). Walter Short (. . .).

From Richard Wyse's fine for being excused the office of alderman in Pakyn's mayoralty £3; pledged by John Noble, John Bremley, and Thomas Freman. From Thomas Davy's fine at the same time £3; pledged by John Noble and John Bremley.

(. . .) fines at the election of Robert Warmwell as mayor 8 Hen.VI [1429], as [appears] two leaves on [no. 264]: John Crykemour £3, pledges Robert Warmwell, Thomas Randolf, Robert Gilberd; Henry Baron £3, pledges John Noble, John Bremle; Richard Payn £3, pledges Richard Gatour, Thomas Freman 'mercer'; [all] paid within the year.

[f. 92v.; *faded, stained, and holed*]]

261. [*Heading*:] William Pakyn then mayor of Salisbury.

Assembly: Friday next after St. Katherine 7 Hen.VI [*26 Nov. 1428*].

Present [*in three columns*]: John Marchal, William Cokk', Richard Gatour, John Swyft, Robert Warmwell, William Waryn, Henry Man, John Bremle, John Cammel, Robert Gilberd, John More, [*column two*] William Phebys, Hugh Androw, Robert Pottere, John a Port, John Chippenham, Thomas Freman, Walter Short, George Joce, Stephen Mercer, John Morys, Richard Gage, [*column three*] William Amelyn, John Everard, Thomas Danyel, John Shad, Thomas Randolf, William Phebys, William Dunnyng, John Wodehay, John Wantynch, Thomas Durneford, John Bo(. . .).

Agreed: the city's counsellors William Alisaundr' and William Lord to be retained for their old fees as appear in the account roll of Thomas Randolf, city chamberlain.

Also, the livery of the mayor and the Twenty-Four [on the feast of?] St. John the Baptist; of the green which the king uses should not be counterfeited by any from the city of Salisbury. And that the stewards of the guilds of weavers and fullers of the city are to be charged annually with warning everyone of their guilds to observe that and for making scrutiny for that and to present offenders to the mayor for the time being by their circumscribed oath.

262. Assembly: Friday in Easter week [*?1 April 1429*].

Present, with the sums which they freely granted for the repair of the common ditch [*in three columns*]: John Marchal 3s. 4d., John Shad 6s. 8d., Robert Gilberd 3s. 4d., William Warwyk 6s. 8d., William Waryn 13s. 4d., the mayor as above 13s. 4d., John Noble 6s. 8d., Thomas Freman 6s. 8d., Richard Gage 3s. 4d., William Dunnyng 1s., Henry Hamme 1s., [*column two*] Thomas Durneford 1s., John Hayne 1s. 8d., John Port 1s. 8d., Elias Plomer 1s., William Knoll 1s., Thomas Danyel 1s., Geoffrey Goldsmyth 1s., John Hampton 3s. 4d., Richard Gatour 3s. 4d., John Bottenham 3s. 4d., Thomas Randolf [*blank*], John Boteler 3s. 4d., Robert Pottere 1s., Henry Man 6s. 8d., John Estbury 1s. 8d., John Willy 3s. 4d., John Paule 'fourbour' 1s., William Chepman 1s., William Swyft 8d., William Amelyn [*blank*].

Further ordered: the citizens to be assessed for the said repair. Elected as assessors: Thomas Freman, Thomas Randolf, Robert Gilberd, Richard Gage; as collectors: William Mouhn, John Griffith; their fellows: John More, Walter Short.

Elected as constable in place of the mayor, as John Bottenham's fellow: Thomas Freman 'mercer'.

[f. 93; *faded and stained*]

263. Assembly: Friday next after St. Agatha 7 Hen. VI [*11 Feb. 1429*].

Present [*in three columns*]: John Marchal, Robert Watercombe, Robert Gilberd, John Shad, Thomas Randolf, Richard Gatour, William Warwyk, William Waryn, the mayor as above, Robert Warmwell, Henry Man, John Bremle, John Swyft, [*column two*] George Westby, Richard Gage, John Everard, Stephen Mercer, Walter Short, John Griffyth, Henry Hamme, Richard Balfot, John Bottler, John Teffonte, William Knoll, [*column three*] John Noble, William Mowhn, Walter Skot, Thomas Freman, Henry Hamme, William K(. . .), Simon Poy, Richard Balfot, William Chyld, Thomas Danyel, William Hamelyn, John Willy, Edward Gudyer.

Ordered: the willows growing in the common ditch, planted by Adam Teffonte, to be uprooted and the ground (*solum*) which John Teffonte appropriated to be remade (*reformetur*). All defects of the common ditch to be put right under the mayor's surveyor.

264. Assembly: Monday the eve of All Saints 8 Hen. VI [*31 Oct. 1429*].

Present [*in three columns*]: John Marchal, William Cokkys, William Warwyk, Robert Warmwell, William Waryn, John Bremle, John Chippenham, Walter Short, Gilbert Marchal, [*column two*] Richard Gatour, Thomas Randolf, John Bottenham, Robert Gilberd, John Boteler, Richard Gage, William Avene, Thomas Durneford, John Crikemour, [*column three*] Richard Wyse, Henry Hamme, John More, Robert Watercombe, William Hamelyn, William Taverner, William Halstede.

Allowed to the mayor, besides the £10 of his fee, 5 marks because when prices were high (*in ista caristia*) he came to the community's aid with corn, so that when a bushel of corn was being sold in the market for 1s. 5d. he sold it for 1s. 1d. to his own detriment.

Agreed: the election or nomination of the mayor should respect the five year rule (*observatur per qinque annos*) as was ordered in the mayoralty of John Bromle, 7 Hen. VI [*1428–9*]. It was confirmed in this assembly.

Officers, ministers, and serjeants elected in St. Edmund's church, according to custom at the feast of All Souls 8 Hen. VI [*2 Nov. 1429*]: mayor, Robert Warmwell. [*Incomplete.*]

Fines [*for being excused the office of alderman*]: H. Baron £3, pledges John Noble, John Bremle [paid Boteler *added*]; Richard Payn £3, pledges Richard Gatour, Thomas Freman [paid Boteler *added*]; John Crikemour £3; pledges Thomas Randolf, Robert Gilberd.

[f. 93v.; *faded and stained*]

265. [*Heading:*] Robert Warmwell [*recte* William Pakyn].

Assembly: Saturday next after the nativity of the Blessed Virgin Mary 7 [*recte 8*] Hen. VI [*the year is clearly written, but it is evident from the election to parliament below that it was in fact 1429, when the Saturday named was 10 Sept. For the date of the parliament see* Handbook of British Chronology *(1986), 568.*].

Present [*the names in pairs, in two columns*]: John Shad, William Cokkys, John Swyft, W. Warwyk, Henry Man, W. Waryn, the mayor [William] Pakyn, George Westby, Robert Warmwell, John Bremle, Richard Gatour, John Boteler, William Touker', John Glasier', [*column two*] John Marchal, William Phebys, Geoffrey Goldsmyth, John Estbury, Robert Gilberd, William Avyne, Walter Short, John Chippenham, John More, Elias Plomer, William Mohun, Gilbert Tanner, William Amelyn, Richard Gatour.

Agreed: a pipe of red wine to be given to the duke of Gloucester.

Also: from the £5 in the keeping of John Noble, which was the fine paid by Thomas Freman 'mercer', 5 marks to be paid to John Boteler and Richard Nedler for two maces ('macys') belonging henceforth to the city to be carried before the mayor by the two city serjeants so long as they behave themselves well. [*The word 'macys' is preceded by a faint word, apparently* musis, *which is perhaps a first attempt, not cancelled, at 'macys'.*]

Elected to attend the parliament to be held at Westminster two weeks from Michaelmas [*13 Oct.*] and until the feast of St. Leonard next following [*6 Nov.*] for the king's coronation: Henry Man, John Bremle.

266. Assembly at 'le Councelhous': Wednesday next after St. Nicholas 8 Hen. VI [*7 Dec. 1429*].

Present [*in four columns*]: John Marchal, Robert Gilberd, Richard Gatour, [*column two*] William Waryn, Robert Warmwell, John Noble, [*column three*] William Alisaundr', William Cokk', John Shad, [*column four*] John Boteler, John Swyft, Thomas Randolf.

It was alleged against Thomas Freman 'mercer', and on behalf of the mayor and citizens it was complained, that he feigned a plea of debt on Friday next before Michaelmas last [*23 Sept. 1429*] under the name of one John Horf of Taunton, when there was none such, in the court of Bristol town, and became pledge in a suit against Thomas [*sic, recte* William] Hamelyn of New Salisbury, their neighbour, in a plea of debt, so that he

[William] was placed under arrest in Bristol for three days; and that he [Thomas Freman] meanwhile, riding about in various parts of Somerset, procured and excited various people to bring actions against the said William in the said court in pleas of debt, in which he owed nothing, as was said; and that he procured others to empanel him in a court of law held at New Salisbury on Wednesday next after St. Edmund the king last [*23 Nov. 1429*] to accuse the said William concerning a knife drawn in breach of the peace by one Thomas Gerveys, whom he supported, against the said William, [the offence being] presented against Thomas Gerveys by the alderman of the place where it happened, which the same Thomas [Gerveys] denied and put himself on [the judgement of] the jury. All those failings redounded not only to Thomas Freman's condemnation but also to [the discredit of] the fellowship (*ritus*) of the Twenty-Four. Even so, on the intervention of his friends and at their supplication, all the aforesaid [offences] are forgiven, and so long as he behaves himself well he is received [back] as one of the fellowship, but if in any of the foregoing or in like matters he offends he is to be expelled for ever.

[f. 94a, *an inserted strip of parchment*]

267. The king's writ, dated Westminster 24 Feb. 8 Hen. [VI, *1430*] and signed Haseley, to the mayor and bailiffs for the payment to Henry Man and John Bromlegh, citizens attending the parliament on the morrow of St. Matthew last [*22 Sept. 1429*], of £28 2s. for their expenses in coming, staying for 141 days, and returning, each receiving 2s. a day.

[*On the dorse*] Paid H. Man £14 1s. [*The date of assembly, originally 13 Oct. as in no.* **265,** *was advanced by writs of 3 Aug. to 22 Sept. The sum paid to each should have been £14 2s., and the total £28 4s.*]

[f. 94; *faded and stained*]

268. [*Heading:*] In the mayoralty of Robert Warmwell.

Assembly: Friday next before St. Nicholas 8 Hen. VI [*2 Dec. 1429*].

Present [*in three columns*]: John Barchal [*sic, recte* Marchal], John Shad, Richard Gatour, Robert Gilberd, William Waryn, the mayor [Robert] Warmwell, John Noble, William Cokk', William Chaundeler, Richard Wyse, [*column two*] John More, John Chippenham, Elias Plomer, John Paule, William Chepman, Robert Chamberlayn, John Wiot, John Griffith, Henry Hamme, Robert Pyl, [*column three*] John Coscombe, Richard Balfot, Walter Serjant, Henry Baron, George Joce, John Skot, Stephen Mercer, Richard Gatour, Thomas Randolf.

Ordered: since the mayor has the keeping of the smaller part of [the letter under] the king's seal of the king for creditors and merchants, William Waryn to have the keeping of the larger part during the said mayor's term of office. [*The significance is not clear, and the construction of the entry is illogical, with 'since' (eo quod) balanced by 'provided that' (proviso quod).*]

Also, those retained by the city to have their fee and to be retained as before.

Also, John Boteler to be city chamberlain.

Also, the officials to be established (*ordinentur*) and to have their livery just as of old.

Also, the livery of the Twenty-Four to be furnished (*ordinetur*) for Christmas of rayed (*stragul'*) cloth as of old.

269. Assembly: Saturday the eve of Epihany 8 Hen.VI [*sic: Epiphany, 6 Jan., fell in 1430 on Friday, so either Saturday is an error for Thursday or the eve is an error for the morrow*].

Present [*in three columns*]: John Cammel, Henry Baron, John Shad, John Bottenham, William Pakyn, John Swyft, William Warwyk, William Waryn, the mayor [Robert] Warmwell, John Noble, John Bromle, Richard Gatour, [*column two*] Robert Tanner', John Marchal, John Boteler, Richard Wyse, Walter Serjant, Stephen Coupere, John Chippenham, John Port, John Gage, Richard Payne, [*column three*] William Knoll, Geoffrey Goldsmyth, John Coscombe, Richart Balfot, Richard Coupere, William Brounyng, William Charlyng.

Exhibited: a commission for [levying] one whole fifteenth granted at the parliament on [?] (*in xvᵗ mᶜ*) [*the grant was made on 20 March*] addressed to Richard Balfot 'taillour', Richard Coupere, William Brounyng smith, and William Charlyng.

Fines for [being excused the office of] alderman: Richard Wyse £3, pledges John Noble, John Bromle, paid Boteler by account; John Wyot £3, pledges William Warwyk, John Bromle, paid Boteler by his account.

[f. 94v.; *faded and stained*]

[*Heading:*] Robert Warmwell.

Assessors for a whole tenth within the city: Thomas Randolf, John Marchal, John Hampton, John Teffont; collectors: John Wynchestr', John White, Nicholas Shute, Robert Chamberlayn.

Agreed: Richard Nedler' and William Swyft serjeants to hold the common ditch encircling the city from the mayor and community for the following year, paying 13s. 4d. a year and to scour, mound, and repair the ditch meanwhile.

270. Assembly: 31 March 8 Hen.VI [*1430*].

Present [*in three columns, the first containing a pair of names on each line except that for the mayor*]: Richard Wyse, John Shad, Robert Gilbert, John Bromle, William Warwyk, Henry Man, William Waryn, John Swyft, the mayor Robert Warmwell, Richard Gatour, John Willy, Richard Gage, Stephen Mercer, [*column two*] Richard Balfot, Robert Pyl, Richard Payn, Gilbert Marchal, John Boteler, John Frend, Robert Levyng, [*column three*] John Coscombe, John Chippenham, Geoffrey Goldsmyth, William Brounyng, William Charlyng, William Swengil.

Agreed: the sum of £44 13s. 4d. which the king was to borrow from the mayor and community, which was to come from the common chest and which was to be repaid from one whole fifteenth from the city at the feast of St. Martin [*11 Nov.*], to be received by the mayor, William Waryn, Stephen Mercer, and Richard Gage for replacing in the said chest. For which [they had] a privy seal [letter], which was placed in the mayor's chest in 'le Councelhous', in these words:

[*In French, at length, summarized here*] Needing money for his proposed expedition to France in April to put an end to the war, the king, by letters under the great seal, commissioned the bishop of Bath, Lord Hungerford the Treasurer, John Juyn knight chief baron of the Exchequer, the dean of Salisbury, Humphrey Stafford, Edmund Cheyne, William Boneville, John Stourton, knights, William Darell esquire, and the sheriffs of Wiltshire, Somerset, and Dorset jointly and severally, to treat with the city for a loan of money and to promise surety in the king's name for repayment.

Agreed: the said citizens to lend to the king 100 marks. And as to the £100 which the citizens had lent King Henry V through the cardinal bishop of Winchester and which were to be repaid by him, Sir Walter Hungerford treasurer of England to receive them from the cardinal to lend them to the present king, and to give surety for repaying them to the mayor and community.

Elected as assessors for the expenses of the citizens [in parliament] which amount to £28 2s. for 141 days as appears in the king's writ sewn in here [*no. 267*]: Richard Gatour, Stephen Mercer, Robert Gilberd, John Chippenham; as collectors: Thomas Payn, Richard Plouman, Edward Gudyer, John Crikemour.

[f. 95; *faded and stained*]

271. [*Two entries which have been struck through and appear to be out of place.*] In an assembly on Friday next after Michaelmas [*the year not stated*] it was agreed that there would be two adequate carts, to be found by four men chosen by the mayor and citizens to maintain the said carts, the more able (*validiores*) and all other inhabitants of the city to pay for the carriage of their ordure (*fimi*) at the discretion of the city stewards (*cenescallorum*). Elected for this: Robert Deverel, William Warmwell, Thomas Bowyere, John Nedlere junior, Richard Spencer, and John Nyweman, at whose discretion the above would be provided.

Wednesday the eve of St. Katherine 13 [Ric.] II [*24 Nov. 1389*]. John Bitterleygh,

Thomas Sevenhampton, John Levesham, John Nedlere junior, John Forest, Edward Coffard, William Woderove, Roger Stapilford, and John Moner were given permission to cover the ditch at St. Edmund's for taking a cart in and out. For this permission they bound themselves jointly and severally to John atte Hether, the mayor, in £10 to be paid to him or his successors without delay if when given reasonable notice they refused, declined, or neglected to close the entry and exit.

272. [*Heading, at the top of the page:*] Robert Warmwell.

Assembly: Saturday 2 Sept. 9 Hen.VI [*1430*].

Present [*the names, except for the last, in threes, in two columns*]: John Shad, John Marchal, Richard Gatour; John Swyft, W. Waryn, the mayor; William Alisaundr', H. Man, J. Bromle; John Noble, Thomas Randolf R. Wyse; John Skot, Richard Wyot, Stephen Hert; Richard Jage [*sc.* Gage], Walter Short, John Deverel; John Everard, John Boteler, W. Emelyn; [*column two*] Robert Gilberd, Geoffrey Goldsmyth, Peter de Verw; Robert Pottere, John Frend, John Machyn; William Mohun, Stephen Mercer, J. Coscombe; Richard Balfot, Robert Watercombe, Hugh Androw; Henry Baron.

Thomas Randolf granted for term of his life for maintaining and repairing the upper bridge at Fisherton for the easement of the poor in time of flood [going] with their carts to the city over the bridge with their loads [*garbled or incomplete*].

Named as city serjeant in place of Richard Nedler: Henry Frend, saving to the commons of the city their free choice of serjeants and other officers on election day, viz. at the feast of All Souls [*2 Nov.*].

273. Assembly: Monday the feast of St. Denis 9 Hen.VI [*9 Oct. 1430*].

[f. 95v.; *faded and stained*]

Present [*in four columns*]: Henry Baron, John Marchal, William Cokkys, John Aport, John Coscombe, William Charlyng, [*column two*] John Noble, William Waryn [*those two names paired on one line*], Robert Warmwell the mayor, George Joce, Henry Man [*those two names paired on one line*], John Alisaundr', Richard Balfot, Richard Boteler, [*column three*] Thomas Randolf, Richard Wyse, John Everard, John Chippenham, Thomas Durneford, Richard Gage, [*column four*] Thomas Freman 'mercer', Gilbert Marchal, Thomas Danyel, Stephen Mercer, William Mohun, Wi [*incomplete*].

Agreed: the old assessors, Thomas Randolf and his fellows, and the old collectors, John Wynchestr' and his fellows, to assess and levy a fifteenth at two weeks from St. Martin next [*25 Nov. 1430*].

Also John Boteler, city chamberlain, to continue in office for the whole year for the usual fee.

Also the city officials, viz. three, to be retained for the whole year for the old wages payable to them.

City serjeants and officers in the mayoralty of Robert Warmwell 9 Hen. VI [*1430*]: reeves, John Hampton, John Wodehay; alderman of New Street, Edward Dauntesey, and he did not take it up etc.; of Market, John Pykk; of St. Martin's, John Coscombe; of Meadow, Richard Balfot; serjeants ('servyntes'), William Swyft, Henry Frend.

Repayments made to the following of sums loaned to the king [*in three columns; each name is preceded by* quit, *and some in the first column are also preceded by* all', *(? for* 'allowed')]: William Alisaundr' £1 (*all'*), William Waryn £1 (*all'*), John Wynchestr' 6s. 8d. (*all'*), William Brounyng 6s. 8d. (*all'*), Robert Watercombe 6s. 8d. (*all'*), Thomas Freman £1 (*all'*), Richard Gage 10s. (*all'*), Nicholas Shute 6s. 8d. (*all'*), John Helier' 6s. 8d., Richard Coupere 6s. 8d., William Jonys 6s. 8d., William Charlyng 6s. 8d., John Hampton 6s. 8d., John White 10s. (*all'*), Richard Gatour 13s. 4d., Richard Boteler 'brewer' 6s. 8d., John Colyngbourne 6s. 8d., [*column two*] John Helyer 'yrmonger' 13s. 4d., John Chippenham 6s. 8d., Thomas Malabre 6s. 8d., William Halstede 6s. 8d., Thomas Randolf [*the surname smudged or crossed out*] 10 marks, Richard Wyse 13s. 4d., William Warwyk £1, John Marchal 6s. 8d., John Noble 13s. 4d., Joan Paule 6s. 8d., John Park 6s. 8d., Peter de Verwe [by H. Frend *interlined*] 6s. 8d., John Griffith 6s. 8d., Geoffrey Goldsmyth 6s. 8d., Richard Payn 13s. 4d., John Shadde 6s. 8d., George Westby 6s. 8d., John Wyot 13s. 4d., Robert Gilberd 13s. 4d., [*column three*] Henry Baron 13s. 4d., Henry Man 13s. 4d., John Crikemour 6s. 8d., John Houchynes 13s. 4d., Thomas Randolf [*again*] 13s. 4d., Stephen Coupere 13s. 4d., John Chaundeler 6s. 8d., Robert Levyng 6s. 8d., Robert Bulk 6s. 8d., John Gower [by H. Frend *interlined*] 6s. 8d., John de Port 13s. 4d., Thomas Danyel 6s. 8d., Gilbert Tannere 6s. 8d., John Coscombe 6s. 8d., Robert Pottere 6s. 8d., John Teffonte 6s. 8d., William Phebys 6s. 8d., John Swyft 13s. 4d., John Hayne 6s. 8d., John Willy 6s. 8d.

[f. 96; *badly faded and stained*]

274. [*Heading:*] Richard Gatour mayor.

Assembly: Saturday next before St. Thomas the Apostle 9 Hen. VI [*16 Dec. 1430*].

Present [*perhaps in column*]: Richard Gatour the mayor, (. . .) Nouble, William Cokkes, (. . .) Balfot, William Pakyn, (Thomas Durn?)eford, Richard Gage, [John Cors?]combe [*and about twelve names illegible*].

Agreed: (William Alisau?)ndr', William Lord, John Boteler, chamberlain (. . .) and officials.

275. Assembly: Friday next after St. James 9 Hen. VI [*27 July 1431*].

Present [*in three columns*]: John S(had?), Richard Gage, Robert Gilberd, John Noble, John Swyft, William Waryn, the mayor [Richard] Gatour, Robert Warmwell, John Bromle,

Thomas Randolf, [*column two*] William Cokkis, Richard Wyse, Thomas Freman, John Boteler, Walter Short, John Clyter, Stephen Mercer, John Chippenham, John Port, John Morys, [*column three*] Geoffrey Goldsmyth, John Alisaundre, Richard Payn, John Griffith, John Coscombe, Edward Gudyer, Thomas Danyel, Robert Chamberlayn, William Charlyng, William Clark, Thomas Durneford.

Elected as coroner in place of the mayor: Robert Gilberd as fellow to William Cokkis.

Agreed and ordered: all houses within the city roofed with straw to be roofed with tiles and not with straw.

Elected as assessors of knights' fees [*sic; i.e. the expenses of the citizens at parliament*]: William Cokkis, John Shad, John Colyngbourne, Thomas Durneford; as collectors: John Alisaundr', John Estbury.

The mayor's account. And later, on the feast of St. Margaret 9 Hen. VI [*20 July 1431; the discrepancy between that date and the date of the assembly, both of which are clear in the MS., may have resulted from either* James *or* Margaret *being written in error for the name of another saint*] at 'le Councelhous' the said collectors paid to the mayor £7, with which he [the mayor] paid to William Pakyn £7 6s., by virtue of the king's writ sewn into this folio [*no. 277*]. And later, on Saturday the morrow of St. Bartholomew next [*25 Aug. 1431*] at the said house there was paid to the mayor £7 12s., with which on Friday the eve of the nativity of St. Mary next [*7 Sept. 1431*] he paid to William Alisaundr' £7 6s. Later, the mayor received from the said collectors £1 8s. 4d., with which he paid to William Broun, Richard Balfot, and William Charlyng 6s. for amends of the fifteenth which they could not levy. [Paid] for a painted clothe ('Peytidcloth') for 'le Councelhous', 5s.; for a mace there, 2½d.; to John Estbury and John Alisaundr', collectors for the expenses of the knights' [*i.e. citizens at parliament*], 6s.; to William Lord for his work and for writing letters to the king and the certificate of tenements held in socage and of rents-seck and everything [?] (*om's* or *on'is*) in the city returned before John Westbury and his fellow justices [*no amount given*]; to William Balfot, 3s. 4d. So Richard Gatour owes on his account £8, which he was to pay at the Purification next [*2 Feb. 1432*]. Later he was to pay £1 at the nativity of St. John [the Baptist] and afterwards £2 term by term until the £8 was fully paid.

[*The calculation above is puzzling. The sums paid by the mayor amount to only 5s. 9½d. less than his receipts. Presumably he had other receipts which failed to be entered in the book.*]

[f. 96v.; *faded and stained*]

276. Copy of a writ from David Cervyngton, sheriff [of Wiltshire], to the mayor and bailiffs of New Salisbury, quoting at length the king's writ for a parliament to be held at Westminster on Friday next before St. Hilary next [*12 Jan. 1431*]. [*At the point where king's writ requires the names of those elected to be returned, the copy ends with*] etc., as written in the mayoralty of William Warwyk by William [*sic, recte* Walter] Paunsfot, sheriff of Wiltshire, 4 Hen. VI, as appears in the eighth folio back [*no. 251*].

276A. Memorandum: Richard Gatour mayor and Henry Man undertook, on Tuesday next after the translation of St. Thomas 9 Hen. VI [*10 July 1431*], to acquit Robert Warmwell towards all who contributed to the loan of £100 to King Henry V. On the same day he [?*recte* they] delivered to the mayor 10 marks, which the same Robert received from Thomas Randolf from the city's goods, and 8 marks, which he received from the wool which the bishop of Winchester delivered to the mayor and community for the said £100.

Also on the said day the mayor deposited 42 marks to be delivered, along with the said sums, to John Honythorn to deliver them to William Alisaundr', who was to receive surety therefor, viz. letters patent with a tally for those sums, viz. £40, in the presence of Robert Warmwell, H. Man, Richard Gage, Stephen Mercer, Thomas Freman, John Boteler, W. Warwyk, W. Lord.

[f. 96a; *an inserted piece of parchment, the dorse blank*]

277. The king's writ, witnessed by the duke of Gloucester, regent (*custode*) of England, at Westminster 20 March 9 [Hen. VI, *1431*], and signed Haseley, to the mayor and bailiffs of the town [*sic*] of New Salisbury for the payment to William Elisaundre and William Pakon, citizens attending the parliament at Westminster on Friday next before St. Hilary last [*12 Jan. 1431*], of £13 12s. [*the correct amount was £14 12s., as in no. 275*] for their expenses in coming, staying for 73 days, and returning, each receiving 2s. a day.

[f. 97; *faded and stained*]

278. [*Heading:*] Henry Man mayor [*though he was not mayor for the first assembly below.*]

Assembly: Tuesday next after St. Denis 10 Hen. VI [*16 Oct. 1431*].

Present: Richard Gatour mayor, William Waryn, Robert Warmwell, Henry Man, John Bromle, John Noble, William Pakyn, John Marchal, Robert Gilberd, John Wyot, John Boteler, Richard Payn, John Port, John Chyppenham, John Colyngbourne, John Houchyn, William Knoll, Walter Short, Geoffrey Goldsmyth, William Halstede, John Alisaundre, John Coscombe, John Gage, John Shadde, Ralph Pakkere, Richard Wyse, John Swyft, Robert Watercombe, Henry Baron, and Thomas Randolf.

Announced by the king's letters patent that the parliament held at Westminster on Friday next after St. Hilary 9 Hen. VI [*12 Jan. 1431*] had granted one whole fifteenth to be paid on the feast of St. Martin [*11 Nov.*] and one third of a fifteenth to be paid at Easter following [*20 Apr. 1432*]. Elected as assessors: William Pakyn, John Aport, John Bromle, John Chippenham; as collectors: Walter Short, William Chyld, Robert Crome, John Purdy; as commissioners: John Coscombe, Roger Brounyng, John Houchyns, Geoffrey Goldsmyth.

279. [Election: 2 Nov.] 10 Hen. VI [*1431*].

In the mayoralty of Henry Man. Serjeants and officers elected: mayor, Henry Man; reeves, John Coscombe, William Halstede; alderman of New Street, William Charlyng; of Market, William Knoll; of St. Martin's, Edward Gudyer; of Meadow, John Hurst of Fordingbridge (*Forþyngbrigge*); serjeants,: Henry Frend, Thomas Yoxford 'chaundler'.

Fines [for being excused office]: William Stamford £3, pledges Richard Gatour, Richard Payn; Bremle r'. William Waryn £3; pledges Richard Gatour, Richard Wyse; Richard Gatour r'. Peter de Verw £3, pledges John Noble, John Wyot; Bremle r'. [*The names with r' appended were added later above the line; the significance of r' is not clear.*]

280. Assembly: Saturday next after St. Edmund the [arch]bishop 10 Hen. VI [*17 Nov. 1431*].

Present: Richard Gatour, Henry Man, John Swyft, John Bromle, William Warwyk, William Cokk', Robert Gilberd, John Marchal, John Shad, John Boteler, Robert Chamberlayn, John Chippenham, John Machyn, William Knoll, William Chrlyng [*sic*], Thomas Randolf, Richard Wyse, Richard Gage.

Elected as chamberlains: John Boteler, John Aport.

Of a fifteenth: memorandum that Roger Brounyng and John Purdy, collectors of the fifteenth in St. Martin's aldermanry [they answer for £17 10s. 7d., *in the margin*], paid on their account to Henry Man, mayor, at the Conception [*8 Dec.*] and the Purification [*2 Feb.*] £17 9s. 7d. and so they go quit for the said year. Ralph Pakker [*not named in connection with the fifteenth in no. 278*] and John Crome, collectors of the fifteenth in Market aldermanry [they answer for £30 6s. 5d., *in the margin*], paid to the mayor on Friday next after the Conception [*14 Dec. 1431*] £19 from the said sum, besides £8 0s. 2d. which they paid to John Coscombe, the king's commissioner for the fifteenth; afterwards they paid by hand of Richard Gage 13s. 4d.; to John Coscombe £9 16s; to the mayor on Thursday next before Whitsun [*5 June 1432*], £1 11s. 7d., and to the same at another time 13s. 4d.; and to the same at another time 7s. 8d. John Houchynes and [Walter Short *crossed out;* William Chyld *interlined*], collectors of the fifteenth [in New Street aldermanry, *in the margin*] paid £21 17s. to John Coscombe. Walter Short [collector in Meadow aldermanry, *in the margin*] paid £5 13s. 3d. to John Coscombe.

[f. 97v.; *faded and stained*]

281. [H*eading*:] Henry Man mayor.

Assembly at the council house (*domum concilii*): Friday next after St. Nicholas 10 Hen. VI [*7 Dec. 1431*].

Present: Henry Man, Robert Warmwell, John Swyft, John Noble, John Bromle, William Pakyn, Richard Gatour, Thomas Randol, Thomas Freman, William Cokkys, Henry Baron, Richard Wyse, Stephen Mercer, John Shad, John Wyot, John Marchal, John Boteler, John Estbury, Simon Poy, Walter Short, Edward Gudyer, William Knoll, William Charlyng, John Coscombe, Robert Gilberd.

Agreed: the mayor's livery to be worn until the bishop's arrival [?] (*differatur usque ad indictionem episcopi*) after Easter, and afterwards to be kept for two years (*habeatur de biennio in biennium*) except for the officials' livery.

Also, Stephen Mercer to hand over to Walter Short the key of the common chest.

Also, William Alisaundre, with the mayor, to encourage Robert Longe, [the bishop's?] bailiff, to have the (. . .) of pleas before him, so that the citizens should not forfeit their profits in the king's court. [?]

282. Assembly: Wednesday next after Palm Sunday 10 Hen.VI [*16 April 1432*].

Present: Henry Man mayor, William Waryn, Robert Warmwell, John Swyft, John Noble, John Bremle, Richard Gatour, Thomas Freman, Richard Wyse, Richard Payn, John Wyot, John Marchal, John Boteler, Richard Gage, Robert Watercombe, Gilbert Marchal, John Skot, John Morys, William Moun, Simon Poy, William Warwyk.

Elected to the parliament to be held by virtue of the king's writ at Westminster 12 May 10 Hen.VI [*1432*]: William Alisaundr', Thomas Freman.

Elected as city constables in place of Thomas Randolf: Thomas Freman, John Wyot.

Memorandum: John Wyot paid to Henry Man, mayor, in the presence of W. Waryn [and] Robert Warmwell at 'le Conselhous' £3. [*The payment may have been for being excused the office of constable.*]

283. Assembly at 'le Counselhous': Friday the eve of St. Luke 11 Hen.VI [*17 Oct. 1432*].

Present: H. Man mayor, William Waryn, John Bromle, William Cokk', John Noble, Robert Gilberd, John Boteler, John Wyot, Richard Gatour, John Wyot [*again*], Richard Wyse, Walter Short, Robert Watercombe.

By virtue of the king's writ, elected to assess the expenses of the said citizens [attending parliament]:

For one half of the third part of a fifteenth to be paid on the feast of St. Martin next [*11 Nov. 1432*] and the other half on the feast of St. Martin then following:

[*the names, in column on the right-hand side of the page, are apparently for both assessments*] as assessors: Stephen Coupere, John Shad, John Hayne, John Colyngbourne; as collectors: William Swayn, Peter de Varwe, Robert Hygon, John Clyve 'tannere'; as commissioners: William Sever', Richard Plowman, John Hampton, John Teffonte.

[f. 97a; *an inserted strip of parchment, the dorse blank*]

284. The king's writ, dated at Westminster 17 July 10 Hen. [VI, *1432*] and signed Haseley, to the mayor and bailiffs for the payment to William Alisaundre and Thomas Freman, citizens attending the parliament at Westminster 12 May last, of £14 8s. for their expenses in coming, staying for 72 days, and returning, each receiving 2s. a day.

[f. 98; *faded and stained*]

285. [*Heading:*] H. Man mayor. [*By the date of the assembly recorded next, being after the usual day of election, 2 Nov., Henry Man's mayoralty might be expected to have ended.*]

Assembly: Friday next after St. Martin 11 Hen. VI [*14 Nov. 1432*].

Present [*in three columns*]: William Waryn, Henry Baron, Robert Warmwell, John Swyft, John Noble, John Bromle, Richard Gatour, John Gilberd, Stephen Coupere, [*column two*] John Shad, John Marchal, John Boteler, Richard Wyse, John Wyot, Richard Gage, Peter de Varw, John Estbury, John Coscombe, [*column three*] Richard Plowman, John Gage, Walter Short, John Deverel, Edward Gudyer, John Colyngbourne, William Cokkys, John Tyssebury.

Ordered: Robert Warmwell to be a city chamberlain with John Boteler.

286. Assembly: Monday next after St. Andrew 11 Hen. VI [*1 Dec. 1432*].

[Present:] H. Baron mayor, [*then in three columns*] William Waryn, Robert Warmwell, Henry Man, John Swyft, John Bromle, William Pakyn, Richard Gatour, Thomas Freman, [*column two*] John Marchal, Richard Payn, Richard Gage, John Shad, Stephen Mercer, Richard Wyse, John Gryffith, [*column three*] Robert Chamberleyn, Walter Short, Robert Levyng, John Estbury, William Ovyng, Pleasant Deye.

Ordered: outside fishmongers (*piscatores forincece*) to stand above the common ditch (*trench'*) of running water within the city; indigenous fishmongers to stand opposite 'le Gildhalle' in the usual place; those bringing oysters and shellfish ('shulfyssh') to sell them at Cheese Corner ('Chescorner') in the usual place; milk, butter, cheese, apples, pears, and all such fruits to be sold at the cross opposite John Gage's tenement; those bringing rabbits for sale in the city not to sell them in lodging-houses but (*nisi*) in the common market. [*The syntax of the last clause is faulty.*]

Also, John Boteler to have the common ditch (*com'foss'*) around the city paying 3s. 4d. a year and to report those committing offences in the said ditch.

[f. 98v.; *faded and stained*]

287. [*Heading*:] H. Baron mayor.

Assembly: Saturday next after one week from St. Martin 11 Hen. VI [*22 Nov. 1432*].

Present: William Waryn, Robert Warmwell, Henry Man, John Swyft, John Noble, John Bremle, Richard Gatour, William Warwyk, William Cokkys, John Boteler, Richard Gage, Walter Short, John Chippenham, Thomas Durneford, John Hobbys, William Swayn, John Skot.

Agreed: the Twenty-Four, with the stewards of each guild, (. . .) the bishop of Salisbury (. . .) on Monday the feast of St. (Clement?) [*the feast of St. Clement, 23 Nov., fell on Sunday in 1432, on Monday in 1433*] in his first visitation after his installation as bishop. (. . .) given one piece of silver-gilt value £9 and (. . .) pipes of wine value £4 (. . .).

288. Assembly: Friday (. . .).

Present [*the names, except for the last, in pairs, in two columns*]: Henry Baron mayor, William Waryn; Robert Warmwell, Henry Man; John Swyft, Richard Gatour; Richard Gage, Richard Wyse; Stephen Mercer, Robert Gilberd; Thomas Freman, John Bromle; John Shad, John C(. . .); John Coscombe, John S(. . .); Richard Payn, John M(. . .); John Crom, William Knoll; Ralph Pakkere, John Chatour; William Clyter.

The mayor lent £10, William Waryn £1, Robert Warmwell £2, William Warwyk £2 of which 6s. 8d. was in the hands of John Coscombe, Henry Man £1, John Bromle £1, Richard Wyse 13s. 4d., Stephen Coupere 13s. 4d., Robert Gilberd 13s. 4d., Richard Gatour 13s. 4d., Thomas Freman 13s. 4d., John White £1, John Wyot 13s. 4d., Richard Payn 13s. 4d., these sums lent for the repair and building of the tenements of the mayor and community in the city, the said £10 being the mayor's wages lent with the other sums above until etc.

289. Assembly: Friday next after the nativity of St. John the Baptist 11 Hen. VI [*26 June 1433*] for electing citizens to the parliament to be held on 8 July at Westminster.

Present [*in four columns*]: Henry Baron mayor, Robert Longe, William Alisaundr', Robert Warmwell, Henry Man, John Swyft, John Bromle, Richard Gatour, [*column two*] Thomas Freman, John Cammel, John Wyot, Robert Gilberd, Richard Wyse, John Shad, John Willy, William Cokkys, [*column three*] Richard Payn, John Marchal, John Swyft, Pleasant Deie, John Gerveys, John Oy, John Morys, Robert Watercombe, [*column four*] Walter Short, John Gage, John Colyngbourne, John Tutsay.

Elected: William Warwyk, Richard Gatour.

[f. 98a; *an inserted piece of parchment, mutilated, the dorse blank*]

290. Writ from John Seymour, sheriff of Wiltshire, dated at his exchequer in Fisherton 2 April 10 Hen. VI [*1432*] to the mayor and bailiffs, quoting the king's writ in full (except for the dating clause) for elections to the parliament to be held at Westminster on 12 May next. The sheriff required a response without delay.

[f. 99; *faded, stained, and holed*]

291. [*Heading:*] H. Baron mayor.

Assembly at 'le Counselhous': Tuesday next after the Assumption 11 Hen.VI [*18 Aug. 1433*].

Present: the mayor, William Waryn, Robert Warmwell, Henry Man, Richard Gatour, Thomas Freman, John Bromle.

Ordered: all the stewards of each guild in the city to give notice to every member of each guild to greet (*obviendum*) the duke of Bedford and the duke of Gloucester who intend to be in Salisbury on (. . .) with their wives.

Also, the prostitutes to have their houses [*manciones*] or brothel [*lupanarium*] in Friary Lane ('Frerenestret') at the cottages.

292. Assembly: (. . .) 12 Hen.VI [*1433*].

Present: H. Baron mayor, William Waryn, Robert (Char?)lyng, (. . .), (John Cos?)combe, William Pakyn, John White, Stephen Mercer, Richard W(yse?), [*two names illegible*], Richard Payn, Robert Gilberd.

Elected as assessors for the fourth part of the fifteenth: the old assessors, viz. Stephen Coupere, John Shad, John Hayne, John Colyngbourne; as collectors: Peter de Veraw, John Clyve 'tannere', John Androw 'mercer', Robert Cove.

Paid to the mayor by John Boteler and Richard Wyse, as appears in the roll of their account for outside (*forinc'*) expenses, £9; paid to the said Henry Baron £4 18s. 8d., as appears in the account of the said Henry and Richard Wyse among the particulars of the assised rents in the same roll.

Ordered: the city clerk to receive, for making a charter relating to a free tenement, 1s., for the writing 8d., for the enrolling 4d., and no more unless the matter of the charter demands more examination and more difficulty, then to receive what he can agree with the parties.

[f. 99v.; *faded, stained, and holed; below the heading the top quarter is either blank or illegible*]

293. [*Heading*:] William Waryn mayor.

Assembly in the Guildhall (*Guildaula*): Friday next before St. Thomas the apostle 12 Hen. VI [*18 Dec. 1433*].

Present [*in four columns*]: Robert Warmwell, Henry Man, John Bromle, William Pakyn, Thomas Freman, William Cokkys, John Shad, Richard Wyse, John Boteler, William Phebys, John Chippenham, William Charlyng, John Swyft, [*column two*] Richard Gage, Robert Cove, John Hampton, John Gryffyth, John Gerveys, Thomas Durneford, Edward Gudyer, Nicholas Shute, John Fadir, Thomas Glovere, Robert Ferour, William Mouhn, John Hobbys, [*column three*] Robert Hygon, John Machyn, Robert Chamberlayn, Peter de Verw, John Coscombe, John Crykemour, John Wyot, John Whelere, Ralph Pakker', John Gy, John Colyngbourne, [*column four*] Thomas Stoppe, Richard Balfot, Robert Pottere, Gilbert Marchal, Walter Short, Stephen Coupere, John Anketill', William Halstede, William Swayn, Richard Cofe, John Marchal, Richard Plowman.

Ordered and constituted as city chamberlains: John Boteler, Richard Wyse.

Also ordered: weights to be kept for merchandise (*mercimon' et aliis mercandizis*), and to be prepared by the chamberlains as soon as they can with an iron beam ('bem') and a scale, and the chamberlains to take a suitable house for weighing. Elected to operate it: Simon Poy. And afterwards Simon and [*incomplete*].

294. Assembly at 'le Councelhous': Thursday next after St. Juliana 12 Hen. VI [*18 or 25 Feb. 1434*].

Present [*in four columns*]: William Waryn mayor, William Alisaundr', Henry Man, John Swyft, Henry Baron, Robert Warmwell, John Bromle, Richard Gatour, Robert Gilberd, Stephen Mercer, John Boteler, [*column two*] Richard Wyse, William Cokkys, John White, Robert Watercombe, John Skot, John Gryffyth, Thomas Archebaud, William Chyld, Ralph Pakker', Stephen Lythenard, [*column three*] John Wheler', Thomas Danyel, John Glovere, William Charlyng, Thomas Durneford, John Marchal, John Wyot, John Chippenham, John Shad, Richard Gage, Walter Short, John Deverel, [*column four*] Elias Plomer, John Fadyr, John Coscombe, John Gerveys, Peter de Varw, John Hampton, Robert Cove, William Knoll, John Alysaundr', John a Port, Robert Pottere, Simon Poy.

[f. 100; *faded, stained, and holed*]

[*Heading*:] William Waryn mayor.

By virtue of the king's writ below [*no. 296*], elected as assessors for the expenses of the citizens [at parliament]: John Bromle, John Wyot, William Chepman, William Chrlyng [*sic*]; to collect and levy the same: Robert Bulk, Simon Poy, Henry Shad, Robert Cove.

Ordered: the justices of assize to have a gift from the city as used to be done of old.

Also: the common cart (*biga*) for taking away ordure (*fimis*) and other filths (*sordis*) (. . .) for work (. . .).

295. Assembly at the Guildhall (*Gildaulam*): Wednesday next before St. Gregory 12 Hen. VI [*10 March 1434*].

Agreed: the assessors for the expenses of the knights [*i.e. citizens at parliament*] to assess also the fifteenth (payable) at Easter (. . .), viz. John Bromle, John Wyot, William Chepman, William Child [*but William Charlyng is named above*], and that the collectors elected for those expenses should collect the fourth part of the fifteenth, with others below as their fellows: for New Street ward, Robert Bulk, Anselm Skynnere, [Robert Tanner *added and crossed out*]; for Market, Simon Poy, Thomas [Malabre *crossed out*] Mabre; for St. Martin's, Robert Crome, John Whelere; for Meadow, Thomas Pese, John Bridmere.

Ordered: outside (*extranei*) butchers to stand behind Butcher Row ('le Bocherwe').

Also, the justices of assize to have oats, bread, and wine, as used to be done of old.

Memorandum: on Thursday in the feast of St. Hilary 13 Hen. VI [*14 Jan. 1435*] there was paid to W. Warwyk, one of the citizens at parliament, £11 16s.; and earlier there was paid to Richard Gatour, the other citizen at parliament, £11 16s.

[f. 100a, *a strip of parchment, blank on the dorse, inserted at the lower edge of the book between ff. 99 and 100*]

296. The king's writ, dated Westminster 3 Feb. 12 Henry [VI, *1434*] and signed Haseley, to the mayor and bailiffs for the payment to William Warwyk and Richard Gatour, burgesses [*sic*] of the city at the parliament at Westminster 8 July last, of £23 12s. for their expenses in coming, staying 118 days, and returning; each receiving 2s. a day.

[f. 100v.; *faded, stained, and holed*]

297. [*Heading:*] William Waryn.

Names of persons assessed for £40 to be loaned to the king. [*Each named has in front of it a large dot, and all except John Hayne, William Pakyn, John Marchel, and William Alisaundr' have also a cross; those marks and the names or initials Freman, Waryn, White, F., and W. which are added to some of the names presumably relate to the payment or repayment of the loan. The total, excluding the two entries which have been crossed out, amounts to £40. The first part of the list is arranged in three columns, the second in two columns.*]

Anselm Skynnere 6s. 8d., John Thoresby 6s. 8d., William Swayn 6s. 8d., John Wynchestre 6s. 8d., John Heliere £1, John Gower 6s. 8d., Clement Fobour 6s. 8d., John Aport 13s. 4d., Robert Levyng 6s. 8d., John Swyft 'dier' 6s. 8d., William Chepman [Freman *added before the name*] 6s. 8d., Robert Pottere 6s. 8d., William Wrythe [Waryn *added before the name*] 6s. 8d., John Colyngbourne 6s. 8d., John Hampton [Freman *added before the name*] 6s. 8d., Walter Carogan 6s. 8d., John Coscombe 6s. 8d., William Charlyng 6s. 8d., Robert Bulk 6s. 8d., John Gy [Freman *added before the name*] 6s. 8d., John Hayne 6s. 8d. [*followed by an undeciphered abbreviation, possibly* fan], [*column two*] John Crykemour 6s. 8d., William Knoll 10s., William Brounyng 6s. 8d., Nicholas Shute 6s. 8d., [Robert Bouer 6s. 8d. *crossed out*], John Goldsmyth 6s. 8d., Richard Ploumman 6s. 8d., [John (*cf. no. 314*)] Bover 'bocher' 6s. 8d., John Chaundeler 6s. 8d., Thomas Pakker 6s. 8d., John Clyter 6s. 8d., John Bote 6s. 8d., Thomas Payn 6s. 8d. [F. *added after the amount*], William Prangnel 6s. 8d. [per W. *added after the amount*], Edward Gudyer 6s. 8d., William Phebys 6s. 8d. [W. *added after the amount*], John Griffith 6s. 8d., William Halstede 6s. 8d., William Pridy 6s. 8d., [*column three*] John Clyve 'brewer' 6s. 8d., John Everard 6s. 8d. [White *added after the amount*], John Houchyn 6s. 8d., Thomas Brasier 6s. 8d., John Clyve 'tannere' 6s. 8d., Richard Gage 10s., Nicholas Pyl 6s. 8d., John Estbury 6s. 8d., George Westby 13s. 4d., John Androw 'mercer' 6s. 8d., Richard Brennevir 6s. 8d., John Moris 6s. 8d., Stephen Hendy 6s. 8d., [William Cokkys 6s. 8d. *crossed out; see below*], John Gerveys 6s. 8d., [*column one*] Robert Warmwell £1 6s. 8d., Henry Man £1 6s. 8d., John Bremle £1, Richard Gatour £1 [Freman *added before the name*], John Swyft 13s. 4d., Thomas Freman £1 13s. 4d., John White £1 13s. 4d., Richard Wyse £1, Richard Payn £1, Henry Baron £1, William Pakyn 13s. 4d. [Freman *added before the name*], [*column two*] Stephen Mercer £1, John Wyot £1, John Boteler 13s. 4d., John Shadde 6s. 8d. [F. *added after the amount*], Robert Gilberd £1 6s. 8d., John Marchel 6s. 8d. [Freman *added after the amount*], John Noble 6s. 8d., William Warwyk £2, William Cokk' 6s. 8d., William Alisaundr' £1.

[f. 101; *faded, stained, and holed*]

298. [*Heading:*] In the mayoralty of William Waryn's.

Assembly: Thursday next after Michaelmas 13 Hen. VI [*30 Sept. 1434*].

Present: Richard Gage, Robert Gilberd, William Warwyk, [*then in three columns*] Henry Baron, Richard Gatour, John Marchal, Richard Wyse, John White, John Boteler, Thomas Durneford, John Tissebury, [*column two*] Robert Warmwell, John Swyft, John Bromle, Henry Man, Robert Cove, John Wyot, William Charlyng, Robert Chamberleyn, [*column three*] William Chapman, John Coscombe, John Fadir, Thomas Glovere, William Chapman [*again*], John Everard.

Ordered and constituted: Stephen Hendy to hold 'Pynnokkesyn', paying 7 marks a year until its new structure, which has been begun, is built, then paying yearly what can be agreed with the mayor and community; and he is to have preference in the placing [*or* the letting] of the messuage (*preferatur in locacione eiusdem mesuag'*).

Also, the butchers to stand in the place already assigned and ordered for them, viz. behind the butchers' stalls established of old by the city's common ditch (*trench'*).

Also, the old collectors and assessors [to be continued], viz. John Bromle and his fellows and the collectors Robert Bulk and his fellows, whose names are written on the other side of the preceding folio [*nos. 294–5*].

[*There follows, in English, the beginning of the account included below, in no. 311, of events at Ghent, breaking off, at the end of the third of the Flemings' articles, with a reference to f. 104.*]

[f. 101v.; *faded, stained, and holed*]

299. Election of the mayor and other officers in St. Edmund's church, [2 Nov.] 13 Hen. VI [*1434*].

Mayor, John White; reeves, William Charlyng, William Knoll; alderman of New Street, William (Ov?)yng; of Market, John Oy; of St. Martin's, Richard Cook; of Meadow, John Younge of Harnham; serjeants, Thomas Yoxford, Henry Frend.

Whose pledges entered bonds to the mayor and community to indemnify them against the king and all others. The bonds remain in Henry Man's keeping.

300. Assembly: Friday next after St. Andrew 13 Hen. VI [*3 Dec. 1434*] in the mayoralty of John White.

Present [*in six columns*]: William Cokk', Stephen Mercer, John Swyft, William Waryn, Robert Warmwell, William Warwyk, Robert Gilberd, William [Halstede *crossed out*, Pridy *added*], Richard Walker, Nicholas Pyl, John Estbury, John Bromle, William Gloucestre, Ralph Pakker', John Alisaundr', William Pakyn, [*column two*] John Marchal, John Wyot, John Boteler, Richard Gage, William Halstede, George Westby, Gilbert Marchal, Edward Gudyer, Robert Pyl, Robert Chynton, John Clyve, John Stokle, John Parson, Thomas Payn, John Dun, Peter Dawe, [*column three*] John Shadde, John Fadyr, Richard Balfot, Richard Boteler, Robert Chamberleyn, Robert Cove, William Gy, John Hampton, John Hornpipere, Nicholas Purbyk, William Cokkys [*again*], John Slegge, John Hobbys, Richard Lavyngton, John Machyn, Thomas Whityng, [*column four*] John Oy, Simon Poy, Henry Shadde, John Crikemour, John Tutsay, John Honythorn, John Coscombe, John Cammel, John Hayne, John Pope, Walter Short, John Adkyn, Richard Shirle, John Marchal [*again*], John Gerveys, John Tyssebury, [*column five*] William Phebys, John Pekham, John Leycestr', John Wheler', Thomas Stoppe, Thomas Tarry, William Clytyr, John Bote, John Gage, John Aport, Richard Ecton, John Page, William Chepman, Thomas Danyel, William Prangnel, William Child, Thomas Parrok, [*column six*] Richard Gatour, John Everard, Robert Pottere, John Colyngbourne, John Mone, John Oy [*again*], William Wrythe, Nicholas Shute, John Asshford, Richard Wyse, John Shadde [*again*], Thomas Mabre, Richard Payne,

Thomas Freman, Stephen Mercer [*again*], John Houchyn, Thomas Bugbrigge, William Knoll. [*The list is apparently continued below.*]

Ordered: anyone summoned to the assembly and failing to attend without reasonable excuse to be amerced according to the old amercement of 6d., to be levied by one of the chamberlains and the city serjeant.

Also: the livery for the king's arrival, if he comes to the city, to be green, under the supervision of Robert Warmwell, Henry Man, Richard Gage, and John Hampton.

Also: the city officials to be retained as before and to have their livery for Christmas, etc.

[*List, apparently continuing that above, with which none of the names overlap, in seven columns:*] William Selwode, John Goldsmyth, John Thoresby, Henry Chubbe, [*column two*] John Stonard, William Swayn, Robert Levyng, Stephen Hendy, [*column three*] Richard Plowman, Clement Fourbour, Robert Bulk, John Wynchestr', [*column four*] John Bover, John Heliere, John Chaundeler, Thomas Pakker, [*column five*] William Brounyng, John Auncel, John Ferour, Richard Mylys, [*column six*] William Alisaundr', William Charlyng, John Wodehay, Richard Boteler, [*column seven*] Walter Dytton, Walter Carogan, Henry Baron, William Ovyng, [f. 102; *faded and stained*] [*in two columns*] William Hore, John White mercer, John Gower, [*column two*] Henry Man, John Auncel, John Beshampton.

301. [*Heading, at the top of the page:*] John White mercer mayor.

[Assembly]: Wednesday next after the Conception 13 Hen. VI [*15 Dec. 1434*].

Elected as chamberlains in the place of John Boteler [and] Henry Baron: Henry Baron, Richard Wyse. [*John Boteler and Richard Wyse had been appointed as chamberlains in Dec. 1433: above, no. 293.*]

302. Assembly in the Guildhall (*Gildaula*): Friday next after St. Scholastica 13 Hen. VI [*11 Feb. 1435*].

Present: the mayor, John Marchel, John Wyot, Stephen Mercer, William Cokk', Richard Gatour, Henry Man, John Swyft, William Warwyk, William Alisaundr', Robert Warmwell, Henry Baron, Richard Wyse, Robert Gilberd, John Boteler, Robert Watercome, Robert Cove, John Estbury, Johne Slegge, John Machyn, Thomas Danyel, John Crikemour, John Everard, Richard Plowman, John Skot, William Ovyng, John Oy, John Fadyr, William Swengyl, Henry Shad, William Chrlyng [*sic*], Richard Balfot, John Coscumbe.

Ordered: the assessors and collectors to assess the fourth part of the fifteenth payable at Easter; they themselves to be assessed by the mayor and four of the leading men of the city, as used formerly to be done.

Also: the new house which Robert Levyng holds in 'Pynnokkesyn' to be placed on the land where there is already an old house called [*blank*].

The two tenements late of William Asshele chaplain in Castle Street ('Castelstret') to be sold to the dean and chapter.

Also: Stephen Hendy 'taillour', tenant of 'Pynnokkesyn', to have the tenement which he holds there for 7 marks [now], and after the construction of the new house for 8 marks, for the duration of the term.

303. Assembly of the Twenty-Four: Saturday next after St. Laurence 13 Hen. VI [*13 Aug. 1435, on the assumption that St. Laurence was the martyr; if it was the archbishop, the assembly was on 5 Feb., and the record was entered in the wrong place in relation to no. 302*].

[Present, *in six columns, each with two names*:] John White mayor, William Waryn, William Warwyk, Robert Warmwell, Henry Man, William Pakyn, Thomas Freman, Stephen Mercer, John Wyot, Richard Payn, John Shad, John Marchal.

Ordered: a third macebearer, viz. a serjeant, to be appointed to serve the mayor and attend on him, and to perform the office of chamberlain in levying rents and supervising the maintenance and repair of lands and tenements, to receive wages as do the chamberlains, viz. £2, and to perform the office of subwarden of Holy Trinity hospital in buying food for the poor there, repairing their tenements, and all else belonging to that office according to the foundation, receiving for that annually £1 16s. 8d. (*xxxvj s' viij d'*) [*but it should be £1 6s. 8d., xxvj s' viij d', if the following figure is right*], total salary for both duties 5 marks, receiving in addition annually from the mayor for the time being a gown and food and drink.

[f. 102v.; *faded and stained*]

304. Transcript of the king's letters patent, dated Westminster 6 Aug. 13 Hen. [VI, *1435*] to William Westbury, Robert Hungerford knight, John Whyte mayor of New Salisbury, and John Westbury, appointing any three of them, or two of them provided that one is either William Westbury or John Westbury, to deliver, at New Salisbury, the gaol in the castle of Old Salisbury of Richard Hode 'bocher', doing justice according to the laws and customs of England, saving amercements and other things due to the king. The king has ordered the sheriff of Wiltshire to bring Richard Hode before them.

305. Assembly: Friday [7 Oct. 14 Hen. VI *crossed out*] next after Michaelmas 14 Hen. VI [*7 Oct. 1435*].

Present: John White mayor, John Marchal, Robert Gilberd, John Swyft, Robert Warmwell, William Waryn, Henry Man, John Bromle, Henry Baron, Richard Wyse, William Cokkis,

John Port, John Oy, John Skot, John Pakyn, John Fadyr, Robert Chynchon, Thomas Stoppe, John Crykemour, John Wheler, John Adkyn, Richard Balfot, Peter de Varw, Robert Cove, John Gage, Thomas Durneford, John Purdy, Stephen Coupere, Walter Short, William Charlyng.

Elected, by virtue of the king's writ, as citizens [to parliament]: John Bromle, Richard Ecton.

306. Assembly: Friday 7 Oct. 14 Hen. VI [*1435*]. [*The heading appears to have been repeated in error. It and the record which follows (the wording of which suggests that the clerk started with a much fuller and more important record in mind) refer to the 'underwritten citizens', but there is no such list.*]

Ordered: the articles written below to be observed:

First, the officials to be established (*habeantur*) in the city as was of old.

Also, William Pakyn to replace John Bromle as assessor because the said John has set out for parliament.

[f. 103; *faded and stained*]

307. Account of William Waryn, mayor, Friday after Michaelmas [*presumably 1 Oct. 1434*].

He asked for allowance for the officials' liveries, £1 12s.; for the board (*tabula*) of the chaplain of St. George, £2 13s. 4d.; for his [the mayor's] wages, £10; for various lords' officials, £1; for J. Baas, the bishop of Salisbury's collector (*collat'*), 4s. Sum total, £15 9s. 4d.

Of which he received from Thomas Freman, £3; from the city butchers, £4. There remained to be paid to the mayor, £9 9s. 4d. [*recte* £8 9s. 4d., *as suggested below*]. Richard Wyse was assigned to pay him at Christmas next £6 7s.; and to be paid to him by John Skot for the 'almeshous' by virtue of a statute merchant £2

Memorandum: on Monday next before St. Martin [*8 Nov. 1434*] in the presence of John White mayor, William Waryn, Robert Warmwell, Richard Gage, John Boteler, Nicholas Shute, John Colyngbourne, and Thomas Durneford there was delivered to Walter Short from the common chest £3; to Edmund the chaplain of St. George £2 13s. 4d.; to the said Walter at the same time 14s.; to William Lord for his livery from the common chest, 8s. 4d.; to the said Walter from the money arising from the brotherhood of St. George, £1 0s. 8d.

[f. 103v.; *faded and stained*]

308. Account of John White, mayor, Monday next before St. Martin 14 Hen. VI [*7 Nov. 1435*].

Owed to the mayor for his wages £10; for the board (*tabula*) of the chaplain of St. George £2 13s. 4d.; for officials, 10s.; for one bringing a privy seal [letter] 3s. 4d.; for Lord Hungerford for 3 gallons of wine 2s. 8d.; delivered to Richard Ecton £1 13s. 4d. Sum £15 2s. 8d.

Of which, paid to the said mayor from the money arising from the brotherhood of St. George on the account of William Baker and William Halstede £1 19s. 4d. And paid to the same in readiness (*de prompt'*) from the £25 loaned to the king, of which he answers for [?] (*ressn*) £5 and all sums of defaulters [?] (*def'torum*).

[f. 104; *faded, stained, and holed*]

309. [*Heading:*] Stephen Coupere mayor.

Election of the mayor and other officers in St. Edmund's church, [2 Nov.] 14 Hen. VI [*1435*].

Mayor, Stephen Coupere; reeves, Peter de Varwe, John Slegge; alderman of New Street, Robert Cove [*evidently in error, since he was elected for St. Martin's and there is no other record in the book of the election of two aldermen for a ward*], John Clyve 'brewer'; of Market, John Everard; of St. Martin's, Robert Cove; of Meadow, John Wheler' 'webbe'; serjeants, Thomas Yoxford, Henry Frend.

[f. 104v.; *faded, stained, and holed*]

310. [*Heading:*] In the mayoralty of Stephen Coupere.

Assembly: Friday next after St. Lucy 14 Hen. VI [*16 Dec. 1435*].

Present: John Helyer', John Shad, John Wyot, Richard Wyse, John Swyft, William Warwyk, Henry Man, William Waryn, Robert Warmwell, Henry Baron, John Whyte, William Cokkis, John Gilberd, John Boteler, William Chaundeler, William Swayn, John Gerveis, John Estbury, George Westbury, John Marchal, John Oy.

Ordered: William Alisaundr' and William Lord to be retained as the city's counsel for their old wages and livery; the city officials to have their livery as is customary; Richard Gage to keep the key of the common chest; everyone to weigh [their goods] at the city weigh[house] according to statute.

311. Assembly: Friday next after Epiphany 14 Hen. VI [*13 Jan. 1436*].

Elected as auditors of the account of debts due to the city: the mayor for the time being, William Waryn, Robert Warmwell, Henry Man, William Warwyk, John White, William Pakyn, Thomas Freman.

Transcript of a report [*in English*] of the duke of Burgundy's negotiations at Ghent with the Flemings for their support in his siege of Calais. The support was given on the duke's acceptance of five articles, of which the second was that no Englishman be allowed to sell English cloth at any market within the duke's lordships, and the fifth that the Flemish towns should have the wool [stored or sold] at Calais. A large force was preparing to besiege Calais. [f. 105] On this, the king sent three privy seal letters to the mayor of Salisbury, which are transcribed in full in the book. The first [*in French*], dated Westminster 14 Feb. [*1436*] and addressed to the mayor and other good folk of Salisbury, summoned the mayor to appear at Westminster two weeks from Easter next [*22 April*] to hear what the Council shall decide. The second [*also in French*], dated Westminster 14 Feb. and addressed to the mayor and community of Salisbury, required a loan of 300 marks for the army to be sent to France under the duke of York. The third [*in English*], dated Westminster 26 March and addressed to the mayor, bailiffs, and inhabitants of Salisbury, enclosed the report of the negotiations at Ghent and the massing of the force against Calais, and [f. 105v.] required the city to send to the king as many persons 'defensables and habiles' for the war to raise the siege, certifying to the county sheriff within eight days of receipt of the letter the number of people to be sent.

Copy [*in Latin*] of the response of the mayor, bailiffs, and inhabitants made to Edmund Hungerford knight, sheriff of Wiltshire, on Tuesday, the sixth day [*17 Apr. 1436*] after the receipt on 11 April of the king's letter: twelve men were ready to set out.

[*The above documents relating to the defence of Calais are printed in* H.M.C. Var. Coll. IV, *pp. 197–200.*]

Copy of the king's letters patent, dated Westminster 14 March 14 Hen. [VI, *1436*], addressed to Stephen Coupere mayor of the town [*sic*] of New Salisbury, William Waryn, Robert Warmwell, Henry Man, Thomas Freman, and John Wyot, ordering the mustering of all light horsemen and bowmen within the city and its suburbs.

[f. 104a; *a strip of parchment, blank on the dorse, inserted at the lower edge of the book between ff. 104 and 105.*]

312. The king's writ, dated Westminster 12 Feb. 14 Hen. [VI, *1436*] and signed Prestwyk, to the mayor and bailiffs for the payment to Richard Ecton, one of the citizens at the parliament at Westminster on 10 Oct. last, of £8 2s. for his expenses in coming, staying 81 days, and returning, receiving 2s. a day. And as much for [John] Bremle.

[f. 106; *faded, stained, and mutilated*]

313. [*Heading:*] Stephen Coupere.

Assembly at the Council House ('Cou…h…'): Friday next [*blank*] feast of St. Dunstan 14 Hen.VI [*18 or 25 May 1436*].

By virtue of the king's commission addressed to the collectors of a quarter of a fifteenth granted at the last parliament at Westminster, elected as collectors: Richard Walter, John Paunt, John Crykemour, William Knoll; as assessors: Richard Wyse, John Boteler, John A(…) and John C(…).

Memoranda: [1] Thomas Hall, the third city serjeant, was appointed subwarden of the almshouse ('Almeshous') on Wednesday next after (…) 14 Hen.VI, on which day Walter Short then subwarden died; Thomas to account for the period from (Michaelmas?) to the same feast next following.

[2] On Monday next after Holy Trinity 14 Hen.VI [*4 June 1436*], before the mayor, William Waryn, Robert Warmwell, Gilbert Marchal, an account was presented for Margaret, late the wife of Walter Short late subwarden of the almshouse, [who] owed to the said hospice 9s. 4d., to be paid on the feast of St. Margaret next [*8 July*].

[3] On that day before the said auditors the said Margaret owed to the mayor and community on all accounts £1 12s., to be paid at Michaelmas next [*29 Sept.*], on which the mayor and community will pay John Spencer of Alderbury ('Alwardbury') for the tiling [*sc.* of the almshouse?].

[4] William Swyft appointed as steward of Holy Trinity, with John Crome, for the brotherhood of the almshouse on Wednesday next before the Assumption 14 Hen.VI [*8 Aug. 1436*], through the death of said John [*?recte* Walter].

[5] On 23 July 14 Hen.VI [*1436*], there was paid from the mayor's chest, viz. Stephen Mercer's [*apparently in error for* Stephen Coupere's *or* Stephen Coupere 'mercer's'] for the men at arms and the archers [*cf. below, no. 317*] who resisted the duke of Burgundy's siege, £1 18s. 2d., the sum being paid to the men [and] archers by the said Stephen.

[6] The said Stephen had in hand 15s. besides the sum which he received for the archers; that and the £2 which he received from William Swayn in riding to London to be deducted from his wages (*pencione*) when he presents his account.

[f. 106v.; *faded, stained, and mutilated*]

314. Repayments made to the following for the £40 loaned to the king in the mayoralty of William Waryn as appears in the seventh folio above. [*The reference is to no. 297 above. The two lists are in different order but contain the same names, except that Thomas Brasier and Walter Carogan in the first list are represented by Thomas Bukbrigge and Walter atte Bole in the second, the names perhaps being variants for the same men, and there is an additional name, William Payn, in the second list, in which the amounts*] *are in each instance half those of the first, the total of the second list exceeding £20 by the 6s. 8d. repaid to William Payn.*]

[*In three columns:*] John Marchal 3s. 4d., William Wrythe 3s. 4d., Henry Man 13s. 4d., John Bromle 10s., Richard Brendewyr 3s. 4d., John Colyngbourne 3s. 4d., Edward Gudyer 3s. 4d., Robert Gilberd 13s. 4d., John Clyve 'tannere' 3s. 4d., William Alisaundr' 10s., Richard Plowman 3s. 4d., Robert Levyng 3s. 4d., Anselm Skynner 3s. 4d., John Griffyth 3s. 4d., Robert Bulk 3s. 4d., John Boteler 6s. 8d., William Brounyng 3s. 4d., Thomas Bukbrigge 3s. 4d., William Warwyk £1, Thomas Freman 16s. 8d., Walter atte Bole 3s. 4d., William Knoll 5s., Thomas Pakker 3s. 4d., Robert Pottere 3s. 4d., John Clyve 'brewer' 3s. 4d., [*column two*] John Bote 3s. 4d., John Crykemour 3s. 4d., William Chepman 3s. 4d., John Goldsmyth 3s. 4d., William Pridy 3s. 4d., John Clyter 3s. 4d., William Phebus 3s. 4d., John Coscombe 3s. 4d., Thomas Payn 3s. 4d., Nicholas Pyl 3s. 4d., John Chaundler 3s. 4d., John Thoresby 3s. 4d., Robert Warmwell 13s. 4d., John Gower 3s. 4d., Stephen Hendy 3s. 4d., Stephen Mercer 10s., John Swyft 6s. 8d., John White 16s. 8d., Richard Gatour 10s. [*this and the next two bracketed together with the words*] which remain in the mayor's chest, John Morys 3s. 4d., John Houchyn 3s. 4d., John Gy 3s. 4d., John Noble 3s. 4d., John Estbury 3s. 4d., Henry Baron 10s., Richard Payn 10s., [*column three*] William Cokk' 3s. 4d., John Shad 3s. 4d., John Androw 3s. 4d., Nicholas Shute 3s. 4d., George Westby 6s. 8d., Richard Gage 5s., William Payn 6s. 8d., John Gerveis 3s. 4d., Richard Wyse 10s., John Everard 3s. 4d. [*this and the next two bracketed together with the words*] in the hands of (. . .), William Pakyn (6s. 8d. [*illegible, but cf. no. 297*]) Clement Fourbour (3s. 4d. [*illegible, but cf. no. 297*]), William Swayn 3s. 4d., William Prangnel 3s. 4d., John Bover 3s. 4d., John Wynchestr' 3s. 4d., William Halstede 3s. 4d., John Helier 'yrmonger' 10s., John Aport 6s. 8d., John Wyot 10s., John Hayne 3s. 4d., John Swyft 'dier' [*blank, but no. 297 suggests 3s. 4d.*], John Hampton 3s. 4d., William Charlyng 3s. 4d

315. Money collected for the archers at the time of their departure.

[*In five columns:*] the mayor 1s., Ecton 1s., William Pakyn 8d., W. Lord 4d., Swengel 4d., [*column two*] Warmwell 1s., Waryn 1s., Robert Cove 8d., Selby 4d., [*column three*] Henry Man 1s., Whyte 1s., Wyse 8d., Tutsay 4d., [*column four*] Warwyk 1s., Freman 1s. 8d, W. Chaundeler 4d., Yoxford 4d., [*column five*] Baron 1s., Payn 1s., J. Wheler 4d., Swayn 4d. Sum 15s. 4d.

[f. 107; *faded, stained, and mutilated*]

316. [*Heading:*] Stephen Coupere mayor 14 Hen. VI.

To be noted: The mayor Stephen Coupere, by virtue of the king's privy seal letter addressed to him, appeared before the king two weeks from Easter [*22 Apr. 1436*] and with all the mayors of England was asked by the Council what sum of money he could provide for the king for the defence of the realm. Because the Council was informed by Walter Hungerford of the various burdens undertaken by the city in that defence, he was excused from providing any sum.

The sum of 300 marks specified in the said letters was discussed by the mayor and community with Lord Hungerford, according to the privy seal letter sent to him, on 11 April in the chapter house of the canons of Salisbury, with the sum of £25 provided by them for the king, which had been paid on the feast of St. Martin last [*11 Nov. 1435*]. Afterwards, under a privy seal letter, the payment not yet made was to be deferred to the following Easter, and the money was increased to £50. The said Stephen asked to have surety both for the £25 which long ago had been delivered by Richard Ecton and for the £25 newly granted, payable at Whitsun following Whitsun next. For the mayor's expenses in this matter, William Swayn paid to the said mayor £2

317. Names [with the sums paid to them] of the men at arms and archers from Salisbury going overseas to resist the siege of Calais by the duke of Burgundy [*in three columns*]:

Men at arms: Richard Ecton £2 Richard Brigges £2, Walter Huntele £2; [*column two*] Archers: John Peyntour £1, John Bentele 'tannere' £1, John Kyng 'bocher' £1, John Clyter £1, Edmund Thomas £1, Robert Jonessone £1, Robert Parker £1, Richard Westerdale £1, Edmund Bentele £1, Thomas Cabbel 'bocher' £1, John Tykel £1, Robert Hygon £1, [*column three*] William Warman £1, Henry Golde £1, William Bonde £1, John Rous 'tanner' £1, Laurence Drw [*sic*] £1, John Agodeshalf £1, Nicholas Bryd £1, John Seman 'carpynter' £1, William Kene £1, John Bremler 'baker' £1, Richard Gatyn 'smyth' £1, Roger Brynkenham £1.

Each of the men at arms and archers [received], at the city's expense, a coat ('huyk') [bearing] front and back the sign of a red cross with **S** in blue (*blodii coloris*) in the middle of the cross.

Sum total £30 paid by the above mayor to the above persons.

318. Assembly: Friday after Easter 14 Hen. VI [*13 April 1436*].

Present: John Gerveys, John Estbury, George Westby, John Marchal, John Oy, John Helier', John Shad, John Wyot, Richard Wyse, John Swyft, William Warwyk, Henry Man, William Waryn, Robert Warmwell, Henry Baron, John Whyte, William Cokkys, Robert Gilberd, John Boteler, William Chaundeler, William Swayn, and others.

By the authority of the king's writ, elected as assessors for the expenses of the citizens [at parliament]: William Pakyn, John Boteler, William Cormaille, Nicholas Shute; as collectors: Robert Levyng, Richard Plowman, John Adekyn, Thomas Stoppe. [*In the margin:*] Citizens [at parliament]: Richard Ecton, John Bromle.

[f. 107v.; *faded, stained, and mutilated*]

319. [*Heading*:] 14 Hen. VI

Citizens assessed for the £25 to be loaned to the king, together with the other £25 previously loaned totalling £50 to be repaid at Whitsun [*19 May*] 1437 according to the Act passed in the last parliament, the assessment made the morrow of the close of Easter [*16 April 1436*]:

[*In two columns. Each name, except for those of John Shad, John Bremle, Richard Ecton, William Alisaundr', and Richard Gatour, is preceded by* sol' *(paid). In addition, as indicated below, some names are preceded by a cross and some are followed by a note.*] William Waryn 13s. 4d., Robert Warmwell 13s. 4d., Henry Man 13s. 4d., John Swyft 10s., Henry Baron 13s. 4d., John White 16s. 8d., + William Warwyk 13s. 4d. 'payd', Richard Wyse 10s., Richard Payn 10s., John Wyot 10s., John Gilberd 13s. 4d. 'payd', + John Shad 6s. 8d. 'payd' R [? *sc.* recessu, *on reduction to*] 3s. 4d., John Marchal 5s., John Helyer' 13s. 4d., John Bromle [*blank*], William Pakyn 6s. 8d., William Cokk' 5s., Richard Ecton 6s. 8d., William Alisaundr' [*blank*], Richard Gatour [*blank*], + Thomas Freman 13s. 4d., John Boteler 6s. 8d., Thomas Whityng 6s. 8d., + John Honythorn 5s. 'payd' R [? *sc.* recessu, *on reduction to*] 3s. 4d., John Stokle 3s. 4d., William Leoker 'tannere' 3s. 4d., John Combe 3s. 4d., Thomas Pyse 3s. 4d., Richard Bowyere 3s. 4d. 'payd', John Cachers 3s. 4d., John Thoresby 3s. 4d., William Selwode 3s. 4d., John Mowne 'touker' 3s. 4d., William Prangnel 3s. 4d., Thomas Payn 3s. 4d., George Westby 3s. 4d., William Halstede 6s. 8d., Richard Lavyngton 3s. 4d., John Adkyn 'dier' 3s. 4d., Stephen Hyewode 6s. 8d. 'payd', John Dun 'drover' 3s. 4d., John Goldsmyth 6s. 8d., [*column two*] Robert Levyng 3s. 4d., Richard Plowman 3s. 4d., John Wynchestr' 3s. 4d., Robert Bulk 5s., Stephen Hendy 3s. 4d., Clement Fourbour 3s. 4d., John Aport 13s. 4d., Richard Gage 6s. 8d., Nicholas Pyl 5s., Walter Corogan 5s., John Colyngbourne 5s., John Coscombe 6s. 8d., William Charlyng 6s. 8d., + John Slegge 6s. 8d. F(reman?), John Stafle 3s. 4d., Robert Pottere 5s., Edward Gudyer 5s., Nicholas Shute 6s. 8d., William Knoll 8s. 4d., + John Crykemour 3s. 4d. Freman *in ofrie* [?] on reduction [?] (*recessu*), + William Chepman 3s. 4d., John Gerveys 6s. 8d., John Clyve 'brewer' 5s., John Androw 6s. 8d. on reduction to [?] (*recessu*) 2s., Thomas Pakker' 6s. 8d. [John Parke *crossed out*], + William Pridy 5s. 'payd', John Assheford 5s., + William Wrythe 3s. 4d. by Warmwell (*a Warmwell*), John Wyot 'brewer' 5s., John Page 3s. 4d., William Brounyng 6s. 8d., Robert Cove 6s. 8d., Anselm Skynnere 3s. 4d., William Child 3s. 4d., + John Hampton 3s. 4d., John Clyve 'tannere' 6s. 8d. [by?] Richard Gage, + John Estbury 6s. 8d., William Hore 6s. 8d., William Walker 3s. 4d., Henry Shad 3s. 4d., John Gower 3s. 4d., + John Tissebury 6s. 8d. paid Wyot, Thomas Gyle 3s. 4d., Thomas Androw 3s. 4d. .

[f. 108; *faded and stained*]

320. [*Heading*:] Stephen Coupere mayor.

Memorandum: Robert Levyng and Richard Plowman, collectors for the expenses of the citizens at parliament in Coupere's mayoralty, on Monday next after St. Mary Magdalene [*23 July 1346*] in the presence of William Waryn, Robert Warmwell, Henry

Man, William Pakyn, paid to the mayor £3 2s. 3d. and earlier, with the sum at which Richard Ecton was assessed viz. 5s., the sum of £8 2s., making a total of £11 4s. 3d.

Memorandum: John Adekyn and Thomas Stoppe, collectors for the expenses of the citizens at parliament in Stephen Coupere's mayoralty, on the said Monday paid to the mayor £4 12s.

321. The names of persons assessed for the men at arms and archers whose names are written in the second folio back [*no. 317. A similar heading is put at the top of ff. 108v. and 109.*]

321A. New Street aldermanry.

[*In three columns*] William Colyn 'baker' 1s. 8d., William Basket 1s., Robert Cove 3s. 4d., William Selewode 3s. 4d., John Perant 3s. 4d., Richard Knyght 1s., John Aley, a 'Flemyng' 6s. 8d., Stephen Corvisor, a Dutchman ('Duychissman') 6s. 8d., Thomas Bokbynder 1s., Thomas Paule 1s., John Thoresby 3s. 4d., Henry Chubbe 1s. 8d., Anselm Hebbyng 1s. 8d., Thomas Coughton 1s., William Swyft 1s., Gerard Taillour 1s., Richard Brandewyr 1s., George Cerle 1s., Edward Say 1s., John Parson 'tannere' 1s., Nicholas Dene 'corvisor' 1s., Stephen Barbour 1s., John Corvisor 1s., William Alisaundr' 13s. 4d., Robert Ostiler 1s., Henry Baron 13s. 4d., [*column two*] William Swayn 5s., Robert Levyng 3s. 4d., Stephen Hendy 3s. 4d., Richard Plowman 5s., Clement Fourbour 3s. 4d., Robert Bulk 5s., John Stavele 1s., Robert Warmwell 13s. 4d., John Wynchestr' 5s., John Bover 1s. 8d., John Chaundeler 1s. 8d., John Cachers 6s. 8d., John Helyer 10s., Stephen Sadiler 1s. 8d., John Veysy 'glasier' 1s. 8d., Thomas Brouderer 1s., Richard Barbour 1s., William Leoker 1s. 8d., Robert Longe 1s. 8d., John Ecton 'corvisor' 1s., John Batyn 'smyth' 1s. 8d., John Bishampton 1s. 8d., Mr. John Ferour 1s. 8d., John Wodehay 1s., Walter Carogan 3s. 4d., Samuel [? *corrected from, apparently,* Arthur] Corvisor 1s., [*column three*] Thomas Pakkere 5s., William Brounyng 3s. 4d., Anselm Taverner 1s. 8d., William Geves 1s., John Frank 1s., William Waryn 13s. 4d., William Gore 'baker' 1s. 8d., John White 13s. 4d., Peter de Varw 1s. 8d., George Westby 3s. 4d., Henry Man 13s. 4d., John Gower 3s. 4d., William Foghler' 1s., Robert Heryng 'bocher' 1s., John White 'taillour' 1s., Guy Galisshmaker 1s., Stafford Ostiler 1s., Robert Soubury 1s., John Berton 'cook' 1s., John Chippenham 'bocher' 1s., John Wexchaundeler 1s., Richard Miles 'baker' 1s. 8d., William Charlyng 10s., Richard Boteler 1s. 8d., Walter Dicton 1s. 8d., William Ovyng 1s. 8d.

Sum £12 5s. 4d. [*recte £12 4s. 4d.*]

[f. 108v.; *faded and stained*]

321B. Market aldermanry.

[*In three columns*] John Swyft 'dier' 3s. 4d., Richard Flecchere 1s., John Randolf 'fletcher' 1s., Thomas Terry 1s., John Clyter 3s. 4d., John Shether 2s., John Gerard 5s.,

John Bertovils 1s. 8d., Geoffrey Bonvalet 1s. 8d., John Bote 'baker' 1s., John Gage 1s. 8d., John Aport 10s., John Warde 1s. 8d., Thomas Foul 1s., John Page 1s. 8d., Ralph Pakker 1s., Thomas Payn 3s. 4d., Richard Lavyngton 3s. 4d., John Shergold 1s. 8d., John Marchal 3s. 4d., Robert Gilberd 13s. 4d., [column two] Thomas Danyel 1s. 8d., William Prangnel 1s. 8d., John Gilberd 1s. 8d., Robert Tarant 1s., William Glovere 1s., John Alisaundr' 1s., William Writhe 3s. 4d., John Oy 1s., John Mone 1s. 8d., John Colyngbourne 6s. 8d., Robert Pottere 1s. 8d., John Swyft 10s., Walter Hende 1s., William Murie 1s., Phillip Dier' 1s., Thomas Freman 13s. 4d., Stephen Coupere 13s. 4d., Richard Payn 10s., Thomas Mabr' 1s. 8d., Simon Poy 1s., William Warwyk 13s. 4d., John Shad 3s. 4d., [column three] Richard Wyse 'drapere' 10s., John Wyot 10s., John Androw 5s., Thomas Gyl 2s., William Pope 1s. 8d., John Wyot 'brewer' 1s. 8d., John Asshford 1s., Stephen Hywode 1s. 8d., John Tutsay 1s. 8d., John Everard 3s. 4d., Nicholas Shute 5s., John Don 'drovere' 1s. 8d., John Clyve 'tannere' 6s. 8d., Gilbert Marchal 1s. 8d., William atte Wode 1s., Henry Corvysor 1s., Richard Gage 6s. 8d.

Sum £10 18s. 4d. [recte £10 16s.]

321C. St. Martin's aldermanry.

[In three columns] William Hardyng 'Fysshere' 1s., Richard Walker 1s. 8d., Edward Gudyer 2s., William Hore 6s. 8d., Henry Shad 1s. 8d., John Hampton 6s. 8d., Thomas Copter 1s., John Horn discharged [?] (dis' per hang' lav' ?), John Estbury 3s. 4d., John Cammel 1s. 8d., Nicholas Pyl 3s. 4d., John Brewere 1s., [column two] William Chepman 'touker' 3s. 4d., Thomas Wylmyndon 1s. 8d., Thomas Androw 3s. 4d., Edmund Penston 1s., Richard Cokelote 1s. 8d., John Noke 1s., John Boteler 6s. 8d., John Coscombe 6s. 8d., William Halstede 5s., Robert atte Mer' 8d., John Lacok 1s. 8d., [column three] Nicholas Purbyk 1s. 4d., Thomas Pese 1s. 8d., John Bromle 10s., Richard Balfot 1s., John Crykemour 1s. 8d., William Wotton 1s., William Pridy 3s. 4d., John Slegge 1s. 8d., John Clyve 6s. 8d., William Cokk' [blank], John Stokle 1s. 8d., John Atkyn 1s. 8d., William Gloucestr' 1s.

Sum £4 15s. 4d.

[f. 109; faded and stained]

321D. Meadow aldermanry.

[In three columns] John Judde 'carpynter' 3s. 4d., Hugh Heliere, Thomas Benet 'helier' [i.e. tiler] [bracketed together] 1s., Thomas Leoker' 1s., William Aldrygge 1s., [column two] William Leoker' 1s., John Hobbys 1s. 8d., Robert Waltercome [sic] 1s., Walter Plowman 1s., Thomas Stoppe 1s. 8d., [column three] John Wheler 1s., John Leycestre 1s., Henry Spencer 1s. 8d., John Wayte 'carp[enter]' 1s., William Sopere 1s.

Sum 18s. 4d.

322. Assembly: Wednesday next after the Exaltation of Holy Cross 14 Hen. VI [*19 Sept. 1436*].

Present [*in four columns*]: Richard Payn, John Marchal, William Pakyn, John Bromle, John Swyft, Henry Man, John White, John Hampton, John Boteler, William Halstede, [*column two*] Richard Gage, William Hore, Gilbert Marchal, William Swayn, John Gower, John Crykemour, Richard Walker, William Knoll, Peter de Varw, [*column three*] John Everard, Robert Cove, John Coscombe, John Machyn, John Adkyn, Robert Chamberleyn, Richard Balfot, John Aport, [*column four*] John Estbury, Thomas Halle, William Chrlyng [*sic*], Edward Gudyer, Henry Shad.

Elected as assessors for the fourth part of the fifteenth to be paid on the feast of St. Martin [*11 Nov.*], which earlier by virtue of letters patent ought to be paid on the morrow of Michaelmas [*30 Sept.*]: John Aport, Richard Payn, Richard Wyse, John Coscombe.

[f. 109v. *blank*]

[f. 110; *faded and stained*]

323. Elections [2 Nov.] 15 Hen. VI [*1436*].

Mayor, Thomas Freman; reeves, John Alisaundre, Thomas Stoppe; alderman of New Street, William Swayn; of Market, John Tyssebury; of St. Martin's, John Atkyn; of Meadow, Richard Walker; serjeants, Thomas Yoxford, Henry Frend.

[f. 110v.; *faded and stained*]]

324. Assembly: Wednesday next after St. Edmund the king 15 Hen. VI [*21 Nov. 1436*].

Present [*in four columns*]: John Shad, John Marchal, Richard Payn, William Pakyn, John Swyft, William Warwyk, Robert Warmwell, William Waryn, Henry Man, John Bremle, Henry Baron, Stephen Coupere, Robert Gilberd, [*column two*] Richard Wyse, Robert Wyot, William Cokk', Richard Gage, Robert Watercombe, Peter de Varw, John Slegge, Richard Cove, John Estbury, Nicholas Shute, Simon Poy, John Oy, [*column three*] John Gage, John Gerveys, Robert Pottere, William Chepman, William Hore, Richard Plowman, John Tyssebury, John Adkyn, Richard Walker, John Hobbes, John Colyngbourne, Robert Ferour, [*column four*] Henry Shad, John Tutsay, John Machyn, John Hampton.

Elected as chamberlains: John Wyot, Robert Cove.

325. Assembly: Friday the eve of the Conception 15 Hen. VI [*7 Dec. 1436*].

Present [*in four columns*]: John Marchal, John Shad, William Cokkis, William Warwyk, William Waryn, Robert Warmwell, Henry Man, John Bremle, Stephen Coupere, Richard

Wyse, Richard Payn, John Boteler, William Alysaundr', [column two] Richard Gage, Robert Ferour, Richard Balfot, Peter de Varw, Robert Chamberlayn, Robert Cove, Gilbert Marchal, Simon Poy, John Wodehay, John Asshford, William Charlyng, Edward Gudyer, John Coscombe, William Ludelowe, [column three] John Estbury, William Swayn, Walter Corogan, John Tyssebury, John Adekyn, Richard Walker, John Alisaundr', John Skot, George Westby, Richard Gower, Thomas Wylmondon, John Crykemour, John Tutsay, [column four] John Elys 'plomer', Richard Plowman, John Gerveys, William Sever'.

Elected for the parliament to be held 21 Jan. next: [Robert Okebourne, John Whyte, William Lodelowe, all crossed out], William Pakyn and George Westby.

William Lord delivered to the mayor on the same day a written bond by which John Saymore 'chivaler' is bound to John Gylys [in a sum not specfied in the record] for the use of the community of Salisbury.

[f. 111; faded, blotted, and stained]

326. [Memorandum]: on Wednesday next before Christmas 15 Hen.VI [19 Dec. 1436] Stephen Hendi surrendered [Pinnock's inn] to the mayor and community. Richard Gage gave £2 for repairing 'Pynnokesyn' and Robert Warmwell £1.

Memorandum: on Saturday the eve of Epiphany 15 Hen.VI [5 Jan. 1437] Thomas Freman mayor was pardoned by those named below the £3 which he was condemned to pay to John Wyot and Robert Cove, the city chamberlains, for his unpleasant behaviour (ingrata gubernacione): W. Waryn, Henry Man, W. Warwyk, John Wyot, Robert Cove, William Swayn, Richard Payn, Richard Wyse, John Swyft, William Pakyn, Richard Gatour, Robert Gilberd, John Marchal.

327. Assembly: Friday, 8 March 15 Hen.VI [1437].

Present [in four columns]: Thomas Freman mayor, William Waryn, Robert Warmwell, [column two] Henry Man, John (. . .), John Bromle, [column three] Henry Baron, Stephen Mercer, Richard Wyse, [column four] John Boteler, John Wyot, Robert Gilberd.

Agreed: whereas £3 was assigned during the mayoralty of William Waryn to remove the butchers' stalls to the common ditch (trench'), they are to be moved back to their former place by the market.

328. Assembly: Saturday next before two weeks from Easter 13 Hen.VI [13 April 1437].

Present [in two groups, the first in five columns]: John Shad, Robert Gilberd, Stephen Mercer, John Swyft, William Warwyk, Richard Wyse, John Wyot, Richard Payn, Richard

Gage, John Coscombe, [*column two*] John Oy, Nicholas Shute, John Alisaundr', William Chyld, Thomas Stoppe, John Pottere, John Elys 'plomer', John Gower, John Adekyn, John Tyssebury, Robert Canne, [*column three*} Simon Poy, John Gage, John Gerveys, William Chepman, John Clyve, John Colyngbourne, Edward Penston, John Crykemour, Ralph Pakker', William Swengil, Thomas Copter, [*column four*] John Gilberd, John Skot, Robert Watercombe, John Auncel, Thomas Wylmyndon, John Hobbys, Peter Dawe, Thomas Halle, John Tutsay, William Charlyng, Henry Frend, [*column five*] Robert Hygon, Edward Gudyer, John Hampton, William Lord, [*after a gap, in two columns*] John Auncel [*again*], Thomas Fadir, Thomas Whytyng, John Berton, William Prangnel, John Wyot 'brewer', John Mone, Thomas Mabr', Walter Hyende, William Smyth, [*column two*] Stephen Hywode, Walter Bryd, John Rowe, William Swyft, Thomas Parrok, John Berton 'cok' [*i.e. cook*], Philip Dier', and many others to the number of 100 in all. [*The first group, numbering 47, with the addition of the mayor may have constituted the Forty-Eight. The large attendance is not explained by the nature of the business recorded below.*]

[f. 111v.; *faded and stained*]

[Ordered]: those supervising the common ditch (*foss'*) to punish delinquents, so that the ditch be reformed to its original shape.

Discussed in the presence of the [bishop's] bailiff, Robert Longe: that his hearing of pleas should be held before the same bailiff for paying to him the cost of accounts [?] (*quod cogn' sua placitorum habeatur coram eodem ballivo pro comp' costagiis sibi solvend'*).

[Ordered]: the butchers' stalls to be placed by the market where they were before.

329. Assembly: Friday next before Whitsun 15 Hen. VI [*17 May 1437*].

Present [*in three columns*]: John Marchal, John Wyot, Robert Gilberd, Stephen Mercer, John Bromle, William Waryn, Henry Man, William Warwyk, Richard Wyse, John Shad, William Alisaundr', William Pakyn, [*column two*] Robert Cove, John Estbury, Gilbert Marchal, John Boteler, Peter de Varw, Richard Walker', Richard Gage, John Machyn, William Charlyng, John Wheler', Robert Higon, Simon Poy, [*column three*] Robert Ferour, John Crykemour, John Gerveys, John Gage, John Skot, John Tissebury, John Adekyn, William Gloucestre, Richard Plowman.

Elected as assessors for the expenses of the citizens [at parliament]: Robert Gilberd, William Kokkys, John Colyngbourne, William Prydy; as collectors: John Tutsay, Henry Blakemour, Clement Fourbour, William Leoker 'tannere'.

Elected as city constable in the place of Thomas Freman: Richard Wyse, with John Wyot.

[Ordered:] six large candles (*tortices*) to be provided for the brotherhood of St. George from the money arising from the brethren, for carrying the bodies of the deceased of the brotherhood in the presence of the mayor for the time being and the brethren.

[f. 111a; *an inserted strip of parchment, blank on the dorse, the left-hand side torn away*]

330. The king's writ, dated (Westminster?) 17 March 15 Hen. [VI, *1437*] and signed Bate, to the bailiffs of the town [*sic*] of New Salisbury for the payment to William Pakyn and George Westby, burgesses [*sic*] at the parliament at Westminster 21 Jan. last, of £14 8s. for their expenses in coming, staying 72 days, and returning, each receiving 2s. a day.

[f. 112; *faded and stained*]

331. Assembly: Saturday next after Corpus Christi 15 Hen. VI [*1 June 1437*].

Present [*in three columns*]: John Shad, Richard Gage, Robert Gilberd, William Warwyk, William Waryn, John Bromle, Henry Baron, Stephen Coupere, William Pakyn, [*column two*] Robert Watercombe, Thomas Durneford, John Slegge, Richard Balfot, John Coscombe, John Wheler', Richard Walker, John Elys, John Skot, [*column three*] William Swayn, William Hore, John Kele(. . .), John Gerveys.

Agreed: John Slegge to be one of the city auditors in place of George Westby.

332. Assembly: Wednesday next after St. Matthew 16 Hen. VI [*25 Sept. 1437*].

Present [*in four columns*]: William Cokkys, John Helier', Richard Wyse, Stephen Coupere, William Warwyk, Henry Man, John Wyot, Robert Gilberd, Richard Payn, Peter de Varw, [*column two*] Robert Cofe, Thomas Stoppe, Robert Chamberlayn, John Adekyn, William Swayn, John Skot, John Coscombe, William Knoll, Richard Plowman, [*column three*] Thomas Halle, Simon Poy, Richard Gore, John Weston, John Machon, Richard Gage, Nicholas Shute, John Crikemour, John Tutsay, Thomas Durneford, John Estbury.

Agreed: two others than the ordinary assessors to be elected to assess foreign (*extraneos*) merchants, and the sum so assessed to be levied for the king's use; if necessary the merchants to be distrained. [Elected as assessors for the purpose]: John Slegge, John Estbury.

Richard Payn. [*The names stands isolated on the page.*]

[f. 112v.; *faded and stained*]

333. Election of city officers All Souls 16 Hen. VI [*2 Nov. 1437*].

Mayor, Thomas Freman; reeves, John Gage, Richard Balfot; alderman of Market ward, John Clyve 'tannere'; of St. Martin's, Henry Shad; of New Street, Henry Frend; of Meadow, John Oke chaplain; serjeants, Thomas Yoxford, Walter Huntele.

William Hore, excused [the offices] of alderman and reeve, [to pay] 6 marks, pledges Thomas Freman and William Pakyn; John Crykemore, [excused the office] of reeve, £1 6s. 8d., pledges Thomas Freman and William Pakyn.

[f. 113; *faded and stained*]

334. [*Heading:*] Thomas Freman mayor.

Assembly: Monday a week from St. Martin 16 Hen. VI [*18 Nov. 1437*].

Present [*in four columns*]: Robert Watercombe, John Marche, Richard Payn, Stephen Mercer, John Bromle, John Swyft, Henry Man, Richard Wyse, John Boteler, William Hore, Peter de Varw, John Slegge, [*column two*] Richard Plowman, John Skot, Gilbert Marchal, William Swayn, Richard Gage, John a Port, William Knoll, William Charlyng, John Tissebury, John Estbury, Robert Cove, [*column three*] Henry Frend, Edward Clyve, Henry Shad, Walter Carogan, John Crykemour, John Wheler', John Wyot, Richard Balfot, Robert Gilberd, John Shad, [*column four*] John Adekyn, Simon Poy.

Elected by virtue of the king's letters patent as collectors of the half of a fifteenth [to be] paid on the feast of St. Martin [11 Nov.]: Richard Plowman, Stephen Hendy, Robert Gilberd, Edward Gudyer; as assessors: William Hore, John Boteler, [John Wynchestr' *crossed out*], John Alisaundr', Robert Cove.

335. Assembly: Monday next after the close of Easter 16 Hen. VI [*21 April 1438*].

Present: William Hore, Robert Tannere, Richard Wyse, John White, Henry Man, Robert Warmwell, William Warwyk, Stephen Coupere, John Wyot, William Cokkes, John Marchal, John Shadde, [*then in three columns, the names in pairs except those of Peter de Varw and John Gower*] John Slegge, Robert Watercombe, Simon Poy, Gilbert ('Gybon') Marchal, John Coscombe, Nicholas Shute, [*column two*] Richard Gage, John Clyve, Peter de Varw, John Elys, Henry Shad, [*column three*] John Gower, Richard Walker, John Alisaundr', Henry Frend, John Skok [*sic*].

Ordered: the mayor to approach the dean and chapter, the bishopric being vacant, for permission to make a pit in the market to take the ordure from the market area (*pro fimis circa mercatum imponendis*).

[f. 113v.; *faded and stained*]

[*Heading:*] Thomas Freman mayor.

[The mayor's account.] Payments made by Thomas Freman to the following persons for the £50 loaned to the king in the mayoralty of Stephen Coupere, as appears in the seventh folio back [*no.* **319**]: John Crekemour, 3s. 4d.; Henry Man, 13s. 4d.; John Boteler, 6s. 8d.

Sum of Clement Fourbour and William Leoker, collectors of the expenses of the citizens [at parliament], [paid?] £9 13s. 4d., for which he [*sc.* the mayor] asked for (*petiit*) an allowance for W. Alisaundr' 2s., for George Westby 3s. 4d., for Robert Okebourne 1s., and for strangers 3s. 8d., for which there was paid to the mayor £9 1s. 3d. [remainder £1 3s. 11d. *crossed out*, 13s. 4d. *crossed out*], and so he [*or* they] went quit. [*The calculations is not clear.*]

Memorandum: John Paraunt 'goldsmyth' and W. Knoll, collectors of the fourth part of a fifteenth in the mayoralty of Thomas Freman 16 Hen. VI [*1436–7*], accounted for £5 15s. 9d. They further accounted for £5 1s. 8d. for the fourth part of a fifteenth in the said mayoralty.

2d. [*the figure standing isolated from the entries before and after*].

336. Assembly: Friday next after Corpus Christi 16 Hen. VI [*13 June 1438*].

Present [*in four columns*]: the mayor, Robert Warmwell, William Pakyn, John White, Henry Baron, Robert Gilberd, Richard Gage, Henry Man, William Warwyk, John Swyft, Stephen Mercer, Richard Wyse, John Wyot, William Cokk', John Camel, Peter Dawe, [*column two*] John Marchal, Richard Payn, John Shadde, Ralph Pakker', Robert Watercombe, Symon Poy, Richard Plowman, William Swayn, Gilbert Marchal, Robert Cofe, Nicholas Shute, John Alisaundr', John Crikemour, John Wyot [*again*], [*column three*] William Hore, Edward Godyer, John Eylys 'plomer', Peter de Varw, Richard Balfot, John Gower, John Pette, John Wheler', John Adekyn, Henry Shad, John Skot, Thomas Pakyn, Thomas Whityng, [*column four*] John Tissebury, Henry Frend, Thomas Halle, William Knoll, Walter Carogon, Clement Fourbour, William Child, John Coscombe, John Tutsay, Richard Artour, Robert Lavyng, John Courteys, W. Pridy, Stephen Sadiler.

[f. 114; *faded and stained*]

Ordered: Richard Gage, Nicholas Shute, John Aport to go through Market aldermanry to assess people for the sum to be given King Henry VI upon his first coming to Salisbury; William Swayn, Robert Cofe, Richard Plowman to assess the people of New Street aldermanry; John Estbury, John Hampton, William Halsted to assess the people of St. Martin's aldermanry; Robert Watercombe, John Wheler', John Hobbys to assess the people of Meadow aldermanry.

Memorandum: William Cormaile, collector in Meadow aldermanry of the fourth part of a fifteenth in the mayoralty of Stephen Coupere 14 Hen. VI [*1435–6*] and of Thomas Freman 15 and 16 Hen. VI [*1436–8*], on Tuesday next after St. Peter and St. Paul [*1 July*

1438] accounted for those years by four rolls, two for the said Stephen's time and two for the said Thomas's. The sum of the four rolls was £26 15s. 8d., of which he paid to the said Stephen £6 14s. 6d. for one roll and £6 8s. 4d. for the other, the total paid to Coupere being £13 2s. 10d. And he paid for the whole sum to the said Thomas on the same day for one roll £6 for the other £5 5s. 5d., and £1 6s. 8d. for the last session [?] with all the allowances; the total sum paid to Thomas being £12 12s. 1d., and so he went quit.

337. To be noted: on Wednesday next before St. Peter in Chains 16 Hen. VI [*30 July 1438*] two casks of wine and £14 were given to the bishop of Salisbury on his induction, from the mayor and the following [*in four columns*], William Waryn, Robert Warmwell, Henry Man, William Warwyk, [*column two*] Henry Baron, John Swyft, John White, Richard Wyse, [*column three*] William Hore, Robert Cove, Richard Plowman, Robert Watercombe, [*column four*] John Wheler, John Aport, Richard Gage, William Swayn.

[f. 114v.; *faded and stained*]

338. [*Heading:*] Thomas Freman mayor

Memorandum: on Saturday next after St. Peter in chains 16 Hen. VI [*2 Aug. 1438*], in the presence of [*in five columns, three names in each column*] Thomas Freman mayor, William Waryn, Henry Man, John Swyft, Robert Warmwell, William Warwyk, William Pakyn, Robert Cove, Stephen Coupere, John Wyot, John Aport, Richard Gage, Robert Watercombe, Richard Wyse, William Swayn, £13 was withdrawn from the common chest and delivered to the mayor to pay to the king and to the bishop of Salisbury, Mr. William Ascu [*i.e. Ayscough*].

339. Memorandum: on Friday next after St. Peter in chains 16 Hen. VI [*8 Aug. 1438*] the citizens written below agreed that the king should have as a gift from the city £40 [*crossed out*: of which the mayor would make up the shortfall of £16 8s. and should receive the rent of St. George's hospice until the money was repaid to him]: William Waryn, Robert Warmwell, Henry Man, William Warwyk, Richard Gage, John Marchal, Robert Gilberd, Robert Cove, John White, John Coscombe.

340. Memorandum: on Wednesday next after Michaelmas 17 Hen. VI [*1 Oct. 1438*] on the deliberation of the mayor and other good citizens there were elected as assessors for the half of a fifteenth to be paid on the feast of St. Martin [*11 Nov.*] by William Swayn, the king's collector by letters patent: John Boteler, William Hore, Robert Cove, John Alisaundr'; as collectors: John Shethere for New Street; John Bertevile for Meadow; Thomas Pakker for Market; Philip Adam 'barbour' for St. Martin's.

[*Struck through and marked* 'because later':] Also agreed: the mayor to have [the income from] the hospice called 'Georgesyn' until he has received £10 6s. 8d. owed to him on his account of the £40 given to the king and the £14 and the two casks of wine owed to him by the city chamberlains. Also £19 [2s. 10d. *crossed out*, 2s. 5d. *interlined*] to be paid.]

341. Assembly at the Guildhall (*Guildaulam*): Monday the eve of St. Simon and St. Jude 17 Hen. VI [*27 Oct. 1438*].

The mayor Thomas Freman accounted for the two years of his mayoralty before the citizens, [present: *in four columns*] William Hore, William Cokk', John Wyot, William Warwyk, Robert Warmwell, Henry Baron, John White, Stephen Mercer, [*column two*] John Honythorn, William Swayn, Robert Watercombe, Gilbert Marchal, Walter Caragon, John Tutsay, Ralph Pakker', John Skot, [*column three*] Henry Frend, John Clyve 'tannere', Henry Shad, John Adekyn, John Gerveys, Richard Gage, John Slegge, Robert Cove, [*column four*] Richard Balfot, John Machyn, John Coscombe, Thomas Archebaud, John Shadde, Thomas Halle, Richard Payn, Henry Man, George Westby.

[f. 115; *faded, stained, and holed*]

In the presence of Robert Warmwell, John White, and William Pakyn [auditors; *William Pakyn is not in the list of those present*], agreed: Thomas Freman mayor to have [the income of] the hospice of 'Georgesyn' until he has received £10 6s. 8d.

Also owed by [John Wyot and Robert Cove city chamberlains *crossed out*; the mayor and community *interlined*] on their accounts made on Monday the eve of St. Simon and St. Jude 17 Hen. VI [*27 Oct. 1438*] £19 2s. 5d. From them he received £19 2s. 5d.; from Stephen Henry £2; from John Crikemour, for being excused the office of reeve, £1 6s. 8d.; from Simon Poy, one of the stewards of the brotherhood of St. George, on his account, £1 13s. 8d.; from William Hore, for being excused the office of alderman, £2; from Robert Cove, for the goldsmith's tenement in High Street (*alto vico*), £3 6s. 8d.; from Robert Cove, £3 in part payment of the aforesaid £19 2s. 5d.; from William Hore, as a fine for [being excused] the office of reeve in 17 and 18 Hen. VI [*1438–40*], £2.

[*Four lines almost wholly illegible.*]

Memorandum: all the rolls of the half of a fifteenth in the mayoralty of Thomas Freman 17 Hen. VI [*1438*] – one part remains in the keeping of the said assessors [named] in one part of the next folio, together with the paper books through which the people of the city were assessed (*omnes rotuli medietatis xv tempore Th' Freman maioris anno regni regis H. sexti xvii° altera pars predictorum rotulorum reman' in custodia assessorum predictorum in altera parte prox' foll' simul cum paupir' per quas persone civitatis sunt assessi*).

[f. 115v; *faded, stained, and holed*]

342. Election of the mayor and other officials [*2 Nov. 1438*].

Mayor, Henry Man; reeves, Nicholas Shute, Richard Walker; alderman of New Street, Thomas Byere; of Market, Thomas Temse; of St. Martin's, Thomas Androw; of Meadow, John Gower; serjeants, Henry Frend, Walter Huntele.

[*Written on the right-hand side of the page, and repeated and struck through at the foot*] Fined: Henry Shad, for being excused the office of reeve, £2, pledge John Shad; to be paid to the mayor Henry Man at Michaelmas next [*29 Sept. 1439*].

[f. 116; *faded and stained*]

343. [*Heading*:]: H. Man mayor.

Memorandum: John Shethere, on Saturday the eve of St. Edmund [the archbishop] 17 Hen. VI [*15 Nov. 1438*], as collector for New Street aldermanry, paid to Henry [*recte* William] Swayn, the king's collector in the county of Wiltshire, in the presence of the mayor in the 'Councelhous', for the said aldermanry, which was assessed (*se extendit*) at £9 14s. 9d., £9 12s. He was allowed 2s. 9d. and withdrew quit.

John Bertevile, collector for Meadow aldermanry, answered for the aldermanry, assessed at £1 18s. 4d., which he paid to William Swayn, the collector, in the presence of the said mayor [and] Richard Gage. He withdrew quit, and he was allowed 1s. 6d.

[Philip *crossed out*, John *interlined*] Adam 'barbour', [collector for St. Martin's *in the margin*], answered for £9 [15s. 4d. *crossed out*, 14s. 8d. *interlined*], of which he paid to the said collector in the presence of the said mayor and Richard £8, and afterwards he paid £1 0s. 8d. in the presence of the mayor and Richard Gage. And so he paid £9 0s. 8d., and 14s. was allowed to the said John for certain persons [named] in a list (*secula* [recte *cedula*]) sewn into this [book] [*nos. 343A–K*]. And he withdrew quit.

Thomas Pakker', [collector of Market aldermanry *in the margin*] answered for £14 9s. 7d., of which he paid by the hand of Thomas Yoxford his deputy in the presence of the said mayor and Richard £8. Afterwards he paid £6 6s. 1d. in the presence of the mayor, Robert Warmwell, and Richard Gage, the auditors, on Wednesday next after the Conception [*10 Dec. 1438*]. He withdrew quit, and he was allowed 3s. 6d.

To be noted: the said sums were placed in a bag which was delivered to the mayor to look after and to pay to William Swayn, when he returns from the king's Exchequer.

Sum £27 8s. 4d.

The mayor paid that sum to William Swayn on Wednesday next after the Conception 17 Hen. VI [*10 Dec. 1438*]. Afterwards the said collectors on their account paid to the mayor £7 8s. 9d. Sum total £34 17s. 2d., of which [*blank*].

Afterwards the mayor paid, on Wednesday next before the Conception in the said year [*3 Dec. 1438; either there is a mistake in the MS. or 'afterwards' refers to the first payment above*], in the presence of Robert Warmwell, Richard Gage, and Thomas Yoxford, to the said William Swayn £6 11s. [8d. *crossed out*, 9d. *interlined*]. So there remained in the mayor's keeping 17s. [beyond the said £34 *crossed out*] from which he paid to William Swayn 3s. 4d. for a writ of *constat*.

[*A double leaf inserted between ff. 116 and 117, the first leaf unnumbered, the second numbered f. 116b; faded and mutilated, the second leaf also holed*]

343A. [*An assessment of the inhabitants, apparently, in view of the reference in nos. 341 and 343, for the tax of which the payment is there recorded.*]

[*In two columns*] William Pakyn 2s., John Brake 'helyer' 2d., John Parke 1d., John Thomesene 2d., Thomas Leche 6d., Margaret Coupere 1d., Cristina Golddyng 1d., John Gobeler 1d., John Kent 1d.; sum [*blank*].

343B. William Tayllour 2d., John Bokelond 2d., Nicholas Corys' 2d., Robert Towkere 1d., Stephen Hywode 8d., Walter Huntle 7d., William Shuppton 8d., Richard Cok' 1d., John Potter 2d., John Tuttesay 1s., John Everard 1s. 4d., James Towker 2d., Thomas Pymperne 2d., Nicholas Shutte 1s. 8d., John Leovvyng 2d., Thomas Duche 'tayllour' 2d., Robert Hygon 4d., John Nele 6d., Thomas Bugbrgge [*sic*] 1s. 4d., Roger Brownyng 10d., John Duchman 'corvyser' 2d., John Frye 2d., Thomas Brasyer 8d., John Cardemaker 4d., William Best 4d., John Chapman 2d., [*column two*] Nicholas Barbour 6d., Thomas Taverner 2d., John Cras 6d., Robert Keche 2d., John Agoddeshalf 2d., John Walysser 2d., Robert Cardemaker 2d., Thomas Cabbell 2d., William Barbour 3d., Robert Grever 2d., Robert Meryot 2d., John Felde 4d., Richard Goldsmyth 2d., John Weston 1d., Nicholas Howchon 8d. [*the rest of the page is missing*].

343C. [*On the verso, in three columns*] Richard Sturmy 2d., John Bowode 2d., William Boteler 2d., John Stone 2d., William Baker 1s. 4d., John Gyngle 1d., William Basket 8d., John Goldingham 1d., Robert Fynle 3d., Thomas Panne 2d., Peter Bery 2d., John Feysey 8d., Bartholomew Skynnere 1d., Peter Masselyn 2d., John servant (*serviens*) of the rector 1d., Walter Browne 4d., Robert Couf 1s. 4d., Richard Hunte 2d., John Upton 4d., Richard Plowman 2s., Thomas Silke 8d., John White 'tayllour' 1d., John Waterman 4d., Thomas Seward 2d., Joan Drapere 2d., John Kele 4d., Stephen Barbour 5d., John Botell' 2d., John Hode 4d., John Barbour 3d., John Devyle 2d., John Chapman 8d., Richard Panter 2d., Hugh Helyer 6d., [John Paraunt *crossed out*], John Eylys 6d., John Chaundeler 6d., John Peryn 'skynnere' 2d., John Alee 'corvysor' 8d., Stephen Corvyser 8d., Richard a Chamber 8d., Henry Osteler 2d.; sum [*blank*].

343D. [*column two*] William Fause 4d., Thomas Bokebynder 2d., Thomas Paule 8d., John Thursby 2s., John Stamford 6d., Robert Canne 4d., William Tannere 8d., Henry Chubb 1s., Richard Cok' 2d., Richard Stere 8d., Agnes Eceshale 10d., Robert Recton 4d., John Leche 6d., Thomas Goldsmyth 8d., William Barbour 2d., William Bruwderer

2d., Robert Levyng 10d., Anselm Skynnere 1s., Thomas Cofton 10d., William Swayn 2s., John Burton 2d., John Jeweler 10d., Stephen Hendy 2s., Henry Osteler 2d., Clement Furbour 2s., Alice Hardyng 8d., Henry Smyth 2d., Robert Bulke 1s. 8d., Richard Fourbour 2d., [blank] Sadeler 2d., John Staveley 1s. 4d., Robert Warmwell 5s., Richard Tayllour 1d., John Wynchester 1s. 8d., Gerard Tayllour 2d., John Barbour 2d., Ralph Bowyer 2d., William atte Wode 4d., Thomas Bruwderer 8d., John Bover 1s., Guy Galogemaker 6d., John Pynner 8d., Richard Bowyer 8d., John Peuterer 1s., [column three] John Chaundeler 1s., John Helyer 2s.; sum [blank].

343E. Stephen Sadeler 6d., Thomas Pakker 2s., Richard Knyght 6d., John Newbury 2d., Robert Brid 2d., William Brownyng 2s., Joan Sheppyster 1d., John Wayte 2d., Thomas Smyth 1d., Richard Wytte 1d., John Walesford 2d., Thomas Purewell 6d., John Chippenham 8d., Richard Bocher 2d., William Fouler 4d., Robert Heryng' 6d., John Baker 3d., Richard Edmund 2d., John Kyng 2d., John Wellys 4d., John Short 2d., John Sewter 2d., John Parrok 6d., John Auncell 8d., Thomas Fysshere 2d., Henry Colyngbourne 2d., Walter Fissher 2d., John Byllyk 8d., William ('Gylam') Leche 4d., John Mercer 2d., George Carpenter 2d., John Franke 1s., William Sayes 2d., John Cornyssh' 1d., John Cros 2d., William Waryn 3s., William Coverer 1s., William Flecche 1d., John White 'mercer' 5s., William Cardmaker 2d., Peter Devaryw 1s. 4d.; sum [blank].

343F. [f. 116b] [in three columns] Hugh Glasyer 2d., George Westby 6d., John Hay 8d., John Angold 2d., John Cloterig 1d., John Dancastell' 1d., Peter Whitbred 1d., Henry Man 3s. 4d., Robert Latener 1d., John Dymmok 4d., Reginald Brewer 2d., John Mone 1d., John Lormen 4d., William Haben's wife 2d., Richard Barbour 4d., Thomas Balle 2d., Nicholas Dene 5(. . .), Richard Artour' (. . .), John Bisshampton (. . .), John Bernet 2d., Philip Coke 2d., Thomas Barbour 4d., Thomas Browne 'drover' 4d., John Wodehurst 6d., Matthew Cardemaker 1d., Cristina Baker 6d., John Lowes 1d., William Charlyng 2s., John Wodehay 2d., Laurencia Boteler 6d., Robert Roo 4d., Richard Sadeler 4d., the same Richard's servant (famulus) 2d., Walter Corogon 1s. 8d., William Swyft 4d., Walter Dytton 6d., John Fareham 1d., Henry Baron 3s. 6d., Thomas Beyre 1s. 8d., William Ovyng 6d.; sum [blank]. [Added] Henry Stokes chaplain [blank].

343G. [column two] Market ward:

John Swyft 'dyer' 1s., John Butte 2d., John Weyrdrawer 2d., Richard Fleccher 2d., Thomas Danyell 2d., John Fleccher 4d., Thomas Tarry 8d., William (Gatour?) 1s. 8d., John Clyter 2d., Henry Drew 2d., Gerard Goldsmyth 2d., John (. . .) 2d., Robert Mason 1d., Simon Eylys 8d., John (. . .)er 8d., John (Danyell?) 6d., John Sheder 8d., John Luyter 6d., John Browne 8d., Simon Barbour 2d., Joan Cokkes 1d., Nicholas Dover 1d., John G[a]ttour 6d., Edward Potekary 4d., John Bartevyle 8d., Thomas Mercer 1s., Richard Tykell 4d., John Wyly 6d., John Syvvar' 2d., Thomas Porter 6d., John Bote 1s. 3d., Robert Okebourne [blank], John Gage 1s., George Deverell' 2d., Bartholomew Goldsmyth 2d., Edmund Fissher 2d., John Peyntour 4d., Stephen Jolyfet 8d., [John a Park crossed out], Richard Barbour 2d., John Warde 10d., [column three] John Roddon

2d., Alice Noble 8d., Richard Ecton 1s., John Tayllour 2d., William Bydewode 2d., John Wyllyam 2d.; sum [*blank*].

343H. John Ely 4d., Robert Baker 6d., John Bosampton 1d., William Newbury 2d., Richard Rounde 2d., Robert Pleyer' 2d., Thomas Hele 1d., John Bruton 1d., John Eston 4d., John Stevenys 2d., Thomas Mog' 2d., William Yorke [*the initial letter is Middle English yogh*] 2d., Thomas Sendale 2d., John Bromale 2d., John Page 1s., Ralph Pakker 10d., Thomas Payn 1s. 4d., Richard Lavyngton 1s., William Demenysstr' 2d., Perquin Dyer 1d., John Shergold 4d., John Marchall 8d., Robert Gylberd 5s., John Shupton 4d., Thomas Danyel's wife 4d., James Hamme 2d., John Dubber 3d., John Britford 2d., Thomas Burgeys 4d., William Perys 2d., John Glover 2d., William Townesend 4d., Margaret Gylberd 2d., John Parker 2d., Robert White 2d., William Taverner 2d., [f. 116b verso] [*in three columns*] Agnes Mason 4d., John Purdy 2d., Edward Say's wife 2d., Robert Rydon 4d., Robert Russell 4d., Henry Spencer' 4d., Robert Tarant 4d.; sum [*blank*].

343I. William Glovere 3d., Edmund Brasyer 3d., John Auncell 2d., William Rogger 2d., Robert Preterien 4d., William Cake 2d., William Gerenyng 2d., Nicholas Clerdr 2d., Robert Cake 2d., Robert Britford 2d., Thomas Stevenys 2d., Roger Tayllour 2d., William Hygon 4d., Stephen Lythenard 2d., Thomas Holme 2d., William Swyngell 3d., William Tene 2d., John Wayte 2d., John Alysaundre 1s., John Rovell 4d., Thomas Durneford 1s., Nicholas Tayllour 4d., William Writhe 1s. 8d., William Baker 1d., John Oy 6d., John Corteys 4d., John Helyer 3d., John Mone 1s. 8d., John Colyngbourne 1s. 4d., William Basele 1d., Robert Potter 1s., John Bythewode 4d., John Swyft 2s., [*column two*] John Sherley 1d., Thomas Foule 8d., Alice (*Alysia*) Nutkyn 2d., Alice Mason 2d., Robert Ferrour 3d., William Smyth 6d., Walter Hende 8d., John Barbour 1d., John Warham 2d.; sum [*blank*].

343J. Philip Dyer 4d., Thomas Halle 2d., Stephen Mercer (. . .), Thomas Saylere (. . .), Simon Poy (. . .), William Warw(. . .) 4d., John Shadde (. . .), [Richard (. . .) *crossed out*], John Wyot (2s.?), Matyn [*sic;?* Martin or Matthew] Tayllour 4d., John Androw 7d., Thomas Gyle 10d., William Pope 6d., Geoffrey Bonvalet 1s. 4d., John Garland 1d., John Landesdale 6d., John Sadeler 1d., John Wyot 1s., John Stonard 1d., John Assheford 1s. 4d., John Seeman 1d., Thomas Lauerens 2d., William Kenerig 1d., William Yonge 1d., Thomas Norton 1d., John Smyth 1d., John Wheler 1d., Elizabeth More 6d., John Honythorn 1s. 2d., Richard Gatour 1s., Bartholomew Cok' [3d. *crossed out*, 2d. *interlined*], Richard Gage 1s. 6d., [*column three*] Thomas Wayte 1d., Robert Welle 1d., John Gerveys 1s. 8d., John Tissebury 1s. 4d., John Norman 1s., William Chylde 1s., Thomas Parrok' 1s., William Bookbynder 6d., Robert Synbury 8d., Richard Lynde 6d.; sum [*blank*].

343K. John Glowcestr' 1d., Olive (*Olyva*) Parche 1d., John Bedeford 1d., William White 'helier' 6d., (. . .)estard 6d., (. . .)fildere 4d., (. . .)rche 4d., (. . .) Barbour 1d., William Edyngdon 1d., Joan Ancketille 3d., (Nicholas?) Clyfford 1d., John Donne 4d., William Taverner 2d., John Machon 2d., Edward Doll' 4d., John Frankeleyn 2d., Joan Monere

4d., John Holme 6d., John Clyve 1s., Edward Godeyer 2d., John Mylde 2d., John Weyse 2d., John Dol 2d., Henry Maste 2d., Robert Coteler 1d., Gilbert Marchal 1s., John Berton 8d., Thomas Whityng 1s., Peter Dawe 4d.

[f. 116v.; *faded and stained*]

344. [*Heading:*] H. Man mayor.

Assembly: Wednesday next after the Conception 17 Hen. VI [*10 Dec. 1438*].

Present [*in three columns*]: the mayor, John Wyot, Robert Gilberd, Richard Gage, John Swyft, Thomas Freman, William Warwyk, Stephen Coupere, William Cokkys, Richard Payn, [*column two*] John Hampton, Robert Chynchon, Nicholas Shute, Robert Cove, Thomas Payn, John Crikemour, John Coscombe, Robert Watercombe, John Skot, Thomas Androw, [*column three*] John Gower, John Alisaundr', William Pette, John Tissebury, Richard Wyse.

Agreed: the officials to have their livery and fees secured to the mayor at their true value (*muniend' maiori securite de valore*).

Also, the mayor's livery to be deferred until Easter because of the shortness of time [? *the assembly being too close to Christmas*].

Also, no one of the city to receive any grain brought to the city for storing (*hospitandum*), which leads to scarcity, under penalty.

345. Assembly: Friday in Easter week 17 Hen. VI [*10 Apr. 1439*].

Present [*in four columns*]: the mayor, William Warwyk, Robert Warmwell, William Pakyn, Henry Baron, Richard Wyse, Richard Payn, John White, [*column two*] Richard Gage, John Coscombe, John Estbury, John Gower, John Temse, John Skot, John Adekyn, John Aport, [*column three*] Thomas Pakyn, William Swayn, John Gerveys, Edward Gudyer, Simon Poy, Henry Shad, Thomas Mason, [*column four*] Thomas Androw, William Pope, John Wheler', John Crykemour, Walter Corogon, William Chepman, William Charlyng, William Swengil.

Agreed: to be offered to the Lord Hungerford, the dean of Salisbury, John Sturton 'chivaler', [and] William Darel, the king's commissioners under privy seal letters by which he asks for 100 marks to be loaned on sufficient surety to be provided by the last parliament, the sum to be offered and collected 50 marks and to be loaned to the king. [*The syntax is muddled.*]

Assessors: for New Street, Robert Warmwell, William Swayn; for Market, Thomas Freman, Richard Gage; for St. Martin's, John Boteler, John Coscombe; for Meadow, John White, Robert Watercombe.

Elected to assist the said assessors: the mayor, William Pakyn, Henry Baron, John Aport.

[f. 117; *faded and stained*]

To be noted: the said 50 marks were levied from the persons written below, and on Monday next after St. Mark [*27 Apr. 1439*] were delivered by Henry Man mayor to John Hunyþorn to be taken to London and delivered to John Stourton knight. The same John [Honythorn] was to bring back to the mayor and community sufficient surety for the repayment of the said 50 marks.

[*Added later, overwriting the headings for the first two wards:*] Repayments of the said sum made to the persons below by John Wyot mayor 20 Hen.VI [*1441–2*]. [*The list, in two columns on the recto and in a single column on the verso, has 'paid' (*sol*'), evidently added later, after each amount, with in some instances, as indicated below, a note before or after 'paid'. Before the name Henry Baron is written 'quit', and, as indicated below, don' is written before fourteen of the names, its significance being obscure.*]

345A. New Street ward:

Robert Cove 6s. 8d., John Parham 10s., John Thoresby 6s. 8d., John White 'mercer' £1 6s. 8d., Robert Levyng 3s. 4d., Nicholas Hebbyng 6s. 8d., William Swayn 6s. 8d., Stephen Hendy 6s. 8d., Clement Fourbour 6s. 8d., Robert Bulk 6s. 8d., John Stafele 3s. 4d. R.W. [*?i.e. by Robert Warmwell*], Robert Warmwell £1, John Wynchestr' 6s. 8d., John Bouer 3s. 4d., John Shethere 3s. 4d., John Gy 3s. 4d., John Cathers 5s., John Chaundeler 3s. 4d., John Helier' 'irmonger' £1, Stephen Sadiler 3s. 4d.Y.[*?i.e. by Thomas Yoxford*], John Auncel 3s. 4d. Thomas Y. [*as the last*], William Waryn 13s. 4d. Y. [*as Stephen Sadiler*], H. [*the initial standing alone on its line*], John Gower 6s. 8d., William Charlyng 10s., Walter Carogon 6s. 8d., Henry Baron £1 Hor' [*?i.e. by William Hore*], Thomas Byer' 'mason' 10s.; sum £11 8s. 4d.

345B. [*column two*] Market ward:

(*don'*) John Swyft 10s., Walter Hende 3s. 4d., Stephen Coupere £1 6s. 8d., Thomas Freman £1 6s. 8d., Richard Payn 10s. Wiot [*?i.e. by John Wyot*], Simon Poy 3s. 4d., William Warwyk £1 6s. 8d., Richard Whyse £1, John Wyot £1, Thomas Payn 5s., Stephen Hywode 5s., John Tutsay 3s. 4d., John Everard 5s. Thomas Ox'[*?i.e. by Thomas Yoxford*], Nicholas Shute 6s. 8d. by Richard Gage, (*don'*) William Wrythe 3s. 4d., John Mone 5s., John Colyngbourne 5s., John Swyft 'dier' 3s. 4d., John Clyter 6s. 8d., Thomas Pakker' 10s., John Aport £1, (*don'*) Robert Baker 3s. 4d., John Warde 3s. 4d., Ralph Pakker' 3s. 4d., John Page 3s. 4d., (*don'*) John Asshford 3s. 4d., William Prangnel 3s. 4d. assigned W. Warwyk, William Swengil 3s. 4d., William Pakyn 13s. 4d., (*don'*) Thomas Whytyng 3s. 4d. by Richard Gage, Richard Gage 6s. 8d., (*don'*) William Child 3s. 4d. by Richard Gage, John Gerveys 6s. 8d., William Knoll 6s. 8d., (*don'*) Thomas Bugbrygge £2, Richard Lavyngton 3s. 4d., Robert Gilberd £1, John Clyve 'tannere' 6s. 8d., (*don'*) John Holm 3s. 4d. from Warwike, (*don'*) John Best 3s. 4d., Thomas Shirwode 3s. 4d.; sum £16 11s. 8d.

[f. 117v.; *faded and stained*]

345C. St. Martin's ward:

Edward Gudyer 5s., William Hore 13s. 4d., (*don'*) Thomas Lambard 3s. 4d., Henry Shad 3s. 4d., John Hampton 6s. 8d., John Estbury 5s., John Boteler 6s. 8d., (*don'*) John Coscombe 6s. 8d. Poy [?*i.e. by Simon Poy*], (*don'*) William Halstede 6s. 8d., William Wilmot 3s. 4d., (*don'*) John Crykemour 3s. 4d., John Slegge 5s., John Clyve 3s. 4d., William Meriot 3s. 4d. by Wiot, (*don'*) John Adekyn 3s. 4d., William Purdy 3s. 4d.; sum £4 1s. 8d.

345D. Meadow ward:

William Sopere 5s., John Hobbis 6s. 8d., John Wheler' 3s. 4d. by W. Warwyk, Thomas Archebaud 3s. 4d., Robert Watercombe 6s. 8d.; sum 25s.

Sum total £33 6s. 8d.

[f. 118; *faded and stained*]

346. Assembly: Friday next before St. Luke 18 Hen. VI [*16 Oct. 1439*].

Present [*in three columns*]: John Marchal, George Westby, Stephen Mercer, Robert Warmwell, Henry Baron, Richard Gage, Robert Watercombe, Nicholas Shute, John Whyte, Robert Cove, [*column two*] John Alisaundr', Henry Shad, John Wheler', [John?] Gowher, Thomas Byer', Ralph Pakker, William Swayn, William Cokkys, William Chapman, William Pette, [*column three*] Walter Carogon, John Adekyn, John Skot, Richard Wyse, Simon Poy, Edward Gudyer, Thomas Payn, John Crikemour.

[Agreed:] the mayor to have his pension, as was granted by the community; William Lord to account before the city auditors, and what is owed to him on his account to be provided for him, in whatever way it is paid.

347. Assembly: Friday next after St. Simon and St. Jude 18 Hen. VI [*30 Oct. 1439*].

Present [*in three columns*]: John Camel, Stephen Coupere, John Swyft, Robert Warmwell, William Pakyn, William Cokkis, John Colyngbourne, Robert Chynchon, Richard Gage, William Swayn, Richard Balfot, Walter atte Bule, Robert Watercombe, John Crykemour, Thomas Benet, Robert Hampton, Edward Gudyer, William Knoll, William Pette, [*column two*] John Willy, Gilbert Marchal, Richard Whithorn, John Estbury, Thomas Mew, Richard Payn, Simon Poy, George Westby, John Alisaundr', John Baken, John Deverel, John Wodehay, Henry Frend, Peter de Varw, William Child, John Boteler, John Marchal 'dier', John Aport, [*column three*] John White, Ralph Pakker, Thomas Temse, John Adekyn, Thomas Byer', John Gowher, Richard Plowman, John Gerveys, Thomas

Coscombe, John Clyve 'tannere', Thomas Payn, John Clyve 'brewer', Nicholas Shute, Thomas Copt', William Pope, Thomas Durneford.

[f. 118v.; *faded and stained*]

348. [*Heading:*] H. Man.

Assembly: Tuesday next after St. Simon and St. Jude 18 Hen. VI [*3 Nov. 1439*].

Present [*in four columns*]: Robert Cove, John Everard, Robert Gilberd, William Cokkis, William Pakyn, Henry Baron, Richard Payn, John Boteler, William Hore, [*column two*] William Warwyk, John Marchal, William Halstede, John Willy, William Swayn, George Westby, Richard Gage, Robert Watercombe, [*column three*] Richard Plowman, John Gerveys, Richard Balfot, John Tutsay, Ralph Pakker, John Skot, John Colyngbourne, William Swengel, Thomas Copt', Peter de Varw, [*column four*] William Charlyng, Thomas Mewe.

Elected for parliament: [John White *crossed out*], Richard Payn, William Lodelowe.

Election (*Elexio*) of the mayor and city officials:

Mayor, William Warwyk; reeves, John Everard, Robert Cove; alderman of New Street, Henry Chubbe; of Market, John Parch; of St. Martin's, John Copter; of Meadow, John Tutsay; serjeants, Thomas Yoxford, Walter Huntele.

[f. 119; *faded and stained*]

349. [*Heading:*] in the mayoralty of William Warwyk.

Assembly: Saturday the eve of St. Nicholas 18 Hen. VI [*5 Dec. 1439*].

Present [*in three columns*]: H. Frend, William Pette, (Richard?) Plowman, Gilbert Marchal, John Crikemour, John Hobbys, Simon Poy, Henry Chubbe, John Copt', Richard Gage, George Westby, William Swyft, [*column two*] William Hore, Robert Warmwell, John Swyft, Richard Wyse, Nicholas Shute, William Cokkis, John Aport, William Pakyn, John Boteler, John (Shad?), Henry Man, [*column three*] Robert Chynchon, Anselm Hebbyng, William Halstede, H[enry] Blake(moure?), John Tutsay, John Wheler, John Gower, William Charlyng, John Wynchestre, John Mone, William Wrythe, John Wyot 'brewer', John Clyve 'brewer', Ralph Sandes.

Articles noted on the part of the mayor:

Whether fees ought to be paid this year as they were formerly paid?

Whether Thomas Hall should be the third serjeant attending on the mayor, and what wages he should have? Deferred.

Which lords' officials should have wages or gifts? Answer, the king's and the duke of Gloucester's.

Whether it was proposed to have city officials this year? Answer, no.

Whether the bishop's steward and bailiff should be rewarded (*opulentur*) in the courts of law at the mayor's expense, remitting nothing from their fee?

Whether the bailiff should be retained for green wax, to be made good among the citizens (*retineatur pro viridi cera salvand' inter cives civitatis*)?

Ordered: the city cooks to cook their meat as and [*a blank space*] at retail [?].

[*A list, in four columns, the purpose of which is not apparent; fifteen of the thirty-five names are in the list of those present, above.*] Robert Cove, John Shad, John Everard, Richard Payn, Thomas Freman, John Swyft, Henry Man, Robert Warmwell, [*column two*] John White, Stephen Coupere, William Hore, John Boteler, Richard Gage, Richard Balfot, Thomas Payn, Elias Plomer, Thomas Durneford, [*column three*] Simon Poy, Peter de Varw, Gilbert Marchal, Richard Cove, John Marchal, William Swyft, Edward Gudyer, William Chepman, John Skot, [*column four*] Henry Frend, Laurence Pakker', George Westby, Nicholas Shute, John Gower, William Pette, Henry Elyot, William Swengel, Richard Lowode.

[f. 119v.; faded and stained]

350. Assembly: Friday the eve of St. Gregory 18 [Hen.VI, *11 March 1440*] for contributing for barriers ('barrers') within the city [*with amounts attached to the first eleven names*].

Present [*in two columns*]: William Warwyk mayor £1, Richard Gage 3s. 4d., William Hore 3s. 4d., Stephen Coupere 3s. 4d., John White 5s., Robert Warmwell 5s., Henry Man [3s. 4d. *crossed out*] 5s., John Swyft 1s. 8d., Thomas Freman [3s. 4d. *crossed out*] 5s., John Wyot 1s. 8d., Richard Pay 3s. 4d., John Everard, Robert Cove, John Shad, John Marchal, Gilbert Marchal, Richard Plowman, John Clyve 'brewer', Peter de Varw, Robert Gilberd, William Swayn, John Colyngbourne, William Cokkys, Richard Plowman, Peter de Varw [*again*], John Wheler, William Halstede, William Charlyng, John Copter, Walter Carogan, Edmund Penston, John Alisaundr', William Pette, Henry Chubbe, John Aport, John Boteler, Robert Chynchon, John Tutsay, John Gower, John Mone, William Wrythe, John Gerveys, Richard Balfot, Ralph Pakker', John Skot, William Swengil.

Ordered: the steward of each guild in the city summoned to this assembly to see that the men of each guild fit for military service (*defensabiles*), both light horsemen and archers, are mustered, and so mustered parade before the mayor and his fellows, the king's commissioners, on Monday next before St. George next [*18 Apr. 1440*], etc.

Also, the old constitution viz. that 2 lb. of wax from those who do not come to the mayor's assembly to be observed, as confirmed in the mayoralty of John White. Added to the same: if anyone legitimately summoned by the city serjeants does not come, [his name] to be written by the city clerk to the serjeants or one of them, to levy for the city's use 2 lb. of wax or the price of it from the goods and chattels of the defaulter, unless he has a reasonable cause of absence; the serjeant to receive from the defaulter for his labour 1d.; and if the serjeant does not levy the said amercement he is to pay to the chamberlains 2d. for the city's use for each defaulter.

[f. 120; *faded and stained*]

Elected to attend (*assidend'*) the men for making the barriers: Robert Warmwell, John White.

[*A strip of parchment inserted between ff. 119 and 120, blank on the dorse, unnumbered in the main foliation*]

351. The king's writ, dated Westminster 24 February 18 Hen. [VI, *1440*] and signed Kirkeby, to the mayor and bailiffs for the payment to William Ludlowe and Richard Payn, citizens at the parliament at Westminster on the morrow of St. Martin last [*12 Nov. 1439*], of £17 12s. for their expenses in coming, staying 88 days, and returning, each receiving 2s. a day.

[f. 120 (*cont.*)]

352. Assembly: Friday next after Corpus Christi 18 Hen. VI [*27 May 1440*].

Present [*in four columns*]: John Shad, John Aport, Robert Cove, John Wyot, William Pakyn, Robert Okebourne, Henry Man, Henry Baron, Stephen Coupere, Richard Payn, [*column two*] John Boteler, Robert Chynshon, Richard Gage, Gilbert Marchal, Thomas Pakker, John Gerveys, Richard Plowman, Simon Poy, Walter Hende, Walter Corrogan, [*column three*] Thomas Payn, John Crykemour, Ralph Pakkere, Edward Gudyer, William Knoll, Henry Frend, John Skot, William Pette, Thomas Stoppe, Henry Chubbe, [*column four*] Thomas Copter, William Charlyng, William Swyft, William Sopere, Henry Elyet, John Elys, John Alisaundr', John Slegge, John Paraunt.

Elected as assessors for the fourth part of a fifteenth to be paid on the nativity of the St. John the Baptist [*24 June 1440*]: Richard Wyse, [Robert Cove *crossed out*], William Hore, Simon Poy, Richard Plowman; collectors: for New Street, William Brownyng; for Forum, Clement Fourbour; for St. Martin's [William Cokkys *crossed out*, Thomas Byer' *interlined*]; for Meadow, John Thorsby.

[Ordered:] everyone to appear in his best clothes (*meliori apparatu*) on the eve of St. John the Baptist [*23 June*] and of St. Peter and St. Paul [*28 June*], and a muster to be held on the feast of St. Matthew then next following [*21 Sept. 1440*].

[f. 120v.; *faded and stained*]

353. [*Heading:*] William Warwyk mayor.

Assembly: Wednesday next before the nativity of St. John the Baptist 18 Hen. VI [*22 June 1440*].

Present[*in four columns*]: Robert Cove, William Cokkis, Thomas Freman, the mayor, W. Pakyn, Stephen Coupere, Henry Man, Robert Warmwell, John Wyot, Richard Gage, [*column two*] Thomas Copter, John Gower, John Swyft, John Skot, John Estbury, Henry Frend, Ralph Pakker', Walter Hende, Thomas Mewe, William Swengel, [*column three*] John Deverel, Peter de Varwe, Gilbert Marchal, William Swayn, John Chepman, William P(akyn?), Henry Shad, Thomas Copteore [*again*], Nicholas Shute, Thomas Payn, [*column four*] William Chylde, William Knoll, John Aport, Thomas Temse, John Tutsay, William Hore, William Charlyng, Thomas Mone, Richard Walker', John Wheler', William Pette, Richard Balfot.

Ordered: William Russel not to enter the city to perform the office of clerk of the market in the city.

Also, the assessors and collectors specified on the other part [of this folio] to be assessed by William Swengel, Robert Warmwell, William Pakyn, Richard Gage.

Also, to be paid to George Westby, William Baker', and William Balfot 'laborer' for allowances in connection with the discussion with (*iuxta parliamentum coram*) the abbot of Malmesbury and John Saymour, the king's royal commissioners in this matter, £1. [*Added*, Afterwards it was paid to them by the mayor. *The whole entry has been struck through.*]

Also, the 30s. which the mayor paid to Susan More for 'Pynnokkesyn' to be paid to the mayor by the chamberlains.

Also, the mayor to be paid for his pension during his mayoralty.

Elected to write down the names of those who contributed to making the walls around the city: John Parant 'goldsmyth', Thomas Pakkere. [*The two names, written on the right-hand side of the page, could apply either to the preceding or to the following item, which they overlap, or to both, but it seems more likely that the collectors of the following item are those named on the next folio.*]

Collectors within the city by virtue of the king's letters patent.

[f. 121; *faded and stained*]

[*Heading:*] Collectors.

Market ward. To be noted: Thomas Byere is to pay, by hand of John Tutsay, [to?] the king's collector, £7. [*Added*: There remained 13s. 3d.; he paid 10s. and is quit.]

New Street ward. Clement Fourbour, the collector, (. . .) [*or a gap*] £4 11s. [*Added*: He paid 4s. 11d. and is quit.]

St. Martin's ward. William Brownyng, the collector (. . .) [*or a gap*] £4 7s. [*Added*: 3s. 6d., there remained 6s. 3d.; paid.]

Meadow ward. John Thoresby, the collector (. . .) [*or a gap*] 18s. 8d.

Sum total, £16 16s. 8d.

[Deducted for abatements for the fourth part of a fifteenth, £2 2s. 6d. *crossed out*.]

Sum of a whole fifteenth of the city of Salisbury, £75 0s. 2½d.

Sum of the fourth part, £18 15s.

Deducted for abatements for the fourth part, £2 2s. 6d.

The sum delivered by the said collectors to be paid to the king, £16 2s. 6d.

So from the £16 16s. 8d. there remains 14s. 2d., which was paid to mayor.

John Paraunt and Thomas Pakkere, collectors of a tenth and half of a tenth in the city, [are charged with] £56 5s. 1½d., from which a deduction, in proportion to £7 on a whole tenth, is made of £5 5s.; balance, £51 1½d., of which they paid by two tallages £47 12s. 6d. They owe £3 7s. 7½d., of which 17s. 6½d. is for the fourth part and £2 10s. 1d. is for the half.

[f. 121v.; *faded and stained*]

354. Assembly: Friday next after the nativity of the Blessed Virgin Mary 19 Hen.VI [*9 Sept. 1440*].

Present [*in four columns*]: Robert Cove, Robert Okebourne, Henry Man, the mayor, Stephen Coupere, John Skot, Richard Payn, William Hore, [*column two*] John Copter, the husband [Thomas Hayne *interlined*] of Edward Dubbere's daughter, John Tutsay, Peter de Varw, John Perrant, William Halstede, Richard Gage, Gilbert Marchal, Thomas Halle, [*column three*] William Pette, John Gerveys, Nicholas Shute, John Durneford, Edward Gudyer, William Charlyng, John Skot [*again*], John Estbury, [*column four*] Henry Frend, Simon Poy, Ralph Pakker, Richard Cove, John Hampton, Henry Shad, William Swengil, Henry Chubbe, Thomas Payn, William Child.

Ordered: Richard Gage, who has newly built the north gate [*de novo edificavit portam bor'*] on the road towards Sarum castle, to have the said [house *crossed out*] gate, with the houses there after he has built them, for a term of eighty [years] from Michaelmas next.

Also, the common seal to be placed under six locks and six keys in a chest and [*incomplete*].

Also, those assessed to pay various sums for the building of the said gate to be distrained to pay the said sums.

Also, the mayor to have his pension as other mayors have, viz. £10.

Also, Richard Wyse, for being excused [the office of] assessor for the half of a fifteenth, of the fourth part of a fifteenth, and of the half of a fifteenth payable according to the letters patent made and directed to John Parant and Thomas Pakker and paid to Robert Cove, to pay [a fine of] 3s. 4d.

[f. 122; *faded and stained*]

Fines: [Thomas Mewe 'mason' made fine *crossed out*] Thomas Mewe 'mercer' made fine for being excused (*exonerand'* [*altered from or to* excercend']) the office of alderman and reeve, £4, to be paid at Easter next £2, at Michaelmas following £2, pledge Henry Man.

William Pope made fine for being excused the office of alderman and reeve (. . .) £4, to be paid at Easter next £2, at Michaelmas following £2, pledge William Pakyn.

John Glovere of Taunton made fine for being excused the office of alderman, £2, to be paid on the feast of St. Peter in chains next [*1 Aug. 1441*], pledge William Warwyk. [*Added*: Paid to the mayor by William Warwyk.

Memorandum: a document containing a bond for £1 6s. 3d. was delivered to William Pakyn to bring to 'le Counselhous', the document relating to the 50 marks paid to the king.

Fines: Thomas Hardyng of London made fine for being excused the office of alderman, £2, pledges William Warwyk and William Pakyn, to be paid on the feast of St. Peter in chains next [*1 Aug. 1441*] etc. [*Added*: Paid to the mayor William Warwyk, *and the entry struck through.*]

Walter Carogan, for being excused the office of alderman and reeve, £4, pledge John Port, to be paid £2 at Easter next and the other £2 at Michaelmas following. [*Added*: John Aport paid it to the mayor, *and the entry struck through.*]

William Pette, for being excused the office of alderman [and reeve *interlined*], £4, pledge John Boteler, to be paid at Easter next £2 and the other £2 at Michaelmas following. [*Added*: paid to the mayor William Warwyk *and the entry struck through.*]

Thomas Mogge 'couper' made fine for being excused the office of alderman and reeve, £4, pledges John Everard and Gilbert Marchell. [*Added*: paid to William Warwyk mayor *and the entry struck through.*]

[f. 122v.; *faded and stained*]

355. [*Heading:*] W. Warwyk.

Assembly: Friday next after St. Luke 19 Hen.VI [*21 Oct. 1440*].

Present [*in four columns*]: the mayor W. Warwyk, Robert Warmwell, Henry Man, Stephen Coupere, John Wyot, Richard Payn, Richard Wyse, William Cokkys, Robert Cove, William Hore, John Boteler, John Everard, Thomas Freman, John Shad, John Aport, [*column two*] Richard Gage, Gilbert Marchall, John Tutsay, Richard Plowman, John Estbury, Thomas Mewe, William Swayn, William Charlyng, John Kele, John Clyve 'tannere', Simon Poy, John Skot, [*column three*] John Wynchestr', John Gower, Nicholas Shute, Henry Chubbe, John Slegge, John Clyve 'brewer', John Wylly, William Pope, Henry Shadde, Thomas Payn ('wefer'?), William (. . .)ld, John Sopere, John Crykemour, [*column four*] Robert Levyng, Thomas Copt', Anselm Hebbyng, Edward Gudyer, Thomas Halle, John Marchal, John Alisaundr'.

Elected as assessors for the half of a fifteenth: William Hore, John Aport, William Halstede, [Richard Plowman *crossed out*], John Gower; the old collectors as in the second folio back [*no. 352*].

[Ordered:] Thomas Hall, the third mace-bearer, to have from the mayor and community for his salary 6s. 8d. and his food (*esculeta*) and livery from the mayor [and the community *crossed out*].

Fine: Thomas Byer' made fine for being excused the office of reeve, £2, to be paid at the nativity of St. John the Baptist next [*24 June 1441*] £1; and at Michaelmas following £1.

[f. 123; *faded and stained*]

356. Election (*Elexio*) of the mayor and other officers [*2 Nov. 1440?*].

Mayor, William Warwyk; reeves, John Clyve 'tannere', John Whelere; alderman of New Street, Thomas Selk; of Market, William Swengil; of St. Martin's, John Fowey; of Meadow, Thomas Knoyel; serjeants, Thomas Yoxford, Walter Huntle.

Robert Warmwell granted to the mayor and community, for being excused the office of mayor, 10 marks and £1 6s. 8d. in rent.

William Swyft, after his account, granted that he would pay for the brethren of St. George for his time as steward of St. George's 13s. 4d.

[f. 123v.; *faded and stained*]

357. [*Heading:*] Warwyk.

[*Payments by collectors of the half of a fifteenth. The initial amounts paid for each ward make up the total of £25 specified in no. 358; the amounts paid 'afterwards' make a total of 3s. more than the £6 10s. also specified there.*]

Collector for Market ward: To be noted, Thomas Byer' on the eve of St. Katherine 19 Hen. VI [*24 Nov. 1440*] paid in the presence of the mayor, Robert Warmwell, Henry Man, and Richard Gage, the auditors, £10, afterwards £3 13s. 4d., immediately afterwards 6s. 8d., and afterwards 2s. 4d. paid to the mayor.

Collector for New Street ward: Clement Fourbour paid £7, afterwards 14s., immediately afterwards by Richard Gage 6s., and afterwards paid 8s. 5d. [in Thomas Yoxford's keeping *interlined*]. Allowed to him, 2s. 8d. [which he paid to the mayor as appears below *interlined*]. The said 6s. will be paid to Ricard Gage at the next audit (*collecta'*), and so he [*sc.* Clement Fourbour] went quit. [*Added*: The mayor paid the 6s. to Richard Gage on the Wednesday [*19 Apr. 1441*] in Easter week.]

Collector for St. Martin's ward: William Brounyng [paid] £6, afterwards £1, for the half of a fifteenth which amounted to [*blank*]. Afterwards he paid 2s. 3d., and 4s. was allowed to him, and he went quit.

Collector of Meadow ward: John Thoresby £2.

At the same time the mayor paid 10s. until it should be levied, and afterwards he received from Clement Fourbour 2s. 8d. and from Thomas Yoxford 8s. 5d., and so there remained in the mayor's hands 1s. 1d., which he owed to the city.

358. Assembly: Friday next after St. Lucy 19 Hen. VI [*16 Dec. 1440*].

Present [*in four columns*]: the mayor, Robert Warmwell, Henry Man, William Pakyn, John [*surname omitted*], Robert Cove, Thomas Freman, William Swayn, John Shad, John Everard, Stephen Mercer, [*column two*] John Boteler, John Gerveys, Edmund Penston, William Pette, Thomas Pakyn, John Hende, William Swengel, Henry Frend, Thomas Stoppe, Peter de Varw, Thomas Payn, [*column three*] Simon Poy, John Skot, John Ystbyry, Richard Payn, Walter Caragon, John Wheler', John Gower, John Wheler' [*again*], Richard Gage, Edward Gudyer, [*column four*] John Mone 'touker', John Gage, William Charlyng, John Colyngbourne, William Pope, Thomas Mewe, Robert Hygon, John Alisaundr', Thomas Stoppe [*again*].

Elected as coroner after the death of Robert Gilbert: Robert Cove.

[Elected] to assess [the levy] for the expenses of the citizens [*sc.* at parliament] amounting to £17 12s., of which half was paid to the said citizens, viz. £8 16s., to each of them £4 8s.: William Swayn, John Estbury, Walter Corrogan, William Pette.

Memorandum: William Warwyk mayor delivered to Thomas Pakker and John Parant 'goldsmyth', the king's collectors by letters patent, £25; and by hand of Geoffrey Bolleyn of London, as appears in a memorandum about the said half of a fifteenth made between the said mayor and the collectors, £6 10s.

[f. 124; *faded and stained*]

[*Heading*:] W. Warwyk.

Elected to levy and collect the same: Robert Cronin, Henry Blakemour.

[Elected] to supervise and order the construction of the great ditch (*fossatum*) of the city, which is the city's responsibility, and from which some persons with free tenements have defaulted, and to inquire who is willing to contribute, and how much, to making gates and ditches, and if necessary to assess them for the completion of the work: [*in a column to the right of the foregoing*] the mayor, Robert Warmwell, Henry Man, William Pakyn, John Boteler, Thomas Freman, John Everard, Richard Gage, John Skot, John Alisaundr', John Hampton, Nicholas Shute, Henry Frend.

[Ordered:] the mayor to be paid his pension by the chamberlains.

359. Assembly: Wednesday next after St. Hilary 19 Hen. VI [*18 Jan. 1441*].

Present: William Warwyk, Robert Warmwell, Thomas Freman, Richard Wyse, H. Man, John Aport, Robert Cove, John Shad, Richard Gage, Walter Hende, Ralph Pakker', Walter Carogon, John Boteler, William Halstede, [*then in three columns*] [*no forename*] Clyve 'brewer', Nicholas Shute, Thomas Payn, Edward Gudyer, William Swengil, [*column two*] Thomas Stoppe, Thomas Gerveys, John Hampton, Henry Frend, William Knoll, [*column three*] Gilbert Marchal, John Honythorn, Thomas Copter, John Mone 'touker'.

Ordered: to pay the king as a loan 50 marks, to be repaid on the feast of St. Martin [*11 Nov.*].

Memorandum: on Wednesday next after St. Vincent 19 Hen. VI [*25 Jan. 1441*] there were sent to London by Robert Okebourne a charter of King Richard [II] concerning the liberties of the city and a letter patent about the same by the hand of William Pakyn.

Memorandum: John Boteler to have the grazing of the great ditch (*magn' fossat'*) of Salisbury for 2s. a year, for which he has paid to Robert Cove 4d., and there remains [due] 1s. 8d.

[f. 124v.; *faded and stained*]

360. Persons assessed to the 50 marks loaned to the king with the other 50 marks granted to the king in the mayoralty of H. Man. Repayments of the said sums made by John Wyot mayor to the following persons 20 Hen. VI [*1441–2*].

[*In three columns. Each amount is followed by 'paid' (*sol'*), with in some instances, as indicated below, a note, before or after* sol', *of the person through or to whom the repayment was made; a few names are preceded by* don', *the significance of which is obscure.*]

360A. William Waryn £1 [13s. 4d. *crossed out*], Robert Warmwell £1, Henry Man 13s. 4d., William Pakyn £1, Stephen Coupere £1, Thomas Freman £1, Richard Wyse £1, John Wyot 13s. 4d., William Hore 13s. 4d., John Aport £1, John Everard 5s. quit [?], Robert Cove 13s. 4d., John Estbury 6s. 8d., John Boteler 6s. 8d., (*don'*) John Swyft 3s. 4d., William Swayn 40s., John Helier' £1, Richard Payn 10s., Thomas Pakker' 10s. Wiot, John Page 3s. 4d., John Mone 'touker' 5s. W. War., Richard Lavyngton 3s. 4d., (*don'*) John Asshford 3s. 4d., William Swengel 3s. 4d., John Alisaundr' 3s. 4d., William Sopere 5s., John Colyngbourne 5s., Walter Hende 3s. 4d. Warwik, Stephen Hyewode 5s., Thomas Payn 5s., Simon Poy 3s. 4d., William Child 3s. 4d. by Richard Gage, [Thomas *crossed out*] John Gerveys 6s. 8d., John Wyot 'brewer' 3s. 4d. Wiot, John Honythorn 3s. 4d. Wiot, Richard Gage 6s. 8d., Nicholas Shute 6s. 8d., (*don'*) Thomas Whytyng 6s. 8d., John Clyve 'tannere' 6s. 8d. to the mayor and Gage, John Holm 'tannere' 3s. 4d. to the mayor and Gage, William Knoll 6s. 8d., (*don'*) Thomas Bugbrygge 3s. 4d., William Clyter 6s. 8d., Simon Gylys 3s. 4d., William Halstede 6s. 8d.; sum £20 16s. 8d.

360B. John Warde 'touker' 3s. 4d., [*no forename*] Shirwode 'mercer' 3s. 4d., (*don'*) Thomas Mabre 3s. 4d., (*don'*) John Wyse 3s. 4d., (*don'*) William Smyth 3s. 4d., John Hobbes 6s. 8d., Thomas Stoppe 3s. 4d., John Wheler 'webbe' 3s. 4d., William Charlyng 10s. & 10s. [?], John Chatour 'smyth' 1s. 8d., John Bertevile 3s. 4d., John Best 'smyth' 3s. 4d., Thomas Helier' 3s. 4d., Robert Chynchon 3s. 4d., (*don'*) William Wotton 3s. 4d., (*sol'* [?*recte don'*]) William Pridy 3s. 4d., John Ykeswell 3s. 4d. Wiot, (*don'*) Thomas Puse 3s. 4d. by Wotton, Henry Shad 3s. 4d. Wiot, Thomas Baron 6s. 8d., Stephen Sadiler 3s. 4d. Y. [?*i.e. Yoxford*], John Shether 3s. 4d., John Chippenham 3s. 4d., Stephen Hendy 6s. 8d., William Brounyng 6s. 8d., John Wynchestr' 6s. 8d., Edward Gudyer 5s., Clement Fourbour 6s. 8d., (*don'*) John Crykemour 3s. 4d., John Gower 6s. 8d., (*don'*) Thomas Mewe 6s. 8d., John Stafele 3s. 4d., John Hampton 6s. 8d., John Thoresby 6s. 8d., Robert Levyng 3s. 4d., Anselm Hebbyng 6s. 8d., Robert Bulk 6s. 8d., John Bover 3s. 4d., John Gy 3s. 4d., Anselm Graunt 3s. 4d. Y. [?*i.e. Yoxford*], Walter Carogan 6s. 8d., John Clyve 'brewer' 3s. 4d., John Everard 5s. Th. Ox. [?*i.e. Thomas Yoxford*], William Wilmot 3s. 4d., John Parrok 3s. 4d.; sum £10 8s. 4d.

360C. John Brouderer 3s. 4d., John Slegge 5s., John Tyssebury 3s. 4d. Wiot, (*don'*) John Adekyn 3s. 4d., Bartholomew de Champ 3s. 4d., John Boteler 'mercer' 3s. 4d. Wiot, Thomas Cofton 3s. 4d., John Ferour 3s. 4d., Robert Roo 3s. 4d., William Glovere 3s. 4d. Warwyk, William Meriot 3s. 4d. to the mayor and Gage, William Lyghtfot £1; sum £2 18s. 4d.

[f. 125; *faded and stained*]

361. [*Heading*:] Warwyk mayor.

[*Payments by collectors of the fourth part of a fifteenth. The arithmetic is not clear.*]

St. Martin's ward: William Brownyng, the collector, paid to the mayor for the [half of a *crossed out*] fourth part of a fifteenth on Wednesday next after the Annunciation 19 Hen. VI [*29 Mar. 1441*] £4. And afterwards he paid 12s. 3d. [*corrected from* 8d.], and was allowed 1s. 9d. which could not be levied, and 3s. for his clerk [of which 2s. for Hore, and so *interlined*] the mayor received 7s. 6d. [*corrected from* 10d., *corrected from* 6d.], and he [*sc.* William] went quit. [And allowed to him for W. Hore 2s. *crossed out.*]

New Street ward: Clement Fourbour, the collector, for the fourth part of a fifteenth, on Monday next after the Annunciation 19 Hen. VI [*29 Mar. 1441*] paid to the mayor £4. And afterwards he paid £1 11s. 1d., from which he was allowed 3s. 4d. for William Swayn, 1s. which could not be levied, and 3s. for his clerk, and there remained £1 3s. 9d. in the mayor's hands.

Market ward: Thomas Bier' 'mason,' the collector, for the fourth part of a fifteenth, on the said day paid to William Warwyk the mayor [£1 7s. 11d. *crossed out*] £8. Afterwards, on Wednesday in Easter week [*19 Apr.*] he paid £1 4s. Besides this, he was allowed 5s. 3d. for what could not be levied and for his clerk.

Meadow ward: John Thoresby, the collector, for the fourth part of a fifteenth, on the said day paid to the mayor £1 7s. 11d.

Memorandum: the mayor delivered to the king's collectors Thomas Pakker' and John Parham [*recte* Parant] £17 [2s. 6d. *crossed out*] on Wednesday next after the Annunciation 19 Hen. VI [*29 Mar. 1441*] and afterwards on the same day to the said John Parant £4 7s. 11d., of which £3 7s. 7½d. was from the old half of a fifteenth.

362. Assembly: Friday in Easter week 19 Hen. VI [*21 Apr. 1441*].

Present [*in four columns*]: the mayor, Robert Warmwell, Henry Man, Stephen Coupere, William Cokkys, William Swayn, John Wyot, John Boteler, William Hore, Thomas Mewe, Richard Wyse, [*column two*] Richard Gage, Henry Frend, Simon Poy, Walter atte Bole, John Gerveys, John Crikemour, John Tutsay, Henry Shad, Thomas Selk, John Aport, [*column three*] William Halstede, William Charlyng, John Willy, Edward Gudyer, Thomas Stoppe, John Marchal, Robert Chynchon, William Pope, William Swengel, [*column four*] Thomas Durneford, Nicholas Shute.

Agreed: on the feast of St. Martin next [*11 Nov. 1441*] to pay to William Swayn for his expenses and labour in making [arrangements] for two tallies and two letters patent relating to the apportionment (*allocac'*) of the 100 marks loaned to the king by the mayor and community, at the rate of 1d. for each noble, the sum of 16s. 8d. [*added, which was paid to William Swayn by John Wyot mayor.*] [*The noble was evidently assigned the value, in the context, of 8s. 4d.*]

Memorandum: there remained in the mayor's hands on Wednesday in Easter week 2s. 7d., saving the audit of his account.

[f. 125v.; *faded and stained*]

Stewards elected by the 'mercers', 'grocers', [and] 'drapers' for completing the ditch, William Hore, William Swayn; [*then in tabular form*] stewards of the guild (*artis*) of weavers, Nicholas Shute, Thomas Payn; [*then in tabular form in two columns*] of the brewers (*pandoxatorum*), William Halstede, Walter Carrogon; of the fullers, Ralph Pakk', Stephen Hywode; of the tailors (*sissorum*), Stephen Hendy, John Stavele; of the shoemakers (*sutorum*, 'curriours'), John Ecton, Simon Wylys; of the bakers, William Colyn, William Swengil; of the innkeepers (*ostill'*), Clement Furbour, John Stafford; of the 'dubbers', 'parchmeners', [and] 'glovers', John Crykemour, John Slegge; of the barbers (*barbitons'*) [and] cooks, Nicholas Wedergrove and Thomas Hurde; of the 'goldsmyth' [*sic*], 'blacksmythes', [and] 'brasiers', Walter Hende, John Parant; of the 'sadilers', cutlers ('cotelers'), pewterers ('peutres'), 'pynneres', [and] 'cardmakers', Stephen Waryn, John Cathero; [*column two*] of the fishmongers (*piscatorum*) [and] vintners ('vynters'), John Parrok, John Bertevile; of the 'bochers', John Chippenham, John Baker; of the 'tanners', Thomas Stoppe, John Clyve; of the 'diers', John Eston, John Lavyngton; of the 'carpinters', 'bowiers', 'coupers', 'masones', tilers ('heliers'), limeburners ('lymberners'), [and] 'flecchers', John Rede, John Cras 'helier' alias Fulbrok; of the 'skynners', Anselm Hebbyng, William Meyson; of the 'chandelers' [and] attorneys at law, [John Skot *crossed out*], [*no forename*] Penston, Thomas Yoxford.

[f. 126; *faded and stained*]

[Elected] as constables: William Hore and Richard Payn.

[f. 126a; *a paper fragment, the right-hand side missing, inserted between ff. 125 and 126*]

363. [*Apparently a note relating to the will of William Charlyng.*]

On Wednesday the morrow of St. Luke [*19 Oct., ?1440*] (. . .) in the presence of John Pa(. . .) concerning the goods and chattels of William Charlyng (. . .) W. Bowier then present (. . .) sale of wines of the same (. . .) from which he sought an allowance of 25 marks and 6 (. . .) and of 6d. paid at another time and of (. . .).of the value of one (florin?) (. . .) 5s. (. . .) and of 1s. 6d. for two silver spoons (. . .) handed to the same. And also 12d. paid (. . .) and likewise allowed to the same for bread bought (. . .) allowed to him. And likewise for his labour and (. . .) And so the total sum allowed to him £21 (. . .) committed which was in the keeping of R. Enterb' (. . .).

[f. 126a verso]

[*The writing at right angles to that on the recto*] (. . .) after his death (. . .) John Nedler senior (. . .) in the city of New Salisbury in Castle Street ('Castlestret') between the tenement of John Wylys (. . .) (returned?) by law to Amice my servant (*ancille*) daughter of my son Thomas 10 marks, and the residue (. . .) a pair of saddle-cloths (*huchiarum*), a [?] (*coceperter'*?), a brass pot, a dish, and 20s. in silver (. . .)

[f. 126 (*cont.*)]

364. Assembly: Wednesday the eve of St. Peter and St. Paul 19 Hen. VI [*28 June 1441*].

Present [*in three columns*]: the mayor, Henry Man, William Swayn, Richard Payn, John Wyot, John Boteler, Robert Cove, John Marchal, John Yrmonger, Robert Warmwell, William Hore, [*column two*] Simon Poy, Walter Hendy, Thomas (Selk?), William Swengil, Richard (Tutsay?), William Pette, John Hywode, Thomas (. . .), John (. . .), Robert Chynchon, John Skot, Richard Gage, John Crykemour, John Gerveys, [*column three*] John (Wyly?), William Charlyng, John Hampton, William Bertovile, Peter Pheylp, Thomas (Swyfte?), John Clyve 'tannere', Henry Frend, Henry Eliot, William Knoll, Edward Gudyer, John Gower.

[*In a later hand*] 'The great ditche.'

To finish the ditch (*fossatum*) around the city of Salisbury: Henry Man £1, John Helier 6s. 8d., William Swayn £1, John Marchel 40s., Robert Cove 13s. 4d., Richard Gage 6s. 8d., [William Hore £2 *crossed out*], Richard Payn £1 of which 13s. 4d. for the tenement acquired by the mayor and community, late Richard Spencer's, for the [?] (*costat'*) of William Lord, John Wyot 6s. 8d., John Boteler 6s. 8d., John Adekyn 1s., John Willy 3s. 4d., Gilbert Marchal 1s. 8d., Simon Poy 3s. 4d., Walter Hende 3s. 4d., William Knoll 6s. 8d., William Charlyng 6s. 8d., John Gerveys 1s. 8d., Peter Phelyp 1s., John Crykemour 6s. 8d. from [?] what was lent to the king (*de promtu domino regi*), Thomas Selk 1s. 8d., William Swengil [paid to the mayor *interlined*] 1s., Richard Cokelot 1s. 8d., John Skot 1s. 8d., William Pette 3s. 4d.. Thomas Stoppe 2s., Henry Frend 1s., John Tutsay 1s., John Mone 3s. 4d., John Gower 1s. 8d., Henry Shad 1s. 8d., John Clyve 'tannere' 3s. 4d., Thomas Mog 'couper' 1s., Thomas Baron £1 from the loan of Henry Baron his father, Stephen Hyewode [paid to the mayor *interlined*] 8s. 4d., William Hore £1.

[f. 126v.; *badly faded and stained*]

365. Assembly: Wednesday next after St. Peter and St. Paul 19 Hen. VI [*5 July 1441*].

[*Continuation of the list of contributions toward finishing the ditch. In a single column.*]

John Sether 2s., John Cathero 3s. 4d., William Meriot 2s., John Bedewynde 1s., John Walyssh 1s. 8d., Thomas Brouderer 1s. 8d. loaned to the king [?]; Thomas Payn 4s., Anselm Hebbyng one perch [?*i.e. length of digging*], William Chyld [*no amount*]; John Hampton labour for ten days, William Ferour 3s. 4d. loaned to the king [?] and the same for piece-work ('taske') 3s. 4d., Cristina sister of Cristina [*sic*] Baron one perch, the mayor W. Warwyk one perch, William Swayn 4 perch.

[f. 127; *faded and stained*]

366. Assembly: Wednesday next after St. Peter in chains 19 Hen. VI [*2 Aug. 1441*].

Present[*in two columns*]: John Estbury, William Swayn, John Aport, Robert Cove, Robert Okebourne, Richard Payn, William Hore, Richard Gage, Simon Poy, William Swyft, Nicholas Shute, Anselm Graunt, John Tissebury, [*column two*] Thomas Payn, Richard Cokelot, Henry Frend, Thomas Selk, William Swengil, Thomas Adekyn, William Knoll, John Marchal, John Alisaundr', John Durneford, John Tutsay, Walter Hende.

Agreed: [*blank*].

Memorandum: Henry Blakemour and Robert Crom on Friday next after St. Peter in chains 19 Hen. VI [*4 Aug. 1441*] accounted on their rolls for £9 18s. 1d., from which there was allowed to them in sums reduced in value (*disparagatis*) 9s. 8d., and so there remained 13s. 2d. [*the calculation is not clear*] which was put towards the building of the great ditch. And so they went quit. Afterwards there was allowed to Simon Poy 2d., to William Lord 2d., and to Thomas Halle 2d., and so there remained 12s. 8d. for the said ditch, which William Warwyk the mayor paid in the presence of Thomas Yoxford and Simon Poy to the labourers working on the ditch.

[f. 127v.; *faded and stained*]

367. Assembly: Wednesday next before St. Simon and St. Jude 20 Hen. VI [*25 Oct. 1441*].

Present [*in three columns*]: the mayor W. Warwyk, Robert Warmwell, Henry Man, William Pakyn, Richard Wyse, William Hore, John Estbury, John Marchal, John Wyot, William Swayn, Richard Gage, [*column two*] William Halstede, Walter Carogan, Thomas Selk, William Swengil, Henry Frend, Richard Cokelot, John Gower, Nicholas Shute, Henry Shad, [*column three*] Robert Chynchon, William Chyld, John Hampton, William Charlyng, Thomas Payn, Thomas Durneford, John Willy.

Agreed: the mayor to be allowed his pension, viz. £10; for the board of the chaplain of St. George £2 13s. 4d.; for the king's officials 13s. 8d.; for the duke of Gloucester's officials 3s. 4d.; for Lord Hungerford 1s. 8d.; for two cartloads of firewood (*focal'*) on the eve of the nativity of St. John [the Baptist] and on the eve of St. Peter [and St. Paul], 3s. 4d.; for two casks (*covell'*) of good ale on the said eves 3s.; for the officials' livery £1 1s. 11d.

Memorandum: William Warwyk the mayor paid to Thomas Pakker and John Goldsmyth, the king's collectors in the city, 13s. 5d. [in full *crossed out*, towards *underlined*] payment of the half [paid *interlined*] of a fifteenth, and 2d. for a bag in which to put the tallies, on Wednesday next after St. Martin 20 Hen. VI [*15 Nov. 1441*] [*added*: to be repaid from the half of a fifteenth on the feast of St. Martin [*11 Nov.*].

[f. 128; *faded and stained*]

368. Election on All Souls' day 20 Hen.VI [*2 Nov. 1441*].

Mayor, John Wyot; reeves, William Clyter, Thomas Temse; alderman of New Street, John Hayn; of Market, Thomas Payn; of St. Martin's, John Gosselyn of Bristol; of Meadow, Thomas Benet; serjeants, Thomas Yoxford, Walter Hu[n]tle.

[f. 128v.; *faded and stained*]

368A. [*Crossed out and unfinished*: Memorandum: John Wyot mayor of the city of New Salisbury received].

To be noted: In the mayoralty of H. Man, 17 Hen.VI [*1438–9*], there was loaned to the king by the said mayor and the community 50 marks. And in the mayoralty of William Warwyk, 19 Hen.VI [*1440–1*] 50 marks. Sum total of the loan 100 marks. And on this there was delivered to the mayor and community a tally from the king's Exchequer with letters patent under the great seal [to the effect that] the collectors of the county of Wiltshire and the collectors of the city should repay to the mayor and community the 100 marks on the feast of St. Martin in the said year [11 Nov. 1441].

By virtue of those letters W. Warwyk received that day from the collectors of the county by the hand of John Gylys £33 6s. 8d., from which was allowed to the same William for the said collectors for the said payment 6s. 8d. And on this the same William Warwyk delivered to John Wyot mayor on the said day £33.

And in addition the said John Wyot mayor received from the collectors of the city the following sums on the days written below:

From Thomas Byer' 'mason', collector of Market aldermanry for the fourth part of a fifteenth, by the hand of J. Frank £12 14s. 2d.

From Clement Fourbour, collector of New Street aldermanry on Friday next after St. Lucy the said year [*15 Dec. 1441*] £9 13s. 4d.

From W. Brownyng, collector of St. Martin's, by the hand of Thomas Yoxford, on the same day and year £6 7s. 7d.

From John Thoresby, collector of Meadow aldermanry, on the same day and year £2 15s.

From W. Pakyn 10s.; from Richard Gage 5s.; from Thomas Pakker' 1s 4d.; from Margaret Haynes 6s. 8d.; from W. Wrythe 2s.; from Thomas Byer' 10s.

Sum total received, £66 5s. 1d.

The said John Wyot also received £1 11s. 7½d., viz. an allowance for each 'noble' of 2d.

From which he paid to W. Swayn, for having the king's sureties for the said 100 marks, 16s. 8d.

So there remained in the said John Wiot's hands 13s. 11½d. He paid to William Warwyk 13s. 4d., remainder 1s. 7½d. He paid to Thomas Pakker, the collector, as an allowance for expenses 5s., and to John Paraunt, the other collector, for his allowed expenses 5s.

[f. 129; *faded and stained*]

368B. Men assessed for the 40 marks advanced to the king in the mayoralty of John Wyot 20 Hen. VI [*1441–2*] [*in two columns. Each item except for seven of those crossed out (John Adekyn, John Alisaundr', John Walysshe, John Ferour, William Charlyng, John Hampton, and Thomas Baron) and three of those not crossed out (John Everard, John Swyft, and Thomas Pakker') is preceded by 'paid' (sol')*]:

[Thoms Mew £1 *crossed out*], Richard Hayne 3s. 4d., [Henry Shad 3s. 4d. *crossed out*], Thomas Goston [*sic, ?recte* Cofton] 'corvesor' 3s. 4d., John Cachero 3s. 4d., [John Ypysewell 3s. 4d. *crossed out*], Bartholomew Champ 3s. 4d., William Swengil [5s. *crossed out*] 3s. 4d. 'the most resseym' [?], Anselm Graunt 3s. 4d., Stephen Hiewode 6s. 8d., John Colyngbourne 5s., John Asshford 3s. 4d., John Best 'smyth' 6s. 8d., Thomas Whytyng 6s. 8d., [John Adekyn 3s. 4d. *crossed out*], [John Mone 5s. *crossed out*], William Sopere 3s. 4d., John Warde 3s. 4d., John Page 3s. 4d., Thomas Bugbrygge 3s. 4d., [William Wilmot 3s.4d. *crossed out*], John Wheler 3s. 4d., Nicholas Shute 6s. 8d., John Wyot 'brewer' 3s. 4d., [John Bover 3s. 4d. *crossed out*], Stephen Hendy 3s. 4d., Robert Bulk 3s. 4d., Robert Levyng 3s. 4d., William Charlyng [15 *crossed out*] 13s. 4d., John Clyve 'brewer' 6s. 8d., [John Alisaundr' 3s. 4d. *crossed out*], [John Walysshe *crossed out*], William Chyld 3s. 4d., [Thomas Shirwode 3s. 4d. *crossed out*], John Chatour 'smyth' 3s. 4d., John Wyse 3s. 4d., Thomas Pyse 3s. 4d., John Gerveis [6s. 8d. *crossed out*], William Clyter 6s. 8d., Walter Hende 3s. 4d., William Lyghfot 13s. 4d., [John Hobbes 'brewer' 6s. 8d. *crossed out*], Thomas Mabre 3s. 4d., Thomas Stoppe 3s. 4d., [John Ferour *crossed out*], John Shether 3s. 4d.; Sum, £10 10s.

368C. [*Column two*] Robert Roo 3s. 4d., [John Eston 3s. 4d. *crossed out*], William York 3s. 4d., John [Schute *crossed out*] Slegge 3s. 4d., [Thomas (. . .)erenderer *crossed out*] 3s. 4d., [John Hench 3s. 4d. *crossed out*], William Meryot 3s. 4d., Edward Gudyer 3s. 4d., [Thomas Stoppe 3s. 4d. (*again*) *crossed out*], Simon Poy 3s. 4d., [John Boteler 'mercer' 3s. 4d. *crossed out*], Richard Payne 13s. 4d., John Port' £1, [William Charlyng (*again*) 10s. *crossed out*], William Prydy [3s. 4d. (. . .) 13s. *crossed out*] 3s. 4d., William Hore 13s. 4d., Henry Man 13s. 4d., Robert Warmwell [£1 (. . .) *crossed out*] £1, William Pakyn £1, Stephen Coupere [8s. 4d. *crossed out*] 10s., Thomas Freman 13s. 4d., Richard Wyse [13s. 4d. *crossed out*] £1, John Everard 6s. 8d, Robert Cove 13s. 4d., John Estbury 6s. 8d, John Boteler (. . .) 6s. 8d., [John Swyft *crossed out*], William Swayn 13s. 4d., John Helier' [£1 *crossed out*] 13s. 4d., William Warwyk [£1; 13s. 4d. *crossed out*] £1, William Knoll 13s. 4d., John Wynchestr' 3s. 4d., Thomas Pakker' [6s. 8d. *crossed out*] 10s, [John Hampton *crossed out*], William Wotton 3s. 4d., [Thomas Baron *crossed* *out*], William Halstede 13s. 4d., Robert Okebourne 6s. 8d., Walter Carogon 6s. 8d., John Athursby 3s. 4d., Thomas Payn 3s. 4d., Guy Rotor 3s. 4d., Anselm Hebyng 3s. 4d., Thomas Tempsse 6s. 8d., [Richard Gage 6s. 8d. *crossed out*], [John Marbe 3s. 4d. *crossed out*].

[f. 129v.; *faded and stained*]

369. Memorandum: on the feast of St. Philip and St. James 20 Hen.VI [*1 May 1442*] it was agreed by the mayor, Robert Warmwell, William Pakyn, John Aport, H. Man, Thomas Freman, William Warwyk, Stephen Coupere, Robert Cove, Richard Wyse, John Estbury, Richard Payn, William Swayn, John Boteler, W. Hore, John Marchal, W. Halstede, W. Knoll, [and] Thomas Mewe, that Thomas Yoxford, for the delivery of the 40 marks advanced to the king from the community of Salisbury, should ride to the treasurer of England to collect as surety for repayment from a fifteenth in the city, the king's [letters] patent and a tally from the Exchequer, as agreed between [on one hand] Sir Walter Hungerford, knight, and the abbot of Malmesbury and [on the other] the mayor and community (. . .) in (. . .) of the church of St. Mary of Salisbury.

370. Assembly: Friday next before Whitsun 20 Hen.VI [*18 May 1442*].

Present [*in three columns*]: John Wyot mayor, Robert Warmwell, (. . .), William Pakyn, Thomas Freman, Stephen Coupere, William Hore, William Swayn, Richard Wyse, Richard Payn, John Marchal 'dier', William Warwyk, John Estbury, John Aport, Robert Cove, [*column two*] William Knoll, William Charlyng, John Wheler', Walter Bryd, John Crikemour, Thomas Durneford, John Mone 'touker', John Skot, Nicholas Shute, Simon Poy, Peter de Varw, Edmund Eggeworthe, Walter Hende, [*column three*] Ralph Pakker, John Boteler, Thomas Halle, William W(. . .)nos, Thomas Payn.

Agreed: for the repayment of the 40 marks advanced to the king, to obtain the king's letter patent with a tally from the king's Exchequer, otherwise they [the 40 marks] are to be returned.

Thomas Freman and Richard Payn undertook to build a gate at the ditch of Ed[mund] (*una' porta' apud fossatu' Ed'*) [*sc.* at St. Edmund's church?] similar to the gate of the Close on the way to de Vaux college (*domum scole de Valle Sar'*), before the feast of St. John the Baptist following the nativity of St. John next after this [*i.e.* by 24 June 1442].

Agreed: to pay to W. Swayn by the hands of the chamberlains' at the time £8 5s. 4d. [by instalments], beginning on the nativity of St. John the Baptist [*24 June*] in the year 1443, at each nativity of St. John £2 [*the wording is garbled and repetitive*] until the said £8 5s. 4d is fully paid.

William Lord, the city clerk, resigned his office into the hands of the mayor [for the benefit of Philip Morgan *interlined*]. The mayor promised that he would treat the said Philip amicably in sealing the agreement made and discussed between William and

Philip, reserving to William his pension for the nativity of St. John the Baptist next [*24 June 1442*]. Furthermore William will be excused from performing every office in the city, without [having a fine] imposed on him.

[f. 130; *faded and stained*]

371. Assembly: Monday next after Holy Trinity 20 Hen. VI [*28 May 1442*].

Present [*in three columns*]: the mayor, Robert Warmwell, Henry Man, Thomas Freman, Robert Cove, William Knoll, William Halstede, Richard Payn, John Boteler, William Charlyng, William Pakyn, [*column two*] John Deverel, Richard Hayne, John Gerveys, Thomas Halle, Simon Poy, John Skot, William Pette, Henry Frend, Thomas Payn, William Swyft, William Chyld, John Hampton, [*column three*] Nicholas Shute, Richard Walker, Henry Shad, Richard Hayne 'taillour', Edward Gudyer, John Parant 'goldsmyth'.

Elected as assessors for the king's fifteenth: Market ward, William (Slege?), John Mone 'touker'; New Street ward, Richard Payn, Henry Frend; St. Martin's ward, William Halstede, John Hampton; Meadow ward, John Slegge, Thomas Stoppe; as collectors: New Street ward, John Parrok 'fysshere'; Market ward, Nicholas Barbour; Meadow ward, John Crikemour; St. Martin's ward, John Parson junior.

Admitted to the office of city clerk: Philip Morgan.

Afterwards on Monday the feast of St. Barnabas in the said year [*11 June 1442*] John Wyot the mayor delivered to Richard Walker and Edward Gudyer, the king's collectors by virtue of the king's letters patent, £8 10s.

And on the said day Nicholas Barbour, collector of Market ward, paid to the mayor £3 8s. 9d.; John Parrok, collector of New Street ward, paid to the mayor £2 17s. 3d.; John Parson junior, collector of St. Martin's ward, paid to the mayor £2 16s. 4d.; John Crykemour, collector of Meadow ward, paid to the mayor 15s.

[f. 130v.; *faded and stained*]

371A. [*An assessment, possibly to the fifteenth. In two columns. Most of the names are preceded by a cross and, written over it, 'paid' (sol'); those names without 'paid' are marked in the list printed below with †.*]

†Richard Hayne 3s. 4d., Henry Shad 5s., Thomas Cofton 'corvesor' 3s. 4d., John Cachero 3s. 4d., Bartholomew Champ 3s. 4d., William Swengill 3s. 4d., Anselm Graunt 3s. 4d., Stephen Hyewode 6s. 8d., John Colyngburne 5s., John Asshford 3s. 4d., John Best 'smyth' 6s. 8d., Thomas Whytyng 6s. 8d., John Mone 6s. 8d., William Sopere 3s. 4d., †John Warde 3s. 4d., John Page 3s. 4d., †Thomas Bugbrigge 3s. 4d., William Wylmot 6s. 8d., †John Wheler 3s. 4d., †Nicholas Shute 6s. 8d., †John Wyot 'brewer' [3s. 4d. *crossed out*] 6s. 8d., Stephen Hendy 3s. 4d., Robert Bulke 3s. 4d., Robert Levyng 3s. 4d.,

William Charlyng [10s. *crossed out*] 13s. 4d., John Clyve 'brewer' 6s. 8d., William Chylde 3s. 4d., John Chatour 'smyth' 3s. 4d., †John Wyse 3s. 4d., John Gerveys 10s., Thomas Pese 3s. 4d., William Clyter' 6s. 8d., Walter Hende 3s. 4d., William Lyghfote £1, †[John Hobbes 'brewer' 6s. 8d. *crossed out*], Thomas Mabre 3s. 4d., Thomas Stoppe 3s. 4d., John Parham 'golsmyth' [*sic*] 3s. 4d., John Hampton 6s. 8d., Robert Chynchon 3s. 4d., John Shetere 3s. 4d., †Robert Roo 3s. 4d., Thomas Gyle 3s. 4d., †Thomas Brouderer 3s. 4d., William Meryot 3s. 4d., Edward Gudyer 3s. 4d., †Simon Poye [3s. 4d. *crossed out*] 6s. 8d., †Richard Payne £1; sum £12 [3s. 4d. *crossed out*] 6s. 8d.

371B. [*column two*] †John Porte [£1 *crossed out*] £1 10s., William Predy 3s. 4d., William Hore £1, Henry Man 10s., William Pakyn £1 6s. 8d., Stephen Couper £1, Thomas Freman 13s. 4d., Richard Wyse [£1 *crossed out*] $1 3s. 4d., †John Everard 13s. 4d., Robert Cove £1, John Estebery 13s. 4d., John Boteler 'brewer' 6s. 8d., †William Swayne 40s., John Helyer 13s. 4d., †William Warwyk £2, William Knolle £1, John Wynchestr' [3s. 4d. *crossed out*] 6s. 8d., Thomas Pakker' [10s. *crossed out*] 6s. 8d., †William Wotton 3s. 4d., William Halstede £1, Robert Okeburne 6s. 8d., †Walter Corogan 6s. 8d., John Thursby 3s. 4d., †Thomas Payne 3s. 4d., Guy Rotor 3s. 4d., †Anselm Hebyng 3s. 4d., Thomas Tempse 6s. 8d., †Richard Gage 6s. 8d., †John Chypman 'bocher' 3s. 4d., [*no forename*] Leker' 'tanner' 3s. 4d., John Honythorne 6s. 8d., John Combe alias (*aliis*) Parson 'tanner' 3s. 4d., Richard Lavyngton 'dyer' 3s. 4d., John Stone, innkeeper ('ostelet') 3s. 4d., John Eston 'dyer' 3s. 4d., William Yorke 'dyer' 3s. 4d., Thomas Schyrwode 3s. 4d., John Boteler 'mercer' 3s. 4d., John Marke 3s. 4d., John Epysswyll 3s. 4d.; sum £21

[f. 131; *badly faded and stained*]

372. Assembly: Wednesday next after St. Simon and St. Jude 21 Hen.VI [*31 Oct. 1442*].

Present [*in three columns*]: John Wyot 'mercer' mayor, Robert Warmwell, Henry Man, William Warwyk, Richard Wyse, William Pakyn, Thomas Freman, Robert Cove, William Knoll, William Swayn, John Marchal, [*column two*] Thomas Durneford, William Pette, John Skot, Simon Poy, John Crikemour, Walter Hende, William Sopere, Walter Corynger, John Gerveys, John Byn(. . .), Robert Chynchon, [*column three*] John Adeton, William Coupere, Anselm Hebbyng, John Mone, John Slegge, Henry Shadde, William Charlyng, Thomas Copter, Thomas Stoppe, Edward Gudyer, William Barbour.

Agreed: (Thomas?) Freman to have the ditch next to (. . .) for a term of four years paying 1s. 6d. a year. And (. . .).

The prostitutes to live in Culver Street (*via de* 'Culverstret').

[Elected as] chamberlains: William Halstede, William Charlyng.

Account of John Wyot mayor 21 Hen.VI: for the said mayor's fee £10; for the board of the chaplain of St. George and his clothing 4 marks; for [the fee of *crossed out*] William Alisaundr' and William Lord and their clothing £1 12s.; for the city officials' clothing

£1 1s. 11d.; for two cartloads of firewood (*focal'*) on the feasts of the Nativity of St. John and of Peter and Paul 3s. 4d.; for two casks (*cowellae*) of good ale at the same time 3s.; for a gift to the bishop of Salisbury, a lamb, a heron ('hayron'), a fawn ('foun'), 7s.; for three dozen chickens to the same bishop and six quail (*quaillae*) 8s.; to four king's officials 6s. 8d.; to the duke of Gloucester's officials 6s. 8d.; to the cardinal's officials 6s.; to the earl of Suffolk's official 2s.; to the earl of Huntingdon's official 2s. 8d.; to the chancellor of England's officials 2s.; to the earl of Somerset's official 3s. 4d.; to Lord Neville's official 1s.; in wine for 'sire' Robert Roos and his fellow ambassadors [?] (*abassat'*) 1s. 4d.; [f. 131v.; *faded and stained*] to the sheriff of Wiltshire in bread and wine 2s. 4d.; to the escheators of Wiltshire and Southampton 6s. 8d. and 1s. 4d.; to John Sturton knight 1s. 4d.; to the said knight's servant bearing the fourth of a fifteenth 1s. 8d.; to Richard Brid, the bishop of Salisbury's steward, 1s. 4d.; for the writer of charters sent to the citizens at parliament 4d.

Sum total £18 11s. 3d.

(. . .) Robert Warmwell (. . .) the said letter patent (. . .). [*Three lines illegible.*]

[f. 132, *unnumbered and blank*]

[f. 132v.; *faded and stained*]

373. [*Heading:*] Mayor [? *to be read in conjunction with the (missing) heading on the facing recto*].

Election on All Souls' day 21 Hen.VI [*2 Nov. 1442*].

Mayor, William Pakyn; reeves, William Swengil, Thomas B(iere?); alderman of New Street, John Staph(lege?); of Market, William Burly; of Meadow, Robert Aylward; of St. Martin's, William Ramet; serjeants, Thomas Yoxford, Walter Huntley.

Simon Poy made fine for being excused the offices of alderman and reeve, £4, pledges William Warwyk, John Wyot. John Paraunt 'goldsmyth' made fine for being excused the offices of alderman and reeve, £4, pledges Thomas Freman, Robert Warmwell.

[f. 132a; *an unusually long and narrow strip of parchment, made of two pieces, faded and worn*]

374. [*Notes apparently for or from the record of assemblies. Cf. nos. 203–4, 214–16.*]

Robert Poynant mayor, 6 and 7 Hen.V [*1418–19*].

Outside (*forinc'*) victuallers to be separated from resident (*intrincicis*) ones. A penalty of ½ mark for receiving any grain after the ninth hour. Prohibition of ducks and other animals. Thomas Rede to build (. . .). Subwarden of the 'almeshous': W. More elected as appears in another part of the folio. Robert Warmwell owed £1 19s. 4d. The farm (*firma*) of John Parch. Order [for attendance] at elections, penalty 2 lb. of wax. Chamberlains in the place of the old ones: John Bremle, Robert Gilberd. The farm of 'Georgesyn'. The farm of the tenement by Fisherton.

[*The second piece.*] Chamberlains, (. . .), Richard Gatour. John Wichford remitted payment of £3 for a fine. Henry Frend (. . .) how paid £2 to John Bromle. From money placed in the [common] purse and paid [John] Bromley and Robert Gilberd, collectors for the tenth and for the third part of a tenth granted in parliament in the mayoralty of John Judde held at Westminster 16 Nov. [1417]. John Teffonte one of the commissioners and John Parch and others his fellows. From the loan (*chivancia*) advanced to the king, viz. from two bonds (*obl'*). (. . .) by the mayor against [Thomas] Biston for [*or* by] John Lympnour. Concerning £1 6s. 2d. paid to the said chamberlains which remains from the mayor was found in the said purse. Broken and false gold delivered to Henry Man: £25 delivered to the same Henry to pay to the Treasurer. William Lord appointed city clerk. How the chaplain of St. George is to attend on the mayor.

Robert Warmwell mayor, 7 and 8 Hen.V [*1419–20*].

[*On the dorse at the left-hand end*] Robert Warmwell.

[f. 133b; *an inserted strip of parchment, blank on the dorse*]

375. The king's writ, dated Westminster 1 May 20 Hen. [VI, *1442*] and signed Kirkeby, to the mayor and bailiffs for the payment to Robert Longe esquire (*armigero*), one of the citizens at the parliament at Westminster on the day of the conversion of St. Paul [*25 Jan. 1442*], of £7 4s. for his expenses in coming, staying seventy-two days, and returning, receiving 2s. a day.

[f. 133c; *an inserted strip of parchment, blank on the dorse*]

376. The king's writ, dated Westminster 20 Nov. 21 Hen. [VI, *1442*] and signed Kirkeby, to the mayor for the payment to Thomas Freman 'marchant', one of the citizens [*etc. as no. 375*].

[f. 133; *faded, stained, and creased*]

377. Assembly: Friday next after St. Nicholas 21 Hen.VI [*7 Dec. 1442*].

Present [*in five columns*]: Henry Man, William Warwyk, Richard Payn, Richard Wyse, John Peraunt, John Wyet, [*column two*] John Marchall, William Knollys, Thomas Temse, Simon Poy, John Cleve, John Wheler', Thomas (. . .), (. . .), [*column three*] Robert Cove, Thomas Pakyn, John Scotte, Stephen Hywode, Richard Balfot, John Thursby,

Nicholas Shute, [*column four*] Richard Heyn, Walter Carogon, Richard Plowman, William Ra(. . .) John (Pakyn?), William Charlyng, Edward (. . .) ner, Edward Gode₃ere, John Crikmore, Henry Frend, John Schadde, Ralph Pakker', Thomas Payn, (William Okeborne?).

Agreed: Thomas Pakyn (. . .) to have the costs (. . .) paying (. . .).

Also, the officials (. . .) for the preceding year (. . .).

Ordered: [*largely illegible, mentioning the weighing of goods and a weigh-beam (balanc')*].

Memorandum: the king on Wednesday next before St. Thomas the apostle [*19 Dec. 1442*] delivered to the mayor by a messenger of his Exchequer his privy seal letter in these words etc. [*followed by a blank space; the letter is bound into the book below as f. 133a, below no. 380.*]

[f. 133v.; *faded, stained, and creased*]

378. Memorandum: on 10 Jan. [*year omitted*] Hen.VI [*1443*] Thomas Freman 'marchant' brought the king's writ, sewn in here [*above, no. 376, much of which is transcribed on this page*] for the payment to him of £7 4s., of which sum, in the presence of the mayor, Robert Warmwell, John Wyot, and Nicholas Shute, he granted and released to the said mayor and citizens £3 12s., and there was owed to him £3 12s.

[*Six lines, largely illegible, mentioning*] John Wyot, the mayor William Pakyn, and the citizens.

379. Assembly: Friday next after St. Gregory 21 Hen.VI [*15 Mar.ch 1443*].

Present: [*in the margin,* the mayor], William Warwyk, Robert Warmwell, John Wyot, William (. . .), Richard Payn, John (Pakker?), William P(. . .), Gilbert Marchal, (. . .), Walter Corogan, William Pette, Thomas Yoxford, John (. . .), Stephen Hywode, William (. . .), John (. . .), (. . .), John Alisaundr', (. . .).

Elected to assess [the levy] for the expenses of the citizens at the parliament held at Westminster on the day of the conversion of St. Paul 20 Hen.VI [*25 Jan. 1442*]: Market ward, John (Chynchon *or* Honythorn), (. . .); New Street, (. . .), Henry Frend; St. Martin's, William Halstede, John Hampton; Meadow, John Slegge, Thomas Stoppe; as collectors: New Street, John Parrok fishmonger ('fyssher'); Market, Nicholas Barbour; Meadow, John Crikkemore; St. Martin's, John Person junior.

Memorandum: on 10 June 21 Hen.VI [*1443*] Robert Longe esquire brought the king's writ, sewn in here [*etc., reciting part of no. 375 above, but breaking off after the date of the parliament and leaving the entry incomplete*].

[f. 133a; *an inserted piece of parchment, stained, blank on the dorse; its tag, bearing the address to the mayor and citizens and formerly closing the document through two slits on each side, is stuck on the same mount*]

380. [*The king's privy seal letter, in English; summary*] The king has heard from John Seymour, knight, that the mayor and citizens have granted him 50 marks as a loan ('chenissh'), which he had hoped to receive before now but has still not been paid. He therefore asks that it should be sent to the Exchequer, on which the mayor and citizens will have sufficient assignment of money granted [in taxes] by the last parliament. Dated Westminster 21 Nov. [*1442*].

[f. 134; *faded and stained*]

381. [*Heading:*] Pakyn.

Assembly in the Council House (*domo consilii*): 3 April 21 Hen. VI [*1443*].

Present: [*in the margin*, the mayor], Robert Warmwell, William Warwyke, William Hore, William Swayn, Robert Cove, John Aport, Simon Poy, John Botiller, Thomas Freman, Richard Payn, John Peraunt, Richard Wyse.

[*A new paragraph*] Walter Carogan, Robert Bulke, John Alisaundre, John Mone, William Lyghtfote, Richard Plowman, John Cachero, John Charlyng, Stephen Hendy, John Wynchester, Clement Fourbour, Richard Walker, Anselm Hebbyng.

Granted to the king: an aid in relief of Bayonne (*Baion*) and Bordeaux (*Burdeux*) and for his safe keeping of Gascony (*Gasconie*) and Guyenne (*Gyane*) etc., 40 marks, of which the mayor and his brethren gave 20 marks and the community of the city 20 marks.

[f. 134v.; *faded and stained*]

W[illiam] Pakyn [mayor]

382. [*Heading:*] W. Pakyn.

Assembly: Friday next after the Assumption 21 Hen. VI [*16 Aug. 1443*].

Present: John Wyot, William Swayn, Richard Payn, William Halstede, Robert Cove, John Peraunt, Simon Poy, Thomas Pakyn, [Richard Gage *interlined*], Gilbert Marchal, John Alisaundre, William Lyghtfote, Richard Plowman, Thomas Yoxford, Thomas Durneford, John Sterlyng, [Stephen Hendy, Nicholas Shute *interlined*], Henry Frend, Edmund Brasyer, William Randul, Peter de Varwe, Anselm Hebbyng, William Mory smith ('ferrour'), John Mone 'touker', Edward Goodyere, William Swyngell, John Crikemore, Henry Shadde, John Couper, John Cachero, John Charlyng.

Considered: the king's writ for attendance before the king in Chancery, on pain of £100, on 25 (. . .) to show [*the rest of the entry is largely illegible, but evidently relates to the payment of part of a fifteenth.*]

383. Memorandum: on 20 Aug. 21 Hen. VI [*1443*] Nicholas Barbour, collector for Market ward of the expenses of the citizens at the parliament held at Westminster on the day of the conversion of St. Paul [*25 Jan. 1442*], paid to William Pakyn mayor £2, and on 26 Sept. the same Nicholas paid to the mayor £1; John Parrok [fishmonger ('fisshere') *interlined*], collector for New Street, paid £2; John Person junior, collector for St. Martin's, paid £2 6s. 8d.; John Crikkemore, collector for Meadow, paid 17s. 8d.

384. Memorandum: on 4 Sept. 22 Hen. VI [*1443*] John Pernaunt 'goldsmyth' paid to William Pakyn mayor, for being excused the offices of alderman and reeve, £1 14s. 7d. [*The whole entry is struck through.*]

385. Memorandum: on Monday next before St. Katherine 22 Hen. VI [*18 Nov. 1443*] John Parrok fishmonger ('fyssher'), collector for New Street ward, paid to William Pakyn, mayor, out of £8 12s. for half of a fifteenth payable on the feast of St. Martin last [*11 Nov. 1443*] £8, and was allowed, [because (who owed it) was unknown *interlined*], 8s., and he owed 3s. 9d. [*the arithmetic is puzzling*]; Nicholas Barbour, collector for Market, out of £11 18s. 5d. and an additional 4s. 4d. as appears by his indentures, paid £11 17s. 8d., and was allowed 5s. 1d. because it was not known where it was owed, and he went quit; John Crikkemore, collector for Meadow, out of £2 13s., paid £2 11s. 5d., and he owed 1s. 7d.; John Person junior, collector for St. Martin's, out of £11 6s. 2d., paid £9 16s. 8d., and he owed 19s. 6d., of which he paid 3s. 4d., and he owes 16s. 2d. [*the entry is faint, but the figures are clear enough and they are wrong by 10s.*]

Memorandum: the mayor paid to the collector of the fifteenth for the city, Edward Godeyre, £17 and to Richard Walker £17.

[f. 135; *faded and stained*]

386. Assembly: 3 Oct. 22 Hen. VI [*1443*].

Present: [*in the margin,* the mayor], Thomas Freman, Robert Cove, John Marchall, William Knolles, Richard Payn, William Halstede, John Paraunt 'goldsmyth', Thomas Pakyn, John Atkyn, Nicholas Shute, John Mone, Edward Godeyre, Henry Frende, Thomas Oxford, John Wheler, John Hampton, Thomas Payn, John Alisaunder, John Crikkemore, William Pope, William Charlyng, Thomas Stoppe, Peter de Varowe, Henry Shadde, and John Adam etc.

Elected as assessors and collectors of the half of a fifteenth payable at the feast of St.

Martin [11 Nov.] next: those elected for assessing and collecting the expenses of the citizens at parliament [*cf. no. 379*].

William Pakyn, mayor, asks to be allowed his various expenses during his mayoralty, which the assembly duly allowed, viz. for his pension, £10; for the board of the chaplain of St. George and his clothing, 4 marks; for the city officials' clothing, £1 1s. 11d.; to the king's officials, 6s. 8d.; to the duke of Gloucester's officials, 6s. 8d.; to the duke of Somerset's official, 3s. 4d.; to the cardinal of England's official, 2s.; to Lord Hungerford's official, 1s. 8d.; to the chancellor of England's official, 1s. 8d.; for the expenses of Robert Hungerford, John Beynton knights, William Alisaunder, and John Atteberge, commissioners for the muster and other services viz. for a dinner [£1 *crossed out*] not allowed by the auditors; in wine given to Lord Hungerford, Robert Hungerford, and Philip Courteney, 2s. For two cartloads of firewood (*focal'*) at the feasts of St. John the Baptist and of St. Peter and St. Paul, 3s. 4d.; [for two casks of good ale at the same feasts, 3s. *crossed out*] not allowed by the auditors etc. Sum [£15 10s. 7d. *crossed out, £14 7s. 8d., which was allowed in the chamberlains' account interlined. The arithemetic seems to be faulty*.]. Towards this, he received from John Parnant 'goldsmyth', as appears in the next folio, £1 14s. 7d.; [*the next five items have all been struck through*] from Peter Dawe for the weighing (*pond'*) this year, 16s. 8d.; from Simon Poy as part of a fine for being excused the offices of alderman and reeve, £1 6s. 8d. and from the same Simon at another time, 13s. 4d.; from the chamberlains, £8 13s. 4d.; memorandum: on 23 Dec. 22 Henry VI [*1443*], the said former mayor [there was paid for all the above *crossed out, received from William Hore £2 13s. 4d. interlined*].

[f. 135v.; *badly faded and stained*]

387. Election: All Souls' day 22 Hen. VI [*2 Nov. 1443*].

Mayor, William Hore; reeves, Thomas W(. . .), Thomas (. . .); alderman of New Street, (. . .); of Market, Thomas El(. . .); of St. Martin's, William Spaldyngton clerk; of Meadow, John Lowde; serjeants, Edmund Eggesworth, Ralph Pakker.

Elected and sworn to the number of the Twenty-Four: Walter Carogan, Nicholas Shute, William Charlyng and John Wyse 'draper'.

John Wyse 'draper' made fine for being excused the offices of alderman and reeve, £4, pledges John Wyot, Simon Poy. Peter Dawe, made fine for the keeping of the common weigh-beam this year, £1 13s. 8d.

[f. 136; *faded and stained*]

388. [*Heading:*] Hore.

Assembly: Saturday next before St. Katherine 22 Hen. VI [*23 Nov. 1443*].

Present: Robert Warmwell, William Pakyn, John Wyot, William Halstede, John Peraunt, Richard Payn, Robert Cove, John Estbury, Walter Carogan, William Charlyng, William Knollys, John Marchall, John Boteler, John Wise, Thomas Freman, Robert Chynchon, Anselm Hebbyng, Peter de Varewe, Henry Frende, John Mone 'touker', William Lyghtfote, John Willy, Stephen Hendy, John Crikemore, Thomas Pakker, John Atkyn, William Cove, John Alisaundre, John (. . .), John (. . .)one 'brewer', Thomas Mabre, (. . .), (. . .) Swengil, John Scotte, William More, Thomas W(. . .), John Cleve 'tanner', Thomas (. . .), John (. . .)er, John Thorsby, (. . .), William (Lavyre?), John Colynghurst.

[*Several lines largely illegible, relating to the grant of a tenement for rent and to a levy for the construction of the ditch during the mayoralty of John Wyot, of which what follows appears to be a list. Some of the contributions are not in money but in perches of digging, indicated in the MS. by* P.]

[*In two columns*] John Wheler and William Swayn (. . .), William Halstede ½ perch, William Knoll 1 perch, John Pragnel 'fyshmonger' 6s., William Charlyng (. . .), Richard Payn 1 perch, Robert Cove 1 perch, John Estbury and Simon Poy 1 perch, John Marchall agreed to give 5s., John Boteller agreed to give 6s. 8d., Walter Carogan and John Wyse agreed to do 1 perch, Thomas Pakker [1s. 8d. *crossed out*], the executors of Stephen Mercer agreed to do ¼ perch, Richard Walker 1s. 8d., Stephen Hendy and Thomas Yoxford 1 perch, William Lyghtfote ½ perch, John Thursby agreed to give 3s. 4d., John Colyngbourne 3s. 4d., John Cleve 'brewer' 3s. 4d., John Alisaunder 1s. 8d., John Scotte 1s. 8d., William Wilmot 3s. 4d., [John *crossed out*, Richard *interlined*] Balfot 1s., William Walssh 1s., John Mone 'touker' 3s. 4d., John Crikemore 1s. 8d., John Willy 1s. 8d., Henry Frend 1s. 8d., William Swyft 'brewer' 1s. 8d., John Whelere 'brewer' 3s. 4d., William Swyngel 1s. 8d., Walter Hynde 3s. 4d., John Atkyn 'dyer' 3s. 5d., [*column two*] (. . .), John (. . .) 1s., Thomas M(. . .) 1s. 8d., John Durneford 1s. 8d., William M(. . .), Edward Godyer 1s. 8d., Anselm Hebbyng agreed to do ½ perch, Peter de Varewe 1s., Robert Chynchon ½ perch, Edmund Brasyer 1s. 8d., John Aport 13s. 4d.

[? *in a later hand*] A Rakr'.

Agreed: It is agreed that from each aldermanry there should be chosen one man to assess all the (inhabitants?) within the city who can pay each quarter of the year 1d. or ½d. for the wages of a man called 'le Raker' to carry away the (ordure? *fimos?*) (. . .) by the city. Granted by the assembly: the money arising to be paid for a man (. . .) of the mayor for the time being. [*The entry is very faint and the reading uncertain.*]

[f. 136v.; *faded and stained*]

389. [*Heading:*] William Hore.

Assembly: Saturday in Whitsun week 22 Hen. VI [*6 June 1444*]

Present: [*in the margin,* the mayor], William Alisaundre, William Warwik, John Aport, Robert Cove, John Estbury, Walter Carogan, John Marchall, [William Swayn *interlined*],

John Boteler, Robert Okeburne, [Thomas Freman, John Peraunt *interlined*], William Halstede, William Knollys, Nicholas Shute, William Lyghtfote, Anselm Hebbyng, John Wylly, Thomas Oxford, John Hampton, John Gerveys, John Wynchestre, Thomas Durneford, William Swyngell, Walter Hynde, Richard Hayne, John Alisaunder, John Wheler, John Mone 'touker', Walter (Chyld?), John Walssh, Richard Hayne 'taillor', John Scote, Edward Goodyere, Thomas Copter, William Childe, Thomas Pakker, William (. . .), Thomas F(. . .), John S(. . .), Stephen Hendy, William More 'ferrour', John Wyot 'brewer', John (. . .), John Cove 'bruer', Robert Barlowe, John Atkyn, Thomas Payn, William (Sibyst?), John Stone, John Mone 'gentilman'.

Agreed: William Hore mayor, his brethren, and their counsel agreed to ride to the bishop of Salisbury, William Ascuth [*i.e.* Ayscough], [to discuss] the revival of the city's liberties as they were of old, viz. concerning the bridges, ale-tasters, brewing, the mill, etc., and at their discretion to give to the bishop silver at the city's expense for granting those liberties.

Also, all (. . .) to be granted to the mayor and other citizens for the use of the hospital (*domus*) of the Holy Trinity.

390. Assembly: Friday next after the nativity of St. John the Baptist 22 Hen. VI [*26 June 1444*].

Present: [*in the margin*, the mayor], Robert Warmwell, Thomas Freman, Richard Payn, William Halstede, Nicholas Shute, [William Swayn, William E(. . .) *interlined*], Robert Cove, John Estbury, Simon Poy, John Marchall, Walter Carogan, John Boteler, John Mone 'gent', Richard Plowman, John Willy, John Hampton, William Lytfote, Thomas Yoxford, Henry Frend, John Wheler, Thomas Stopp, John Thursby, William Swyngell Edward Godyere, John Hampton [*again*], Richard Hayne 'taillour', John Boner, Stephen Hywode, William Mory, John Mone, Anselm Hebbyng, John Alysaunder, Thomas Pakker Thomas Mogge 'couper', Walter Hynde, John Crikkemore.

Agreed: in each future year, at one of the assemblies, four auditors to be chosen, two from the Twenty-Four and two from the commons, to audit, with the mayor, the chamberlains' accounts of all rents and other profits of the city.

Elected in the assembly as chamberlains: William Knollys, Anselm Hebbyng; [John Mone 'gent' as controller (not agreed, *interlined*), and that they have for their stipend this year *all crossed out*]; as auditors [besides] the mayor: Robert Warmwell, William Swayn, Robert Longe 'squyer', and John Mone 'gent'.

[f. 137; *faded and stained*]

[*Heading*:] W. Hore

The king sent to the mayor and community Mr. Adam Moleyns, dean of the church of Salisbury, keeper of his privy seal for an advance of money under sufficient security etc. who brought to the mayor a letter sealed with the king's seal.

391. Assembly: 27 July 22 Hen.VI [*1444*].

Present: [*in the margin*, the *m*ayor], Robert Warmwell, Thomas Freman, John Wyot, William Swayn, Richard Payn, John Peraunt, Nicholas Shute, Robert Cove, John Estbury, William Knollys, Walter Corogan, John Wyse, John Boteler, William Halstede, Edmund Penston, John Atkyn, Stephen Hendy, John Gerveys, John Batyn, William Colyns, John Honythorn, Robert Chynchon, John Mone, William Pette, John Hampton, John Thursby, Henry Frende, Robert Bulk, John Wynchester, Richard Hayne taillour, Henry Shadde, Thomas Maber, Walter Brydde, John Cleve 'tanner', Thomas Brymmore, Thomas Yoxford, John Willy, John Pynnere, John Soper 'wever', John Colyngburn, John Crykermore, Walter (Lor?)de, Oliver Benham, John Marchall 'dyer', John Asseford, Edward Godeyer, Thomas Andrewe, John Wheler, John Colyngburn [*again*], John Bysshampton, and others.

Agreed: the mayor and community to advance to the king at the request of the keeper of the privy seal £40 provided that they have sufficient security for repayment [in time] for the queen's visit.

The names of the men assessed to the said £40 to be advanced during the mayoralty of William Hore [*a cross preceding each name except for eight, Thomas Temse, John Noble, William Charlyng, Walter Huntley, Richard Walker, John Norman, John Stone, and John Horman*]:

[*in three columns*] William Alysaundre 13s. 4d., Robert Warmwell £2, William Warwyk £2, William Pakyn [*blank; 10s. would make the sum for the column correct*], Thomas Freman 10s., John Wyot 10s., William Swayn £1, John Aport £1 6s. 8d., Robert Cove 13s. 4d., William Knollys 13s. 4d., William Halstede 13s. 4d., Simon Poy 13s. 4d., John Perraunt 13s. 4d., John Everard 13s. 4d., Walter Carogan 13s. 4d., John Wyse 10s., Thomas Temse [*blank*], John Botelere 10s., John Estbury 13s. 4d., Richard Payn 13s. 4d., Nicholas Shute 13s. 4d., Henry Shadde 3s. 4d., Thomas Cofton 3s. 4d., Edward Godeyere 3s. 4d., William Colyn 'baker' 3s. 4d., Thomas Feld 3s. 4d., John Boteler 'mercer' 3s. 4d., Bartholomew Champ 3s. 4d. [Sum] £17 6s. 8d.

[*column two*] John Thursby 3s. 4d., John (Gerveys?) 3s. 4d., John Aley 3s. 4d., Thomas Yoxford 6s. 8d., Stephen Hendy 6s. 8d., Clement Fourbour 6s. 8d., Robert Bulke 6s. 8d., John Wynchester 6s. 8d., John Shethere 3s. 4d., William Glover 3s. 4d., John Aleyn 'pynner' 3s. 4d., John Chatour 3s. 4d., Richard Sadeler 3s. 4d., John Halle 6s. 8d. r[eceived?] 6s. 8d., Thomas Hurde 'barbour' 3s. 4d., Guy Rotour 3s. 4d., Richard Bowyer 3s. 4d., John Cacheroo 3s. 4d., John Chippenham 6s. 8d., John Parrok 3s. 4d., Anselm Graunt 3s. 4d., John Etour 3s. 4d., Edward Boner 3s. 4d., Richard Lavyngton 3s. 4d., Richard Shirgold 3s. 4d., Walter Dytton 3s. 4d., John Assheford 3s. 4d., William Soper 3s. 4d., William Swyngell 3s. 4d. [Sum] £6.

[*column three*] Thomas Gyle 6s. 8d., John Wyot 'bruer' 6s. 8d., John Cleve 'tanner' 6s. 8d., Thomas Wytyng 6s. 8d., Stephen Gage 3s. 4d., William Child 3s. 4d., Thomas Bukbrigge 3s. 4d., Simon Newman 3s. 4d., Thomas Sampson 3s. 4d., William Best 6s. 8d., Thomas Hill 3s. 4d., Edmund Penston 3s. 4d., Walter Bridd 3s. 4d., William Meriot 3s. 4d., William Barlowe 3s. 4d., John Noble 3s. 4d., William Wotton 3s. 4d., William

Predy 3s. 4d., John Slegge 3s. 4d., Thomas Pese 3s. 4d., Robert Chaundeler 3s. 4d., Thomas Andrewe 3s. 4d., Thomas Leber 3s. 4d., Richard Spynler 3s. 4d., John Person 'tanner' 3s. 4d., Edward Doll 3s. 4d., John Veyse 3s. 4d. , Nicholas Scote 3s. 4d., William Prangnell 3s. 4d., William Chepton 3s. 4d., John Hampton 3s. 4d., William Charlyng 13s. 4d. [Sum] £6 13s. 4d.

[f. 137v.; *faded and stained*]

[*in two columns*] John Batyn 3s. 4d., John Crekemore 3s. 4d., John Walsche 3s. 4d., William Lyghtfot 13s. 4d., Thomas Packer 6s. 8d., Thomas Lyon 3s. 4d., Henry Ostler 3s. 4d., John Chatour 3s. 4d., Geoffrey Bonvalet 6s. 8d. [?], Richard Sadler 3s. 4d., Henry Frend 3s. 4d., John Besamton 3s. 4d., John Halstede 3s. 4d., Simon Laverok 3s. 4d., John Parrok 3s. 4d., Denis ('Denys') Goldsmyth 3s. 4d., John Chaundeler 3s. 4d., Walter ('Wat') Hynde 3s. 4d., John Colyngbourne 3s. 4d., John Lombard 3s. 4d., William Mory 3s. 4d., John Wyse 3s. 4d., Thomas Mabre 3s. 4d., William Clet' 3s. 4d., John Aleyn 'penner' 3s. 4d., John Knygt 3s. 4d., Thomas Payn 6s. 8d., Edward Dolle 3s. 4d., John Cleve 'tanner' [*again*] 6s. 8d., John Stafley 3s. 4d., Walter ('Wat') Huntley 3s. 4d., Richard Walker 3s. 4d. , Thomas Bremmor 3s. 4d., William Wilmot 3s. 4d. , Thomas Stoppe 3s. 4d., John Whyler 3s. 4d., John Gerveys 6s. 8d., John Norman 3s. 4d., Roger Bastard 3s. 4d., John Togode 'brewer' 3s. 4d., John Stone 3s. 4d., John Horman 3s. 4d. [Sum] [£6 6s. 8d. 13s. 4d. *crossed out*] £8 6s. 8d.

[*column two*] Thomas Valeys 3s. 4d., John Holme 3s. 4d., John Whitby 3s. 4d., John Chynchon 3s. 4d., John Tysbury 3s. 4d., Thomas Vowell 'corvasor' 3s. 4d., John Frank 3s. 4d., John Revylle 3s. 4d., William Sylle 'sevyer' 3s. 4d., John Don 3s. 4d. [Sum] £1 13s. 4d.

[f. 138; *faded, stained, and holed*]

392. Assembly: Friday next before All Saints 23 Hen. VI [*30 Oct. 1444*].

Present: William Warwyk, William Pakyn, John Port, William Swayn, Robert Cove, Nicholas Shute, William Knolles, William Halsted, [Richard] Wyse, Walter Carogan, Simon Poy, John Honythorn, John Skot, Thomas Oxeford, Thomas Payn, John Alisaundr', John (. . .)ger, John Cleve 'tanner', Nicholas Wedergrove, Thomas Durneford, Richard Payn, John Marchall, John Wynchester, Thomas Copter, Stephen Hendi, John Cachero, John Wills, John Mone 'webber', Edward Boner, John Togod, Thomas Bremmer, John Willy, Peter Dawe, Edward Godyer, William Doune, Thomas Stop, John Attkyn, John Hampton, Henry Shadde, John Crikemore, Richard Hayne 'taillour', William Mory 'smyth', William Pope, John Wheler.

The names of the men who are assessors for 23 marks for the appeasement of the bishop for having the old customs within the city as we had them of old: [*blank*].

William Warwyk for each bridge [which he has *interlined*], 1s. 1d.; each bridge above the pool (*stangum*) of the Avon [?, *the word, which has been altered, appears to be* aefron *but could be* avon *overwritten with* Ep(iscop)i], 1s. 1d.; each tapster [?] (*tapp'r*) assessed within the city, 6d.

Election of collectors for the bridges and for tapsters: John Willy, Thomas Durneford.

Elected to keep the key of the common chest: John Wynchestour, Stephen Hendy.

[f. 138v., *blank*]

[f. 139; *faded, stained, and torn*]

393. [*Heading:*] W. Hore mayor.

Assembly: Friday the feast of St. Edmund the king 23 Hen. VI [*20 Nov. 1444*].

Present: [*in the margin,* the mayor], William Warwyk, [Robert Warmwell *interlined*], John Wyot, Robert Cove, Thomas Freman, William Knollys, John Boteler, Nicholas Shute, William Lyghtfote, Gilbert Marchall, Richard Payn, Walter Carogan, [*a long gap*] John Scotte, John Hampton, John Wynchester, John Mone 'touker', John Wheler, Edmund Penston, John Alisaunder, Edward Boner, [John *crossed out,* Robert *interlined*] Chynchon, Thomas Durneford, Walter Bridde, Henry Shadde, Thomas (Bremmore?), John (. . .), Thomas Yoxford, William Pope, Thomas Pakyn, Edward Godeyere.

[*The mayor's account.*] (. . .) for the city officials' clothing, £1 4s.; for a present given to the dean of Salisbury, £1 6s. 8d.; for the king's officials, 6s. 8d.; for the duke of Gloucester's officials, 6s. 8d.; for the officials of (. . .), 6s. 8d.; for the officials of (. . .), 6s. 8d.; for the officials of (. . .), 3s. 4d.; for the officials of (. . .), 3s. 4d.; for the officials of (. . .), 3s. 4d.; for the officials of (. . .), 3s. 4d.; (. . .) 3s. 4d. For (. . .) a charter (. . .), 4s.; for, £1 5s.; for (. . .), 16s.; for the repair (. . .), 6s. 8d.; for Thomas Browderer for an interlude at the feast of the nativity of St. John, 5s. 2d. for the earl of Warwick's official, 1s. 8d.; for 2 yards [of cloth] quartered in colour and with thirty stripes (*ij virg' quart' col' et xxx rayes*) for Robert Longe's livery, £1 0s. 9d.; for the like for William Alisaunder's livery, £1 0s. 9d.; for the like for Philip Morgan's livery, 19s. 8d. Sum £23 3s. 8d., which the said chamberlains allowed in their account to be paid to the mayor.

Memorandum: William Halstede and his fellow, former chamberlains, before Robert Longe esquire, Robert Warmwell, William Swayn, and John Mone, the auditors assigned [for the purpose], accounted for all rents and other profits arising in the city during the mayoralties of William Pakyn and William Hore. They had a surplus of 9s. 7d. [*presumably of expenses over income*], which it was agreed that William Knollys and his fellow should pay to them.

Memorandum: William Hore, former mayor, accounted before the said auditors for £8 which he received from a tenement called 'le Otemelcornere', viz. in rent paid to the cathedral church of Salisbury this year, £1; paid to Edmund Penston for his work on the condition of the tenement (*pro labore suo quod habet statum inde etc.*), £2; paid to Mr. Thomas Swyft for the like, £2; rent repaid to the bishop of Salisbury this year, 5s. 2d.; (. . .) to Christina Chapman and her costs (*custag'*) at Tisbury, 11s.; paid to Edmund Penston and Philip Morgan for their expenses relating to (*versus*) Tisbury for the sealing of charters, 6s. 8d.; paid for making the great ditch according to the said Christina's order, £1; allowed to the same William Hore for his work and good will in the said work, 17s. 2d. And he was quit. [*There is in fact 2d. not accounted for.*]

[f. 139v.; *faded, stained, and torn*]

394. Election: All Souls' day 23 Hen. VI [*2 Nov. 1444*].

Mayor, William Swayne; reeves, Thomas Andrewe, Thomas Payne; alderman of New Street ward, Thomas Yoxford; of Market, William Mory; of St. Martin's, Walter Bridde; of Meadow, Stephen Hendy; serjeants, Edward [*sic, ?recte* Edmund] Brasyer, Ralph Pakker.

Fines: John Everard granted to the mayor and his brethren, for being excused the office of mayor in perpetuity, £3, pledge John W(. . .); William Lyghtfote was elected and sworn to the Twenty-Four and for being excused the offices of alderman and reeve [was fined] £4, pledges William Swayn and William Warwike; Thomas Pakker made fine for being excused the offices of reeve and alderman, £4, to be paid at the feast of All Saints next £2 and at the same feast following £2, pledges William Swayn and John Estbury; Walter Hynde 'smyth' made fine for being excused the offices of reeve and alderman, £4, to be paid at the feast of St. Michael next £2 and at the said feast then next following £2, pledges Thomas Freman and Simon Poy.

Thomas Yoxford was elected chamberlain for the community, and Anselm Hebbyng was excused.

[f. 140; *badly faded and stained*]

395. [*Heading:*] W. Swayne.

The mayor's council, summoned to 'le Conselhous': Saturday next after Epiphany 23 Hen. VI [*9 Jan. 1445*].

The names [of those] who were given notice to come to the said council and did not come, for their default a forfeit as in (. . .).

[*About ten lines illegible.*]

396. Assembly: Saturday next after Hilary [23] Hen. [VI, *16 Jan. 1445*].

Present: [*in the margin*, the mayor], Robert Warmwell, William Warwyk, (. . .) Pakyn, Thomas Freman, John Wyot, John Aport, John Marchal, Thomas Temse, P(. . .), John (Mone?), Robert Cove, William Halstede, John Estbury, Simon Poy, John Wyse, William Lyghtfote, John Boteler, William Alisaundr', (John Parant?).

Granted: (. . .) the Twenty-Four had, were released.

[*In the margin,* Penalty.] Richard Hayne (. . .). John Gerveys (. . .) 6s. (. . .) *given notice to come and did not come.* John Slegge (. . .).

Agreed: all citizens having a house (*hospicium tenentes*) in the city to have each for himself a gown (*togam*) of blue (*blod'*) colour worth at least 5d. [*the reading is uncertain*], for the queen's visit, the gowns to be ready by 1 March under penalty for each of 6s. 8d. to be paid to the chamberlains if anyone fails on the day for riding to meet the queen (*die equit' erga Reg'*).

Also, at the king's parliament to be held in the kingdom of England in future, no one to be elected unless they are citizens and resident within the city, and if anyone from the city comes to the election and says to the contrary he is to pay to the chamberlains on each occasion (*totiens quotiens*) £1. And no one from the city is to give a voice in electing the serjeants or the priest of St. George unless those who would be elected are dwelling and resident in the city, under the said penalty etc.

Also, the mayor to make an indentured contract between himself and the men [in charge of] the existing common cart [*i.e. for refuse*] (*homines pro communi carect' exist'*) as was earlier agreed for five years for such reasonable pay as may be agreed between them.

The names of those elected to audit the chamberlains' accounts for the mayoralty of W. Swayne: Robert Warmwell, William Pakyn [*added,* he is dead; Robert Cove], Edmund Penston, John Scotte.

[f. 140v.; *badly faded and stained*]

397. [*Heading:*] W. Swayne.

Assembly: Friday in Easter Week 23 Hen. VI [*2 April 1445*].

Present: [*in the margin,* the mayor], Robert Warmwell and all others from the number of the Twenty-Four, and others from the number of the Forty-Eight, besides those whose names are written below, viz. [*left blank*].

[*In column on the left-hand side of the page*] Richard Hayne 1 lb. [*of wax*], John Colyngbourn 1 lb., Thomas Pakker 1 lb., William Pette 1 lb., John Cachero 1 lb. [*On the right*] Names of those summoned to attend the court who did not come.

Agreed: the tenement in which John Wheler lives in St. Martin's Street ('Martynstret'), the six cottages towards St. Edmund's church, the tenement called 'Helyersplace' in Castle Street ('Castelstret'), [and] the tenement called 'Bolesplace' by the tenement late William Cokkes's to be sold and the moneys spent on the building and repair of other dilapidated (*ruinos'*) houses of the mayor and community etc., with the advice and at the discretion of the mayor and others chosen for the purpose, viz. [*in column on the left-hand side of the page*] Robert Warmwell, the mayor, William Warwik, Stephen Hendy, John Honythorn, John Wynchester, Thomas Payn, [*on the right*] elected to sell the said tenements.

398. Assembly: Saturday next after the translation of St. Thomas the martyr 23 Hen. VI [*10 July 1445*].

Present: [*in the margin,* the mayor], Robert Warmwell and all of the number of the Twenty-Four and others of the number of the Forty-Eight, besides those whose names are written below, viz. [*left blank*].

Agreed: the mayor and community to grant and demise to William Swayn a tenement [with all its appurtenances *interlined*] by Fisherton bridge called 'Bovers', to have and hold to the same William and his assigns from Michaelmas next for the term of eighty-one years, paying yearly to the mayor and community and their successors £2 at the four terms of the year; and the said William has built there a new 'skaldynghous' at his own cost and expense, and all butchers resident within the city are to slaughter and scald there and not elsewhere. William will repair [and] maintain the said tenement with all its appurtenances. [*The whole entry is apparently cancelled by the word* vacat *in the margin.*]

[f. 141; *faded and stained*]

399. [*Heading:*] W. Swayne.

Assembly: Saturday next after the nativity of the Blessed Virgin Mary 24 Hen. VI [*11 Sept. 1445*].

Present: Robert Warmwell and all of the number of the Twenty-Four and others of the number of the Forty-Eight, besides those whose names are written below [*left blank*].

John Cleve 'brewer', [fined] 1 lb. of wax, William Child, 1 lb. of wax, because given notice to come and they did not come.

Elected to the Forty-Eight, for Thomas Pakyn and Thomas Yoxford: Thomas Bukbrigge, Thomas Brynmore.

Elected to assess men dwelling in the city on movable goods for the half of a fifteenth and tenth granted to the king: New Street, Robert Cove, Stephen Hendy; Market. Nicholas Shute, John Alysaunder; St. Martin's, John Estbury, John Walssh. Meadow, William Lyghtfote, John Wheler; to collect the same: New Street, John Hall, John Parrok; Market, John Wyot 'bruer', Edward Boner; St. Martin's, [William Meryot *crossed out,* John Toogode *interlined*], John Batyn; Meadow, Thomas Stoppe, Thomas Leker.

The king ordered John Thursby and William Cormayll by letters patent to collect the half of a fifteenth and tenth, granted to the king, from laymen in the city etc. on 3 June 23 Hen. VI [*1445*].

[f. 141v.; *badly faded and stained*]

400. [*Heading*:] W. Swayne

Assembly: the eve of St. Simon and St. Jude 24 Hen. VI [*27 Oct. 1445*].

Penalties forfeited: John Cleve 'brewer' because he did not come 1 lb. of wax; Ralph Pakker', one of the serjeants, because he did not give notice to William Lyghtfote, one of the Twenty-Four, 1 lb. of wax.

Elected as chamberlain: Thomas Payne [to serve] with William Knollys.

Agreed: the mayor to have his wages and allowances, as other mayors in the future, £10. For the said mayor's pension this year, £10; for the board and clothing of the chaplain of St. George, £2 13s. 4d.; for the city officials' clothing, (£1 ?); in a gift to Lord Hungerford, 12s. 6d.; to the king's official, (. . .); to the duke of Gloucester's official, (. . .); to the earl of Dorset's officials, (. . .); to the cardinal of England's official, 3s. 4d.; to the duke of Exeter's official, 3s. 4d.; for two (cartloads of firewood) on the eve of St. John the Baptist, 3s.; to (. . .)'s official, 3s. 4d.; for two casks of good ale on the eve of St. John [and] of St. Peter, (. . .); to the archbishop of Canterbury of England's official, 3s. 4d.; in a gift to four of the king's heralds ('herowdis') at the queen's visit, 6s. 8d. Sum £16 14s. 10d., which the chamberlains paid to the mayor.

Agreed: all those who wish to make fine to be excused any office not to be allowed by the mayor unless they pay in hand or give surety by a bond under the mayor, the said [ordinance *interlined*] to be held in perpetuity.

Also, the mayor for the time being not to receive [any money from] the tenements of the mayor and community, or from the fines or any other payment belonging to the mayor and community except by the hands of the chamberlains, under penalty of forfeiting the mayor's pension for that year, this ordinance to be held in perpetuity.

Memorandum: William Knollys and the other chamberlain accounted before William Swayn mayor and the other auditors assigned for his mayoralty for all accounts and allowances. The chamberlains owed £6 6s. 4d., which William Knollys agreed to pay at the nativity of St. John the Baptist next [*24 June 1446*] etc.

Assessors: Market, Simon Poy, Thomas Payne 'wever'; New Street, Stephen Hendy, Anselm Hebbyng; St. Martin's, William Hore, Richard Walker'; Meadow, William Halsted', John Wheler'; collectors: Market, John Mone 'touker', John Hoode 'glover'; New Street, John Thursby, Guy Rocher; St. Martin's, John Slegge, Thomas Pese; Meadow, Thomas Benet tiler ('helyer'), Richard Spyndeler'.

Collectors by virtue of the king's commission, assigned to John Dogode and Edward B(oner?), dated 16 July 24 Hen.VI [*1446*] .

[f. 142; *badly faded and stained*]

401. [*Heading:*] Richard Payne mayor.

Election: All Souls' day 24 Hen.VI [*2 Nov. 1445*].

Mayor, Richard Payne; reeves, John Cleve 'brewer', Thomas Copter' [*to the right are some words of which only a few letters are legible*]; alderman of New Street, Anselm Hebbyng; of Market, William Sope(re); of St. Martin's, Robert Meteyeve; of Meadow, William Wotton; serjeants, Ralph Pakker', Edmund Eggesworth.

John Mone 'towker' made fine for being excused the offices of alderman and reeve, £4, to be paid at Christmas next £1 6s. 8d., and at Christmas then following £1, and at the Christmas after that £1, and 13s. 4d. paid in hand which William Hore held, which the same John advanced to the king was repaid to the same William Hore. [*In the margin* 'quyt'].

Stephen Hendy made fine for being excused the office of reeve, £2, to be paid at Michaelmas next. [*In the margin* 'quyt'].

John Honythorn made fine for being excused the offices of alderman and reeve, £4, to be paid at Michaelmas next £2, and at Michaelmas following £2, pledge Simon Poy. [*In the margin,* 'quyt'].

John Hall 'mercer' made fine for being excused the offices of alderman and reeve, £4, to be paid at Michaelmas next £1 6s. 8d., at the Michaelmas following £1 6s. 8d., and at the Michaelmas after that £1 6s. 8d. [*In the margin* 'quyt'].

Elected to the Twenty-Four: Stephen Hendy and John Honythorn.

[f. 142v.; *badly faded and stained*]

402. [*Heading:*] Richard Payne mayor.

Assembly: Friday next after Hilary 24 Hen.VI [*14 Jan. 1446*].

Present: [*in the margin*, the mayor], John (. . .) others of the number of the Twenty-Four and other citizens of the number of the Forty-Eight.

[*About six line wholly illegible or blank.*]

403. Assembly: Friday next after St. Dunstan in the year of the said mayor [*20 May 1446*].

No default in the number of the Twenty-Four. Defaults in the number of the Forty-Eight: John Gerveys, William Soper, Walter Hynde, William Mory, each [fined] a pound of wax.

Elected to the number of the Forty-Eight for others who are to be commended to God: Thomas Bokebrigge, Walter Huntle, John Halsted, Thomas Gyle, John Lumbard.

The king by his writ ordered the mayor to have and levy the expenses of the citizens at the parliament at Westminster on 25 Feb. 23 Hen. VI [*1445*], amounting to £40 8s. for 202 days for each of them, viz. William Hore and Richard Hayn.

Elected from the Twenty-Four to assess [the levy for] the said expenses: John Aport, Simon Poy constable, Walter Corrogan, John Wyse, John Parant constable; from the Forty-Eight: John Wynchester, Thomas [Pakker' *crossed out*] Stoppe, Stephen Hiwode, [Anselm Hebbyng *crossed out*, Thomas Whitynge *added*]; as collectors: Reginald Wynle 'bruer' from New Street, Simon Newman from Market (*mercato*), Thomas Gile from St. Martin's, William [Carevic'r *crossed out*] Beste 'smyth' from Meadow. The mayor, John Wyot, and William Swayn, were appointed to assess both the assessors and the collectors, and Thomas Payn and Anselm Hebbying with them.

[f. 143; *stained*]

404. [*Heading*:] R. Payne mayor.

Assembly: Saturday next after St. Peter [in chains] 24 Hen. VI [*6 Aug. 1446*].

The king sent a privy seal letter to the mayor and community to appear before his commissioners, viz. the dean of Salisbury cathedral, Robert Hungerford, John Stourton, and John Baynton knights, appointed to treat with the mayor and community for the advance to the king of a certain sum of money.

Memorandum: on Thursday next after St. Martin 25 Hen. VI [*17 Nov. 1446*] William Cormayle and Thomas Payn, chamberlains, accounted before Robert Warmwell and the other auditors, and there before the mayor and auditors there was delivered £13 10s. 6d. for the use of the mayor and community, everything being accounted for, and so they went quit, as appears in their account. From the £13 10s. 6d. Robert Warmwell and William Swayn delivered to John Wheler and Clement Fourbour, stewards of the brotherhood of St. George this year, 20 marks, and the stewards accounted for that and the issues and profits of the brotherhood annually before the mayor and other auditors with the chamberlains. For the 20 marks the stewards and Stephen Hendy and John Thursby were bound in writing to Robert Warmwell, William Swayn, Simon Poy, and Thomas Payn for the use and benefit of the mayor.

405. Assembly: 12 Nov. 25 Hen. VI [*1446*].

Present: thirteen from the Twenty-Four, twenty-eight from the Forty-Eight.

Agreed: the mayor to have his pension and allowances as other mayors have been used to have, and the other allowances written below, viz. for the mayor's pension this year, £10; for the board and clothing of the chaplain of St. George, £2 13s. 4d.; for the city officials' clothing, £1 3s.; in a gift to the duke of Gloucester, 14s. 8d. in a gift to Lord Hungerford, 11s. 8d.; to the king's official, 6s. 8d.; to the duke of Gloucester's official, 6s. 8d.; to the cardinal of England's official, 6s. 8d.; to the duke of York's official, 3s. 4d.; to the duke of Exeter's official, 3s. 4d.; to the marquess of Dorset's official, 3s. 4d.; to the archbishop of Canterbury's official, 3s. 4d.; to the earl of Devon's official, 3s. 4d.; to the marquess of Suffolk's official, 3s. 4d.; to Robert Hungerford's official, 1s. 8d.; in expenses and costs of riding to Sonning to show to the bishop of Salisbury the charters for various articles, 10s.; in gifts to the prior of the Charterhouse on two occasions, 4s. 3d.; [for two cartloads of firewood on the eve of St. John the Baptist and of St. Peter, for two casks of good ale at the same time, *crossed out*]; given to John Uffenham and John Mone for [? the detailing *or* the reduction (*the word looks like* menucione)] of the fifteenth in New Salisbury, 6s. 8d. Sum, £18 5s. 3d.

Agreed: two keys of the common chest to be delivered one to Thomas Payn and another one other to [John Wynchester *crossed out*] Henry Frend.

Names of those elected to audit the chamberlains' accounts in the mayoralty of Richard Payn: Robert Warmwell, William Swayn, John Mone 'gent', John Skott.

Agreed in the presence of the mayor, Robert Warmwell, William Swayn, John Scott, and John Mone, the auditors, and also of William Halstede, William Knollys, and Thomas Payn that the said chamberlains pay to Richard Payne 13s. 4d. which Richard advanced to the mayor and community for the work of William Lord, to be had as an allowance due in the next account, and to John Peraunt £1 13s. 4d. which he paid to William Pakyn as part of his fee.

[f. 143v.; *stained*]

406. Election: All Souls' day 25 Hen. VI [*2 Nov. 1446*].

Mayor, John Port; reeves, Anselm Hebbyng, John Parche; alderman of New Street, John Thursby; of Market, Stephen Hywode; of St. Martin's, John Man; of Meadow, John Parrok; serjeants, Edmund Eggesworth, Ralph Pakker.

[f. 144; *stained*]

407. [*Heading:*] Port.

Assembly: Saturday next before St. Thomas the apostle 25 Hen. VI [*17 Dec. 1446*].

Names [and fines] of those who were given notice of this assembly and did not come [*in column*]: from the Twenty-Four: William Lyghtfote, 2 lb. of wax; Stephen Hendy,

2 lb. of wax; John Wyse, 2 lb. of wax; John Estbury, 2 lb. of wax; from the Forty-Eight: Anselm Hebbyng, 1 lb. of wax; John Halstede, 1 lb. of wax; Thomas Gyle, 1 lb. of wax.

Agreed: the present mayor to have in relief of his costs all the fees and other charges granted before this time as he used to have.

Also, the officials to have their wages and livery as they used to have in earlier years.

Also, the collectors of a fifteenth and tenth granted to the king always in the future to have for their work £1 for a fifteenth and tenth, 10s. for half a fifteenth and tenth, and so on *pro rata*.

408. Assembly: Wednesday 18 Jan. 25 Hen. VI [*1447*].

Elected to attend the parliament at Cambridge on St. Scholastica's day, viz. 10 Feb. next, each receiving for his work 1s. a day and not more, viz. Thomas Temse and [Philip Morgan *crossed out*] John Mone 'gent', Thomas and Philip [*sic*] agreeing to attend for the said fee.

[f. 144v.; *stained*]

409. [*Heading*:] John Aport mayor.

Assembly: Wednesday [*incomplete*].

Present: from the Twenty-Four: John Wiot, Robert Cove, Simon Poy, John Estbury, Walter Corrogan, William Halsted, Stephen Hendy, Nicholas Shute, Thomas Tempse, John Gerveys, John Perrant, William Swayn; from the Forty-Eight: Thomas Durneford, Nicholas Barbour, John Crikemore, John Thursby, Richard Walters, Edward Godeyer, Guy Rotor, (Anselm Hebbyng?), Walter Hynde, John Cachro, Thomas Pakker, (. . .), Edmund Penston, Thomas Stoppe, John Slegge, William Swyft, John Skot, William Pette, Edward Boner, Thomas [illegible], Henry Frend, John Slegge [*again*], William Chyld, John (. . .), Thomas Payn, John Clyff 'tanner', John Mone 'towker', Henry Elyot, John Asshford, Richard Ha(yne?), Thomas Gile, Walter Bryd, John Parrok.

Walter Hone, John Togode, William Pope, John Halle by 1 [lb.?], William Durneford, Richard Hayne 'taillour', Stephen Hak were given notice and did not come (. . .) penalty of wax.

Granted to Thomas Temps and John Mone for their time at the parliament held at Bury [St. Edmunds, *to which the parliament originally summoned to Cambridge was resummoned*] on the feast of St. Scholastica, £4, viz. each receiving 1s. a day.

The names of those to assess the men of the city [for the payment to Thomas Tempse and John Mone], from the Twenty-Four: Robert Cove, John Honythorn; from the

Forty-Eight: Thomas Pakker, Anselm Hebbyng; collectors of the expenses of the knights [*i.e. citizens at parliament*]: New Street, Richard Bowier; Market, John Shergold; St. Martin's, William Meriet; Meadow, John Hert 'carpenter'.

410. The mayor's council at the Council House (*domo consilii*): Monday next after the nativity of St. John the Baptist 25 Hen. VI [*26 June 1447*].

Before the mayor, John Wyot, Walter Carogan, Robert Cove, Simon Poy, William Cormaile, John Honythorn, John Wyse, and others, came John Holme, John Cleve, Edmund Bentley, John Toker, Richard Sexsy, and John Penell, 'tanners', and put themselves on the mayor's mercy because they did not come to watch with the said mayor on St. John's eve as they were summoned to do. They asked to be admitted to fine and they were admitted, as appears on their heads [?] (*prout patet super eorum capita*), and they were sworn on the book to observe those things etc. Nicholas Wedirgrove, John Maideman, Richard Campion [John Barbour *crossed out,* William Jones, and Thomas Herde *interlined*], barbers (*barbitons'*), came and put themselves on the mayor's mercy as above for the same cause, etc. John Luter 'corveser' [came] and put himself on the mayor's mercy in the same way and form for the same reason.

[f. 145; *faded and stained*]

411. Assembly: Friday next before St. Margaret 25 Hen. VI [*14 July 1447*].

William Swayn [fined] 2 lb. [of wax], John Wyot 2 lb., Walter Carogan 2 lb., John Jervays 2 lb., John Estbury 2 lb., from the number of the Twenty-Four because they did not come when they were summoned; John Wynchester 1 lb., Anselm Hebbyng 1 lb., Thomas Pakker 1 lb., John Hall 1 lb., John Cleve 'brewer' 1 lb., Richard Plowman 1 lb., John Slegge 1 lb., from the number of the Forty-Eight, because [they did not come when] they were summoned.

[Agreed]: all the citizens to have a blue gown (*tog' blod'*), as in the mayoralty of W. Swayn, for the king's visit.

Also, the king to have as a gift for his visit (. . .).

Also, William Devenyssh to have his tenement in which he lives for 13s. 4d. [a year for term of his life *interlined*], repairing his tenement himself under the community's supervision, and to receive his estate from the mayor and community for making improvements by the city's grant.

412. Assembly: Friday after the Assumption 25 Hen. VI [*18 Aug. 1447*].

Agreed: the king to have as a gift from the community twelve gifts [?] (*bon'*) on his visit to the city; and after his departure, at the mayor's appointment, the citizens to come together to view and grant a day of bounty [?] (*bonitatis*) [*or perhaps* limitatis] so that the money for the said twelve gifts can be levied.

Also, the men [who are] citizens elected John Lye and Michael Skyllyng to be of the city counsel [for term of their lives *crossed out*], each receiving £2 at two terms of the year from the chamber, and they are to come and attend the city council as often as and whenever they are required or one of them is required.

Also, John Wheler to have his tenement and for term of ninety-eight years on certain conditions, viz. that the said John Wheler [*incomplete*].

[f. 145v.; *faded and stained*]

413. [*Heading:*] J. Aport mayor.

Assembly: 15 Sept. 26 Hen.VI [*1447*].

Present: twenty from the number of the Twenty-Four and all from the number of the Forty-Eight, and many others.

Agreed: outside (*extranees*) butchers to have their stalls in the weekly market place as often as and when they wish, and the resident (*intrinc'*) butchers to have their stalls in their own houses and not in the market; and if any resident butcher sells [or makes to sell *interlined*] meat outside his house the meat or the price of it to be forfeit. Stephen Hendy, William Lyghtfote, and all others of the said numbers [*i.e. of the Twenty-Four and the Forty-Eight*] granted that if the mayor for the time being holds an assembly to the contrary (. . .) he is to lose his fee for that year.

Agreed further: William Devenysch to have and hold his office of serjeant of the mayor [and community of New Salisbury, called *interlined*] 'mayresergaunt' on this condition, that the said William should behave well to the mayor and community and their successors, and that the said William should have from the common weigh-beam, while he holds his said office, 13s. 4d. sterling [a year].

414. Assembly: Monday next after St. Simon and St. Jude 26 Hen.VI [*30 Oct. 1447*].

Present: [*in the margin*, the mayor; *no others named*].

Agreed: all outside fishmongers (*piscatores*) in the city to have their stands and stalls on the common ditch for selling fish, and not elsewhere, and they and each of them to sell their fish by their own hands and not through another, under penalty of forfeit etc.

Also that there are to be four keys for the common chest in which the common seal is kept, one to be kept by the mayor, one by another of the Twenty-Four, and two by persons of the Forty-Eight.

Election of auditors for this year: [*in the margin* the mayor], John Wyot, William Hore, from the Twenty-Four; Anselm Hebbyng, John Hall, from the Forty-Eight.

Agreed: the mayor to have his pension and his other allowances as other mayors have used to have, viz. for the mayor's pension this year, £10; for the board and clothing of the chaplain of St. George, £2 13s. 4d.; in a gift to the duke of Gloucester's men, 10s.; in wine given to the prior of the Charterhouse, 8d.; to the king's official, 6s. 8d.; to the duke of Gloucester's official, 6s. 8d.; to Henry, cardinal of England's official, 6s. 8d.; to the duke of York's official 3s. 4d.; to the duke of Exeter's official, 3s. 4d.; to the marquess of Dorset's official, 3s. 4d.; to the chancellor of England's official, 3s. 4d.; to the earl of Devon's official, 3s. 4d.; to the marquess of Suffolk's official, 3s. 4d.; to the earl of Shrewsbury's official, 3s. 4d.; for the carriage of a pipe of wine which was given to the duke of Gloucester, 5s.; in 'gildyng' for the mace, 5s.; for clothing two city officials, 16s. Sum £16 13s. 4d.

[f. 146; *stained*]

415. Election: All Souls' day 26 Hen. VI [*2 Nov. 1447*].

Mayor, John Wyot; reeves, William Wotton, Robert Meteyeve; alderman of New Street, John Welweton; of Market, John Wyse 'vynter'; of St. Martin's, Roger Mayn; of Meadow, John Hert; serjeants, Edmund Eggesworth, Ralph Pakker.

John Cammell, John Hall, Thomas Payn were elected to the number of the Twenty-Four.

John Chatour 'smyth' made fine for being excused the offices of alderman and reeve, £4, to be paid at Michaelmas £2 and at the same feast then next following £2, pledge John Walssh 'brewer' [of that there was received at the hands of Simon Poy and John Wynchestr' chamberlains £2 *added later*].

416. Assembly: Wednesday next after the Conception 26 Hen. VI [*13 Dec. 1447*].

Present: nineteen from the Twenty-Four and twenty-four from the Forty-Eight, etc.

Agreed: Simon Poy and Thomas Payn, the chamberlains, and other chamberlains for the time being to have all their allowances on being examined and sworn by the auditors. Simon Poy, John Wynchester were elected chamberlains for this year.

[f. 146v.; *stained*]

417. [*Heading:*] Wyot mayor.

Assembly: Friday next after the translation of St. Thomas the Martyr 26 Hen. VI [*12 July 1448*].

Present [*in two columns*]: Robert Cove, Walter Carogan, John Gerveyse. Thomas Payn, Simon Poy, William Lyghtfote, John Esterbury, John a Port, Richard Payn, William Cormayle, John Honythorn, William Hore, Stephen Hendy, [*column two*] Edmund Langto[n], Henry Frend, William Pette, John Dogode, John Mone 'gent', Clement Forbour, John Cleve 'tanner', William Wilmot, Henry Shad, John Halstede, Thomas Whytyng, John Lumbard, John Walysch, Thomas Stopp', William Soper', John Wheler', Richard Hayne 'taylour', Walter Brydd, Stephen Hake, Thomas Copter, Richard Walker, John Slegg, William Wotton, John Wynchester, Edward Bonere, William Child, John Mone 'touker', Walter Hende, William Mory, Thomas Valeys, John Wylly.

Agreed: citizens living over the common ditch (*trenchea*) on the southern side ought for their part to scour the ditch (*fossat'*) and mend it at their own cost and expense, and the citizens living on the northern side of the said ditch for their part likewise ought to scour and mend it at their own cost and expense.

Also, all citizens and all of enough wealth (*de mag' sufficienc'*) to have a gown of blue blod') colour [5d. (*i.e. in value*) *interlined*] and a hat of red colour for the king's visit, under penalty of 13s. 4d. of each of them.

f. 147; *faded and stained*]

418. Election of the mayor and other officers at the end of the mayoralty of H. Man, on All Souls' day 11 Hen. VI [*2 Nov. 1432*] in St. Edmund's church, as is the custom, with fines [*i.e. for being excused office*]. [*It is not clear why the election of 1432 is so far out of place.*]

Mayor, Henry Baron; reeves, Robert Pottere, William Chepman; alderman of New Street, John Chaunceler [*sic, recte* Chaundeler?]; of Market, John Alysaundr'; of St. Martin's William Mohun; of Meadow, Thomas Archebaud; serjeants, Henry Frend, Thomas Yoxford.

Fines: John White 'mercer' £5 for being excused [the offices of] alderman and reeve, paid to Robert Warmwell £5; John Park for being excused the office of alderman £2, paid to Robert Warmwell £2 by account; John Everard for being excused the offices of alderman, reeve, and all others except king's serjeant £5, to be paid half at Michaelmas next and the other half at Michaelmas following, pledges [Robert Warmwell *crossed out*], John Bremle, and Robert Gilberd; John Gerveys for being excused the offices of alderman and reeve £5, to be paid half at Michaelmas next [*in the margin*, in Robert Warmwell's account] and the other half at Michaelmas following, pledges Richard Gatour, John Wyot; John Colyngbourne for being excused the office of reeve £2, half to be paid at Michaelmas next [*in the margin*, by Robert Warmwell's account] and the other half at Michaelmas following, pledges Richard Gatour, Robert Gilberd. Sum £19.

John Hobbys 'brewer' by the Friars Minor for £4 which he will pay through 5s. rent arising from the tenement which William Clerk [occupied] in Castle Street ('Castelstret'), conveyed to the mayor and community, was excused the offices of alderman and reeve.

Richard Shirle [*incomplete.*]

John Estbury for a fine of £2 in the time of H. Man paid to John Boteler, as appears in the said John [Boteler]'s account, and £2 for [being excused the offices of] aldermar and reeve; John a Port for a fine of £3 in the time of H. Man 10 [Hen.VI, *1431–2*] paid to John Boteler, as appears in the account of the same; John Gilberd of Odstock for fine of £2 paid to John Boteler.

[f. 147v.; *faded and stained*]

419.Various ordinances and constitutions made for the city's use in various mayoralties beginning with Walter Shirle 10 Hen. IV [*1408–9*]. [*The ordinances, except for the las and with a few minor errors and omissions, are printed in translation in* H.M.C. Var Coll. IV, *pp. 193–5.*]

In the time of Walter Shirle, [it was ordered] that there should be two chamberlains to receive the debts owed to the city, to pay the debts which the city owes, to repair houses, and to pay, meet, and discharge other charges on the city; and that there should be a comptroller for them; for this were elected as chamberlains John Becket and John Judde, and as their controller Thomas Rede, who were to account annually to the mayor and other auditors assigned to them.

At the same time there was presented to the king, being at Clarendon, at the nativity of the Blessed Virgin Mary £26 13s. 4d.

In the same year John Moner in a full assembly of the citizens gave his tenement at the upper bridge of Fisherton, which John Crabilane held, to the hospice of the 'Almeshous'

In the time of John Beket [it was ordered] that all of the Twenty-Four should come to the mass to be offered for a dead member under penalty of 2 lb. of wax unless they had a reasonable cause of absence.

In the time of John Levesham, by the mediation of the bishop of Winchester, chancello of England, and Edward duke of York, the city advanced to King Henry V £100 in the second year of his reign, as appears in the said John's account.

In the time of William Waryn [it was ordered] that any freeholder who, being given notice to attend the assembly, made default should incur a penalty of 6d. and ale (*et s'*) for each default, as appears among the memoranda of the same mayor, 3 Hen.V [*1415–16*].

Also that people bringing victuals into the city for sale should not sell them in inns or secretly or before daylight but in the places ordained for the purpose.

Also that horses carrying victuals or other commodities to the city should after being unloaded be taken by their drivers or others to a resting place outside the market and the common street, so that no harm or damage should happen to passers by from them

Also that victuallers coming to the city with cheese, milk, grapes, plums, apples, pears, and other fruits should in future be made to keep to the place facing Richard Oword's tenement, now John Gage's, where the new cross is being built.

Also that the common ditches (*trench'*) running through the middle of the city should henceforth be kept free of dung and other unsuitable matter.

Also that covert tenures and feoffments should henceforth be held and reputed null and void because contrary to the city's customs.

Also that outside (*extranii*) butchers should not be moved from the places assigned to them by the mayor without reasonable cause and common and solemn assembly of the citizens and commoners.

Also that all outside victuallers both butchers and fishmongers should be altogether separated in their stands from the city victuallers.

Also that no one living in the city should receive any grain put out for sale in the market into his house after the ninth hour for storage, under penalty of ½ mark, nor any fish or meat under the same penalty.

Also that in every election, both for mayor and for citizens at parliament and other officials, each person should be free to nominate whom he wishes, but that no one should be finally elected on the nomination of just one person.

19A. In the time of John Judde it was ordered that the chamberlains and collectors of tallage and all others owing money to the city should be held to render account whenever required by the mayor for the time being, and for this audit were appointed as auditors the mayor for the time being, Walter Shirle, William Waryn, Richard Gage, [and] John Everard, and that those auditors and all others for the time being should have a day every year, the feast of St. Luke [*18 Oct.*], for certifying to the mayor and community at the next assembly then following as to the foot or fine [*i.e. the bottom line*] of the account.

There was presented to John Chaundeler, bishop of Salisbury, on his installation 40 marks, a sum which was loaned by certain persons and paid back to them, as appears in the mayoralty of the said John Jude, 5 Hen. VI [*recte Hen. V, 1417–18*].

f. 148; *faded and stained*]

In the mayoralty of John Salesbury 17 Ric. II [*1393*] it was ordered that King Henry IV should have 100 marks and two silver-gilt cups (*ij cup' arg' et deaur'*) and the queen 50 marks, and also that Robert Halom, bishop of Salisbury, should have £20, to be levied and collected from the whole city. [*Two or more entries appear to have been elided: a gift to Henry IV cannot have been made during Richard II's reign, and Robert Hallum did not become bishop until 1407.*]

In the time of Robert Poynant 6 Hen. V [*1418–19*] it was ordered that those having pigs, geese, or ducks should be prohibited from putting them outside their houses.

In the mayoralty of Robert Warmwell 8 Hen. V [*1420*] it was decreed that no deed should henceforth be sealed under the mayoral seal except by the city clerk deputed for the purpose.

In the time of Henry Man it was ordered that the mayor for the time being [should have] £10 for all expenses and charges met during his mayoralty, to be paid in the following way, half at Easter at the chamberlains' hands and the other half at the end of the year, but that if the mayor should die after Easter and before the end of his year then that half should remain in the chamberlains' hands for the use of the city, except that the city officials should have their liveries at the city's expense and that the chaplain of St George, viz. Edmund [*blank*], should be at the board of the mayor for the time being receiving 8 marks a year, for which the mayor should receive £2 13s. 4d. for his board at the chamberlains' hands and that he [*sc.* the chaplain] should be attendant on every mayor. And if the king or another secular lord or prelate comes to the city nothing should be given to him except by order of the assembly of citizens.

419B. In the mayoralty of William Waryn it was ordered that butchers should not slaughter their animals in front of Butcher Row ('le Bocherrewe') in the common street but behind it, because of the foulness, putrifaction, and nastiness of the [offal from] said animals.

Also that they should not render down their [*blank*] by day but at night, and that they should not carry away the offal or intestines of their animals by day but at night.

Also that poulterers and all other victuallers bringing goods to the city for sale should sell them in the common market and not in inns and specially when it is light (*cum cl'i* [*the reading is uncertain;* H.M.C. Var. Coll. IV, *p. 195, reads it as* rabbits, *sc. cuniculi; q. no.* **286**] and not at night but during the day.

If it happens that the chaplain of St. George is ill the mayor for the time being should pay him 1s. for each week that he lies [in bed].

In the mayoralty of John Bromle 6 Hen. VI [*1427–8*] it was ordered that outside fishmongers (*piscatores extranii*) should be separated from resident (*intrincec'* fishmongers as above [*i.e. like the butchers?*], and that the outside fishmonger should have their stands over the common trench behind the stand of the city fishmongers.

Also that the owners of all animals put out for sale should keep to their place at Barnwell Cross ('Bernewellcros') and Culver Street ('Colverstret') to sell them there.

Also that anyone who has been mayor of the city should be quit from performing that office for five years after occupying the office.

In the time of Robert Warmwell [it was ordered] that 5 marks be paid to John Boteler and Richard Nedler serjeants for carrying before the mayor the two maces ('macys'), to be looked after in future for the city by the two serjeants, as long as they behave themselves well (*quamdiu honeste se habuerint*).

[f. 148v.; *faded and stained*]

420. [*Heading:*] John [Wyot mayor *on the facing page*].

Assembly (*Convencio*): Saturday the feast of St. Matthew 27 Hen. VI [*21 Sept. 1448*].

Present [*in three columns*]: from the Twenty-Four: Thomas Payne, Stephen Hendy, John Ysbury, Simon Poye, Richard Payne, Thomas Freman, John Wyot, John Port, Robert Cove, John Jerveys, John Halle, John Parrok 'goldsmyth', John Wyse 'draper', [*column two,* from the Forty-Eight:] Henry Frende, Anselm Hebbyng, Edmund Penston, John Wyse vintner ('vynter'), Roger Mayne, Thomas Stope, John Mone 'touker', William Pette, Walter Brydde, Richard Cokelet, William Wylmot, John Clyve 'tanner', William Wotton, John Wynchester, Thomas Whytyng, John Mone 'jentilman', John Dogode, Guy Rother, John Slegge, John Chacchero, John Thursby, Thomas Gyle, Richard Spyndeler, Richard Stelbrygge, Thomas Mogge, John Colinesby, John Wheler'.

John Mone 'touker', collector of the fourth part of a fifteenth in Market aldermanry, accounted for £19 3s. 1d., of which he paid to John Wyot mayor in money £18 15s. 1d.; allowed to him 4d. for Peter Jonson, and to the same for William Knoll 6s. 8d., and for Edmund Eggesworth 1s. Quit.

John Thursby, collector in New Street, accounted for £14 12s. 8d., of which he paid to John Wyot mayor in money £13 13s. 4d.; allowed to him for various men beyond hope (*desperatis*) 16s. 4d. because it could not be levied, and he owed 3s. for Ansel Hebbyng.

Richard Spynler, collector in Meadow, accounted for £3 17s. 9d., of which he paid to John Wyot mayor in money £3 11s. 8d.; allowed to him for various unknown men, because he did not know where to levy what was due, 6s. 1d. Quit.

John Slegge, collector in St. Martin's, accounted for £15 2s.. of which he paid to John Wyot mayor in money £13 9s.; allowed to him for various unknown men, because he did not know where to levy [what was due] 13s. Quit.

Sum total received by John Wyot mayor, £50 9s. 7d. [*recte* £50 9s. 1d.].

Of which the mayor accounted for the payment to be made to John Dogood and Edward Boner, the king's collectors of the fourth part of a fifteenth, on the feast of St. Martin 27 Hen. VI [*11 Nov. 1448*] of £33 10s., and in payment to the same collectors for their wages for carrying the said money, 10s.; and in money paid to William Swayn for money lent by him for the king's visit, £11, which was given to the king; and in money paid to John Mone for his clerk, 8d.; and allowed to the same [*sc.* John Mone *or* the mayor?] for various necessary expenses 8s.; and so there remained in the said mayor's hands £5 0s. 11d. [*Added later*, In payment to William Cormayle mayor, William Swayn, and John Wynchestr' on St. Margaret's day 27 Hen.VI [*20 July 1449*] £4.]

[f. 149; *faded and stained*]

421. [*Heading*: John *on the facing page*] Wyot mayor.

Assembly (*Convencio*): Wednesday next before All Saints 27 Hen.VI [*30 Oct. 1448*].

Present [*in four columns, the first two presumably for the Twenty-Four, the third and fourth for the Forty-Eight*]: Simon Poy, John Cammell, John a Port, Robert (. . .), Robert (. . .), Walter Carogan, John Gerveyse, John Honythorn, Thomas Payn, John Wyse, William Lyghtefote, Stephen Hendy, [*column two*] William Cormayle, Nicholas Shute, William Swayn, John Estbury, John Halle, John Peraunt, [*column three*] William Pette, John Hode, John Mone 'touker', Anselm Hebbyng, John Wheler', John Wyse, John Cacchero, Nicholas Barbour, Richard Hayne, John Lumbard, William Sopere, John Aschford, Henry Shad, John Cleve, John Slegge, [*column four*] Henry Frende, John Scotte, John Mone 'gent', John Walsch, Guy Roter, John Parche, William Wylmot, Thomas Copter, John Dogode, Thomas Mogge.

Agreed: the present mayor to have all his allowances just as other mayors have been used to have, viz. for the said mayor's pension this year, £10; for the board and clothing of the chaplain of St. George, £2 13s. 4d.; to the king's official, 6s. 8d.; to the duke of York's official, 3s. 4d.; to the duke of Exeter's official, 3s. 4d.; to the duke of Somerset's official, 3s. 4d.; to the chancellor of England's official, 4s. 4d. [*recte* 3s. 4d.]; to the marquess of Suffolk's official, 3s. 4d.; to the duke of Buckingham's official, 3s. 4d.; to the earl of Devon's official, 3s. 4d.; to Lord Stourton's official, 3s. 4d.; for the city officials' clothing, 16s.; for three gowns of Kendal cloth (*de Kendale*) bought for the city serjeants for the king's visit, 18s.; for various gifts and other necessary costs made for the king's visit, £1 9s. 8d. Sum £17 10s. [*recte* £17 10s. 4d.]

Election of chamberlains for next year, viz. John Perant 'goldsmyth', Anselm Hebbyng.

Election of auditors for this year, viz. the mayor, William Swayn, Robert Cove, John Wheler, John Slegge.

[f. 149v.; *faded and stained*]

422. Election: All Souls' day 27 Hen.VI [*2 Nov. 1448*].

Mayor, William Cormaile; reeves, John Parrok, William Oke chaplain; alderman of New Street, William Hardyng clerk; of Market, John Shupton 'dubber'; of St. Martin's, Nicholas Stote 'carpenter'; of Meadow, [*blank*]; serjeants, Geoffrey Ponyng, Richard Hayne 'taillour'.

Agreed at the election: Philip Morgan may resign his office to the use of Edward Chiltern [if the community wish to have him in the said office *interlined*], and the said Edward to have the said office of clerk of the mayor and community with the fee and the reward belonging to the office as William Lord had them, so long as he remains in the city and behaves himself well towards the mayor and community.

Fines: on this the same Edward made fine for being excused the offices of alderman and reeve for £4, to be paid at Michaelmas next £1 6s. 8d. from his stipend, on the same feast following £1 6s. 8d. from his said stipend, and on that feast following thereafter £1 6s. 8d. from his said stipend, pledges Thomas Freman and Simon Poy [*in the margin*, paid to John Wyse £1 6s. 8d. in the time of W. Lyghtfote]; John Walssh made fine for being excused the offices of alderman and reeve for £4, to be paid at Michaelmas next £2, and at Michaelmas following £2, pledges Simon Poy and John Estbury; John Dogood made fine for being excused the offices of alderman and reeve for £4, to be paid now and in the form written above, pledges John Wyot and John Wyse; John Large made fine for being excused the offices of alderman and reeve for £4, to be paid as above, pledges, William Lyghtfote and Thomas Freman; John Launderier made fine for being excused the offices of alderman and reeve for £4, to be paid as above, pledge William Cormailes; Richard Hayne 'taillour' made fine for being excused the office of alderman for £2, to be paid at Michaelmas next, pledge John Estbury. [*The last five items crossed out, presumably on payment of the fine in full.*]

[f. 150; *faded and stained*]

423. [*Heading:*] William Cormayle.

Assembly: Friday next before St. Thomas the apostle 27 Hen. VI [*27 Dec. 1448*].

Present [*in six columns*]: [*in the margin*, the mayor], John Wyot, William Swayn, William Hore, Richard Payn, Robert Cove, Nicholas Shute, John Aport, Simon Poy, Robert Cammell, [*column two*] John Estbury, William Lyghtfote, Thomas Payn, Thomas Temse, Walter Carogan, John Jerveys, John Wyse, Stephen Hendy, John Perant, [*column three*] Edmund Penston, John Scott, John Wynchester, Roger Mayne, John Dogood, John Mone, John Mone 'touker', William Shipton, [*column four*] John Cacchero, John Wheler, Walter Hynde, William Swyngell, William Mory, Clement Forbour, Thomas Whityng, Richard Walker, [*column five*] Anselm Hebbyng, John Wyly, Walter Bryd, John Slegge, John Cleve 'tanner', John Walssh, Thomas Stoppe, William Child, [*column six*] Ralph Paker, Thomas Copter, Richard Hayne 'taillour', Richard Cokelot, John Fulbroke, John Thursby, Thomas Bukbrigge , Walter Freman.

Agreed: the mayor to have this year the wages, fees, and all other expenses (*onera*) which before this time were customary, as other mayors had, and the officers and liveries as before.

Agreed: Simon Poy and his fellow, late chamberlains, and all others to appear before the mayor and auditors in the council house (*domo consilii*) on Wednesday next after Hilary next [*15 Jan. 1449*] under penalty of £2 for each of them.

Election of constables: [John Estbury *crossed out*], Thomas Temse, Nicholas Shete.

424. Assembly: Wednesday next after St. Wulfstan 27 Hen. VI [*22 Jan. 1449*].

Present: John Wyot, John Port, Robert Cove, Simon Poy, John Perrant, John Wyse, Nicholas Shute, Thomas Payn, William Lyghtfote, William Hore, Richard Payn, John Estbury, Walter Carogan, [John Gerveys *interlined*], Edmund Penston, John Scot, John Mone, John Halste, Richard Walker, John Wyse, Thomas Bugbrigge, John Cachero, John Thursby, Anselm Hebbyng, Henry Frend, Richard Plowman, John Shepton, P [*significance unclear*] Stephen Hendy, Nicholas Stote, John Wynchester, Thomas Stoppe, John Slegge, John Wheler, Richard Cokelot, William Child, William Wotton, John Honythorn, Thomas Copter, Richard Stalbrigge, William Wilmot, Thomas Whityng, John Mone 'touker', Walter Bryt, Ralph Pakker, William Swayn, John Wyot 'bruer', Roger Mayne, John Cleve 'brewer', Henry Shadd, John Cleve 'tanner', Nicholas Wedirgrove, Stephen Hake, Thomas Mogge, John Dogood, John Fulbroke, Guy Roter, Walter Hynde, Edmund Langto[n], William Mory, John Assheford, Robert Meteyeve, John Chippenham, John Noble, John Frank, William Soper, Richard Marchall, William Swyngell, John Crikmore. [*Each of the last three lines, beginning respectively with* Stephen Hake, John Assheford, *and* William Swyngell, *is heavily indented.*]

Agreed: Philip [Morgan] to have and hold his office of clerk of the mayor and community as he had it before this time, and Edward Chiltern not to have the said office. [*Cf. no. 422.*]

Also, John Lye to have 40s. a year from the mayor and community for his good counsel to be given to the mayor and community, and to have for that a charter sealed under the common seal.

Also agreed: John Wheler to have and hold his tenement where he lives in St. Martin's Street ('Seyntmartynstrete'), to have and to hold to him and his assigns for the term of 98 years following, paying thence paying £2 6s. 8d. a year and all other rents and services due from it, and repairing it well at his own cost and expense

[f. 150v.; *faded and stained*]]

425. [*Heading:*] W. Cormayle mayor.

Assembly: Wednesday 5 Feb. 27 Hen. VI [*1449*].

Present: [*in the margin,* the mayor], John Wyot, Richard Payn, William Swayn, John Aport, Robert Cove, Simon Poy, Thomas Temse, Walter Carogan, John Hall, Thomas Payn, John Wyse, Stephen Hendy, William Lyghtfote, John Parrant, John Jerveys [*presumably members of the Twenty-Four*];

Richard Walker, John Willy, John Mone, John Scott, Roger Mayn, Clement Fourbour,

Anselm Hebbyng, Henry Frend, Thomas Stoppe, John Mone 'touker', William Child, Edward Chilterne, John Halstede, John Wynchester, John Wily, Thomas Felde, Robert Meteyeve, John Dogood, Thomas Lyon, John Thursby, John Cleve 'tanner', John Hayne, Henry Shadde, Thomas Mogge, Walter Bridd, Richard Cokelot, William Meriot, John Shipton, Walter Hynd, Thomas Pakker, William Soper, John Batyn [*presumably members of the Forty-Eight*].

Names of those elected to attend the parliament to be held at Westminster 12 Feb. next: John Whitoxmede, Philip Morgan; for half wages, and they may (. . .).

426. Assembly: Friday next after the Ascension 27 Hen. VI [*23 May 1449*].

Present: William Cormayle [*in the margin*, the mayor], William Swayn, Richard Payn, William Lyghtfote, Nicholas Shute, Thomas Payn, John Aport, John Gerveyse, John Estbury, John Peraunt, Walter Carogan, John Wyse, John Wyot 'mercer' [*presumably members of the Twenty-Four*];

Edmund Penston, John Mone, John Scot, John Wynchester, John Mone 'touker', John Slegge, William Childe, John Wyly, John Dogood, John Shypton, Anselm Hebbyng, John Halstede, Walter Hynde, Guy Roter, John Cacchero, Thomas Bugbrigge, John Chyppenham, John Cleve 'tanner', William Sopere, William Wylmot, William Wotton, Thomas Whytyng [*presumably members of the Forty-Eight*].

Nicholas Shute, John Halle are elected as city constables.

427. Assembly: Friday Friday in Whitsun week 27 Hen. VI [*6 June 1449*].

Present: William Cormayle mayor, William Hore, John Wyot, Richard Payn, John Port, Robert Cove, Simon Poy, John Honythorn, Walter Coragan, [Walter (*blank*) crossed *out*], John Wyse, John Halle, Stephen Hendy, John Gerveyse, William Lyghtfote [*presumably members of the Twenty-Four*];

Edmund Penston, John Mone 'gent', Roger Mayn, Edmund Langeto[n], Richard Gylberd, Thomas Pakkere, Anselm Hebbying, Richard Walkere, John Wynchestr', John Cleve 'tanner', Thomas Mogge, Nicholas Wedergrove, Thomas Copter, Thomas Bowyer' esquire, John Mone 'touker', Henry Shad, John Shupton, Nicholas Stote [*presumably members of the Forty-Eight*].

Constables: John Halle for New Street, John Wyse for Market, Roger Mayn for St. Martin's, John Wheler for Meadow.

Agreed: [*incomplete*].

[f. 151; *faded and stained*]

428. Assembly: Tuesday next after Corpus Christi 27 Hen. VI [*17 June 1449*].

Present [*in two columns, with* per disc' *and, lower down,* Jur' (*'sworn'*) *written to the left of them*]: William Cormailes mayor, William Swayn, Thomas Freman, William Hore, John Wyot, Richard Payn, Simon Poy, Robert Cove, Stephen Hendy, Walter Corrogan, John Aport, Thomas Payn, John Wyse, Nicholas Shute, J. Honythorn, J. Gerveys, John Perham 'goldsmyth' [*presumably members of the Twenty-Four*], [*column two*] Edmund Penston, Roger Mayn, Thomas Pakker, Thomas Slegge, Walter Huntley, J. Mone G [*i.e. 'gent'*], Thomas Lyon, William Chyld, Thomas Whityng, Clement Rawlyn, Anselm Hebbyng, Henry Frend, J. Wynchester, J. Cachero, William Wutton, J. Parche, Guy Rotor, J. Skot, Thomas Copter [*presumably members of the Forty-Eight*].

429. Assembly: Saturday next before the nativity of St. John the Baptist 27 Hen. VI [*21 June 1449*].

Present: [*in the margin*, the mayor], William Swayne, Thomas Freman, Richard Payne, William Lyghtfote, Robert Cove, Nicholas Shete, Thomas Payn, Simon Poy, Stephen Hendy, John Wyse, John Gerveys, John Halle, John Portt, John Estbury [*presumably members of the Twenty-Four*];

Edmund Penston, John Slegge, Anselm Hebbyng, John Wyly, Stephen Hake, Guy Ruttour, John Cacheroo, Richard Cokelot, John Mone 'touker', Thomas Whityng, John Wheler, Roger Mayne, John Parche, John Asshford, Henry Shadde, Thomas Lyon, John Wynchester, Nicholas Wethirgrove, John Scotte, Thomas Bugbrigge, John Mone 'gent' [*presumably members of the Forty-Eight*].

430. Assembly: Wednesday next after the nativity of St. John the Baptist 27 Hen. VI [*25 June 1449*].

Present: [*in the margin*, the mayor], Thomas Freman, John Wyot, William Hore, William Swayn, John Aport, Richard Payn, Robert Cove, William Lyghtfote, John Halle, John Wyse, Simon Poy, John Peraunt, Stephen Hendy, Thomas Payn, Nicholas Shute, John Gerveyse [*presumably members of the Twenty-Four*];

John Wynchestr', Anselm Hebbyng, Henry Shadd, Thomas Whytyng, Richard Cokelot, Walter Bryd, John Mone 'touker', Clement Raulyn, Walter Huntele, John Halstede, Nicholas Wedergrove, Guy Roter, John Cacchero, Thomas Bugbrigge, John Wylly, John Scot, Henry Frend, Roger Mayn, Thomas Mogge, William Wotton, John Mone 'gent' [*presumably members of the Forty-Eight*].

431. Assembly: Wednesday next after St. Swithin 27 Hen. VI [*8 July 1449*].

Present: [*in the margin*, the mayor], William Swayne, Robert Cove, William Hore, Simon Poy, Thomas Payn, John Gerveyse, John Wyot, Nicholas Shute, John Wyse, John

Halle, Stephen Hendy, John Aporte, John Peraunt, William Lyghtfote, Walter Carogan, John Estbury, Richard Payn, John Cammell [*presumably members of the Twenty-Four*];

Edmund Penston, John Mone 'gent', Richard Walker, John Cacchero, John Wheler, Clement Raulyn, Henry Shad, Anselm Hebbyng, Guy Rotor, Nicholas Wedergrove, John Cleve 'tannere', John Mone 'touker', John Scotte, Thomas Whytyng, William Wotton, Roger Mayn [*presumably members of the Forty-Eight*].

Agreed and granted: William Stafford esquire to have £5 sterling a year from the mayor and community for his good counsel and help to be given to the mayor and community, and to have for that a charter sealed under the common seal.

Agreed: the bishop of Salisbury to have as a gift [*incomplete*].

Agreed: Lord Stourton to have as a gift [*incomplete*].

Agreed: the mayor ought to choose at his discretion five from the Twenty-Four, with himself as a sixth, and six from the Forty-Eight, viz. the mayor, John Wyot, William Hore, William Swayn, Richard Payn, John Aport, Edmund Penston, John Mone 'gent', John Scot, John Wynchestr', Roger Mayn, and Anselm Hebbyng. [*The purpose of the group is not apparent.*]

[f. 151v.; *faded and stained*]

Names of the men assessed for £66 loaned to the king in the mayoralty of William Cormayle 27 Hen. VI [*1448–9*]. Memorandum: of the said £66, £38 came from the common chest.

[*In two columns; each name, except Thomas Pakker, William Wotton, and those marked as paying nothing, is preceded by 'paid'* ('sol'):] the mayor William Cormaill £2 3s. 4d., Thomas Freman 10s. by [his] wife, John Wyot nil, William Hore 13s. 4d. by W. d [?], William Swayn nil, Richard Payn £1, John Aport £1, Robert Cove 13s. 4d., Simon Poy £1, Nicholas Shute £1, John Peraunt £1, William Lyghtfote £1, John Wyse 13s. 4d. by W. d [?], John Gervayse £1 6s. 8d., John Estebury 6s. 8d. by (. . .), John Boteler nil, William Halstede 10s., Stephen Hendy £1, Walter Carogan £1, Thomas Payn 13s. 4d., John Camell £1, Thomas Temese nil, John Halle 26s. 8d., John Honythorn nil, Edward Chylterne nil, Edmund Penston nil, John Wynchestre 13s. 4d., Thomas Pakker 6s. 8d., John Wyly 6s. 8d., Thomas Lyon nil, Guy Roter nil, Richard Bowyer nil, John Cacchero nil, Nicholas Wedergrove 6s. 8d., Thomas Bugbryg nil, Simon Newman nil, Thomas Sampson nil, John Conesby 6s. 8d., Thomas Whytyng 6s. 8d., John Wyot 'brewer' 6s. 8d., William Beste 6s. 8d., John Lavendre 6s. 8d., Henry Shad 3s. 4d., Philip Nowell 6s. 8d., John Horn 6s. 8d. paid by W. Cormayle, John Cleve 'tannere' 6s. 8d. by W. d [?], John Large 6s. 8d., William Wotton 3s. 4d., Thomas Felde 3s. 4d., John Thorseby 3s. 4d., Richard Sadeler 3s. 4d., John Slegge 3s. 4d., John Cleve 'brewer' 3s. 4d. by W. d [?], Thom Pese 3s. 4d. by W. d [?], Thomas Gyle 3s. 4d., Walter Hynde 10s., [*column two*] John Mone 'touker' 6s. 8d., John Asshford 'taylour' 3s., Thomas Mabr' 6s. 8d., Simon Laverok 6s. 8d., John Wheler 3s. 4d., John Gylle 'bocher' 3s. 4d., William Barlowe 3s. 4d.

by Wyot, James Thomelyn 3s. 4d., William Sopere 3s. 4d., Luke Brasier' 3s. 4d., John Gode 6s. 8d., William Meryet 6s. 8d., William Wylmot 3s. 4d., Thomas Stoppe 3s. 4d., William Chylde 3s. 4d., John Chyppenham 6s. 8d., Nicholas Edmond 3s. 4d. by Luke, John Parrok 3s. 4d., John Boteler 'merser' 3s. 4d. .

[An incomplete version, struck through for cancellation, of the next paragraph.]

Memorandum: William Cormaile mayor received from the common chest this year £38; and from various men who advanced money to the king as in this folio £28 13s. 4d.; from the four collectors of one half of a fifteenth and tenth granted in the same year £46 0s. 10d. [*corrected from* £46 7s. 1d.]. Sum total received this year £112 14s. 2d. [*corrected from* £113 0s. 5d.], from which the said men are paid £28 13s. 4d., and to John Halsted and John Cammell, the king's collectors, £66 as appears by four tallies; and he [the mayor] owed £18 0s. 10d., from which [was paid *crossed out*, was allowed to William Cormayle *interlined*] for various expenses at Winchester £7 18s. 8d.; and so there remained £10 2s. 1d. [*recte* £10 2s. 2d.], which he delivered into the common chest; and so he went quit. [*The paragraph has been much amended.*]

[f. 152; *stained*]

432. [*Heading:*] W. Cormayle mayor.

The mayor, Thomas Freman, John Wyot, William Hore, William Swayn, Richard Payn, John Aport, Robert Cove, Simon Poy, Nicholas Shute, John Wyse, John Halle, William Lyghtfote, John Gerveyse, Thomas Payn, John Peraunt, John Estebury, John Honythorn, Walter Carogan [*presumably members of the Twenty-Four*];

John Mone, Edmund Penston, Thomas Pakker, Edward Chylterne, Roger Mayn, John Wynchester, Simon Laverok, Henry Shadd, Thomas Whytyng, John Thorseby, John Wyse, John Mone [*the other*], John Wylly, Thomas Lyon, Nicholas Wedergrove, Guy Roter, John Cacchero, William Meriet, John Chippenham, Clement Rawlyn, John Batyn, William Mory, William Wylmot, John Lavender, William Soper', John Wheler, William Chylde, John Slegge, William Wotton, John Cleve 'tannere', John Cleve 'brewer', John Horn, Anselm Hebbyng [*presumably members of the Forty-Eight*].

At the mayor's council in the Council House (*domo consilii*) [Wednesday next before St. Denis 28 Hen.VI [*8 Oct. 1449*] at which assembly it was agreed that Robert Cove, Nicholas Shute, and Thomas Payn, should be excused and quit of the office of mayor in perpetuity for 40 marks sterling, to be paid £20 in hand [*i.e. immediately*] and £6 13s. 4d. at Michaelmas next under a bond.

433. Assembly: Friday next before St. Luke 28 Hen.VI [*17 Oct. 1449*].

Present: the mayor, John Wyot, William Hore, William Swayn, Richard Payn, John Aport,

Robert Cove, Simon Poy, Nicholas Shute, John Wyse, John Halle, William Lyghtfote, John Gerveyse, Thomas Payn, John Peraunt, John Estebury, John Honythorn, Walter Carogan [*presumably members of the Twenty-Four*];

Edmund Penston, Edward Chylterne, Thomas Pakker, John Mone 'gent', Roger Mayn, John Wynchestr', Simon Laverok, Henry Shad, Thomas Whytyng, John Wyly, John Wheler', Clement Rawlyn, John Thorsby, John Mone 'touker', Anselm Hebbyng, John Wyse vintner ('vynter'), Nicholas Stote, John Shupton, John Chyppenham, William Wylmot, John Cleve 'brewer', John Slegge, John Lavendr', William Sopere, William Wylmot [*again*], John Batyn, William Mory, John Cleve 'tannere', William Wotton, William Chylde [*presumably members of the Forty-Eight*].

Agreed: the mayor to have all his allowances as other mayors have been used to have, viz. for the mayor's pension this year, £10; for the board and clothing of the chaplain of St. George, £2 13s. 4d.; for the city officials' clothing, 12s. 8d.; for the king's official, 6s. 8d.; to the duke of Exeter's official, 3s. 4d.; to the duke of Suffolk's offical, 3s. 4d.; to the chancellor of England's official, 3s. 4d.; to Lord Stourton's official, 1s. 8d.; to the earl of Wiltshire's official, 1s. 8d.; in a gift to Lord Stourton, 10s.; in a gift to William Stafford, 6s. 4d.; in a gift to William Ludlowe, 3s. 4d.; given to the bishop of Salisbury's steward, Richard Haselden, and to John Hedle, the bishop's servant, to each 10s.; for various expenses in riding to Devizes to the bishop of Salisbury and being there, John Aport and others, 13s. 8d.; given to a groom of the Crown [*valect' corone*], being there, as appointed by the bishop of Salisbury, £1; to John Chafyn for riding to London and to Windsor to the bishop of Salisbury and Lord Stourton 'pour le Tretez' [?], 11s. 8d.; in a gift to the sheriff of Wiltshire, 3s. 4d.; given to Christopher, William Stafford's servant, 3s. 4d.; given to Giles, Lord Stourton's servant, 3s. 4d.; given to John Rows, the Lord Chancellor's servant, 6s. 8d.; given to John Rokez, the bishop of Salisbury's servant, 6s. 8d.; to Alexander Hody for having his good advice, £1; to John Nedam for advice, £1; given to Lord Hungerford's pursuivant ('a le pursefaunt'), 6s. 8d.; for the cost of riding to the bishop of Salisbury from [*or at*] Marlborough, 12s. 8d. Sum £22 3s. 8d.

[*Isolated at the foot of the page*] Robert.

[f. 152v.; *stained*]

434. [Assembly]: [no date]

[Present:] the mayor, Thomas Freman, William Hore, William Swayn, John Aport, Robert Cove, Simon Poy, John Cammell, Nicholas Shute, John Wyse, John Honythorn, Thomas Payn, John Gerveyse, John Estebury, William Lyghtfote, Walter Carogan, John Halle [*presumably members of the Twenty-Four*];

Richard Hayne 'gent', [Richard Gilberd *interlined*], Edward Chiltern, John Mone 'touker', John Wylly, John Halsted', William Wotton, William Colyn, John Slegge, Walter Freman, William Childe, [Robert Longe 'corveser' *crossed out*], John Brydmour, John Attekyn, Robert Longe 'corveser', Richard Ploman, John Stephenez, John Mone 'gent',

Richard Brom(le?), John Scotte, William Shupton 'dubber', Henry Frend, John Wyse vintner ('vynter'), Richard Stalbrygg', John Chyppenham, Roger Mayne, John Parch, Anselm Hebbyng, John Batyn, Richard Walker, Edmund Penston [*presumably members of the Forty-Eight*].

Election to parliament: William Swayn, Edmund Penston; for half wages only to be received by them unless at the discretion of the mayor and community they are to be otherwise remunerated for their deserts and labours.

435. [Assembly]: [no date]

[Present:] the mayor, John Wyot, William Swayn, [Richard Payn *interlined*], Robert Cove, John Cammell, Walter Carogan, Simon Poy, Nicholas Shute, John Gerveyse, John Wyse, Thomas Payn [*presumably members of the Twenty-Four*];

Edmund Penston, John Mone 'gent', John Scotte, Roger Mayn, John Wynchestr', Henry Frende, John Slegge, John Wylly, Nicholas Wedergrove, Nicholas Stote, John Shupton, John Attekyn, John Halsted, John Chyppenham, John Parrok, Edward Chyltern [*presumably members of the Forty-Eight*].

[Elected:] New Street: John Halle, John Wyly, [Robert Cove in [Wyly's] place *added*]; Market: John Perant, Thomas Whytyng; St. Martin's: John Estebury, Henry Shad; Meadow: William Wotton, John Wheler' – as assessors for one half of a fifteenth and a tenth granted 28 [Hen. VI, *1449–50*]. New Street: Richard Bowyer'; Market: John Lavendr'; St. Martin's: Robert Chaundeler; Meadow: Thomas Leker – as collectors for the same.

John Lavender [collector] for Market ward answered for his part for £18 0s. 5d., of which he paid to William Cormaile by indenture £16 3s. 4d. He owed £1 17s. (1d.) to be paid to the same on his account etc. And he is quit.

Richard Bowyer collector for New Street answered for £13 18s. 5d., of which he paid to the mayor by indenture £11 6s. 8d. He owed £2 11s. 9d., of which was allowed to him 13s. 4d. for William Swayn [which he ought to pay to William Cormaile *crossed out*; because he was at parliament at the time of the assessment *interlined*], and for various other small amounts which could not be levied [6s. 6d. *crossed out*, 12s. 2d. *interlined*], and he owed [2s. 8d. *crossed out*, £1 6s. 3d. *interlined*] which he was to pay on his account to William Cormaile.

Thomas Lekere collector for Meadow answered for £3 15s., of which there was allowed to him for the various amounts which could not be levied 3s. 6d. [And he owed *crossed out*] paid £3 4s. 6d. to William Cormaile by indenture. He owed 7s. 1d. which he was to pay to W. Cormaile on his account. [*The calculation is out by 1d.*]

John Parch collector for St. Martin's [*but cf. above*] answers for £12 7s. 9d., of which he paid to William Cormaile by indenture £2, and there was allowed to him 11s. (9d.) for various amounts which could not be levied. He owed [£1 19s. 11d. *crossed out*] £1 17s. [7d. *crossed out*] which he was to pay to W. Cormaile.

Sum total received net £40 (11s. 6d.?).

[f. 153; *stained*]

436. Election: All Souls' day 28 Hen. VI [*2 Nov. 1449*].

Names of the number of the Twenty-Four [*in four columns*]: William Cormaile, Thomas Freman, John Wyot, William Hore, William Swayn, Richard Payn, [*column two*] John Port, Robert Cove, Simon Poy, Nicholas Shete, William Lyghtfote, John Cammell, [*column three*] John Honythorn, Walter Carogan, John Estbury, John Hall, John Jervays, Thomas Payn, [*column four*] John Wyot, John Parant, William Halstede [*added*, he has died], Thomas Tempse, John Boteler [who] was discharged because he told the mayor and the fellowship (*societat'*) that he could not manage his affairs (*se advisare*) or work. And in place of the same John –

Elected to the said number: Thomas Pakker, sworn; Edmund Penston in the place of Stephen Hendy, deceased, and the said Edmund has not yet been sworn.

Mayor, John Cammell; reeves, John Thursby, William Soper'; alderman of New Street, Guy Roter; of Market, John Hode; of St. Martin's. John Horne; of Meadow, Thomas Lekere; serjeants: Geoffrey Ponyng, Richard Hayne.

Fines [*all the entries have been crossed out, presumably on payment in full*]: John Wyly 'draper' made fine for being excused the offices of alderman and reeve £4, to be paid [£2 *interlined*] at Michaelmas next, and at the said feast following £2, pledges William Swayn and Robert Cove. [*Added in English*, 'Resett by M[ayor?] (. . .) (have?) £2'; *the words and the meaning are not clear.*]. Simon Laverok made fine for being excused the offices of alderman and reeve £4, to be paid at Michaelmas next £2, and at the said feast following £2, pledges Simon Poy and John Halle. John Wyse vintner ('vynter') made fine for being excused the office of reeve £2, to be paid at Michaelmas next £1, and on the said feast following £1, pledges Simon Poy and John Wyse 'draper'. John Chyppenham 'bocher' made fine for being excused the offices the offices of alderman and reeve £4, to be paid at Michaelmas next £2, and at the said feast following £2, pledges William Swayn and John Estebury. [*Added in English*, 'They have resett £2'.]

[f. 153v.; *stained and mutilated*]

436A. [*Transcript, in English, the spelling modernized here:*] By the king. A remembrance as for the credence that Thomas Borton, one of our yeomen of the crown royal, open and declare unto them of the shires of Somerset and Dorset and Wiltshire and to the good towns of the same shires. First he shall say unto them that the king wills if any writing or language come to them touching any sedition or commotion of the people, that they give not credence thereto, but in as much as in them is, stir the people to the contrary of all such writing, and that they take no heed of no writing nor speech but to such as they may verily know is to the king's intent and will, and to perform that as far as their lives and goods may stretch against all manner of men of what estate, degree, or condition soever that they be, and that they send to the king word by writing of their intent after the form above written, and that if any so do the king will be to them as good and tender lord as him ought to be to his kind, true, and faithful subjects and liege men.

437. [*Heading:*] John Cammell mayor.

Assembly: Thursday next after the nativity of the Blessed Virgin Mary 29 Hen. VI [*10 Sept. 1450*].

Agreed: [*blank*].

Present: John Cammell mayor, Thomas Freman, John Wyot, William Hore, William Swayn, Richard Payn, John Port, William Cormayle, Robert Cove, John Halle, Simon Poy, William Lyghtfote, Edmund Penston, John Mone 'gent', John Wynchestr', Anselm Hebbyng, John Wyly, Henry Frend, Thomas Feld, Thomas Whityng, Guy Rotuor, William Wutton, Thomas Copter, William Swyngell, John Chippenham, Richard Furbour, William Child, John Person, Thomas Leker, John Wyse vintner ('vynter'), William Mory, John Willy, John Wheler, John Kyngescote, John Batyn, John Rede, Thomas Johnis, Robert Chaundeler, Robert Metgyff, John Judde 'carpenter'.

438. Assembly: Wednesday next after [the translation of] St. Edward the king 29 Hen. VI [*14 Oct. 1450; nos. 437–9 are clearly in chronological order, so the feast referred to is the translation*].

Present: the mayor John Cammell, Thomas Freman, William Hore, Richard Payn, John a Port, William Cormayll, Robert Cove, Simon Poy, Nicholas Shute, Walter Carogan, Thomas Payn, and others of the Twenty-Four; Edmund Penston, John Mone 'gent', John Scot, Richard Gylberd, Anselm Hebbyng, Henry Frend, John Slegge, John Thorseby, John Wyly, and others of the Forty-Eight.

Election to parliament: Thomas Freman, Edmund Penston, for half wages.

Agreed: the present mayor to have for his necessary costs £7 11s. 6d. until etc.

Elected for the greater security of keeping the peace: for New Street: John Halle, Thomas Pakker; for Market: Simon Poy and John Wyse 'draper'; for St. Martin's: William Hore, Walter Huntele; and for Meadow: John Wheler, William Wotton.

439. Assembly: Friday next after St. Luke 29 Hen. VI [*23 Oct. 1450*].

Present: the mayor John Cammell, Thomas Freman, William Hore, William Swayn, [Richard Payn *interlined*], Simon Poy, John Halle, Robert Cove, William Lyghtfote, Thomas Payn, Walter Carogan, etc. [*presumably members of the Twenty-Four*]; Edmund Penston, John Mone 'gent', John Scot, Henry Frend, John Wyly, Robert Meteyeff, Clement Rawlyn, Guy Rotore, John Laundevere, John Wyot, William Swyngell, John Slegge, John Wheler', John Dogode, William Sopere, John Horn, John Hode, Thomas Leker, William Wotton, John Cleve 'tanner', Thomas Whytyng [*presumably members of the Forty-Eight*].

Elected as chamberlains: John Wyse 'draper', John Wyly 'draper' [*both names crossed out*]; as auditors: William Swayn, Robert Cove, John Slegge, John Wheler'.

[f. 154; *badly faded, stained, and mutilated*]

440. Assembly: Friday next after St. Nicholas 29 Hen.VI [*11 Dec. 1450*].

Present: [*in the margin*, John Hall mayor], John Wyot, John Hore, William Swayn, Richard (Payn?), William Cormaile, John Cammell, Thomas Copter, (. . .), Thomas Payn, Simon Poy, William Lyghtfote, John Perrant, John Honythorn, Thomas Pakker, John (. . .), John Lyon 'mercer', Robert Chynchon, John Wheler, Anselm Hebbying, John Slegge, Robert Meteyeve, (John?) Cle(ve?), Clement Raulyn, John Fulbroke, John Stoppe, Henry Frend, Guy Rot', Richard S(talbrigge?), John Cachero, John E(stbury?), (Edmund Pen?)ston, John Mone 'touker', Simon Poy, John Chippenham, Nicholas (. . .), (. . .).

[*About four lines wholly illegible.*]

Agreed: the office of chamberlain (. . .) under penalty of (forfeiting wax as appears in the fourth book in the time of H. Swayn?) (*sub pena for' cere ut patet quarto libro tempore H. Swayn*) (. . .)

Names of those elected to the number of the Forty-Eight: (. . .) Mone, John Scotte, Henry Frend, Robert Meteyeve.

Also agreed: outside fishmongers (*piscatores extranei*) to sell their fish by their own hands, and to have their stands above the ditch and not elsewhere.

Outside butchers to have their stands in the market as they used to of old. And the mayor for the time being to keep and observe the said ordinance without changing it, under penalty of forfeiting his fee (. . .).

And that all common prostitutes should have their house in Culver Street ('Culverstrete') and not elsewhere in the city under the penalty of imprisonment at the mayor's discretion etc.

And that Robert Cove, Nicholas Shete, and Thomas Payn be excused in future the office of mayor; granted to them by the mayor and community under their common seal and by fine of £20 which is [to be?] paid on (. . .). [*Cf. no. 432.*]

[*About eight lines largely illegible, mentioning the keeping (of the key to the chest?), Thomas P(. . .), and the mayor.*]

Election of chamberlains: John Wyse 'draper', Robert Chynchon.

Agreed: Geoffrey Ponyng's mace to be mended at the community's cost. [*Geoffrey was elected as one of the serjeants in 1449: above, no. 436.*]

And the sheriff of Devon and the sheriff of Wiltshire to have from the mayor some gift at the mayor's discretion (. . .).

And Richard [Beauchamp], bishop of Salisbury, to have at his installation in Lent 29 [Hen.VI, *1451*] 20 marks as a gift from the mayor and community.

[f. 154v; *faded, stained, and mutilated*]

441. Assembly: Monday 8 March 29 Hen.VI [*1451*].

Present: [William Swayn, John Honythorn *interlined*], Richard Payn, William Cormaile, Nicholas Shete, John Parraunt, John Aport, Robert Cove, Simon Poy, William Lyghtfote, John Slegge, Walter Carogan, Thomas Payn [*presumably members of the Twenty-Four*]; John Mone 'touker', John Wynchest', John Wheler, John Togode, Robert Chynchon, William Soper, Thomas Whytyng, Henry Frend, William Child, William Brid, John Cachero, [John] Lavender, Nicholas Wedergrove, Simon Newman, Richard Walker, John Hod, John Scot, John Thursby, John Hone, Richard Coklote, Anselm Hebbying, Clement Fourbour, Thomas Mogge, John Botler, John Cleve 'tanner', Simon L(averok?) [*presumably members of the Forty-Eight*].

Agreed: all citizens and men dwelling in the city to have liveries for the king's visit, as follows: the stewards of all guilds to write down the names of their men who are able to provide themselves with a gown and to deliver those names to the mayor, and the mayor to have delivered to the stewards a pattern of green cloth, and each man to have one green gown for the king's visit, under the penalty of 13s. 4d.

Also agreed: all carters coming to the city (with oysters? *ostriis*) to stand and sell the oysters above the common ditch and not elsewhere, under penalty (. . .)

Joan, late the wife of William Warwike, gave to the mayor and community for performing an obit the rack (*Rekka*) with its appurtenances located in Endless Street ('Endelestrete') (. . .) to the mayor so that in each assembly they should pray for the souls of William Warwike and Joan.

442. Assembly: Friday 4 June 29 Hen.VI [*1451*].

Present: [*in the margin*, the mayor], William Hore, John Aport, Richard Payn, [William Cormaile *interlined*], Robert Cove, John Estbury, Walter Carogan, Simon Poy, William Lyghtfote, Thomas Payn [*presumably members of the Twenty-Four*]; John Mone, John Scot, John Wynchest', Thomas Whityng, Richard Marchall, Clement Raulyns, John Fulbroke, John Mone 'touker', Richard C(okelot?), John Togood, Thomas Stop, Peter Devarowe, William Lavender, Thomas Glover, Richard Hayne 'taillour', John Cacheroo, John Cleve 'tanner', Richard Child, Henry Shadde, Nicholas Wedergrove, Thomas Valeys, Simon Laverok, John Wyse 'draper', John Wheler, Richard Bellers, Thomas Broderer, Richard Shalston, Guy Galegmaker.

Simon Poy, William Lyghtfote, Robert Cove, and John Wyse 'draper' were elected as constables for this year and sworn.

Agreed: each of the Twenty-Four to have an armed man to accompany the mayor on the night of the eves [*23, 28 June*] of St. John the Baptist and of St. Peter [and St. Paul], under penalty of forfeiting 3s. 4d. to be paid to the chamberlains etc.

443. Assembly: Monday next after St. Peter in Chains 29 Hen. VI [*2 Aug. 1451*].

Present: Thomas Freman, John Wyot, William Hore, John Aport, William Swayn, Richard Payn, Simon Poy, Thomas Payn, Nicholas Shute, John Parr(ant), William Lyghtfote [*presumably members of the Twenty-Four*]; John Mone 'gent', John Scot, John Wynchest', John Slegge, Richard Mascall, John Fulbroke, John Wheler, Henry Frend, Clement Raulyn, Richard Cokelot, John Mone 'touker', Richard Walker, Walter Brid, John Shepton, Thomas Stopp, Simon Newman, John Laundever, Thomas Mogge, John Wyot 'bruer', Nicholas Wedirgrove, William Wotton, Thomas Whityng, William Swyngell, Simon Laveroke, John Chippenham, Robert Meteyeve [*presumably members of the Forty-Eight*].

Agreed: the king to have as a gift from the mayor and community for the defence of Calais 50 lances and 24 archers for 40 days at the city's cost.

The names of those who ought to assess the citizens for the expenses and costs of the said men: collectors: New Street: John Noble, John Smeth 'galegmaker'; Market: John Wyse vintner ('vynter'), Thomas Mabre; St. Martin's: [John Ive junior *crossed out*], Walter Stede, John Dogood; Meadow: William Meryot, Robert Duver; assessors: New Street: Robert Cove, William Lyghtfote; Market: Simon Poy, Thomas Payn; St. Martin's: Richard Walker, John Slegge; Meadow: William Wotton, Thomas Pese.

[f. 155; *faded, stained, and mutilated*]

444. Assembly: Monday the eve of St. Matthew 30 Hen. VI [*20 Sept. 1451*].

The king sent a writ, dated 12 July 28 Hen. [VI, *1450; the day has been corrected from 24, the month has been corrected three times, and the year has been corrected from 29*], to the mayor and community for levying the sum of £11 6s. [John Cu'll *interlined, perhaps the name of the messenger*] for [the wages of] John Whittokkesmede and Philip Morgan, citizens at the parliament held at Westminster 6 Nov. [*29 crossed out, 28 interlined*] Hen. VI [*1449; in fact they were citizens at the parliament of 12 Feb. 1449, as above no. 425*]. The writ is attached to this folio [*but it is no longer*]. Agreed: the citizens to have the wages, viz. £11 6s.

Also granted: to William Swayn and Thomas Penston, elected by the king's letters patent and writ as citizens at the parliament held at Westminster 6 Nov. 28 Hen. [VI, *1449*], [wages of] £17 [*blank*]. And because the said citizens were at Leicester [*to which the parliament was prorogued*], they were remunerated by the community with (. . .) by the king's writ dated 24 Oct. 29 Hen. [VI, *1450*].

Granted: the money recently granted for the relief of the town of Calais ought to be levied to satisfy those citizens for their fees, viz the whole sum of [*blank*] (. . .) as said above, for half their fees as was granted to them, with the said remuneration, because the town of Calais as yet has no need.

Granted: in future there will be watchmen and wardens (*vigilatores et custodes*) of the city by night during these days of unrest, the said watchmen to be sworn [before the mayor and constables *interlined*] to be of good behaviour in their watches, the money for their fees to be levied on the more discreet and better citizens; and any citizen may undertake to watch for them.

Present: J. Hall mayor, William Hore, W. Swayn, Richard Payn, J. Aport, William Cormayle, Robert Cove, W. Lightfote, Thomas Payn, Walter Corrogan, John Wyse, John Honythorn, John Skot, Robert Numan, Robert Metgyff, John Chipnam, John Mone 'touker', W. Swyngell, Thomas Mogg, John Slegg, John Cachero, Thomas Whityng, Richard Hayn, John Wheler, Henry Shadd, John Clyff 'tanner', John Hode, John Thorsby, Richard Cokelot, John Togode, John Lavend', Philip Nowell, Richard Walker, John Fulbrok, Richard Shalston, John Frank, John Ive, Walter Stede, Thomas Feld, William Swyft, John Mone.

[f. 155v.; *faded, stained, and mutilated*]

445. [*Heading:*] John Halle mayor.

Assembly: Friday next after St. Simon and St. Jude 30 Hen. VI [*29 Oct. 1451*].

Present: [*in the margin*, the mayor], Thomas Freman, John Wyot, William Hore, William Swayn, John a Port, William Knolles, John Cammell, Nicholas Shete, Thomas Payn, Robert Cove, William Lyghtfote, Simon Poy, John Parant, John Wyly, [John Wyse *interlined*] [*presumably members of the Twenty-Four*];

John Mone 'gent', John Scote, Edward Chilterne, Richard Marchall, Robert Newman, John Togood, John Wynchest', Thomas Valeys, Clement Rawlyns, John Fulbroke, Anselm

Hebbyng, William Swyft, John Chippenham, John Slegge, William Ramet, John Hode, John Cleve 'tanner', Henry Frend, Walter Brit, Robert Chynchon, Richard Cokelet, Thomas Whytyng, John Wheler, William Meryot, Thomas Feld, John Nachere, John Comesbury, Richard Bowyer, Nicholas Wedergrove, John Mone 'touker', Henry Shadd, John Lavender, John Shepton, Peter de Varow, John Horne [*presumably members of the Forty-Eight*].

Granted: the mayor to have all the allowances and expenses written below as other mayors have had etc. For the mayor's pension this year, £10; for the clothing and board of the chaplain of St. George, £2 13s. 8d.; to the king's official, 6s. 8d.; to the duke of York's official, 3s. 4d.; to the duke of Exeter's official, 3s. 4d.; to the duke of Somerset's official, 3s. 4d.; to the chancellor of England's official, 3s. 4d.; to the earl of Devon's official, 3s. 4d.; to the earl of Wiltshire's official, 3s. 4d.; to Lord Stourton's official, 3s. 4d.; in a gift to Lord Seyntmond [*i.e. Seymour*], 6s. 8d.; in a gift to Lord Stourton, 16s. 8d.; in a gift to the king's commissioners for inquiring into the extent of land, 10s. Sum, £15 16s. 8d.

Furthermore, for the mayor's various great expenses and costs about the visit of the king and his justices for hearing and judging all sorts of treasons, insurrections, and felonies, and also for the installation of Richard [Beauchamp], bishop of Salisbury, there was granted to the same mayor £14.

Sum total received this year £30 [*the sum being rounded up*].

Agreed: Edward Chilterne to have the office of clerk of the mayor [and community *interlined*] with the wages and other profits belonging to that office as long as he behaves himself well, and Philip Morgan is discharged etc.

Also agreed: Philip Morgan, late clerk, to have for term of his life one gown of silk like the mayor and his brothers of the Twenty-Four as often as and when they receive their common livery, at the expense of the mayor and community.

Also agreed: John Hall mayor to receive and have from the common chest a bond deposited there, by which kept Robert Cove, Nicholas Shute, and Thomas Payn, citizens, were bound to William Cormayle, then mayor, John Peraunt, and Anselm Hebbyng, then chamberlains, in 10 marks to be paid at Michaelmas after [the date of] the bond, of which the date is 8 Oct. [*blank*] Hen.VI, in part payment of the expenses made by the said John Hall and allowed to him as expressed above.

Edward Chilterne appeared and presented royal letters signed with the royal signet, of which the tenor is contained below.

[f. 156; *faded and stained*]

[*Heading:*] John Hall mayor.

[*Transcript, in English, the spelling modernized here:*] By the king. Trusty and well beloved, we greet you well, and albeit that we herebefore by our several letters in

consideration of the good service that our well beloved Edward Chilterne, notary, hath
done to us as well within this realm as in our realm of France have desired him to be
chosen unto the office of recorder otherwise called town clerk of our city of Salisbury,
howbeit also that he was chosen thereunto by you mayor [and] commoners of the
livery and number of Twenty-Four citizens of our said city yet nevertheless our said
letters have taken none effect as yet because he was not chosen in common assembly
among you all, as we be informed. Wherefore we write eftsoons unto you desiring and
praying you heartily that at the reverence of this our special writing you will at your
next assembly by your common assent [appoint] this the said Edward unto the foresaid
office of your town clerk to have unto him for term of his life with the fees, profits, and
commodities thereto appertaining as other clerks of that office have had before without
any further delays, wherein you shall do unto us right good pleasure and cause us to be
the rather inclined to show you the favour of our good grace when the case shall
require it. Given under our signet at our city of Winchester the last day of June.

Also, a writ dated 8 June 29 Hen. VI [1451], to the mayor and bailiffs of Salisbury, to
proclaim an Act of parliament that the king should have for his use all the alum from
Foglia [?] ('Alym Foyle') belonging to the merchants of Genoa ('Jeyne') or their agents
in the town and port of Southampton to the value of £8,000 to be delivered to those
deputed by the king, but that repayment be made to the merchants of Genoa or their
agents from the subsidies and customs of merchandise imported into and traded or
exported from thence to the said sum of £8,000 which the merchants of Genoa will
pay to the king and will be appropriated for his use on pain of forfeiture of the third
part of the sales of alum of the kind,

Also, a writ dated 28 Jan. [year omitted, but see next entry] Hen. VI [1451], to the
keepers of the peace and each of them in the town of New Salisbury for suit of peace
[?] on behalf of William Maysaunt against Thomas Hawede 'skynner', John Peryn
'skynner', John Skyrby 'skynner', and John Skynner of Hereford.

Also, a writ of supersedeas, dated 22 Feb. the said year 29 Hen. VI [1451], to the keepers
of the peace in the county of Wilts. and the city of Salisbury and each of them at the
suit of Bartholomew Broke against John Westover after an information made against
the said John as he suggested in that the same John Westover found mainpernors in
Chancery for the said Bartholomew and all the king's people.

Also, a writ dated 7 Dec. the said year [1450], to the keepers of the peace as above for
John Suter against Thomas Petyr and John Oylfot for a surety.

Also, a writ dated 16 April 29 Hen. VI [1451], to the keepers of the peace as above for
John Chaundeler for the safety of his life and limbs against Robert Denby 'boucher' of
New Salisbury.

On Sunday next before St. Bartholomew the said year [22 Aug. 1451] Thomas Valeys of
New Salisbury a merchant in the county of Wilts. acknowledged that he was bound to
Joan widow of William Warwyk late a citizen of New Salisbury in £60 to be paid on
the feast of St. Andrew next [30 Nov.], and unless etc.

On the feast of the Annunciation of the Blessed Virgin Mary the said year [*25 Mar.*
1451], William Magot 'bowchere' and merchant of the city of Salisbury acknowledged
that he was bound to Robert Chaundeler of the said city, merchant, in £10 for various
merchandise bought from him, to be paid to the same on the feast of St. John the
Baptist next [*24 June*], and unless etc.

On 18 Feb. the said year James Michell of New Salisbury acknowledged that he was
bound and owed to John Horn £10 for various merchandise bought from him, to be
paid to the same on the feast of St. Matthew thereafter [*21 Sept.*], and unless etc.

Memorandum: John Perraunt and Anselm Hebbyng, lately chamberlains for the two
years next before John Hall was elected mayor, accounted for the said two years before
William Swayn, Robert Cove, John Slegge, and John Wheler, the auditors assigned, for
all rents and other profits arising in the city for the said two years [*repeated*], and when
everything accountable had been accounted and all allowances allowed [the mayor and
interlined] community owed to the said accountants £8 6s. 9½d.

446. Memorandum: John Hall late mayor accounted before the said auditors on Saturday
next before St. Leonard 30 Hen. VI [*30 Oct. 1451*]. First, for £37 7s. 6d. which he
received from John Laundevere, Richard Bowyer', John Parche, and Thomas Leker',
collectors of the fourth part of a fifteenth granted in the parliament at Winchester and
of the expenses of the citizens at that parliament; for £37 11s. 4d. [*?recte £37 4s. 4d., to
accord with the sum total*] received by him from John Dogode and Walter Stede, William
Meryot and John Chaundeler', John Nobele and John Galagemakere, Thomas Mabre
and John Wyse vintner ('vynter'), collectors of the expenses of the citizens lately being
at the parliament of Winchester and Westminster. Sum total received, £74 11s. 10d.
[And there remained to be received from the said Thomas Mabr' and John Wyse vintner
('vynter') £1 1s. 3d. *crossed out.*]

[f. 156v.; *faded and stained*]

[*Heading*:] John Hall mayor.

John Hall late mayor also accounts for the repayment made by him for a gift given to
the king, for six [*?recte four, to accord with the sum total*] large oxen at a price of £1
6s. 8d. [each], for two smaller oxen at a price of £1 3s. 4d. [each], and for fifty sheep at
a price of £5 [together], sum total £12 13s. 4d.; for a cask of wine, 6 quarters of wheat,
6 pipes of ale given to the reverend father Richard [Beauchamp] bishop of Salisbury at
his installation, £13 13s. 8d.; paid by the same to John Whittokkesmede and Philip
Morgan, burgesses [*sic*] for the city of Salisbury at the parliament at Winchester, for half
their wages, £11 6s. 8d.; paid to William Swayn and Edmund Penston, citizens at the
parliament at Westminster ending at Leicester, for half their wages, £22; to Philip Morgayn
for his expenses in riding to Winchester to find out about the king's visit to the city,
10s.; for the taker of ale for the king for his reward, 6s. 8d.; in a pipe of wine given to Sir
John Saymour, sheriff of Wiltshire, for gaining his good will, £3 5s.; to the undersheriff
for his reward and for having his good will and all else, 13s. 4d.; in a present given to the

duke of Somerset, £1 6s. 8d.; for the expense of writing the rolls for the collectors of the fifteenth and for the expenses of the citizens at parliament and in other small expenses, 8s. 8d. Sum total, £66 4s.

Memorandum: whereas William Swayn and Richard Balteswell, citizens and grocers of the city of New Salisbury, on a disagreement arising between them about a bond in the said William's hands in which it was contained that Richard was obliged to pay £100 sterling on a certain day stated in the document to the mayor and his brethren from the Twenty-Four on certain conditions written on the dorse of the bond and on certain other articles agreed on by certain arbitrators, viz. William Lygtfote and Symon Poye on William Swayn's part and John Wyot and Richard Payn on Richard Balteswell's part, chosen agreeably by the said parties to pronounce, define, award, and arbitrate on the foregoing, and swore [to observe] the statement, award, decision, and decree of the same arbitrators from top to bottom, on 11 Nov. 30 Hen. VI [1451] in the council house before John Hall then mayor and the said arbitrators the parties appeared in person and were present to receive the award in the matter, and after discussion between the same arbitrators they annulled the same document and gave it, divided by them, to the same Richard Balteswell, decreeing that the same Richard Balteswell should behave himself well with regard to the mayor and his fellow citizens of the Twenty-Four elders and their successors, and should not without reasonable cause annoy, disturb, or belittle them or any of them by any mocking (*rixatoriis*) or opprobrious words, and that if it should be lawfully proved that the same Richard acted to the contrary he is to pay £5 to the common chest of the city and the same amount to the fabric of St. Thomas's church when he is duly required to do so; John a Port and Robert Cove being then present there at the pronouncement of this award.

[f. 157; *badly faded and stained*]

447. On 20 April 12 Ric. II [1389] a statute merchant by which Thomas Fyport, of New Salisbury dyer ('dighere'), merchant of the county of Wilts., on 14 Nov. 10 Ric. II [1386] before Robert Play, then mayor, acknowledged that he was bound to Robert Harongeye citizen and merchant of London in £39, was certified by William War[m]well mayor of this city.

On 24 May 7 Ric. II [1384] Thomas Vyport dyer ('digher'), merchant of the county of Wilts., acknowledged that he owed to John Moner, John Baker grocer, Richard Juwel, merchants of the same county, £15 sterling to be paid as is more fully contained in a statute merchant acknowledged before Thomas Hynedon, then mayor of Salisbury; was certified by William Warmwelle on 2 May 12 Ric. II [1389].

On 30 Sept. 5 Ric. II [1381] John Pykot of (Lilesford?) merchant of the county of Southampton acknowledged that he was bound by a statute merchant before Thomas Chandeler, then mayor of Salisbury, in £40 sterling to be paid to Robert Harneges, citizen and merchant of the city of London. It also was certified by William Warmwell, then mayor, viz. on 24 April 12 Ric. II [1389].

John Preston of New Salisbury merchant of the county of Wilts., before John Nedlere, then mayor, and Ralph Tile, the king's clerk, on 21 March 8 Ric. II [*1385*] acknowledged that he owed to Roger Siward now deceased and to John Siward, merchants of the county of Dorset, £140 sterling for various merchandise traded between them, to be paid at New Salisbury on the nativity of St. John the Baptist [24 June] then next following. It was certified during the mayoralty of William Warmwell on 4 May 12 Ric. II [*1389*].

[f. 157v.; *stained*]

448. Election: All Souls' day 30 Hen. VI [*2 Nov. 1451*].

Mayor, William Lyghtfote; reeves, Guy Rotour, Thomas Leker'; alderman of New Street, John Conyngysby *alias* Noble; of Market, Thomas Gyle; of St. Martin's, William Spyndeler'; of Meadow, John Nedeler'; serjeants, Geoffrey Ponyng, John Knyght.

Edmund Penston [was elected *interlined*; and Edward Chylterne were elected *crossed out*] and sworn to the number of the Twenty-Four. John Frank was elected to the number of the Twenty-Four, and was not yet sworn. [*Added,* Later the same John Frank was sworn.] Edward Chiltern was elected and sworn to the number of the Twenty-Four.

Nicholas Wedergrove made fine for being excused the offices of alderman and reeve £4, [£2] to be paid at Michaelmas next, and £2 at the Michaelmas following, pledges [Thomas Freman and William Swayn *crossed out*; John Wyot and John Wyly *interlined*]. John Frank made fine for being excused the office of alderman and reeve £4, to be paid on the same feasts, pledged John Hall and John Wyot. [*Both entries crossed out and each marked in the margin* Fine £4, paid to J. Wyse £2.]

Agreed among those citizens who are of the Twenty-Four elders: in the election of the mayor, to be held each year according to the city's custom, they should not nominate or write to the commons the name of the person who in fact (*realiter*) occupied the office in the preceding year, so that he is accepted as mayor [?] (*ut assumatur in maiorem*), but will write and nominate to the commons for the office three suitable others of his brethren who have not held the office in the five preceding years, according to the orders (*acta*) made earlier; and if any of the number of the said citizens effectively acts to the contrary in this matter he shall pay £10 into the common chest when duly called upon by the mayor for the time being.

[*At the foot of the page are two isolated words,* whence prayers (*unde preces*).]

[f. 157a, *an inserted strip of parchment, blank on the dorse*]

449. The king's writ, dated Westminster, 12 Oct. Hen. [VI, *1451*] and signed Fortes, to the mayor for the payment to Thomas Freeman and Edmund Penston citizens at the parliament at Westminster on the feast of St. Leonard [*6 Nov. 1450*], of £32 16s. for their expenses in coming, staying for 164 days, and returning, each receiving 2s. a day.

[f. 158; *faded and stained*]

450. [*Heading*:] William Lyghtfote.

Assembly: Wednesday next before St. Nicholas 30 Hen. VI [*1 Dec. 1451*].

Present: [*In the margin*, the mayor], William Lyghtfot, William Swayn, Richard Payn, William Cormayll, John Aport, John Hall, Robert Cove, Nicholas Shete, John Wyse 'draper', Thomas Payn, John Perraunt, John Wyly, Edward Chilterne, John Mone 'gent', John Scot, John Wynchester', Anselm Hebbyng, Robert Meteyeve, John Fulbroke, Henry Frend, Guy Rotour, John Mone 'touker', Walter Bryd, William Cok 'spyndeler', John Noble, John Cacchero, John Dogod, Richard Hayne 'tayllour', William Swengyll, John Clyve 'tanner', William Meryot, Nicholas Wedergrove, Thomas Mogge 'couper', Clement Raulyn, Thomas Valeys, John Chippenham, John Hode, William Ramet, Thomas Whytyng, Richard Cokelet.

Agreed: the present mayor to have the fees and allowances as other mayors before this time have been used to have.

And the officials to have their livery as in preceding years.

Also agreed: Geoffrey Ponyng, serjeant at mace, to have the tenement where he lives for keeping prisoners, paying yearly £1 6s. 8d. until the said tenement is adequately repaired by the city chamberlains for habitation and keeping prisoners.

Also agreed: the auditors assigned for other things to consider how to make satisfaction to John Perraunt and Anselm Hebbying, lately chamberlains, for their arrears of £8 6s. 11½d. due to them on their last account.

Also the expenses met by Geoffrey Ponyng on the city's business, viz. £2 5s., were allowed to him.

Also agreed: Geoffrey Ponyng and John Knyght, the city serjeants, to have the common weigh-beam with its weights and appurtenances, paying yearly to the mayor 13s. 4d. And to William Devenysshe, the mayor's serjeant at mace, for his salary 13s. 4d.

451. Assembly: Saturday next after the Purification 30 Hen. VI [*5 Feb. 1452*].

Present [*in five columns*]: William Lyghtfote mayor, Thomas Freman, John Wyot, William Hore, William Swayn, Richard Payn, John Aport, [*column two*] Robert Cove, Simon Poye, John Perrant, Thomas Payn, John Wyly, Edward Chilterne [*presumably members of the Twenty-Four*]; [*column three*] Richard Hayn 'gent', John Mone 'gent', John

Scott, Anselm Hebbyng, John Slegge, John Mone 'touker', John Wyse 'vynter', Henry Elyot, John Thurseby, [*column four*] John Clyve 'tanner', John Chyppenham, Richard Hayne 'tayllour', Walter Brydd, Nicholas Wedergrove, Thomas Leker', Walter Freman, John Wheler', Robert Meteyeve, John Laundevere, [*column five*] Thomas Stoppe, William Child, Richard Marchell, Richard Belhurst, William Wylmot, Thomas Copter', William Soper', Thomas Mogge [*presumably members of the Forty-Eight*].

Agreed: William Swayn, Robert Cove, John Slegge, John Wheler' to be the auditors, as assigned before, and to call the chamberlains to their audit.

Also agreed: the prostitutes called common women to be removed from Culver Street ('Colverstrete') to outside the city, and not to enter the city to stay there for any length of time (*ad permanendum amplius ibidem*) or in any other way except they come in the striped hoods (*capiciis stragulatis*) prescribed for them, on pain of imprisonment.

Assessors for the last fourth of a fifteenth granted in 28 [Hen. VI, *1449–50*] and for the expenses of the citizens at the parliament of 29 [Hen. VI, *1450–1*]: New Street, John Wyly, Henry Frend; Market, Thomas Payn, Thomas Whytyng; St. Martin's, Richard Payn, John Slegge; Meadow, John Wheler', William Wotton; collectors: New Street, Richard Bowyer'; Market, John Laundevere; St. Martin's, John Parche; Meadow, Thomas Leker'.

[f. 158v.; *faded and stained*]

452. Assembly of the reverend father in Christ and lord, Sir Richard [Beauchamp], bishop of Salisbury: 28 April 30 Hen. VI [*1452*].

[Present]:. Mr. John Chedworth, archdeacon of Wiltshire, Mr. Robert Ayscogh, doctor of law, prebendary of the prebend of Charminster and Bere, Mr. John Pyville provost and canon of Salisbury, Sir Thomas Veysy chaplain.

[*In four columns*] William Lightfote mayor, Thomas Freman, John Wiott, William Hore, William Swayn, Richard Payn, John a Porte, William Cnoll, John Cammell, John Hall, Simon Poy, Nicholas Shute, John Honythorn, Edmund Penston, Robert Cove, Thomas Payne, John Wyly, Edward Chylterne [*presumably members of the Twenty-Four*]; John Wynchest', John Mone 'gent', Richard Shaldeston, Richard Canne, John Wyot 'brewer', John Noble, Henry Frend, John Wheler', Richard Walker, Anselm Hebbyng, Thomas Beer, Clement Rawlyns, Peter de Varough, Thomas Copter', John Hayter', Thomas Benet 'tayllour', William Swengyll, [*column three*] Richard Plowman, Walter Brydd, William Soper', John Clyve 'tanner', John Dogode, John Crykmour, Guy Rotour, John Cachero, William Ferrs', John Batyn, Thomas Whytyng, Thomas Mogge, John Scotte, John Lombard, John Mone 'touker', William Colyngbourne, John Wyse 'vynter', [*column four*] Thomas Browderer, William Meryot, John Slegge, Thomas Felde, Richard Haynes tailor, Nicholas Wedergrove, Thomas Glover', William Wylmot, Simon Newman, John Byllyk, John Chaundeler, John Laundevere, William Ramet, Thomas Barbour, John Chepman, William Chyld, John Hode 'glover' [*of whom some but by no means all were members of the Forty-Eight*].

Agreed: to elect certain persons both from the Twenty-Four citizens and from the other commoners for overseeing the common ditch (*fossat'*) of the city.

Elected from the Twenty-Four to oversee the ditch, with the lord: William Lyghtfote mayor, William Hore, William Swayn, John a Port, Richard Payne, John Hall, William Cnoll. Elected from the other commoners: John Slegge, Anscelm Hebbyng, John Wheler, Thomas Whytyng, Thomas Brouderer, Simon Newman, Guy Rotour, Richard Heynes 'tayllour', Nicholas Wedergrove, Robert Chynchon.

[f. 159; *stained*]

453. Assembly: 19 May 30 Hen.VI [*1452*].

Present [*in three columns*]: William Lyghtfote mayor, Thomas Freman, Richard Payn, William Swayn, William Cormayll, John Hall, Symon Poye, Robert Cove, John Honythorn, John Wyse 'draper', Thomas Payn, Nicholas Shute, John Perraunt, Edward Chilterne [*presumably members of the Twenty-Four*];

[*column two*] John Mone 'gent', John Scot, Anselm Hebbyng, John Wynchest', John Noble, John Cachero, William Swyngell, John Mone 'touker', John Wheler', Robert Chynchon, Henry Frend, William Wotton, Walter Freman, Thomas Mogge, John Hode, [*column three*] Richard Haynes 'tayllour', Will Cok 'spyndeler', Robert Meteyeve, John Laundevere, John Clyve 'tanner', Nicholas Wedergrove, John Wyse 'vynter', William Meryot, William Chyld, Henry Shadde, John Dogode, Walter Brydde, John Shypton [*presumably members of the Forty-Eight*].

Constables: John Wyse, John Wyly, elected for this year.

Agreed: to elect certain persons both from the Twenty-Four and from other commoners to supervise the paving (*pavimenta*) of the streets [and] the common privies (*foricas*), ditches, sewers (*cloicas*), and gutters (*gutteas*) emitting their filth into the common ditches of the city, so that by their supervision the sewers and gutters may be stopped up or by the supervision and orders of the persons to be elected they may be cleansed and repaired, along with their banks, and so cleansed and repaired they may be kept in their state of well-being to the adornment of the city.

Elected from the Twenty-Four elders for ordering etc.: Thomas Freman, William Swayn, Richard Payn, William Cnoll, John Hall, Symon Poy, Robert Cove, John Wyse 'draper', Nicholas Shute; elected from the Forty-Eight of the commoners to supervise etc.: John Mone 'gent', John Wheler', Henry Frende, Anselm Hebbyng, William Wotton, Robert Chynchon, Robert Meteyeve, John Dogode.

Also agreed and ordered: no carters or drivers of carts into the city to attach trailers (*ramos*) to their carts or wagons, which so attached or joined are commonly called 'dreyes', [or] to drive them within 'lez barrys' or enclosure (*cepta*) of the city. Nor is anyone in future to bring within the said bars or enclosure of the city on the saddles or the backs of horses or pack-animals the long wooden packs which are commonly called 'trussys' or 'draguhtys' [*sic*] on pain of forfeiting the 'dreyys', 'trussys' or 'draughtys', so that the pavements of the city's streets are not broken up as previously by 'dreyys', 'trussys', or 'draughtys' of the kind, the banks of the common trenches are not destroyed, and the watercourses (*cursus aquar'*) are not altered or blocked by the dragging of mud, as has happened. Advance notice of this matter is to be given by public proclamation.

[f. 159v.; *badly faded and stained*]

454. [*Heading:*] William Lyghtfote mayor.

Assembly: 25 Aug. 30 Hen. VI [*1452*].

Present [*in three columns*]: William Lyghtfote mayor, William Mote, John Porte, Nicholas Shute, Thomas Payne, Robert Cove, John Halle, John Wyot, John Wyly, John Wyse, Simon Poye, John Peryne, William Knollys, Richard Payn, [*column two*] John Cachero, Anselm Hebbyng, John Laundevere, Nicholas Wedergrove, William Swyngell, Thomas Ayon, Robert (Met)efe, Henry Shadde, John Beere, John Clefe 'tanner', John Skotte, John Chippenham, John Mone, Thomas Copter, William Meriot, [*column three*] John Togood, Richard Walker', Henry Frend, Guy Roter', William Chylde, Thomas Mogge, John Nobill', Simon Newman, Walter Birde, Richard Cokelott, John Thoresby, Richard Marchele, William Wotton.

Agreed: Richard Marchall, Robert Metefe, Simon Newman, and John Thoresby, jointly and severally, to gather twenty men called 'le soudyours' to go across the sea and return with Lord Shrewsbury to Aquitaine etc.

Also agreed: Henry Frende, William Mariot, Anselm Hebbyng, and [*blank*] Baker 'touker' to see all the men in the city who are able to advance and put down certain sums of money for payment to the said 'sowdyours', and to deliver their names to the mayor.

[*Transcript of a mandate from the king; printed in Historical Manuscripts Commission 55*, Various Collections IV, *p. 201. In English, the spelling modernized here.*], The king commandeth that all manner labouring men that hold not land and tenements, the which sufficeth to the occupation of half a ploughland, go into service, and that stewards of franchises and constables put all such manner men in service at the request of such men as would have their service according to the statutes thereof made, upon the pain contained in the same statutes, the which is £10 upon the constable for every default; and that all manner artificers go to their craft upon the pain contained in the statute thereof made; and that all stewards of franchises, mayors, constables, bailiffs, and tithingmen of cities, boroughs, hundreds, and towns within the shire of Wilts. arrest or do arrest all manner vagrants, vagabonds, and beggars begging out of the hundred wherein they dwell without the king's authority or warrant, according to the statute thereof made, and that they keep them in ward unto the time they have found surety of their good bearing, and if they find not such surety that they send them to the gaol there to abide according to the statute thereof made; and that none of the king's liegemen give no beggars begging out of the hundred that they they dwell in none good without they have sufficient warrant by the king's authority, or according to the statutes thereupon made, upon pain containing [sic] in the said statutes, and that all manner labourers and servants take such wages as is ordained by the statute; and that all constables make the due sessions of the peace, holden four times by year according to the statutes; and that they bring in their certificates at the sessions of the peace holden within the said shire; if any man find him[self] aggrieved upon the said officers because they do not duly the execution of the premises or any of them, that he come to the justices of the peace of the said shire sitting in the sessions and complain him thereof, and they shall do him remedy according to the statutes.

[f. 160; *stained*]

455. [*Heading:*] William Lyghtfote mayor.

Assembly: 27 Oct. 31 Hen.VI [*1452*].

Present [*in three columns:*]: William Lightfote mayor, Thomas Freman, John Wyot, William Hore, William Cormayll, William Swayn, Robert Cove, John a Port, Symon Poye, John Franke, John Honythorn, John Gerveys, Thomas Payn, John Perrant, Edward Chylterne, [*presumably members of the Twenty-Four*];

John Mone 'gent', John Scott, Anselm Hebbyng, John Mone 'touker', John Dogode, Thomas Lyon, Richard Beller, Clement Rawlyn, Guy Rotour, Thomas Valeys, Henry Frend, Peter Levarowgh, Robert Meteyeve, John Noble, William Swengyll, John Clyve 'tanner', John Cacchero, Thomas Shyppeton, Roger Mayne, Richard Marchell, Nicholas Wedergrove, John Wheler', Richard Walker', John Wyot 'brwer' [*sic*], John Wynchester', Richard Shaldyston, Robert Chynchon, William Meryot, Thomas Mogge [*presumably members of the Forty-Eight*].

Agreed: the mayor to have all the allowances and expenses below as the other mayors have had. For the mayor's pension this year, £10; for the clothing and board of the chaplain of St. George, £2 13s. 4d.; for the king's official, 6s. 8d.; for the duke of Somerset's official, 6s. 8d.; for the chancellor of England's official, 3s. 4d.; for the duke of York's official, 3s. 4d.; for the earl of Westmorland's official, 3s. 4d.; for the duke of Exeter's official, 3s. 4d.; for the earl of Worcester's official, 3s. 4d.; for the earl of Arundel's official, 3s. 4d.; for the earl of Shrewsbury's official, 3s. 4d.; for the earl of Oxford's official, 3s. 4d.; for Lord Ryvers's official, 3s. 4d.; for Lord Stourton's official, 1s. 8d.; for Lord Botreaux's official, 1s.; for the official of Sir Maurice Berkeley knight, 1s.; in a gift to Lord Stourton when he came from Calais, 5s.; in a reward given to the duke of York's messenger bringing a letter to the mayor and community, 1s. 8d.; to the earl of Shrewsbury's messenger coming to collect the city's mercenaries, 6s. 8d.; for the city officials' clothing, £1 3s. 4d.; to a king's messenger called Meryngham, 1s. 8d.

[f. 160v.; *stained*]

Agreed: William Swayn, Robert Cove, John Slegge, John Wheler' to remain as auditors for this year.

Also agreed: the city chamberlains and others who are to render accounts to the city to begin their accounting before the auditors every year in future on the Monday next after St. Luke [*18 October*], after the next account for this year is finished.

Also agreed: the auditors to call before them those who are to account, and those who do not come or, having come, do not account or do not satisfy on their account and the arrears due to the city are to be compelled by the mayor for the year, at the auditors' request, to make their accounts and satisfaction effectively. And if the mayor is negligent or remiss in the foregoing he is to lose £5 from his pension for that year, and each accountant on pain of paying £2 to the city chamberlains, and the stewards of St. George on pain of £1.

Also agreed: William Swayn, John Wyot, Symon Poy, Robert Cove, Anselm Hebbyng, and John Wheler', Richard Beller, Richard Marchall, John Scott, William Meryot, Thomas Glover, and Henry Frend to assist the mayor in assessing the able and sufficient men chosen, nominated, and appointed in an earlier assembly as persons to pay a certain amount of money to certain mercenaries of the city lately going overseas with the earl of Shrewsbury, the amount having been paid and extracted as a loan from the common chest, to be repaid out of the contribution of the men appointed in this way.

Also, Philip Morgan to have £1 6s. 8d. a year from the mayor and community for his good counsel to be given henceforth to the mayor and community, for as long as he behaves well and loyally towards them.

Also, John Scot to have 13s. 4d. a year from the mayor and community for his good counsel to be given hereafter this mayor and community, for as long as he behaves well and loyally towards them.

Account of William Lyghtfote mayor of what is accountable and allowable, before William Swayn, Robert Cove, John Slegge, and John Wheler', the appointed auditors. The said William Lyghtfote stood a debtor to the community in £4 16s., which he paid on his account and so went quit.

[f. 161, *blank*]

[f. 161v.; *faded and stained*]

456. Election: All Souls' day 31 Hen. VI [*2 Nov. 1452*].

Mayor, Simon Poy; reeves, John Hode 'glover', John Shipton 'dubber'; alderman of New Street, Thomas Illesley 'gent'; of Market, John Stoke esquire; of St. Martin's, Robert Eston merchant; of Meadow, William Colyngbourne 'towker'; serjeants, Geoffrey Ponyng, Walter Honteley.

Robert Newman was elected to the number of the Twenty-Four, and not yet sworn.

The same Robert Newman made fine for being excused the offices of alderman and reeve £4, to be paid £2 at Michaelmas next and £2 on the Michaelmas following, pledges Simon Poy and Robert Cove [added, or by Simon Poy £2].

John Stone made fine for being excused the offices of alderman and reeve £4, to be paid at Michaelmas next, pledges John Hall and Simon Poy.

[f. 161a, an inserted leaf of parchment, stained; apparently once part of a roll, since the writing on the verso is inverted]

457. [Assembly]: 8 July 34 Hen.VI [1456].

[Present, in two columns]: John Wyly mayor, Thomas Freman, William Swayne, William Lyghtefote, William Cornemale, Robert Cove, Thomas Whytyng, John Franke, Robert Newman, Simon Poy, John Peraunt, Thomas Lyon, John Wheler [presumably members of the Twenty-Four];

[column two] Andrew Brent, Richard Bellers, John Laundever, John Wyse 'vynter', John Shypton, John Cleve 'tanner', John Dogood, John Stone, William Chylde, Nicholas Barbour, Richard Walker, Robert Meteyiff, Thomas Leker, John Hylle, Thomas Copter, William Cokkes, John Mone, Walter Brydde, John Slegge, John Noble, Henry Frend, Richard Hayne 'taylour', John Scotte, Thomas Mogge, John Wylly, Richard Marchall, John Hode 'glover', John Aysshford, William Mory 'ferrour' [presumably members of the Forty-Eight].

Agreed: William Lyghtefote and Robert Cove for the Twenty-Four and John Mone and Henry Frend for the Forty-Eight to oversee the repair of the tenement late of [blank] Baton 'smyth'.

Also agreed: William Swayne, W. Lyghtefote, Robert Cove, John Mone, and H. Frend with Richard Belers to oversee the repair of the tenement called 'le Lyon' where lately Bover lived. Also they demised the said tenement to John Wyse 'vynter'.

[f. 161a verso; faded and stained]

458. Assembly: 6 Feb. 34 Hen.VI [1456].

Present [in three columns]: John Wyly mayor, John Wyot, John Wyse 'draper', William Swayne, Thomas Payne, Thomas Whytyng, William Knolles, William Hore, John Peraunt, John Wheler, Robert Newman [presumably members of the Twenty-Four];

[column two] Anselm Hebbyng, John Caccherow, Thomas Leker, John Cleve 'tanner', Henry Frende, John Mone 'gentilman', John Wyse 'vyntener', Robert Meteyeff, John stone, Nicholas Barbour, Henry Shadde, John Willy, John Hode, Thomas Mogge, John Dogood, Robert Cokelott, Richard Haynes 'taylour', [*column three*] John Commesby *presumably members of the Forty-Eight*].

f. '171'; *stained and holed*]

459. On 14 Nov. 16 Hen. VI [*1437*] George Westby, John Gower, and William Prangnell, collectors of the fourth part of a fifteenth granted to the king, received at the 'councelhous' in full payment of all the money owed the king £17 0s. 2½d.

The rest of the folio blank.]

f. '172'; *faded, stained, holed, and mutilated*]

460. [*List of*] Charters of liberties and other muniments of the city of Salisbury:

In one chest are contained:

The charter of liberties granted by King Edward [*i.e. Edward I*] son of King Henry .

A commission of the said King Edward recognizing, according to the form of the statute that a market may be held in the city.

Two commissions for the city (. . .).

A commission for making bars.   .

Another commission to discharge (. . .).

A letter patent of the lord Robert [bishop] of Salisbury prohibiting (. . .).

An agreement between Salisbury and Southampton.

Another agreement, between Salisbury and (Wilton?).

Various charters and muniments of (. . .) Asshle and Thomas (. . .) of various tenements.

Largely illegible, apparently relating to the question whether a tenement should revert to the mayor and community on the death of a tenant without issue.]

Three other [letters] patent (. . .).

A charter of John Pynnok (. . .) concerning Pynnock's Inn ('Pynnokesinn') and other lands and tenements outside the city (. . .) to the mayor and community.

In another small chest are contained the muniments of the cottages late John Baker's in Nuggeston; also a charter of rents of 10s. from a cottage late John Thome's, given by William Warmwell.

[f. '172'v.; *two fragments, one at the top, the other at the foot of the page*]

461. Memorandum: on Monday next after All Saints 15 Hen.VI [*5 Nov. 1436*] Stephen Mercer mayor received from William Knolles, collector for Market ward of the fourth part of a fifteenth granted to the king payable on the feast of St. Martin next [*11 Nov.*] £6 8s. 4d. Also on the said day the same mayor received from John Pernaunt 'goldsmyth' collector of the fourth part as above for New Street £5 6s. Also on the said day the same mayor received from Richard Walker and John Crykemour, collectors of the fourth part as above for St. Martin's (. . .) £5 6s. 8d.

462. Memorandum: on 13 Nov. 7 Hen.V [*1419*] the common chest was opened in the presence there of Robert Warmwell, Robert Puynant, John Judde, Walter Nandre, John Swyft, Henry Man, Richard Coof, Robert Gilbert, Walter Short, John Boteler, Stephen Edyngdon, and others, for a charter taken from it concerning the cottages late of John Baker 'grocer' in Nuggeston. The charter was committed to W. Shirle, William Waryn and William Lord [in London *interlined*] to defend the wrongs [done] by Reginald Kynggesbrigge against William Waryn and William Bisshup, who had possession of the cottages in the community's name, and with the assent of the said citizens it was delivered to Thomas Daly to be carried there, and there was given to him ½ mark by Robert Gilbert one of the chamberlains for his expense and work. And the said charter was replaced and delivered by William Lord, and along with other muniments it remains in the chest at the 'counseilhous'.

INDEX OF PERSONS

References are to the numbered entries, not to pages. Roman numerals refer to the introductory pages. Many of the names below relate to more than one person, but two or more people of the same surname and forename are distinguished in the index only where different occupations or other descriptions make it clear that the references are to distinct people. The occurrence of a name more than once in an entry is not indicated except where the repetition of a name in a list suggests that more than one person bore the name. Variant spellings are numerous: to save space, letters which they inlcude only sometimes are set in italic. References to the mayor and to the king which do not include the mayor's or the king's name are not indexed; nor are those to a king named only in a date. The lists of mayors on pp. xxxiii–xxxv is not indexed here.

Abbot, Thos 20, 43, 95, 223D
Abingdon (Abyngdon):
 Nic 223A
 Thos 83
Absolon, Jn 223H
Abyngdon *see* Abingdon
Adam:
 Hen 223B
 Jn 343, 386
 Phil 340, 343
Adekyn *see* Atkin
Adeton, Jn 372
Adkin *see* Atkin
Agodeshalf (Agoddeshalf), Jn 317, 343B
Ailward *see* Aylward
Albon, Jn 219C
Aldrygge, Wm 321D
Alee *see* Aley
Alexander (Alisaund*ere*, Alysaund*ere*, Elisaundre, Elysaundre):
 Jn 156, 210, 273, 275, 278, 294, 300, 321B, 323, 325, 328, 334–6, 340, 343I, 344, 346–7, 350, 352, 355, 358, 360A, 366, 368B, 379, 381–2, 386, 388–90, 392–3, 399, 418
 Wm (W.) 37, 89, 135, 142, 185, 203, 211, 213, 217, 231, 236–7, 242, 245–6, 248–9, 257–61, 266, 272–6, 277, 281–2, 284, 289, 294, 297, 300, 302, 310, 314, 319, 321A, 325, 329, 335, 372, 386, 389, 393, 396
 and see Sanders
Aley (Alee), Jn 321A, 343C, 391
Aleyn:
 Agnes 223D

Jn 391
Alisaunder (Alisaundre) *see* Alexander
All(. . .), Hen 250
Alrigge (Alrygg), Nic 219B, 223F
Alysby, Alson 223F
Amelyn, Wm 243, 247, 252, 261–2, 265
Amerall (scribe), 37
Ancketille *see* Anketill
Androw (Andreau, Andrew*e*, Androw):
 Hugh 234, 236–8, 244, 247, 252, 257–8, 261, 272
 Jn 210, 292, 297, 314, 319, 321B, 343J
 Rob 254
 Thos 210–11, 223G, 224A, 244, 319, 321C, 342, 344–5, 391, 394
Andys, Thos 5
Angold, Jn 343F
Anketill (Ancketille):
 Joan 343K
 Jn 219B, 293
Anthon, Jn 213
Aport *see* Port
Ar(...), Thos 77
Archibald (Archebaud), Thos 294, 341, 345D, 418
Arnald *see* Arnold
Arnhull *see* Harnhill
Arnold (Arnald):
 Joan 89
 Jn 223A
 Rob 89
 Wm 252
Arp(...), Wm 213

Bulmere, Jn 219B
Burdbusshe *see* Birdbush
Burgeys:
    Ralph 219C
    Thos 219C (two such), 343H
Burgundy, duke of 311, 313, 317
Burley, Wm 373
Burnet (Bernet), Jn 343F
Burton *see* Bourton
Bussele, Hugo 4
Busshop (Busshup) *see* Bishop
But *see* Butte
Butcher (Beauchir, Bochere, Botchiure, Boucher):
    Gover 210
    Jn 210, 223F
    Ric 343E
    Wm 167
    (. . .) 39
Buterleigh (Bitterleygh, Buterle*ygh*, Byt*t*erle*ye*):
    Jn 3, 8, 40, 55, 127, 194, 196–7, 200, 219G, 271; as mayor 1–2
    Wal 4
    Wm 33
    (. . .) 3, 53
Butler (Bot*t*ellere, Botiller, Botyler):
    Jn 20, 22–5, 30, 32, 77, 79–80, 97, 102, 138, 164, 170, 211, 223E, 236, 247, 249, 252, 254, 257–9, 262–6, 268–70, 272–6, 278, 280–3, 285–7, 292–4, 297–8, 300–2, 307, 310, 313–14, 318–319, 321C, 322, 325, 327, 329, 334–5, 340, 343C, 345, 345C, 347–50, 352, 354–5, 358–9, 360A, 362, 364, 368C, 369–71, 381, 388–91, 393, 396, 418, 419B, 431, 436, 441, 462
    Jn (brewer) 371B
    Jn (mercer) 360C, 368C, 371B, 391, 431
    Laurencia 343F
    Ric 146, 169, 224B, 254, 273, 300, 321A
    Wm 343C
Butte (But), Jn 138, 223A, 343G
Byde, Wm 155
Bydewode *see* Wood
Byer (Beere, Beyre, Biere, Byere):
    Jn 454
    Thos 342, 343F, 345A, 346–7, 352–3, 355, 357, 361, 368A, 373, 452
    Wal 37, 39
Byke, Jn 219C
Byllyk (Bylk) *see* Bullock
Byn(. . .), Jn 372

Byngley, Wm 33
Byrde *see* Bird
Bysshampton *see* Bishampton
Bysshop (Bysshup) *see* Bishop
Byston *see* Biston
Byterley (Byt*t*erle*ye*) *see* Buterleigh
Bythewood (By *þe* Wode, Bydewode, Bythewode) *see* Wood

C(. . .), Jn 221, 288, 313
Ca(. . .), Wm 25
Cable (Cabbel*l*), Thos 317, 343B
Cachero (Caccheroo*w*, Cachers, Cachro, Cathero, Cathers, Chacchero), Jn (J.) 319, 321A, 345A, 362, 365, 368B, 371A, 381–2, 391–2, 397, 409, 420, 423–4, 426, 428–32, 440–2, 444, 450, 452–5, 458
Caise, Jn 223B
Cake (Cakes):
    Alex 14
    Rob 343I
    Thos 11, 223B
    Wm 36, 223B, 343I
Calet (Calett):
    Jn 56
    Thos 56
Calston, Thos (sheriff of Wilts) 167
Cam (Caym), Hen 223F *and see* Canne
Cambridge (Ca*u*mbrig*ge*), Wm 148, 217; his wife 148
Cammel (Cam*m*el*l*):
    Jn 8, 11, 14, 29, 138, 194–9, 205, 224A, 250, 254, 256–8, 261, 269, 289, 300, 321C, 336, 347, 415, 421, 431, 434–6, 440, 445, 452; as mayor 194, 200, 436–9
    Rob 423
    and see Caundel
Campion, Ric 410
Canne:
    Ric 452
    Rob 241, 257, 328, 343D
    and see Cam
Canning (Canyng):
    Jn 138
    Simon 223H
Canterbury, archbp of 400, 405
Canyng *see* Canning
Capper (Cappe*re*):
    Hugh 223E
    Jn 126–7, 136
    and see Chapour
Cappys, Hugh 219C

Thos 203, 363

Wm 3, 146, 154, 169, 210, 213, 223C, 224A, 254, 258, 269–70, 273, 275, 279–81, 293–5, 297–300, 302, 305, 314, 319, 321A, 322, 325, 328–9, 334, 343F, 345, 345A, 348–50, 352–5, 358, 360B, 362–4, 367, 368B, 368C, 370–1, 371A, 372, 377, 386–8, 391

Charterhouse, prior of 405, 414

Chatour, Jn 288, 360B, 368B, 371A, 391, 415

Chaumb' see Chamber

Chaunceler see Chancellor

Chaundel (Chaundelere, Chaundelir, Chaundiler) see Chandler

Chedford, Thos 223A

Chedworth, Jn (archdeacon of Wilts) 452

Chepman see Chapman

Chepton, Wm 391 and see Shipton

Cherynge, Jn 56

Chesham (Schesham), Ric 110, 133, 169, 192, 219D, 223C

Chew, Jn 213

Cheyne:
Edm 270
Wm 42, 89

Child (Childe, Chylde):
Ric 442
Thos 6, 14, 15, 22–4, 27–8, 33, 42–3, 46, 49, 60, 63–4, 67–8, 71, 76–7, 79, 81, 91–3, 95, 99, 101–2, 106, 113, 115, 119, 128, 138, 263; his wife 223D
Wal 36, 389
Wm 141, 213, 219A, 223C, 224A, 231, 233–4, 238, 246–7, 249, 278, 280, 294–5, 300, 319, 328, 336, 343J, 345B, 347, 353–4, 360A, 365, 367, 368B, 371, 371A, 389, 391, 399, 409, 417, 423–6, 428, 431–4, 437, 441, 451–4, 457

Chiltern (Chilterne, Chylterne), Edw 422, 424–5, 431–5, 445, 448, 450–3, 455 and see Chitterne

Chippenham (Chipnam, Chypman, Chyppenham, Schyppenham):
Jn 30, 33, 54, 84, 92, 97, 101, 115, 124, 128, 138, 169, 203, 210, 212–13, 219A, 220, 223B, 224C, 227, 229, 231, 233–4, 236–8, 244, 246–7, 250, 252–4, 258, 261, 264–5, 268–70, 273, 275, 278, 280, 287, 293–4, 321A, 343E, 360B, 362, 371B, 391, 424, 426, 431–7, 440, 443–5, 450–1, 454
Rob 89

Chirche see Church

Chitterne (Chytterne), Jn 15, 94, 219C and see Chiltern

Christchurch (Cristechurche):
Jn 95, 223F
Ric 77, 80, 92, 134, 142, 146, 167, 223E

Christopher (servant) 433

Chrlyng see Charlyng

Chubbe, Hen 61, 77, 300, 321A, 343D, 348–50, 352, 354–5

Church (Chirche), Rob 160

Churchill (Curchill), Ric 223H and see Kyrchyl

Chychia see Thychy

Chyltern (Chylterne) see Chiltern

Chynchon (Chynshon, Chynthyn, Chynton):
Jn 141, 379, 391, 393
Rob 219A, 223B, 224C, 243, 252, 254, 257, 260, 300, 305, 344, 347, 349–50, 352, 360B, 362, 364, 367, 371A, 372, 388, 391, 393, 440–1, 445, 452–3, 455

Chyppenham (Chypenham, Chypman) see Chippenham

Chyterne (Chytterne) see Chitterne

Cirencester (Susetere), Jn 223C

Clablane, Jn 4 and see Crablane

Clarence, duke of see Thomas

Clark see Clerk

Claronet, Jas 33

Clatford, Geo 219B, 223E

Clefe see Clyve

Clerdr, Nic 343I

Clerk (Clark, Clerke):
Edw 61 223B
Edw (master weaver) 219B
Edw (journeyman weaver) 219C
Jn 89, 91, 94–5, 220, 223A, 223H
Jn (limner) 146, 169, 173, 213–15, 258
Jn (mercer) 219A
Jn (tanner) 223F
Ric 15
Wm 223E, 234, 237–8, 258, 260, 275, 418
Wm (fuller) 224A, 235, 246–7, 257
Wm (tanner) 243
(. . .) 221

Clet' see Clitour

Cleve see Clyve

Clife see Clyve

Clifford (Clyfford), Nic 343K

Clitour (Clet', Clyter, Clytyr):
Jn 223A, 224B, 275, 297, 314, 317, 321B, 343G, 345B
Wm 288, 300, 360A, 368, 368B, 371A, 391

Rob 223G
Wm 219C
Fisher (Fissher, Fys*schere*):
Edm 343G
Jn 103, 223E
Thos 343E
Wal 343E
fitz John, Hen 41
Fletcher (Fletc*chere*):
Jn 224B
Ric 321B, 343G
Thos 56, 343G
Wm 343E
Fobour *see* Furbour
Foghler *see* Fowler
Folham *see* Fulham
Fontaine (Fontaygne), Edw 20
Fonthill (Fontel), Jn 219C
Forbour *see* Furbour
Ford (Forde):
Hugh de 56
Wal 219C
Forest:
Jn 1–2, 4, 8–9, 14, 21–2, 24, 27, 30–1, 36, 43, 53, 55, 61, 64, 70–1, 73, 79, 89, 91, 93–5, 102, 138, 167, 197, 223E (two such), 271
Jn (jun) 138
Jn (sen) 5, 11, 20, 23, 25, 35, 45
Rob 15, 29, 223E
Wm 33
Formage (Furmage), Jn 56, 219A, 223E
Forns', Nic 223A
Forster (For*ystere*, Fu*istour*, Fuyste, Fuysto*ur*):
Jn 25, 56
Pet 219C
Ric 219C
Rob 169
Thos 224A
Thos (fuller) 219D
Thos (dyer) 223A
Wm 20, 23–4, 43, 45, 60, 75–7, 79, 95, 97, 101, 109, 115, 124, 128, 133–4, 142, 146, 156, 163, 166–7, 169–70, 172, 191–3, 197, 203, 211, 223B
Fortes, — 449
Foryster *see* Forster
Foul (Foule), Thos 61, 224B, 321B, 343I
Fouler *see* Fowler
Fourbour *see* Furbour
Fowey, Jn 356
Fowke, Wm 219B

Fowler (Foghler, Fouler):
Thos 219C
Wm 321A, 343E
Fox, Jn 223D
Foxham, Jn 223D
Foxhole (Foxhol), Jn 255
Francis (Fraunc*es*, Fraunses):
Jn 43
Rob 5, 15, 36–7
Frank (Franke):
Jn (J.) 182, 321A, 343E, 368A, 391, 424, 444, 448, 455, 457
— 239
Franklin (Frank*e*layn, Frau*n*keleyn):
Jn 194, 196, 223D, 257, 343K
Jn (weaver) 219B (two such)
Jn (wheeler) 138, 197
Fraunces (Fraunc(. . .), Fraunses) *see* Francis
Fraunkeleyn *see* Franklin
Freeman (Freman):
Jn 236, 259
Thos 216, 221, 224A, 229–30, 237 (two such), 242, 249, 252, 254–5, 258, 260–4, 273, 275, 276A, 281–2, 284, 286, 288–9, 291, 293, 297, 300, 303, 307, 311, 314, 319, 321B, 329, 333, 344–5, 345B, 349–50, 353, 355, 358–9, 360A, 368C, 369–71, 371B, 372–3, 381, 386, 388–91, 393–4, 396, 420, 422, 428–32, 434, 436–9, 443, 445, 448–9, 451–3, 455, 457; as mayor 323, 326–7, 333–6, 338, 341; his wife 431
Thos (mercer) xxx, 225, 231, 256, 260, 262, 265–6, 273
Thos (merchant) xxx *n*, 376, 378
Thos (yeoman) xxx *n*, 238, 254, 258
Wal 434, 451, 453
Wm 423
— 315, 319
Frend (Frende):
Hen (H.) 258, 272–3, 279, 299, 309, 323, 328, 333–6, 341–2, 347, 349, 352–4, 358–9, 362, 364, 366–7, 371, 374, 377, 379, 382, 386, 388, 390–1, 405, 409, 417–18, 420–1, 424–5, 428, 430, 434–5, 437–41, 443, 445, 450–5, 457–8
Jn 257, 270, 272
Frere (Frer'), Wm 219B, 223E
Frith (Frithes), Edw 95, 113, 132, 146, 155–6, 167, 169, 187, 203, 211, 213, 223D
Frog (Frogge), Thos 101–2, 146, 169, 173, 219B, 223C, 224A, 252, 260
Fry (Frye):

Thos 391
and see Hull
Hinde (Hyende), Wal 328, 388–91, 394, 403,
    409, 423–6, 431
Hindon (Hynedon):
    Rob 127, 175, 201
    Thos 40; as mayor 447
Hipswell (Epysswyll, Ypysewell), Jn 368B, 371B
Hiwode *see* Heywood
Hoare (Hore):
    Hugh 197, 199–200
    Jn 223A, 223D
    Wm (W.) 54, 138, 141, 151, 210, 223F, 300,
        319, 321C, 322, 324, 331, 333–7, 340–1,
        345A, 345C, 348–50, 352–5, 360A, 361–
        2, 364, 366–7, 368C, 369–70, 371B, 381,
        386, 400–1, 403, 414, 417, 423–4, 427–8,
        430–4, 436–40, 442–5, 451–2, 455, 458;
        as mayor 387, 389–91, 393
Hobbes (Hobbis, Hobbys), Jn 224C, 238, 287,
    293, 300, 321D, 324, 328, 336, 345D, 349,
    360B, 368B, 371A, 418
Hode (Hod) *see* Hood
Hody, Alex 433
Hogman (Hogemann):
    Jn 42–3, 77, 79, 95, 101–2, 106, 115, 138,
        146, 156, 213, 219A, 223H, 224A
    (. . .) 169
Hogyn *see* Hugon
Holl', Jn 223F
Holloway (Holwey), Jn 219B, 223A
Holme (Holm):
    Jn 343K, 345B, 360A, 391, 410
    Thos 343I
Holurst, Hugh 224A
Holwey *see* Holloway
Hone:
    Jn 441
    Wal 409
Honteley *see* Huntley
Honyballek, Nic 219E
Honythorn (Honyssorne, Honythorne,
    Hunythorn), Jn (J.) 71, 141, 276A, 300,
    319, 341, 343J, 345, 359, 360A, 371B, 379,
    391–2, 397, 401, 409–10, 417, 421, 424,
    427–8, 431–4, 436, 440–1, 444, 452–3, 455
Hood (Hoode):
    Jn 343C, 400, 421, 436, 439, 441, 444–5,
        450, 452–3, 456–8
    Ric 304
Hooper (Houpere):
    Jn 223B

Ric 223D
Hore (Hor) *see* Hoare
Horf, Jn 266
Horman, Jn 391
Horn (Horne), Jn 223H, 321C, 431–2, 436,
    439, 445
Hornpipere, Jn 300
Horsebridge (Hosbrig', Hosbrygge), Wm
    219B, 223C
Horsemill (Horsmul), Jn 138
Horwood (Horwode), Wm 219C
Horyng, Rob 15 *and see* Herring
Hosbrig' (Hosbrygge) *see* Horsebridge
Hoten(. . .), Jn 56
Houchon (Houchynes) *see* Hutching
Hour(. . .), Jn 56
Howchon *see* Hutching
Howles, Alex 56
Howtoon, Ysaac 155
Hubert (Huberd), Ric 56
Huchon *see* Hutching
Hugon (Hogyn), Wm 219C, 223D, 223F *and*
    see Higon
Huish (Huwysche), Jn 223E
Hull (Hulle):
    Jn 223H (two such)
    Jn (weaver) 219C (two such)
    Jn (fuller) 219E
    Wm 8, 11, 14, 27, 29, 33, 36, 42–3, 45, 53,
        76, 126, 132, 139
    and see Hill
Hulton or Hulle, Wm 36
Hungerford (Hungeford):
    Edm (knight, sheriff of Wilts) 311
    Rob (knight) 304, 386, 404–5
    Jn 223A
    Wal (knight, sheriff of Wilts, Lord
        Hungerford) 54, 140, 153, 167, 169, 236,
        253–5, 270, 308, 316, 345, 367, 369, 386,
        400, 405, 433
    Wm 64
    (. . .) 89
Hunt (Huntte):
    Jn 219G, 221, 224A, 225, 227, 229–31,
        233–4, 237–8, 250, 253, 256, 260
    Jn (mercer) 242–3, 254
    Jn (taverner) 224B
    Ric 343C
Huntingdon, earl of 372
Huntley (Honteley, Huntele), Wal 317, 333,
    342, 343B, 348, 356, 368, 373, 391, 403,
    428, 430, 438, 456

Lumbard *see* Lombard
Luter (Lutyer), Jn 343G, 410
Lycfeld *see* Lichfield
Lychenard *see* Lythenard
Lye, Jn 412, 424
Lyghfot (Ly*ghte*fote) *see* Lightfoot
Lyht *see* Light
Lyle (Lylye) *see* Lily
Lymington (Lymyngton), Jn 196
Lymner (Lympner, Lympnour) *see* Limner
Lymyngton *see* Lymington
Lynchwode, Jn 219D *and see* Lythenard
Lynde, Ric 343J
Lyndraper *see* Linendraper
Lyon, Thos 391, 425, 428–9, 431–2, 440, 455, 457
Lyshog', Wm 223A
Lysle, Jn (knight, sheriff of Wilts) 44
Lythenard (Lychenard, Lytenard), Ste 79, 101–2, 106, 110, 112–13, 142, 146, 167, 213, 221, 224A, 237–8, 294, 343I *and see* Lynchwode
Lytle *see* Little
Lyzt *see* Light
Lyztfot *see* Lightfoot

M(. . .):
  Jn 288
  Thos 388
  Wm 388
Maber (Mabour, Mabre) *see* Marlborough
Machin (Machon, Machyn), Jn 180, 216, 219A, 223D, 224A, 236–7, 247, 258, 260, 272, 280, 293, 300, 302, 322, 324, 329, 332, 341, 343K
Magot, Wm 445
Maideman, Jn 410
Malabre *see* Marlborough
Malmesbury, abbot of 353, 369
Malrbr *see* Marlborough
Man:
  Hen (H.) 127, 133–4, 142, 146, 152, 155, 159–60, 169–72, 186–7, 189, 207, 211–16, 225, 227, 231–4, 236–8, 243, 246–50, 252–4, 256–9, 261–3, 265, 267, 270, 272–3, 276A, 278, 280, 286–9, 291, 293–4, 297–9, 300, 302–3, 305, 310–11, 314–15, 318–20, 321A, 322, 324–7, 329, 332, 334–9, 341, 343F, 349–50, 352–5, 357–9, 360A, 362, 364, 367, 368C, 369, 371, 371B, 372, 374, 377, 462; as mayor 219, 219A, 219G, 221–2, 224A, 278–83, 285, 342–3, 344–5,

348, 360, 418, 419A
  Jn 406
Mande, Jn 80
Manning (Mannyng), Thos 37
Manningford (Manyford), Jn 223D
Mannyerg', Jn 223D
Mannyng *see* Manning
Manyford *see* Manningford
Marbe *see* Marlborough
Marchal (Marchal*le*, Marche*lle*) *see* Marshall
Mariot (Mariotte) *see* Meriot
Maritfeis, Hen 223B
Marke, Jn 371B
Marlborough (Maber, Mabour, Ma*labre*, Malrbr, Marbe):
  Jas 223F
  Jn 368C
  Thos 210, 273, 295, 300, 321B, 328, 360B, 368B, 371A, 388, 391, 431, 443, 446
Marshall (Marchal*le*, Marche*lle*, Marshel, Mascall):
  Gilb 264, 270, 273, 282, 293, 300, 313, 321B, 322, 325, 329, 334–6, 341, 343K, 347, 349–50, 352–5, 359, 364, 379, 382, 393
  Gilb (bp of Salisbury's clerk) 216–17
  Jn 203, 212–13, 216, 219A, 221–2, 223A, 224C, 226–7, 231, 233–4, 237–8, 242–4, 247, 249, 252, 254, 256, 258–9, 261–6, 268–9, 272–3, 278, 280–2, 285–6, 289, 293–4, 297–8, 300 (two such), 302–3, 305, 310, 314, 318–19, 321B, 322–6, 329, 334–6, 339, 343H, 346–7, 348–50, 355, 362, 364, 366–7, 369–70, 372, 377, 386, 388–91, 392, 396
  Ric 56 (two such), 219D, 424, 442–3, 445, 451, 454–5, 457
  Rob 61
Martin (Martyn):
  Agnes 223D
  Jn 223G
  Wm 56
Mascall *see* Marshall
Masey, Thos 247 *and see* Massinger
Maslin (Masselyn), Pet 343C
Mason (Mas*s*one, Maysaunt, Meyson):
  Agnes 343H
  Alice 343I
  Jn 219A, 223B
  Jn (chapman) 56
  Jn (weaver) 219B, 223E, 224B
  Nic 54

Jn 6, 20, 29–30, 36, 43, 55, 59, 71, 76, 95,
97, 134, 138, 143, 157, 192, 212–13, 220,
224A, 231, 234, 238
Simon (archdeacon of Salisbury) 182
Sylle, Wm 391
Symond:
Jn 219C (two such), 223G
Wm 219C
Sunbury, Rob 343J
Syre, Wm 138
Syrencot (Sexhampcote):
Rob 195
Thos 195, 199
Syvyar (Sywyer) see Sewer

T(. . .), Wm 142
Tailor (Taillour, Tayllour):
Alson 223G
Eustace 223F
Geof 223A
Gerard 321A, 343D
Hen 223E
Jn 223F, 343G
Jn (clerk) 37
Jn (fuller) 219E
Martin or Mat 343J
Nic 219G, 223C, 343I
Pat 223G
Purs 223G
Ric 56, 223E, 343D
Rob 223A
Rog 219B, 223B, 223G, 343I
Thos 223A
Wm 223B, 223F, 343B
Talbot, Jn 219G
Talwchaundeler see Waxchandler
Tangle, Geo 138
Tanner (Tannere):
Geof 223A
Gilb 146, 187, 213, 219A, 221, 224B, 227,
237–8, 243, 254, 265, 273
Hugh 213, 223H
Jn 151, 153, 219C (two such), 223B, 223C
Rob 113, 142, 166–7, 172–3, 193, 203,
219A, 223H, 259, 269, 295, 335 and see
Tonnere
Sybon [recte Simon?] 223D
Ste 15
Wm 343D
Tarrant (Tarant, Tarent), Rob 223B, 321B,
343H
Tarry, Thos 300, 343G

Taverner:
Alex (Saundr') 223F
Anselm 321A
Thos 56, 343B
Wm 264, 343H, 343K
Tayllour see Tailor
Teffont (Teffonte):
Adam 8, 11, 13–14, 20, 24–5, 27–9, 31,
40, 42–3, 49, 60–1, 64, 75, 77, 79, 91–2,
94, 101, 106, 113, 138, 194, 196–7, 199,
263; as mayor 6, 35–7
Jn 146, 169, 173, 213, 224A, 233–6, 254,
258, 263, 269, 273, 283, 374
Tempse (Temese, Temps):
Jn 345
Thos 342, 347, 353, 368, 368C, 371B, 377,
391, 396, 408–9, 423, 425, 431, 436
Tenant, Jn 223H; his mother 223H
Tene (Teone), Wm 219B, 343I
Terry, Thos 321B
Teynterer (Teyntourer):
Alice 7, 8, 89, 98, 127, 217, 219G
Thos 194
Wm (jun) 7, 89, 98, 127, 140, 217, 219G
Wm (sen) 219G
Therbourne (Thernbourne) see Thorbourne
Thirnynge, W. 41
Thomas duke of Clarence, son of Henry IV,
54, 98, 154, 260
Thomas, Edm 317
Thome, Jn 460
Thomelyn, Jas 431
Thomson (Thomsene, Thomsone, Thomsyn),
Jn 219C, 223D, 343A
Thorbourne (Thernbourne):
Jn 113, 125–7, 138, 194–5, 197, 199, 201
and see Thornton
Wal (sheriff of Wilts) 140
Thoresby (Thorseby, Thursby), Jn 297, 300,
314, 319, 321A, 343D, 345A, 352–3, 357,
360B, 361, 368A, 371B, 377, 388, 390–1,
399–400, 404, 406, 409, 420, 423–5, 431–
6, 438, 441, 444, 451, 454
Thornton (Thorndon):
Jn 136, 169, 223C and see Thorbourne
Ric 224B, 253
Thorp, Hen 42
Thorsby (Thorseby, Thursby) see Thoresby
Thursteyn;
Joan (wife of Thos) 126–7, 206
Thos 126–7, 206
Wm 126–7

343F, 346–9, 353, 459
Hen 223F
Jn 275, 304
Simon 224A
Ste 91
Wm 98, 203, 217, 237, 304
Westerdale, Ric 317
Westmore, Edith 155
Westmorland, earl of 455
Weston:
    Jn 41, 219B, 332, 343B
    Ric 8, 14, 20, 23, 28, 67, 102, 138, 197,
      201, 223E
Westover, Jn 445
Wet, H. 39
Wehtirgrove see Wedergrove
Wever see Weaver
Wexchaundeler see Waxchandler
Wexey, Jn 219D
Weye, Rob 138
Weyrdrawer see Wiredrawer
Weyse see Wise
Wheeler (Wheolere, Whyler):
    Alice 71
    Hen 219C
    Jn 2, 14, 71, 219C, 223B, 293–5, 300, 305,
      321D, 329, 331, 334, 336–7, 343J, 345,
      345D, 346, 349–50, 353, 356, 358, 368B,
      370, 371A, 377, 386, 388–93, 397, 399–
      400, 404, 412, 417, 420–1, 423–4, 427, 429,
      431–3, 435, 437–45, 451–3, 455, 457–8
    Jn (brewer) 388
    Jn (weaver) 309, 360B
    Thos 223B
    Wm 223D
    — 315
Whibete (Wybet):
    Nic 219D
    Jn 223C
Whitbred, Pet 343F
Whitby:
    Hen 219C
    Jn 391
White (Whyhte, Wighte):
    Adam 26, 138, 199
    Alex 56
    Jn 237–8, 257, 269, 273, 288, 292, 294,
      297–8, 310–11, 314, 318–19, 321A, 322,
      325, 335–7, 339, 341, 345, 346–50; as
      mayor 299–301, 303–5, 307–8, 350
    Jn (fuller) 223G
    Jn (mercer) 254, 300–1, 343E, 345A, 418

Jn (tailor) 321A, 343C
Nic 126–7, 136, 201, 210
Ric 219B, 223C
Rob 223A, 224B, 343H
Wm 23, 33, 36, 42, 55, 60, 138, 194–7,
  199
Wm (tailor) 223F
Wm (tiler) 343K
— 315
Whithorn, Ric 347
Whiting (Whitynge, Whytynge):
    Jn 37, 420, 431
    Thos 141, 210, 219A, 223E, 300, 319, 328,
      336, 343K, 345B, 360A, 368B, 371A, 391,
      403, 417, 423–4, 426, 428–33, 435, 437,
      439–40, 442–5, 450–2, 457–8
Whitley (Wytele), Ric 223A
Whitlock, Wm 219C
Whittocksmead (Whittokkesmede,
    Whitoxmede), Jn 425, 444, 446
Whyler see Wheeler
Whyse see Wise
Wicford (Wichford) see Wishford
Wickham (Wykeham):
    Jn 223E (two such)
    Jn (jun) 219B
    Jn (sen) 219B
Wight see White
Wilkes, Jn 223A, 223C
Wilkins (Wilkyns), Jn 219C
Will see Well
Willam (Wyllyam):
    Jn 343G
    Rob of 223E
Willies (Willi, Willyes) see Wylye
Wilmington (Wylmondon, Wylmyndon,
    Wylmyngton):
    Ste 219C
    Thos 321C, 325, 328
Wilmot (Wylmot), Wm 345C, 360B, 368B,
    371A, 388, 391, 417, 420–1, 424, 426, 431–
    2, 433 (two such), 451–2
Wilteshire see Wiltshire
Wilton:
    Jn 219D, 223F
    Wm (W.) 33, 138, 195–6, 199
Wiltshire (Wilteshire, Wylteshire):
    Hen 219C
    Thos 224B
Wiltshire:
    archdeacon of see Chedworth
    earl of 433, 445

escheators of 372
sheriff of 270, 304, 372, 433, 440 *and see*
Beauchamp; Calston; Cervyngton; Darell;
Fynderne; Hungerford; Lysle; Pauncefoot;
Seymour; Stourton; Thorbourne
undersheriff of 446
Wily *see* Wylye
Wimborne (Wymbourne), Jn 223F
Wimpenny (Wynpeny):
Hen 138
Maud 223D
Winch (Wynch), Jn 223D
Winchester (Wynch*estere*, Wynchestour):
Jn (J.) 210, 213, 218, 224B, 269, 273, 297,
300, 314, 319, 321A, 334, 343D, 345A, 349,
355, 360B, 368C, 371B, 381, 389, 391–3,
397, 403, 405, 411, 415–17, 420, 423–33,
435, 437, 441–3, 445, 450, 452–3, 455
Jn (barber) 169, 187
Jn (ironmonger) 173
Penyton de 223F
Winchester, bp of [Hen Beaufort] (chancellor
of England) 83–4, 89, 145–6, 150, 153–4,
169, 172, 270, 276A, 419 *and see* England
(lord) chancellor of
Wind (Wynde):
Ric 56
Wm 219C
Winterbourne (Wynterbourne), Jn 219C
Winterslow (Wynterslewe), Jn 223A
Wiot (Wiott) *see* Wyatt
Wiredrawer (Weyrdrawer), Jn 343G
Wise (W*h*eyse):
Jn (J.) 343K, 360B, 368B, 371A, 388, 391,
396, 403, 407, 410, 421 (two such), 422–
3, 424 (two such), 425–31, 432 (two such),
433–5, 444–5, 448, 453–4
Jn 54 (draper), 219A, 387, 420, 436, 438–
40, 442, 450, 453, 458
Jn (vintner) 415, 420, 433–4, 436–7, 443,
446, 451–3, 457–8
Ric (R.) 257, 260, 264, 268–70, 272–3,
275, 278–83, 285–6, 288–9, 292–4, 297–
8, 300–2, 305, 307, 310, 313–14, 318–19,
321B, 322, 324–9, 332, 334–8, 344–5,
345B, 346, 349, 352–5, 359, 360A, 362,
367, 368C, 369–70, 371B, 372, 377, 381,
392
— 315
Wishford (Wic*h*ford, Wychford):
Jn 14, 127, 146, 155, 165, 170, 202, 211–
12, 374

Reynold 223C
Wm 15, 54, 64, 71, 89, 98, 127, 206, 217,
219G
Witney (Wytteney), Edm 219A, 223D
Witt (Wytte), Ric 343E
Wode *see* Wood
Wodeford *see* Woodford
Wodegrove (Woderove) *see* Woodgrove
Wodehay *see* Woodhay
Wodehurst *see* Woodhurst
Wodeward *see* Woodward
Wodeyate *see* Woodgate
Wodhay *see* Woodhay
Wolf, Rob 77, 79–80, 102, 236, 246–7
Wollop *see* Wallop
Wolmonger *see* Woolmonger
Wood (atte Wode, By þe Wode, Bydewode,
Bythewode, Wode):
Jn 102, 219A, 223A, 343I
Ralph (Radulf) 11, 223B
Ric 219C, 223D
Rog 219B, 223C
Wm 219B, 223B, 321B, 343D, 343G
Woodford (Wodeford):
Rob 138
Rog 27, 36, 42–3, 195
Woodgate (Wodeyate), Jn, 219C
Woodgrove (Wodegrove, Woderove):
Wm 3, 8, 14, 20, 43, 71, 138, 199, 271
(. . .) 66
Woodhay (Wodehay), Jn 211–12, 216, 231,
236, 243, 249–50, 258, 261, 273, 300,
321A, 325, 343F, 347
Woodhurst (Wodehurst), Jn 343F
Woodward (Wodeward):
Hen 219C
Thos 56
Woolmonger (Wolmonger):
Bossom 223F
Hor' 223F
Jn 223F
Wm 223F
Worcester (Worcet'), Jn 56
Worcester, earl of 455
Wotton (Wutton):
Jn 43, 138, 205, 223G
Rob 2
Wm 54, 321C, 360B, 368C, 371B, 391,
401, 415, 417, 420, 424, 426, 428, 430–5,
437–9, 443, 451, 453–4
Wraxall (Wrox*h*ale):
Hen 223G

INDEX OF PLACES AND SUBJECTS

References in arabic numerals are to the numbered entries, not to pages. Roman numerals refer to the introductory pages. Buildings, streets and minor locations are in Salisbury. Towns and villages are in Wiltshire unless stated.

WILTSHIRE RECORD SOCIETY
(As at March 2001)

President: PROF. C.R. ELRINGTON, F.S.A.
General Editor: DR JOHN CHANDLER
Honorary Treasurer: IVOR M. SLCOMOBE
Honorary Secretary: JOHN N. D'ARCY

Committee:
D. CHALMERS
MRS J. COLE
DR D.A. CROWLEY
S.D. HOBBS
M.J. MARSHMAN
MRS I.L. WILLIAMS
K.H. ROGERS, F.S.A., representing the Wiltshire Archaeological and Natural History Society

---

Honorary Auditor: J.D. FOY
Correspondent for the U.S.A.: CHARLES P. GOULD

PRIVATE MEMBERS

ADAMS, Ms S, 23 Rockcliffe Avenue, Bathwick, Bath BA2 6QP

ANDERSON, MR D M, 20 Shakespeare Road, Stratford-sub-Castle, Salisbury SP1 3LA

APPLEGATE, MISS J M, 55 Holbrook Lane, Trowbridge BA14 0PS

ASAJI, PROF K, 5-35-14 Senriyama-nishi, Suita, Osaka, Japan 565-0851

AVERY, MRS S, c/o 46 The Close, Salisbury SP1 2EL

BADENI, COUNTESS JUNE, Norton Manor, Norton, Malmesbury SN16 0JN

BAINES, MRS B M, 32 Tybenham Road, Merton Park, London SW19 3LA

BAINES, MR R T, The Woodhouse, 52 St Mary Street, Chippenham SN15 3JW

BALL, MR S T, 19 The Mall, Swindon SN1 4JA

BARNETT, MR B A, 17 Alexandra Road, Coalpit Heath, Bristol BS17 2PY

BATHE, MR G, Byeley in Densome, Woodgreen, Fordingbridge, Hants SP6 2QU

BAYLIFFE, MR B G, 3 Green Street, Brockworth, Glos GL3 4LT

BEARD, MRS P S, The Anchorage, Port-e-Vullen, Maughold, Isle of Man

BENNETT, DR N, Hawthorn House, Main Street, Norton, Lincoln LN4 2BH

BERRETT, MR A M, 10 Primrose Hill Road, London NW3 3AD

BERRY, MR C, 9 Haven Rd, Crackington Haven, Bude, Cornwall EX23 0PD

BISHOP, MRS S M, Innox Bungalow, Market Place, Colerne, Chippenham SN14 8AY

BLAKE, MR P A, 18 Rosevine Road, London SW20 8RB

BLAKE, MR T N, Glebe Farm, Tilshead, Salisbury SP3 4RZ

BLEASE, MRS S, 9 Royal Field Close,

Hullavington, Chippenham SN14 6DY

BOX, MR S D, 73 Silverdale Road, Earley, Reading RG6 2NF

BRAND, DR P A, 155 Kennington Road, London SE11 6SF

BROOKE-LITTLE, MR J P, Heyford House, Lower Heyford, Bicester, Oxon OX6 3NZ

BROWN, MR D A, 36 Empire Road, Salisbury SP2 9DE

BRYANT, MRS D, 1 St John's Court, Devizes SN10 1BU

BURGESS, MR I D, 29 Brackley Avenue, Fair Oak, Eastleigh, Hants SO5 7FL

BURGESS, MR J M, Tolcarne, Wartha Mill, Porkellis, Helston, Cornwall TR13 0HX

BURNETT-BROWN, MISS J M, Lacock Abbey, Lacock, Chippenham SN15 2LG

CARDIGAN, RT HON EARL OF, Savernake Estate Office, Marlborough SN8 1PA

CAREW HUNT, MISS P H, Cowleaze, Edington, Westbury BA13 4PJ

CARR, PROF D R, Dept. of History, 140 7th Ave South, St Petersburg, Florida 33701 USA

CARTER, DR B J, JP PHD BSc FSG, 15 Walton Grange, Bath Road, Swindon SN1 4AH

CAWTHORNE, MRS N, Dawn, 47 London Road, Camberley, Surrey GU15 3UG

CHALMERS, MR D, Bay House West, Bay House, Ilminster, Somerset TA19 0AT

CHANDLER, DR J H, 53 The Tynings, Westbury BA13 3PZ

CHARD, MR I, 35 Thingwall Park, Fishponds, Bristol BS16 2AJ

CHAVE, MR R A, 39 Church Street, Westbury BA13 3BZ

CHURCH, MR T S, Mannering House, Bethersden, Ashford, Kent TN26 3DJ

CLARK, MR A G, Highlands, 51a Brook Drive, Corsham SN13 9AX

CLARK, MRS V, 29 The Green, Marlborough SN8 1AW

COLCOMB, MR D M, 38 Roundway Park, Devizes SN10 2EO

COLE, MRS J A, 113 Groundwell Road, Swindon SN1 2NA

COLEMAN, MISS J, Swn-y-Coed, Abergwili, Carmarthenshire SA32 7EP

COLLINS, MR A T, 11 Lemon Grove, Whitehill, Bordon, Hants GU35 9BD

COLMAN, MRS P, 28 Abbey Mill, Church Street, Bradford on Avon BA15 1HB

CONGLETON, LORD, West End Farm, Ebbesbourne Wake, Salisbury SP5 5JW

COOMBES, MR J, 85 Green Pastures, Heaton Mersey, Stockport SK4 3RB

COOMBES-LEWIS, MR R J, 45 Oakwood Park Road, Southgate, London N14 6QP

COOPER, MR S, 12 Victory Row, Wootton Bassett, Swindon SN4 7BE

CORAM, MRS J E, 38 The Parklands, Hullavington, Chippenham SN14 6DL

COULSTOCK, MISS P H, 15 Pennington Crescent, West Moors, Wimborne, Dorset BH22 0JH

COVEY, MR R V, Lower Hunts Mill, Wootton Bassett, Swindon SN4 7QL

COWAN, COL M, 24 Lower Street, Harnham, Salisbury SP3 8EY

CRITTALL, MISS E, 3 Freshwell Gardens, Saffron Walden, Essex CB10 1BZ

CROUCH, MR J W, Kensington House, Pensford Hill, Pensford, Somerset BS39 4AA

CROWLEY, DR D A, 16 Greater Lane, Edington, Westbury BA13 4QP

D'ARCY, MR J N, The Old Vicarage, Edington, Westbury

DAVIES, MRS A M, 283 Longstone Road, Iver Heath, Bucks SL0 0RN

DIBBEN, MR A A, 18 Clare Road, Lewes, East Sussex BN7 1PN

DRAPER, MISS R, 12 Sheep Street, Devizes SN10 1DL

EDE, DR M E, 12 Springfield Place, Lansdown, Bath BA1 5RA

EDWARDS, MR P C, 33 Longcroft Road, Devizes SN10 3AT

ELDERTON, MS B, 5 Glebe Close, Blythe Bridge, Stoke on Trent ST11 9JN

ELRINGTON, PROF C R, 34 Lloyd Baker Street, London WC1X 9AB

FAY, MRS M, 40 North Way, Porton Down, Salisbury SP4 0JN

FICE, MRS B, Holt View House, 9 Rosemary Lane, Rowledge, Farnham GU10 4DB

FLOWER-ELLIS, DR J G, Swedish Univ of Agric Sciences, PO Box 7072 S-750 07, Uppsala, Sweden 1972

FORBES, MISS K G, Bury House, Codford, Warminster

FOSTER, MR R E, The New House, St Giles Close, Gt Maplestead, Halstead, Essex CO9 2RW

FOY, MR J D, 28 Penn Lea Road, Bath BA1 3RA

FREEMAN, REV DR J, 1 Cranfield Row, Gerridge Street, London SE1 7QN

FROST, MR B C, Red Tiles, Cadley, Collingbourne Ducis, Marlborough SN8 3EA

FULLER, MRS B, 65 New Park Street, Devizes SN10 1DR

GALBRAITH, MS C, Box 42, 17 Gill Street, Coldwater, Ontario L0K 1EO, Canada

GALE, MRS J, 169 Spit Road, Mosman, NSW 2088, Australia

GARNISH, MRS E A, 9 Rue de Hoek, 1630 Luikebeek, Brussels, B-1630, Belgium

GHEY, MR J G, 18 Bassett Row, Bassett, Southampton SO1 7FS

GIBBS, MRS E, Home Farm, Barrow Gurney, Bristol BS48 3RW

GINGELL, MS B M, 32 Cambridge Lodge, Bonehurst Road, Horley, Surrey RH6 8PR

GODDARD, MR R E H, Sinton Meadow, Stokes Lane, Leigh Sinton, Malvern, Worcs WR13 5DY

GOODBODY, MR E A, Stockmans, Rectory Hill, Amersham, Bucks

GOODFELLOW, MR P S, Teffont Selby, 47 High Street, Mow Cop, Cheshire ST7 3NZ

GOSLING, REV DR J, 1 Wiley Terrace, Wilton, Salisbury SP2 0HN

GOUGH, MISS P M, 39 Whitford Road, Bromsgrove, Worcs B61 7ED

GOULD, MR C P, 1200 Old Mill Road, San Marino, California 91108 USA

GOULD, MR L K, 263 Rosemount, Pasadena, California 91103 USA

GRIFFITHS, MR T J, 29 Saxon Street, Chippenham SN15

GRUBER VON ARNI, COL E E, 11 Park Lane, Swindon SN1 5HG

HAMILTON, CAPTAIN R, 1 The Square, Cathedral Views, Crane Bridge Road, Salisbury SP2 7TW

HARE, DR J N, 7 Owens Road, Winchester, Hants SO22 6RU

HARTCHER, REV DR G N, 3-5 Vincentia Street, Marsfield, NSW 2122, Australia

HATCHWELL, MR R C, Cleeve House, Rodbourne Bottom, Malmesbury SN16 0EZ

HAYWARD, MISS J E, Pleasant Cottage, Crockerton, Warminster BA12 8AJ

HELMHOLZ, PROF R W, Law School, 1111 East 60th Street, Chicago, Illinois 60637 USA

HENLY, MR H R, 99 Moredon Road, Swindon SN2 2JG

HERRON, MRS Pamela M, 25 Anvil Crescent, Broadstone, Dorset BH18 9DY

HICKMAN, MR M R, 184 Surrenden Road, Brighton BN1 6NN

HICKS, MR I, 74 Newhurst Park, Hilperton, Trowbridge BA14 7QW

HILLIKER, MR S, Box 184, Sutherland, NSW 2232, Australia

HILLMAN, MR R B, 18 Carnarvon Close, Chippenham SN14 0PN

HINTON, MR A E, Glenside Cottage, Glendene Avenue, East Horsley, Surrey KT24 5AY

HOBBS, MR S, 63 West End, Westbury BA13 3JQ

HOLLEY, MR R J, 120 London Road, Calne SN11 0AH

HORNBY, MISS E, 70 Archers Court, Castle Street, Salisbury SP1 3WE

HORTON, MR P.R.G, OBE, Hedge End, West Grimstead, Salisbury SP5 3RF

HOWELLS, MS Jane, 7 St Mark's Rd, Salisbury SP1 3AY

HUGHES, PROF C J, Old House, Tisbury,

Salisbury SP3 6PS

HUGHES, MR R G, 60 Hurst Park Road, Twyford, Reading RG10 0EY

HULL, MR J L F, Sandown Apartments, 1 Southerwood Drive, Sandy Bay, Tasmania 7005, Australia

HUMPHRIES, MR A G, Rustics, Blacksmith's Lane, Harmston, Lincoln LN5 9SW

INGRAM, DR M J, Brasenose College, Oxford OX1 4AJ

JACKSON, MR D, 2 Byways Close, Salisbury SP1 2QS

JAMES, MR & MRS C, 18 King Henry Drive, Grange Park, Swindon SN5 6BL

JAMES, MR J F, 3 Sylvan Close, Hordle, Lymington, Hants SO41 0HJ

JEACOCK, MR D, 16 Church Street, Wootton Bassett, Swindon

JELLICOE, RT HON EARL, Tidcombe Manor, Tidcombe, Marlborough SN8 3SL

JOHNSTON, MRS J M, Greystone House, 3 Trowbridge Road, Bradford on Avon BA15 1EE

KENT, MR T A, Rose Cottage, Isington, Alton, Hants GU34 4PN

KING, MR S F, Church Mead House, Woolverton, Bath BA3 6QT

KIRBY, MR J L, 209 Covington Way, Streatham, London SW16 3BY

KITE, MR P J, 13 Chestnut Avenue, Farnham GU9 8UL

KNEEBONE, MR W J R, 20 Blind Lane, Southwick, Trowbridge BA14 9PG

KUNIKATA, MR K, Dept of Economics, 1-4-12, Kojirakawa-machi, Yamagata-shi 990, Japan

LAURENCE, MISS A, 1a Morreys Avenue, Oxford OX1 4ST

LAURENCE, MR G F, Apt 312, The Hawthorns, 18-21 Elton Road, Clevedon BS21 7EH

LEGGATE, MR A, 48 High Street, Worton, Devizes SN10 5RG

LODGE, MR O R W, Southridge House, Hindon, Salisbury SP3 6ER

LONDON, MISS V C M, 55 Churchill Road, Church Stretton, Salop SY6 6EP

LUSH, DR G J, 5 Braeside Court, West Moors, Ferndown, Dorset BH22 0JS

MARSH, REV R, Maybridge Vicarage, 56 The Boulevard, Worthing, West Sussex BN 13 1LA

MARSHMAN, MR M J, 13 Regents Place, Bradford on Avon BA15 1ED

MARTIN, MR D, 21 Westbourne Close, Salisbury SP1 2RU

MARTIN, MS JEAN, 21 Ashfield Road, Chippenham SN15 1QQ

MASLEN, MR A, 8 Alder Walk, Frome, Som BA11 2SN

MATHEWS, MR R, P O Box R72, Royal Exchange, NSW 2000, Australia

MATTHEWS, CANON W A, Holy Trinity Vicarage, 18a Woolley St, Bradford on Avon BA15 1AF

MATTINGLY, MR N, Freshford Manor, Freshford, Bath BA3 6EF

MERRYWEATHER, MR A, 60 Trafalgar Road, Cirencester, Glos GL7 2EL

MILLINGTON, MRS P, Hawkstone, Church Hill, Lover, Salisbury SP5 2PL

MOLES, MRS M I, 40 Wyke Road, Trowbridge BA14 7NP

MONTAGUE, MR M D, 115 Stuarts Road, Katoomba, NSW 2780, Australia

MOODY, MR R F, Harptree House, East Harptree, Bristol BS18 6AA

MORIOKA, PROF K 3-12, 4-chome, Sanno, Ota-ku, Tokyo, Japan

MORLAND, MRS N, 47 Shaftesbury Road, Wilton, Salisbury SP2 0DU

MORRISON, MRS J, Priory Cottage, Bratton, Westbury BA13

MOULTON, DR A E, The Hall, Bradford on Avon BA15

NAPPER, MR L R, 9 The Railway Terrace, Kemble, Cirencester GL7 6AU

NEWBURY, MR C COLES, 6 Leighton Green, Westbury BA13 3PN

NEWMAN, MRS R, Tanglewood, Laverstock Park, Salisbury SP1 1QJ

NOKES, MR P A, Wards Farm, Ditcheat, Shepton Mallet, Somerset BA4 6PR

O'DONNELL, MISS S J, 42 Wessington Park,

Calne SN11 0AU

OGBOURNE, MR J M V, 14 Earnshaw Way, Beaumont Park, Whitley Bay, Tyne and Wear NE25 9UN

OGBURN, CHIEF JUDGE ROBERT W, 317 First Avenue, Monte Vista, CO 81144, USA

OSBORNE, COL R, Unwins House, 15 Waterbeach Road, Landbeach, Cambridge CB4 4EA

PARKER, DR P F, 45 Chitterne Road, Codford St Mary, Warminster BA12 0PG

PARROTT, MRS M G, 81 Church Road, Christian Malford, Chippenham SN15 4BW

PATIENCE, MR D C, 29 Priory Gardens, Stamford, Lincs PE9 2EG

PATRICK, DR S, The Thatchings, Charlton All Saints, Salisbury SP5 4HQ

PERRY, MR S H, Priory Cottage, Broad Street, Bampton, Oxon

POWELL, MRS N, 4 Verwood Drive, Bitton, Bristol BS15 6JP

RADNOR, EARL OF, Longford Castle, Salisbury SP5 4EF

RAYBOULD, MISS F, 20 Radnor Road, Salisbury SP1 3PL

REEVES, DR M E, 38 Norham Road, Oxford OX2 6SQ

ROGERS, MR K H, Silverthorne House, East Town, West Ashton, Trowbridge BA14 6BE

ROOKE, MISS S F, The Old Rectory, Little Langford, Salisbury SP3 4NU

SHELBURNE, EARL OF, Bowood House, Calne SN11 0LZ

SHELDRAKE, MR B, 28 Belgrave Street, Swindon SN1 3HR

SHEWRING, MR P, 73 Woodland Road, Beddau, Pontypridd, Mid-Glamorgan CF38 2SE

SIMS-NEIGHBOUR, MR A K, 2 Hesketh Crescent, Swindon SN3 1RY

SINAR, MISS J C, 1 Alton Road, Wilcot, Pewsey SN9 5NP

SLOCOMBE, MR I, 11 Belcombe Place, Bradford on Avon BA15 1NA

SMITH, MR P J, 6 Nuthatch, Longfield, Kent DA3 7NS

SNEYD, MR R H, Court Farm House, 22 Court Lane, Bratton, Westbury BA13 4RR

SOPP, MR G A, 23952 Nomar Street, Woodland Hills, California 91367, USA

SPAETH, DR D A, School of History and Archaeology, 1 University Gardens, University of Glasgow G12 8QQ

STEELE, MRS N D, 46 The Close, Salisbury SP1 2EL

STERRY, MS K, 8 Watercrook Mews, Westlea, Swindon SN5 7AS

STEVENAGE, MR M R, 49 Centre Drive, Epping, Essex CM16 4JF

STEVENS, MISS M L E, 11 Kingshill Close, Malvern, Worcs WR14 2BP

STEWARD, DR H J, Graduate School of Geography, 950 Main Street, Worcester, Mass 01610-1477, USA

STEWART, MISS K P, 6 Beatrice Road, Salisbury SP1 3PN

STRATTON, MR M J, Manor Farm, Stockton, Warminster BA12 0SQ

SYKES, MRS M, Conock Manor, Conock, Devizes SN10 3QQ

SYLVESTER, MR D G H, Almondsbury Field, Tockington Lane, Almondsbury, Bristol BS12 4EB

TAYLOR, DR A J, Rose Cottage, Lincolns Hill, Chiddingfold, Surrey GU8 4UN

TAYLOR, MR C C, 11 High Street, Pampisford, Cambridge CB2 4ES

TAYLOR, MRS J B, PO Box 3900, Manuka, ACT 2063, Australia

THOMPSON, MRS A M, 18 Burnaston Road, Hall Green, Birmingham B28 8DJ

THOMPSON, MR & MRS J B, 1 Bedwyn Common, Great Bedwyn, Marlborough SN8 3HZ

THOMSON, MRS SALLY M, Home Close, High St, Codford, Warminster BA12 0NB

TIGHE, MR M F, Strath Colin, Pettridge Lane, Mere, Warminster BA12 6DG

TOMKOWICZ, MRS C, 2 Chirton Place, Trowbridge BA14 0XT

TSUSHIMA, MRS J, Malmaison, Church Street, Great Bedwyn, Marlborough SN8 3PE

TURNER, MR I D, Warrendene, 222 Nottingham Road, Mansfield, Notts NG18 4AB

VINCENT, MS M A, 28 Rochester Road, Lodge Moor, Sheffield S10 4JQ

WAITE, MR R E, 18a Lower Road, Chinnor, Oxford OX9 4DT

WALKER, MR J K, 82 Wainsford Road, Everton, Lymington, Hants SO41 0UD

WARNEFORD, MR F E, New Inn Farm, West End Lane, Henfield, West Sussex BN5 9RF

WARREN, MR P, 6 The Meadows, Milford Hill Road, Salisbury SP1 2RT

WEINSTOCK, BARON, Bowden Park, Lacock, Chippenham

WELLER, MR R B, 9a Bower Gardens, Salisbury SP1 2RL

WENDEN, MRS P, 21 Eastern Parade, Fareham, Hants PO16 0RL

WHORLEY, MR E E, 190 Stockbridge Road, Winchester, Hants SO22 6RW

WILLIAMS, MRS I L, 7 Chandler Close, Devizes SN10 3DS

WILTSHIRE, MRS P E, 23 Little Parks, Holt, Trowbridge BA14 6QR

WORDSWORTH, MRS G, Quince Cottage, Longbridge Deverill, Warminster BA12 7DS

WRIGHT, MR D P, Haileybury, Hertford SG13 7NU

YOUNGER, MR C, The Old Chapel, Burbage, Marlborough SN8 3AA

UNITED KINGDOM INSTITUTIONS

Aberystwyth
    National Library of Wales
    University College of Wales
Bath. Reference Library
Birmingham
    Central Library
    University Library
Brighton. University of Sussex Library
Bristol. University Library
Cambridge. University Library
Cheltenham. Bristol and Gloucestershire Archaeological Society
Chippenham. Wiltshire College
Coventry. University of Warwick Library
Devizes
    Wiltshire Archaeological & N.H. Soc.
    Wiltshire Family History Society
Dorchester. Dorset County Library
Durham. University Library
Edinburgh
    National Library of Scotland
    University Library
Exeter. University Library
Glasgow. University Library
Leeds. University Library
Leicester. University Library
Liverpool. University Library

London
    British Library
    College of Arms
    Guildhall Library
    Inner Temple Library
    Institute of Historical Research
    London Library
    Public Record Office
    Royal Historical Society
    Society of Antiquaries
    Society of Genealogists
    University of London Library
Manchester. John Rylands Library
Marlborough
    Memorial Library, Marlborough College
    Merchant's House Trust
Norwich. University of East Anglia Library
Nottingham. University Library
Oxford
    Bodleian Library
    Exeter College Library
    New College Library
Poole. Bournemouth University
Reading
    Central Library
    University Library
St Andrews. University Library

Salisbury
    Bourne Valley Historical Society
    Cathedral Library
    Salisbury and South Wilts Museum
Sheffield. University Library
Southampton. University Library
Swansea. University College Library
Swindon
    English Heritage

Swindon Borough Council
Taunton. Somerset Archaeological and
    Natural History Society
Trowbridge
    Wiltshire Libraries & Heritage
    Wiltshire and Swindon Record Office
Wetherby. British Library Document Supply
    Centre
York. University Library

INSTITUTIONS OVERSEAS

AUSTRALIA
Adelaide. Barr Smith Library, Adelaide
    University
Melbourne
    Baillieu Library, University of Melbourne
    Victoria State Library
Nedlands. Reid Library, University of
    Western Australia
Sydney. Fisher Library, University of Sydney
    Law Library, University of New South
    Wales

CANADA
Halifax, Nova Scotia. Dalhousie University
    Library
London, Ont. D.B.Weldon Library, Univer-
    sity of Western Ontario
Montreal, Que. Sir George Williams
    University
Ottawa, Ont. Carleton University Library
Toronto, Ont
    Pontifical Inst of Medieval Studies
    University of Toronto Library
Victoria, B.C. McPherson Library, Univer-
    sity of Victoria

EIRE
Dublin. Trinity College Library

GERMANY
Gottingen. University Library

JAPAN
Osaka. Institute of Economic History, Kansai
    University

Sendai. Institute of Economic History,
    Tohoku University
Tokyo. Waseda University Library

NEW ZEALAND
Wellington. National Library of New
    Zealand

UNITED STATES OF AMERICA
Ann Arbor, Mich. Hatcher Library, Univer-
    sity of Michigan
Athens, Ga. University of Georgia Libraries
Atlanta, Ga. The Robert W Woodruff
    Library, Emory University
Baltimore, Md. Milton S. Eisenhower
    Library, Johns Hopkins University
Binghamton, NY. State University of New
    York
Bloomington, Ind. Indiana University
    Library
Boston, Mass.
    Boston Public Library
    New England Historic and Genealogi-
    cal Society
Boulder, Colo. University of Colorado
    Library
Cambridge, Mass.
    Harvard College Library
    Harvard Law School Library
Charlottesville, Va. Alderman Library,
    University of Virginia
Chicago.
    Newberry Library
    University of Chicago Library
Dallas, Texas. Public Library

Davis, Calif. University Library
East Lansing, Mich. Michigan State University Library
Eugene, Ore. University of Oregon Library
Evanston, Ill. United Libraries, Garrett/ Evangelical, Seabury
Fort Wayne, Ind. Allen County Public Library
Houston, Texas. M.D. Anderson Library, University of Houston
Iowa City, Iowa. University of Iowa Libraries
Ithaca, NY. Cornell University Library
Las Cruces, N.M. New Mexico State University Library
Los Angeles. Public Library
Minneapolis, Minn. Wilson Library, University of Minnesota
New Haven, Conn. Yale University Library
New York.
     Columbia University of the City of New York

Public Library
Notre Dame, Ind. Memorial Library, University of Notre Dame
Piscataway, N.J. Rutgers University Libraries
Princeton, N.J. Princeton University Libraries
Salt Lake City, Utah. Family History Library
San Marino, Calif. Henry E. Huntington Library
Santa Barbara, Calif. University of California Library
South Hadley, Mass. Williston Memorial Library, Mount Holyoke College
Stanford, Calif. Green Library, Stanford University
Tucson, Ariz. University of Arizona Library
Urbana, Ill. University of Illinois Library
Washington. The Folger Shakespeare Library
Winston-Salem, N.C. Z.Smith Reynolds Library, Wake Forest University

LIST OF PUBLICATIONS

The Wiltshire Record Society was founded in 1937, as the Records Branch of the Wiltshire Archaeological and Natural History Society, to promote the publication of the documentary sources for the history of Wiltshire. The annual subscription is £15 for private and institutional members. In return, a member receives a volume each year. Prospective members should apply to the Hon. Secretary, c/o Wiltshire and Swindon Record Office, County Hall, Trowbridge, Wilts BA14 8JG. Many more members are needed.

The following volumes have been published. Price to members £15, and to non-members £20, postage extra. Available from the Wiltshire and Swindon Record Office, Bythesea Road, Trowbridge BA14 8BS.

1. *Abstracts of feet of fines relating to Wiltshire for the reigns of Edward I and Edward II*, edited by R.B. Pugh, 1939
2. *Accounts of the parliamentary garrisons of Great Chalfield and Malmesbury, 1645-1646*, edited by J.H.P. Pafford, 1940
3. *Calendar of Antrobus deeds before 1625*, edited by R.B. Pugh, 1947
4. *Wiltshire county records: minutes of proceedings in sessions, 1563 and 1574 to 1592*, edited by H.C. Johnson, 1949
5. *List of Wiltshire boroughs records earlier in date than 1836*, edited by M.G. Rathbone, 1951
6. *The Trowbridge woollen industry as illustrated by the stock books of John and Thomas Clark, 1804-1824*, edited by R.P. Beckinsale, 1951
7. *Guild stewards' book of the borough of Calne, 1561-1688*, edited by A.W. Mabbs, 1953
8. *Andrews' and Dury's map of Wiltshire, 1773: a reduced facsimile*, edited by Elizabeth Crittall, 1952
9. *Surveys of the manors of Philip, earl of Pembroke and Montgomery, 1631-2*, edited by E. Kerridge, 1953
10. *Two sixteenth century taxations lists, 1545 and 1576*, edited by G.D. Ramsay, 1954
11. *Wiltshire quarter sessions and assizes, 1736*, edited by J.P.M. Fowle, 1955
12. *Collectanea*, edited by N.J. Williams, 1956
13. *Progress notes of Warden Woodward for the Wiltshire estates of New College, Oxford, 1659-1675*, edited by R.L. Rickard, 1957
14. *Accounts and surveys of the Wiltshire lands of Adam de Stratton*, edited by M.W. Farr, 1959
15. *Tradesmen in early-Stuart Wiltshire: a miscellany*, edited by N.J. Williams, 1960
16. *Crown pleas of the Wiltshire eyre, 1249*, edited by C.A.F. Meekings, 1961
17. *Wiltshire apprentices and their masters, 1710-1760*, edited by Christabel Dale, 1961
18. *Hemingby's register*, edited by Helena M. Chew, 1963
19. *Documents illustrating the Wiltshire textile trades in the eighteenth century*, edited by Julia de L. Mann, 1964
20. *The diary of Thomas Naish*, edited by Doreen Slatter, 1965
21-2. *The rolls of Highworth hundred, 1275-1287*, 2 parts, edited by Brenda Farr, 1966, 1968
23. *The earl of Hertford's lieutenancy papers, 1603-1612*, edited by W.P.D. Murphy, 1969
24. *Court rolls of the Wiltshire manors of Adam de Stratton*, edited by R.B. Pugh, 1970
25. *Abstracts of Wiltshire inclosure awards and agreements*, edited by R.E. Sandell, 1971
26. *Civil pleas of the Wiltshire eyre, 1249*, edited by M.T. Clanchy, 1971
27. *Wiltshire returns to the bishop's visitation queries, 1783*, edited by Mary Ransome, 1972
28. *Wiltshire extents for debts, Edward I - Elizabeth I*, edited by Angela Conyers, 1973

316

29. *Abstracts of feet of fines relating to Wiltshire for the reign of Edward III*, edited by C.R. Elrington, 1974
30. *Abstracts of Wiltshire tithe apportionments*, edited by R.E. Sandell, 1975
31. *Poverty in early-Stuart Salisbury*, edited by Paul Slack, 1975
32. *The subscription book of Bishops Tounson and Davenant, 1620-40*, edited by B. Williams, 1977
33. *Wiltshire gaol delivery and trailbaston trials, 1275-1306*, edited by R.B. Pugh, 1978
34. *Lacock abbey charters*, edited by K.H. Rogers, 1979
35. *The cartulary of Bradenstoke priory*, edited by Vera C.M. London, 1979
36. *Wiltshire coroners' bills, 1752-1796*, edited by R.F. Hunnisett, 1981
37. *The justicing notebook of William Hunt, 1744-1749*, edited by Elizabeth Crittall, 1982
38. *Two Elizabethan women: correspondence of Joan and Maria Thynne, 1575-1611*, edited by Alison D. Wall, 1983
39. *The register of John Chandler, dean of Salisbury, 1404-17*, edited by T.C.B. Timmins, 1984
40. *Wiltshire dissenters' meeting house certificates and registrations, 1689-1852*, edited by J.H. Chandler, 1985
41. *Abstracts of feet of fines relating to Wiltshire, 1377-1509*, edited by J.L. Kirby, 1986
42. *The Edington cartulary*, edited by Janet H. Stevenson, 1987
43. *The commonplace book of Sir Edward Bayntun of Bromham*, edited by Jane Freeman, 1988
44. *The diaries of Jeffery Whitaker, schoolmaster of Bratton, 1739-1741*, edited by Marjorie Reeves and Jean Morrison, 1989
45. *The Wiltshire tax list of 1332*, edited by D.A. Crowley, 1989
46. *Calendar of Bradford-on-Avon settlement examinations and removal orders, 1725-98*, edited by Phyllis Hembry, 1990
47. *Early trade directories of Wiltshire*, edited by K.H. Rogers and indexed by J.H. Chandler, 1992
48. *Star chamber suits of John and Thomas Warneford*, edited by F.E. Warneford, 1993
49. *The Hungerford cartulary: a calendar of the earl of Radnor's cartulary of the Hungerford family*, edited by J.L. Kirby, 1994
50. *The Letters of John Peniston, Salisbury architect, Catholic, and Yeomanry Officer, 1823-1830*, edited by M. Cowan, 1996
51. *The Apprentice Registers of the Wiltshire Society, 1817- 1922*, edited by H R Henly, 1997
52. *Printed Maps of Wiltshire 1787–1844: a selection of topographical, road and canal maps in facsimile*, edited by John Chandler, 1998
53. *Monumental Inscriptions of Wiltshire: an edition, in facsimile, of* Monumental Inscriptions in the County of Wilton, *by Sir Thomas Phillipps*, edited by Peter Sherlock, 2000

VOLUMES IN PREPARATION

Devizes area income tax assessments, 1842–60, edited by Robert Colley; *Wiltshire glebe terriers*, edited by S.D. Hobbs and Susan Avery; *Marlborough probate inventories*, edited by Lorelei Williams; *Wiltshire papist returns and estate enrolments, 1705-87*, edited by J.A. Williams; *The Diary of William Henry Tucker*, edited by Helen Rogers; *Early vehicle registration in Wiltshire*, edited by Ian Hicks; *Wiltshire probate records index*, edited by Lucy Jefferis; *Crown pleas of the Wiltshire eyre, 1268*, edited by Brenda Farr; *The Hungerford cartulary, vol.2: the Hobhouse cartulary*, edited by J.L. Kirby; *The Parish registers of Thomas Crockford, 1613-29*, edited by C.C. Newbury. The volumes will not necessarily appear in this order.

A leaflet giving full details may be obtained from the Hon. Secretary, c/o Wiltshire and Swindon Record Office, County Hall, Trowbridge, Wilts. BA14 8JG.